Trade Marks Retrospective

AUSTRALIA
LBC Information Services—Sydney

CANADA and USA
Carswell—Toronto

NEW ZEALAND
Brooker's—Auckland

SINGAPORE and MALAYSIA
Sweet & Maxwell Asia
Singapore and Kuala Lumpur

Trade Marks Retrospective

Edited by Norma Dawson & Alison Firth

Perspectives on Intellectual Property Series
General Editor: Professor Micheal Blakeney

Editorial Board
Hugh Brett
Professor Gerald Dworkin
Alison Firth
Geoffrey Hobbs Q.C.
Mary Vitoria Q.C.

In association with the Queen Mary Intellectual Property Research Institute, Queen Mary & Westfield College, University of London

LONDON • SWEET & MAXWELL • 2000

Published in 2000 by
Sweet & Maxwell Limited of
100 Avenue Road
Swiss Cottage
London NW3 3PF
http://www.sweetandmaxwell.co.uk
Typeset by Tradespools, Frome, Somerset
Printed and bound in Great Britain
by MPG Ltd, Bodmin, Cornwall

No natural forests were destroyed
to make this product, only farmed
timber was used and replanted.

A CIP catalogue record for this book
is available from the British Library

ISBN 0 421 725 702

All rights reserved. Crown Copyright legislation is reproduced under the terms of Crown Copyright Policy Guidance issued by HMSO.
  No part of this publication may be reproduced or transmitted, in any form or by any means, or stored in any retrieval system of any nature, without prior written permission, except for permitted fair dealing under the Copyright, Designs and Patents Act 1988, or in accordance with the terms of a licence issued by the Copyright Licensing Agency in respect of photocopying and/or reprographic reproduction. Application for permission for other use of copyright material including permission to reproduce extracts in other published works shall be made to the publishers. Full acknowledgment of author, publisher and source must be given.

©
Sweet & Maxwell and Contributors
2000

Foreword

I am delighted to recommend this book both to serious students and experienced practitioners in the trade marks field. The contributors have researched widely and the fruits of those researches have been well marshalled and clearly set down. The results, while confirming that trade mark law is not an exact science, show how an absence of debate on matters of policy has prolonged uncertainty in a number of important areas.

This history of such subjects as what is a trade mark, registrability, passing off and the meaning of goodwill in its geographical context makes fascinating reading and shows that development of trade mark law over the past one hundred plus years has had many twists and turns. In developing their papers the contributors have referred to a large number of decided cases and endeavoured to set such cases in context. In reviewing particular subjects, such as the definition of a trade mark and its relationship to distinctiveness, they have not been averse to expressing views different from those expounded by the courts and this adds to the book's appeal.

The history of trade mark law will be very useful as we move with the Trade Marks Act 1994 into a marriage between the United Kingdom and European law, where the final arbiter will be the European Court of Justice. The contributors foresee the European Court as having an impact on the development of trade mark law in the United Kingdom but there have been too few judgments so far for them to form any conclusive views. Perhaps that will be a subject for a further book in a few years' time.

In the meantime, I congratulate Norma Dawson and Alison Firth for bringing all the contributors together to produce this book. I have enjoyed reading it and I believe that others with an interest in trade marks will likewise find it an enjoyable read.

Norman A. Harkness, OBE
Formerly Assistant Registrar of Trade Marks
United Kingdom

Editors' Introduction

Reading through the preambles to the Trade Marks Acts passed in the United Kingdom since 1875, one could conclude that the first occasion on which the legislature addressed the legal regulation of registered trade marks as a matter of general policy was in 1994. Uniquely, the Trade Marks Act 1994, "an Act to make new provision for registered trade marks", indicates a break with the past. From the enactment of the Trade Marks Registration Act 1875, ("an Act to establish a Register of Trade Marks"), through various pieces of "amending", "extending" and consolidating legislation in 1876, 1877, 1883, 1885, 1887, 1905, 1914, 1919, and 1937, up to the enactment of the Trade Marks Act 1938, ("an Act to consolidate" the 1905, 1919, and 1937 Acts), there appears to be a continuous thread of fundamental principle. What principle? The matter was summarised by Lord Justice Farwell in 1910 in the consolidated actions in *Re Joseph Crosfield & Sons Ltd* ("Perfection" trade mark), *Re California Fig Syrup Co* ("California Syrup of Figs" trade mark), and *Re H.N Brock & Co. Ltd.* ("Orlwoola" trade mark):

> The object of trade mark law, whether before or after the Trade Marks Acts, is to protect honest trading . . . There is no conflict between Parliament and the Courts as some . . . have suggested: the foundation of the whole matter was in the Court of Chancery:[1] it is merely that the principle of protection of fair trade has been simplified and developed by legislation so as to enable a trader who has established that a mark . . . denotes his goods, and his goods only, to register the title and so avoid the necessity of proving it against every defendant.[2]

Indeed, the 1875 Act had been described by the editor of *The Times* published shortly after the Trade Marks Registry opened in January 1876 as a "legislative skeleton" which had only reached the statute-book because of its brevity and the efforts of the Lord Chancellor, Lord Cairns, to push it through Parliament.

Lord Justice Farwell urged continued application of the doctrines of the past. He also sounded a further note of caution and revealed how the establishment of a Register had had a profound impact on the judicial psyche: "in passing off actions the Court determines

---

[1] Carty's essay (below at p.31) charts the further development of passing off.
[2] [1910] 1 Ch. 130 at 150–1.

questions simply inter partes,[3] *but trade marks give rights against all the inhabitants of the United Kingdom."*[4] This crude assessment of the monopolistic nature of trade marks would remain a dominant theme of twentieth century trade mark law, expressing a concern which has shaped judicial attitudes to issues such as registrability, the function of marks and therefore the extent of the exclusive right of the owner of a registered trade mark, and the assignability of trade marks as independent entities separate from business goodwill.

Curiously, the interest of consumers hardly features in what little debate did take place. The protection of consumers against deceptive trading was enshrined in entirely separate, criminal, legislation—the Merchandise Marks Act 1862 and its successors, currently the Trade Descriptions Acts 1968 and 1972. The arguments raised during scrutiny of the Merchandise Marks Acts often echoed those put before Goschen, or Mathys. Indeed, two members[5] of the Goschen Committee had given evidence to the Merchandise Marks Committee convened under the chairmanship of Harry Greer M.P., in 1919–20.[6] However, the Trade Descriptions Acts and the criminal provisions of the Trade Marks Act 1994 still continue in their uneasy parallel course.[7]

Behind the carefully conserved facade of conceptual and doctrinal unity and coherence, however, some important policy changes did occur, forced upon the legislature and the courts as a result of pressure from business and industry in consequence of changes in trading conditions and practices. The Goschen Committee caught the powerful tide of commercial pressure for reform in the 1930s and its recommendations[8] were implemented in the Trade Marks (Amendment) Act 1937 which was immediately repealed and replaced by the Trade Marks Act 1938. The mechanisms in the latter Act for enhanced protection of well-known marks[9] and for protecting registered trade marks generally against non-traditional forms of infringement were conceptually significant advances but in practical terms were obscure and limited in their effect, mere heralds of the major changes which were to come in the 1990s. The business community's major gain in the 1930s was to win the support of the Goschen Committee for a right to assign registered trade marks in gross, a right which reflected and facilitated the growing practice of corporate acquisition and restructuring and the fact that brands were fast becoming major commercial assets in their own right. The Goschen Committee recognised that a right of assignment in gross, and a parallel registered user scheme, could be created without

---

[3] Morcom's chapter demonstrates that the influence of passing off is more pervasive than this: p.21 below.
[4] Above, p.151. Italics added.
[5] Sir E.F. Crowe and Sir D.M. Kerly.
[6] Minutes of Evidence, 1920, HMSO.
[7] For comparisons see Worsdall & Clark, *Anti-counterfeiting* (1998).
[8] Departmental Committee on the Law and Practice relating to Trade Marks, Cmd. 4568 (1934).
[9] On which, see Dawson's chapter, p.57 below.

injury to the public while providing considerable advantages for traders and for the economy generally.¹⁰ Nevertheless, this and the other extensions of trade mark rights proposed by the Goschen Committee met some opposition, as can be seen in this passage from the House of Lords debates on the 1937 Bill:

> I was interested to note that at the outset the right hon. Gentleman pointed out that this Bill is demanded by strong pressure from the commercial community. That reminds us that really the only thing that will get any action out of this Government is the pressure of the commercial community. Indeed, if the trade mark "His Master's Voice" is not taken by some other firm in the same class, I think His Majesty's Government ought to register it immediately for themselves . . . Monopolies are *prima facie* an injustice, but when the operation of monopolies in modern times is simply a method of transferring more and more wealth to people or groups who are already too wealthy, a monopoly develops into a ramp of the worst type.¹¹

While the recommendations of the Goschen Committee and the provisions of the Trade Marks Acts 1937–8 challenged British trade mark orthodoxy, neither the Committee nor Parliament made any serious attempt to interpret the proposed legislative changes and relate them to a discussion of legal policy generally. The Mathys Committee of 1974¹² was even less radical than Goschen, rejecting, for example, "a well supported suggestion" for an action to prevent unfair trading practices such as trade mark dilution,¹³ and a proposal for additional rights in fictional characters¹⁴ and the names of books and TV programmes. With the exception of the proposed extension of existing legislation to service marks (which occurred in 1984¹⁵), the Committee's modest recommendations were left in abeyance following the United Kingdom's entry into a European Community engaged on a programme of harmonisation of trade mark laws. Harmonisation was eventually achieved by the First Council Directive to approximate the laws of Member States relating to trade marks,¹⁶ followed by the Community Trade Mark Regulation of 1994.¹⁷

---

¹⁰ Departmental Committee, paras 102–16. The question of assignment in gross was, in the Committee's view, "the most important matter we have had to consider" (para. 102).
¹¹ H.C. Debs., May 27, 1937, col.532, Mr. Pritt, M.P. for North Hammersmith. For the view of brand owners today, see Cratchley's chapter, below at p.3
¹² Committee on British Trade Mark Law and Practice, Cmnd. 5601 (1974).
¹³ See Norman's chapter in this volume: p.189.
¹⁴ Waelde's chapter, p.211 considers the protection available to the image of a real, deceased, character.
¹⁵ Trade Marks (Amendment) Act 1984. Other minor reforms would follow in the Patents, Designs and Marks Act 1986 and the Copyright, Designs and Patents Act 1988. The Trade Marks Act 1994 repealed all earlier legislation still in force.
¹⁶ 89/104 [1989] O.J. L40/1.
¹⁷ Council Regulation 40/94 [1994] O.J. L11/1.

By 1990, the pressure for fundamental reform in the United Kingdom was irresistible and not only because of pressure from Brussels. The DTI's White Paper, *Reform of Trade Mark Law* published in that year,[18] identified a number of reasons why the 1938 Act no longer fully served the needs of industry and commerce: inadequate protection of well-known marks, unduly restrictive judicial interpretation of the criteria for registrability[19] and the definition of a trade mark,[20] overbroad protection against the use of marks for comparative advertising[21] but an otherwise narrowly-circumscribed action for infringement, the need for general streamlining of the application and registration system, and the undesirability of the restriction on trafficking in a trade mark as interpreted by the House of Lords in the *Holly Hobbie* case.[22] Perhaps the most significant passage of the White Paper is paragraph 12:

> Although the 1938 Act consolidated the law, it has been suggested[23] that parts of it are incomprehensible except in conjunction not only with its predecessors but also with the law before registration began. It is clearly undesirable that those who wish to know what the law on trade marks is should have to indulge in such study. The aim of a new Trade Marks Act will be to provide, as far as possible, a new and self-sufficient law of trade marks, while at the same time simplifying the text of the law.

1990 also witnessed a sea-change in the perceptions of the European Court of Justice[24] of the nature and function of trade marks and the abandonment of its earlier hostility towards them based upon their perceived anti-competitive effect especially when exercised on national lines within the Single Market. In *CNL-Sucal SA v. Hag GF AG (Hag II)*, the Court recognised that trade mark rights constitute "an essential element of the system of *undistorted* competition which the [EEC] Treaty aims to establish and maintain."[25] In the Opinion of Advocate-General Jacobs in *Hag II*, the protection of trade marks is justified in the public interest not only as a means of preventing consumer deception but also because of role which trade marks play within the economy. He adopted the words of Professor William Cornish who described trade marks as "nothing more nor less than

---

[18] Cm. 1203 (1990).
[19] Chapters in this volume by Annand (p.109), by Burrell, Beverly Smith and Coleman (p.137), and by Gredley (p.83) deal with some of the problems of registration.
[20] For collective marks, see Firth's chapter at p.171.
[21] See the chapters by Norman (p.189) and Maniatis (p.229).
[22] *Holly Hobbie Trade Mark* [1984] R.P.C.329.
[23] *Kerly's Law of Trade Marks and Trade Names* (12th ed, 1986), para. 1.02 citing Lord Diplock in *GE Trade Mark* [1973] R.P.C. 297.
[24] Evidence of a similar relaxation of the Commission's attitude may be found in *Re Moosehead & Whitbread* [1991] 4 C.M.L.R. 391.
[25] [1990] 3 C.M.L.R. 571, reversing *Hag 1, Van Zuylen Freres v. Hag AG* [1974] 2 C.M.L.R. 127.

the fundament of most market-place competition."[26] The need to recognise the pro-competitive effects of trade marks was also articulated in the debates leading to the enactment of the Trade Marks Act 1994. Lord Peston stated:

> The non-specialist may not appreciate what is so fascinating to the economist; namely that trade marks which grant a firm a degree of monopoly power and appear to strengthen what is called, imperfect competition, actually promote competition and, unless they are abused, are advantageous to the consumer. They strengthen competition by enabling the producer to identify and promote those goods and services he offers.[27]

Despite this Parliamentary recognition of trade marks' interest to consumers, on this, as many other matters, policy-driven debate remains outstanding.[28] However, threads of development may be detected. The thinking of those interested in trade marks has developed. In this collection, we attempt to reveal policy shifts (or drifts) which have taken place during the twentieth century.

Cratchley reviews the perception of brand owners. Far from cruising up a "ramp of the worst type" to an undeserved monopoly, we see the owners struggling with stern advisers, crowded registers and dedicated imitators.

Developments in judicial thinking are of the greatest significance. Morcom demonstrates that unfair trading in all its forms is likely to attract appropriate remedies. Carty analyses the forms of misrepresentation and damage which constitute actionable unfair trading. As she points out, passing off is not only a form of protection parallel to that provided by trade mark registration but also a tort with a life of its own. It is a valuable tort because policy and concept are often more clearly discernible in judgments of the courts than in Parliament's output.

Morcom and Dawson both refer to the U.K.'s obligations under the Paris Convention for the Protection of Industrial Property. Our obligation under Art 6*bis*, to protect the well known trade marks of Paris Union proprietors, is now firmly entrenched in the Trade Marks Act 1994. However, as Dawson illustrates, cases of marks with international repute have studded the century's law reports.

The theme of international awareness is continued in Gredley's chapter on the registration as trade marks of foreign-language words. Far from being a recent phenomenon, this is a conceptually well-developed area of the law, of especial significance in the age of the Community Trade Mark. Annand examines other problems of

---

[26] W.R. Cornish, *Intellectual Property* (2nd ed, 1989) at p.393.
[27] H.L. Debs., December 12, 1993, cols. 755–6.
[28] This may be because intellectual property in general is seen as a money earner rather than a vote winner. However, it does seem odd that so little Parliamentary time has been devoted down the years to the consumer benefits of trade marks.

distinctiveness in their current and historical contexts, as she explores the fundamental relationship between that requirement and the legal definition of a trade mark.

Burrell, Beverley Smith and Coleman probe the difficulties inherent in registering and protecting three dimensional shapes as trade marks. The legislation is new, but they draw upon earlier wisdom or folly in criticising the possibilities engendered by the Harmonisation Directive, now implemented in all Member States of the European Community. The question of registration is continued by Firth, who analyses the nature of collective marks and considers whether they really lacked protection under earlier Acts.

Use is the essence of a trade mark. Norman, Waelde and Maniatis explore the functions and dysfunctions of trade marks. Norman examines the scope of protection of registered marks down the century, under legislation which has grappled clumsily with referential use and misappropriation of value. Waelde deals with the valuable image of the late Diana, Princess of Wales, and questions the outcome of protection by registration. Her conclusions have implications for any legislative reform in the sphere of privacy and publicity. Maniatis rounds off the issue of use and misuse by cutting through judicial and statutory language to the core issue—what use of a sign can and should be restrained, discouraged or promoted by the trade mark system?

As editors, we should like to thank all the contributors for their pieces. Reading the chapters has given us great enjoyment and much to think about. Our thanks also go to those who helped by refereeing chapters or commenting on our own drafts. We are honoured and grateful to include a preface by Norman Harkness, whose distinguished work at the Trade Marks Registry helped to shape law and practice for many years. Finally, we express our warm appreciation for all the work, help and support from our publishers which has enabled this volume to come into being. We hope that this collection will provide pleasure and interest for readers, and perhaps lead to further work in this fascinating area.

Norma Dawson
Alison Firth

Contents

Foreword	v
Editors' Introduction	vii
Norma Dawson & Alison Firth	
Table of Cases	xv
Table of U.K. Statutes	xxxv
Table of U.K. Statutory Instruments	xxxix
Table of Foreign National Legislation	xli
Table of European Legislation	xliii
Table of International Conventions, Treaties, Agreements and Declarations	xlv

The Brand Owner's View   1
   Liz Cratchley

Leading Cases in Passing Off   19
   Christopher Morcom Q.C.

The Development of Passing Off in the Twentieth Century   31
   Hazel Carty

The Foreign Trade Mark Owner's Experience: An absence of Goodwill?   57
   Norma Dawson

Foreign Language Words as Trade Marks   83
   Ellen Gredley

Developments in Registrability: The Definition of a Trade Mark and its Relationship with the Requirement for Distinctiveness   109
   Ruth Annand

Three-dimensional Trade Marks: Should the Directive Be Reshaped?   137
   Robert Burrell, Huw Beverley Smith & Allison Coleman

Collectivity, Control and Joint Adventure-Observations on
    Marks in Multiple Use   171
  Alison Firth
Scheecter's *The Rational Basis of Trade Mark Protection*
    Revisited   189
  Helen Norman

Commercialising the Personality of the Late Diana, Princess
    of Wales-Censorship by the Back Door?   211
  Charlotte Waelde

Aspects of Trade Mark Use and Misuse   229
  Spyros Maniatis

Index   265

Table of Cases

AD2000 Trade Mark [1997] R.P.C. 168; 20(3) I.P.D. 20029 .... 126, 129, 130, 220, 233
Accurist Watches Ltd v. King [1992] F.S.R. 80 234
Active Line, Case No. I ZB 7/95 105
Aktiebolaget Manus v. R J Fullwood and Bland [1949] L.J.R. 861; [1949] 1 All E.R. 205; 66 R.P.C. 71, CA; affirming (1948) 65 R.P.C. 329.. 181
Al Bassam Trade Mark [1995] R.P.C. 511, CA; affirming [1994] 10 R.P.C. 315... 97, 98
Alain Bernardin et Cie v. Pavilion Properties Ltd ("the Crazy Horse case") [1967] F.S.R. 341; [1967] R.P.C. 581 .. 48, 70, 71, 72, 73, 74, 75, 76, 77, 79, 80, 81
Alexander Pirie & Sons v. Goodall [1982] 1 Ch. 35, CA 115
Alfred Dunhill Ltd v. Sunoptic SA and Dunhill (C) [1979] F.S.R. 337, CA 52, 55
All Weather Sports Activities Ltd v. All Weather Sports (UK) Ltd (unreported 1987, Lexis)...................................... 50
Allen v. Flood [1898] A.C. 1... 36
Allgemeine Elektricitats AG's Application, Re [1957] R.P.C. 127. 94
Allied Domecq Spirits and Wine Ltd v. Murray McDavid Ltd [1997] F.S.R. 864; *The Times*, December 9, 1997, OH............ 206
Aloe Creme Laboratories Inc. v. American Society for Aesthetic Plastic Surgery 192 USPO 170 179
American Coy's Application No. 773, 098 for the Registration of a Trade Mark, In the Matter of (TORQ-SET) [1959] R.P.C. 344 131
American Greetings Corporation's Application, Re [1984] 1 W.L.R. 189; 128 S.J. 99; 1 All E.R. 426; [1984] F.S.R. 199; [1985] E.I.P.R. 6; [1984] R.P.C. 349, HL; affirming [1983] 1 W.L.R. 912; [1983] 2 All E.R. 609; [1983] F.S.R. 581, CA; affirming [1983] 1 W.L.R. 269; 127 S.J. 51 .... P5, 218
Amway Corp v. Eurway International Ltd [1973] F.S.R. 213; [1974] R.P.C. 82... 48, 71
Anheuser-Busch Inc. v. Budejovicky Budvar NP (1984) 128 S.J. 398; [1984] F.S.R. 413; 81 L.S. Gaz. 1369, CA....... 26, 48, 49, 72, 73
Annabel's (Berkeley Square) Ltd v. G. Schock (trading as Annabel's Escort Agency) [1972] F.S.R. 261; [1972] R.P.C. 838, CA 23
APHRODISIA Trade Mark [1977] F.S.R. 133, High Ct of Ireland. 95
Apollinaris Company's Trade-Marks, Re [1891] 2 Ch. 202, CA .. 115
Aristoc Ltd v. Rysta Ltd [1945] A.C. 68; 62 R.P.C. 65..... 217, 235, 254
Artistic Upholstery Limited (on behalf of itself and all other

members of the Long Eaton Guild of Furniture Manufacturers) v. Art Form Limited (LONG POINT), *The Times*, September 21, 1999. .... 174, 186
Associated Newspapers (Holdings) plc v. Insert Media Ltd [1991] 1 W.L.R. 571; [1991] 3 All E.R. 535; [1991] F.S.R. 380; *The Times*, March 11, 1991; *The Guardian*, March 6, 1991; *The Daily Telegraph*, March 14, 1991, CA; affirming [1990] 1 W.L.R. 900; [1990] 2 All E.R. 803; 134 S.J. 636 24
Athlete's Foot Marketing Associates Inc. v. Cobra Sports Ltd [1980] R.P.C. 343. .... 48, 71, 72, 74
Au Printempts Trade Mark [1990] R.P.C. 518, TMR 99
AUDI-MEDT Trade Mark [1998] R.P.C. 863, TMR 225
AUTODROME Trade Mark [1969] F.S.R. 320; [1969] R.P.C. 564.. 201, 203, 243
Avon Trade Mark (1985) R.P.C. 43. 155
Azrak-Hamway International Inc.'s Licence of Right (Design and Copyright) Application [1997] R.P.C. 134; 20(1) I.P.D. 20004, PO 125

BASF plc v. CEP (UK) plc, October 26, 1995, Ch. (unreported) .. 206
BBC v. Talbot Motor Co. Ltd [1981] F.S.R. 228. 48
BBC Worldwide Ltd v. Pally Screen Printing Ltd [1998] F.S.R. 665; 21(5) I.P.D. 21053, Ch D. 258
Bailey (A.) & Co. Ltd v. Clark Son & Morland Ltd [1938] A.C. 557; 55 R.P.C. 253, HL. 122
Baptistin Bodrero's Application (1938) 55 R.P.C. 185 183
Barclays Bank v. RBS Advanta [1996] R.P.C. 307; 15 Tr.L.R. 262; 19(3) I.P.D. 18; *The Times*, February 8, 1996, Ch D. 240, 245
Barnsley Brewery Co. Ltd v. RBNB [1997] F.S.R. 462, Ch D. 38
Barrow's Trade-Marks, In re (1877) 5 Ch.D. 353, CA 86
Baskin-Robbins Ice Cream Co. v. Gutman [1976] F.S.R. 545. .... 48, 73
Baume & Co. v. Moore (A H) [1958] Ch. 907; [1958] 2 W.L.R. 797; 102 S.J. 329; [1958] 2 All E.R. 113; [1958] R.P.C. 226, CA; reversing [1958] Ch. 137; [1957] 3 W.L.R. 870; 101 S.J. 903; [1957] 3 All E.R. 416; [1957] R.P.C. 459; [1957] C.L.Y. 3557 243
Bayerische Motorwerke AG and BMW Nederland BV v. Ronald Karel Deenik [1999] All E.R. (E.C.) 235; [1999] E.T.M.R. 339... 181, 209, 210, 254
Baywatch Production Co. Inc. v. The Home Video Channel [1997] F.S.R. 22; [1997] E.M.L.R. 102; 20(1) I.P.D. 20010, Ch D. 206, 224, 257
Benchairs Ltd v. Chair Centre Ltd [1973] F.S.R. 123; [1974] R.P.C. 429, CA; reversing [1972] F.S.R. 397 150
Benedictus v. Sullivan Powell & Co. (1895) 12 R.P.C. 25 87
Bentley v. Lagonda [1947] R.P.C. 33 243
Bismag v. Amblins (Chemists) Ltd [1940] Ch. 667; (1940) 57 R.P.C. 209 .... 196, 197, 201, 202, 203, 208, 209, 242
Blofeld v. Payne (1833) 4 B. & Ad. 409 193

BLOODSTREAM Trade Mark (Case R 33/1998-2), September
  1998, Second Board of Appeal (unreported) 133
Blundell v. Sidney Margolis (1951) 68 R.P.C. 71 150
Bodega Company, The and Rivière v. Owens (2) (Bodega)
  (1890) 7 R.P.C. 31, CA.. 87
Boköl... 96
Bollinger (J) v. Costa Brava Wine Company Ltd (No. 4) [1961] 1
  W.L.R. 277; 105 S.J. 180; [1961] 1 All E.R. 561; R.P.C. 116 ..... 22, 29,
                                                                    46, 81
Bomford Turner Ltd v. Turner (unreported 1992, Lexis) 52
BONUS GOLD [1998] R.P.C. 859.................................... 132
Boots Co., Re; *sub nom.* Dee Corp., Re [1989] 3 All E.R. 948;
  [1990] R.P.C. 159, CA; affirming [1989] F.S.R. 266 .... 112, 201
Bostick Ltd v. Sellotape GB Ltd [1994] R.P.C. 556; *The Times*,
  January 11, 1994, QBD 128
Bovril, Re Trade Mark [1896] 2 Ch. 600, CA 115
Bowden Wire Co. Ltd v. Bowden Brake Co. Ltd (1914) 31
  R.P.C. 385 197
Bravado Merchandising Services Ltd v. Mainstream Publishing
  (Edinburgh) Ltd [1996] F.S.R. 205; *The Times*, November 20,
  1995, OH............................... 206, 208, 210, 223, 248, 250
Brestian v. Try [1958] R.P.C. 161, CA; affirming [1957] R.P.C.
  443; [1997] C.L.Y. 3554 64
Bristol Conservatories Ltd v. Conservatories Custom Built Ltd
  [1989] R.P.C. 455, CA 23, 29, 38, 44, 45, 238
British American Glass Co. Ltd v. Winton Products (Blackpool)
  Ltd [1962] R.P.C. 230.. 38, 150
British Diabetic Association v. Diabetic Society and Others
  [1995] 4 All E.R. 812; [1996] F.S.R. 1; *The Times*, October 23,
  1995, Ch D.. 215
British Leyland Motor Corp. Ltd v. Armstrong Patents Ltd
  [1986] A.C. 577; [1986] 2 W.L.R. 400; S.J. 203; [1986] 1 All
  E.R. 850; [1986] R.P.C. 279; [1986] F.S.R. 221; 5 T.L.R. 97;
  [1986] E.C.C. 534; 136 New L.J. 211; 83 L.S. Gaz. 974, HL;
  reversing (1984) 128 S.J. 659; [1984] 3 C.M.L.R. 102; [1984]
  F.S.R. 591; 81 L.S. Gaz. 2225, CA; affirming [1982] Com.L.R.
  240; [1983] F.S.R. 50 158
British Northrop Ltd v. Texteam Blackburn Ltd [1973] F.S.R.
  241; [1974] R.P.C. 57................................ 201, 203, 210, 242
British Sugar plc v. James Robertson & Sons Ltd (TREAT)
  [1996] R.P.C. 281; 19(3) I.P.D. 13, *The Times*, February 17,
  1996, Ch D.. 111,
                    129, 130, 131, 134, 141, 147, 148, 149, 154, 160,
                    206, 207, 208, 220, 223, 231, 248, 249, 250, 258
British Telecommunications v. AT & T Communications [1997]
  E.I.P.R. D-1343.. 246
British Telecommunications plc v. One in a Million Ltd; Marks
  & Spencer plc v. One in a Million Ltd; Virgin Enterprises
  Ltd v. One in a Million Ltd; J Sainsbury plc v. One in a

Million Ltd; Ladbroke Group plc v. One in a Million Ltd [1998] 4 All E.R. 476; [1998] Info. T.L.R. 423; [1998] I.T.C.L.R. 146; [1998] Masons C.L.R. 165; 95(37) L.S.G. 37; 148 N.L.J. 1179; *The Times*, July 29, 1998; *The Independent*, July 31, 1998, CA; affirming [1998] F.S.R. 265; 16 Tr. L.R. 554; [1997] Info. T.L.R. 316; [1998] I.T.C.L.R. 7; [1998] Masons C.L.R. 116; 21(2) I.P.D. 21016; 147 N.L.J. 1809; *The Times*, December 2, 1997, Ch D 25, 26, 27, 29, 37, 193, 206, 208, 218, 251
Broadhurst v. Barlow [1872] W.N. 212............................. 86
Bulmer (H P) v. Bollinger (J) SA [1977] 2 C.M.L.R. 625; [1978] F.S.R. 79, [1978] R.P.C. 79, CA...................................... 198
Burgess v. Burgess (1853) 3 De G. M. & G. 896.................... 193
Burgoyne's Trade Mark, In the Matter of (1889) 6 R.P.C. 227 .. 91, 115

C & A Modes and C & A Ireland v. C & A (Waterford) Ltd [1976] I.R. 198.. 75
CIR v. Puller & Co's Margarine Ltd [1901] A.C. 217............. 38
CNL-Sucal SA v. Hag GF AG (Hag II) [1990] E.C.R. I-3711; [1990] 3 C.M.L.R. 571................................... P5, 10, 142, 218
Cadbury Schweppes Pty Ltd v. Pub Squash Co Pty Ltd (Pub Squash) [1981] 1 W.L.R. 193; 125 S.J. 6; [1981] 1 All E.R. 213; [1981] R.P.C. 429, PC 34, 35, 46, 54
California Fig Syrup Company, Re [1910] 1 Ch. 130, CA; (1909) 26 R.P.C. 846.. 120
Calvin Klein Inc. v. International Apparel [1995] F.S.R. 515...... 76
Cambridge University Press v. University Tutorial Press (1928) 45 R.P.C. 355.. 44
Canon Kabushiki Kaisha v. Metro-Goldwyn-Mayer Inc., (Case C-39/97) [1999] 1 C.M.L.R. 77; [1999] R.P.C. 117; F.S.R. 332; E.T.M.R. 1................................. 102, 133, 207, 224, 257, 258
Carl Lindstroem Aktiengesellschaft for Registration of a Trade Mark, In the Matter of an Application by (1914) 31 R.P.C. 261.. 94
Carless, Capel v. Pilmore-Bedford [1928] R.P.C. 205.............. 240
Carson v. Here's Johnny Portable Toilets Inc. 698 F. 2d 831 (6th Cir. 1983)... 215
Carter Medicine Company's Trade Mark (1892) 9 R.P.C. 401 125
Castrol v. Pennzoil F.2d 939, 25 USPQ 2d 1666 (CA 3, 1993)..... 247
Chanel Ltd v. Triton Packaging Ltd formerly l'Arome (UK) [1993] R.P.C. 32, CA.. 201, 242
Charles Goodall & Son v. John Waddington (1924) 41 R.P.C. 658.. 159
Charles of the Ritz Group v. Quality King 832 F.2d 1317, 4 USPQ 2d 1778 (CA 2, 1987).. 247
Chelsea Man Menswear Ltd v. Chelsea Girl Ltd [1987] R.P.C. 189, CA; Affirming [1985] F.S.R. 567 64
Children's Television Workshop Inc. v. Woolworths (N.S.W.) Limited [1981] R.P.C. 187, Sup Ct of New South Wales........ 214

Chocosuisse Union des Fabricants Suisses de Chocolat v.
  Cadbury Ltd [1998] R.P.C. 117; [1998] E.T.M.R. 205; 21(1)
  I.P.D. 21007; *The Times*, November 25, 1997, Ch D .. 45, 46, 47, 52, 81
Ciba Geigy v. Parke Davis & Co. [1994] F.S.R. 8; *The Times*,
  April 6, 1993 245
Clock Ltd v. Clock House Hotel Ltd (1936) 53 R.P.C. 269 64
COCA-COLA Trade Marks, Re [1986] 1 W.L.R. 695; 130 S.J.
  429; [1986] 2 All E.R. 274; [1986] F.S.R. 472; 136 New L.J. 463;
  83 L.S. Gaz. 2090, HL; affirming [1986] R.P.C. 421; [1985]
  F.S.R. 315; 82 L.S. Gaz. 930, CA; affirming [1986] R.P.C. 421111, 124,
                                            125, 127, 139, 141, 144, 145, 157, 158
COFFEEMIX Trade Mark [1998] R.P.C. 717 125
Colgate-Palmolive Ltd v. Markwell Finance Ltd [1989] R.P.C.
  497, CA; Affirming [1988] R.P.C. 283 40
Collins Co. v. Brown (1857) 3 K. & J. 423 .... 64, 65, 68, 69, 76, 80
Collins Co. v. Cohen (1857) 3 K. & J. 428 64
Combe International Ltd v. Scholl (UK) Ltd [1980] R.P.C. 1;
  F.S.R. 464 .... 45, 46
Commissioners of Inland Revenue v. Muller & Co.'s Margarine
  Ltd [1901] A.C. 217 .... 66, 67, 70, 71, 72, 73
Compagnie Générale des Eaux v. Compagnie Générale des
  Eaux Sdn Bhd [1997] F.S.R. 610, HC (Mal) 76
Compaq Computers Corp. v. Dell Computer Corp. [1992] F.S.R.
  93; [1992] B.C.C. 484 .... 201, 242
Conagra Inc. v. McCain Foods (Australia) Pty Ltd Fed Court of
  Australia [1992] 23 I.P.R. 193 .... 48, 76
Consorzio del Prosciutto di Parma v. Marks and Spencer plc
  [1991] R.P.C. 351, CA; affirming [1990] F.S.R. 530 .... 38, 39
Coopervision Inc v. Aspect Contact Lenses Ltd (1987), Lexis 45
Cope v. Evans ("the Prairie Flower case") (1872) L.R. 18 Eq.
  138 86
Copydex Ltd v. Noso Products Ltd (1952) 69 R.P.C. 38 44
Cosmedent Inc.'s Application [1998] E.T.M.R. 658 105
Crawshay v. Thompson (1842) 4 Man. & G. 358 193
Crazy Horse case, The. *See* Alain Bernardin et Cie v. Pavilion
  Properties Ltd
Croft v. Day (1843) 7 Beav. 84 93
Currie v. Barton, *The Times*, February 12, 1998 173

Daiquiri Rum Trade Mark, Re [1969] F.S.R. 89; [1969] R.P.C.
  600, HL; reversing [1967] F.S.R. 229; [1967] R.P.C. 279, CA;
  reversing [1966] F.S.R. 274; [1966] R.P.C. 582; [1966] C.L.Y.
  12180 100
Dalgety Spillers Foods Ltd v. Food Brokers Ltd [1994] F.S.R.
  504; *The Times*, December 2, 1993, Ch D 50
Davidoff (Zino) SA v. A & G Imports [1999] R.P.C. 631; [1999]
  E.T.M.R. 700 .... 181, 232
Davis v. Stribolt; In the Matter of Davis, Bergendahl & Co.'s
  Trade Marks (1889) 6 R.P.C. 207 .... 88, 90, 91

Davis' Trade Marks, In the Matter of (1897) 14 R.P.C. 903 115
Davis's Trade Mark, In the Matter of (USTIKON) (1972) 44
  R.P.C. 412, CA 121
Dawnay Day & Co. Ltd v. Cantor Fitzgerald [1999] E.I.P.R. N-
  178.. 174, 182
Day v. Brownrigg (1878) 10 Ch.D. 294............................... 194
DECLIC Trade Mark, October 7, 1998, OHIM Second Board of
  Appeal (unreported) 129
Dee Corporation plc and Others' Trade Mark Applications. *See*
  Re Boots Co.
Densham's Trade-Mark, Re [1895] 2 Ch. 176; 12 R.P.C. 75 ..... 91, 115
Dent v. Turpin (1861) 70 E.R. 1003..................................... 185
Derry v. Peek (1889) 14 App. Cas. 377................................ 36
Deutsche Renault AG v. Audi AG (Case C-317/91) [1995] 1
  C.M.L.R. 461; [1995] F.S.R. 738; *Financial Times*, December 7,
  1993, ECJ... 142
Dewhurst's Application (Golden Fan), In the Matter of (1896)
  13 R.P.C. 288... 89, 90, 91, 97, 99
Diabolo case, The. *See* Philippart v. William Whitely Ltd and In
  the Matter of Philippart's Trade Mark
DIABOLO Trade Mark (1908) 25 R.P.C. 565....................... 117
Diehl K G's Application, Re; *sub nom.* Diehl Trade Mark [1970]
  2 W.L.R. 944; 114 S.J. 336; [1969] 3 All E.R. 338; [1968] F.S.R.
  571; [1970] R.P.C. 435 181
Direct Line Group Ltd v. Direct Line Estate Agency Ltd [1997]
  F.S.R. 374, Ch D 27, 37
Direct Line Insurance v. Louts Leisure Group Ltd (unreported,
  1993, Lexis) 50
Dominion Rent a Car v. Budget Rent a Car [1987] 2 N.Z.L.R.
  395... 81
Douglass v. Hustler Magazine Inc., 769 F 2d 1128 (7th Cir. 1985
  Posner).. 214
Dun & Bradstreet (Singapore) Pte Ltd v. Dun & Bradstreet
  (Malaysia) Sdn Bhd [1994] 1 M.L.J. 32 76
Duracell International Inc. v. Ever Ready Ltd [1989] F.S.R. 71 201, 242

EANCO Trade Mark (1920) 37 R.P.C. 134 117
Eastman Photographic Materials Company's Application
  (SOLIO) (1898) 15 R.P.C. 476, HL 87, 92, 93, 94, 96, 99, 115,
                                                                                117, 119
Edelsten v. Edelsten (1863) 1 De G.J. & S. 185 .... 65, 113, 193
Edge & Sons Ltd v. Gallon & Son (1900) 17 R.P.C. 537........... 64
Edge & Sons Ltd v. Nicolls & Sons Ltd (1911) 28 R.P.C. 53...... 141
Edginton's Trade Mark, In the Matter of (1889) 6 R.P.C. 513..... 87
Egg Products Ltd for a Trade Mark, In the Matter of an
  Application by (1922) 39 R.P.C. 155.............................. 120
Electrolux v. Electrix (No. 2) (1953) 71 R.P.C. 23, CA; affirming
  (1953) 70 R.P.C. 127; [1953] C.L.Y. 3658 234
Elida Gibbs v. Colgate-Palmolive Ltd [1982] F.S.R. 95 48

Elle Trade Marks, Re; *sub nom.* Hachette Filipacchi Presse v. Safeway Stores plc [1997] F.S.R. 529, Ch D; 20(2) I.P.D. 20018, TMR.. 234
Elliot Optical Coy's application (1952) 69 R.P.C. 169.............. 183
Elvis Presley Enterprises Inc. v. Sid Shaw Elvisly Yours, Court of Appeal, *The Times*, March 12, 1999 .... 166, 167, 169, 221, 222
Elvis Presley Trade Marks [1997] R.P.C. 543 38
Elvis Presley Trade Marks [1999] R.P.C. 673 217
Erven Warnink Besloten Vennootschap v. Townend (J) & Sons (Hull) Ltd ("the Advocaat case"); *sub nom.* Erven Warnink BV v. Townend (J) & Sons (Hull) Ltd [1979] A.C. 731; [1979] 3 W.L.R. 68; 123 S.J. 472; [1979] 2 All E.R. 927; [1979] F.S.R. 397; [1980] R.P.C. 31, HL; reversing [1978] F.S.R. 473, 21, 23, 24, 25, 27, 29, 33, 35, 38, 39, 41, 44, 45, 46, 47, 52, 194
Esanda Ltd v. Esanda Finance Ltd [1984] 2 N.Z.L.R. 748......... 76
Estate of Elvis Presley v. Russen 513 F. Supp. 1339 (D.N.J. 1981) 214, 215
EUROLAMB Trade Mark [1997] R.P.C. 279, TMR 129, 132
European Ltd, The v. The Economist Newspaper Ltd [1998] F.S.R. 283; [1998] E.M.L.R. 536; [1998] E.T.M.R. 307; 21(3) I.P.D. 21022, CA; affirming [1996] F.S.R. 431; [1996] E.M.L.R. 394; 19(7) I.P.D. 19067, Ch D 161, 206, 208
Evans Sons Lescher and Webb Ltd for the Registration of a Trade Mark, In the Matter of an Application by (1934) 51 R.P.C. 423.. 97
Evans v. Eradicure Ltd [1972] R.P.C. 808; [1972] F.S.R. 137 185
Eveready [1998] R.P.C. 631 .... 258, 260
Ewing v. Buttercup Margarine (1917) 34 R.P.C. 232 41
Ewing v. Orr-Ewing (1883) 9 App. Cas. 34....................... 74

Farbenfabriken Co.'s Application [1894] 1 Ch. 645; 11 R.P.C. 8491, 117
Farina v. Silverlock (1856) 6 De G.M. & G. 214 64
Faulder & Co. v. O. G. Rushton Ltd (1903) 20 R.P.C. 477 64
Field, (J.C. & J.) v. Wagel Syndicate: In the Matter of Trade Mark No. 96,997 (Savonol) (1900) 17 R.P.C. 226............... 85, 92
Fletcher Challenge Ltd v. Fletcher Challenge Pty. Ltd [1982] F.S.R. 1.. 28
Fratelli Graffione v. Fransa, (Case C-313/94) ("Cotonelle") [1997] F.S.R. 538, ECJ... 104
Frits Loendersloot v. George Ballantine & Son Ltd [1998] 1 C.M.L.R. 1015... 53, 142
FROOT LOOPS [1998] R.P.C. 240 (Appointed Person)............ 132

GE Trade Mark, Re. *See* General Electric Co. of USA) v. General Electric Co.
GTR Group's Application ("Jois & Jo") [1999] E.T.M.R. 164...... 102
Gallaher (Dublin) Ltd, Hergall (1981) Ltd and Another v. The Health Education Bureau [1982] F.S.R. 464 252

Games Workship v. Transworld Publishers [1993] F.S.R. 705, CA. 203
General Electric Co. (of USA) v. General Electric Co. Ltd; *sub nom.* GE Trade Mark, Re [1972] 1 W.L.R. 729; 116 S.J. 412; [1972] 2 All E.R. 507; [1973] R.P.C. 297, HL; reversing [1970] F.S.R. 113; [1970] R.P.C. 339, CA P5, 64, 81, 182
General Motors Corporation v. Yplon SA, (Case C-375/97), ("Chevy") November 26, 1997 106
Gestetner's Trade Mark [1907] 2 Ch. (1908) 25 R.P.C. 156, CA... 94
Glaxo plc v. Glaxo-Wellcome Ltd [1996] F.S.R. 388, Ch D.. 27, 37, 251
Globelegance BV v. Sarkissian [1974] R.P.C. 603; [1973] F.S.R. 461. .... 48, 71
Golden Fan Case, The. *See* Dewhurst's Application, In the Matter of. ....
Gout v. Aleploglu (1833) 6 Beav. 69n; 49 E.R. 750; 5 Leg. Obs. 495. 86
Gramophone Company's Application [1910] 2 Ch. 423 120
Granada Trade Mark [1979] R.P.C. 303, TMR 161
Grant (t/a Globe Furnishing Co.) v. Leavitt (1901) 18 R.P.C. 361 . 64, 65, 66, 69
Great Tower Street Co., The v. Smith (1889) 6 R.P.C. 165 115
Gromax Plasticulture Ltd v. Don & Low Nonwoven Ltd [1999] R.P.C. 367 174

Hag I–*See* Van Zuylen Freres v. Hag AG
Hag II–*See* CNL-Sucal SA v. Hag GF AG
Hall v. Barrows (1863) 4 De G.J. & S. 150 .... 113, 193
Hanover Star Milling Co. v. Metcalf 240 U.S. 403 (1916) 64, 191
Hans Lauritzen for the Registration of a Trade Mark, In the Matter of an Application by (1931) 48 R.P.C. 392 125
Harris v. Warren and Phillips (1918) 35 R.P.C. 217 40
Harrods Ltd v. Harrodian School [1996] R.P.C. 697; 19(10) I.P.D. 4; *The Times*, April 3, 1996, CA 35, 38, 41, 50, 51
Harrods Ltd v. Harrods (Buenos Aires) Ltd [1999] F.S.R. 187.... 71
Harrods Ltd v. Harrods (Buenos Aires) Ltd [1999] R.P.C. 187 ... 234
Harrods Ltd v. Schwartz-Sackin & Co. Ltd [1986] F.S.R. 490..... 142
Hasbro Inc. v. Clue Computing Inc. No. 97-10065-DPW, 9/2/99, reported in BNA, Patent, Trademark and Copyright Journal Vol. 58, No. 1443. 259
Hassan El-Madi's Application, Re (1954) 71 R.P.C. 348, CA; reversing (1954) 71 R.P.C. 281 97
Henderson v. Munroe (1905) 13 S.L.T. 57. 44
Henderson v. Radio Corp Pty Ltd [1969] R.P.C. 218 53
Hensher Ltd v. Restawhile Upholstery (Lancs.) Ltd [1976] A.C. 64; [1974] 2 W.L.R. 700; 118 S.J. 329; [1974] 2 All E.R. 420; [1974] F.S.R. 173; [1975] R.P.C. 31, HL; affirming on different grounds [1973] 3 W.L.R. 453; 117 S.J. 615; [1973] 3 All E.R.

414; [1973] F.S.R. 477, CA; reversing [1943] 1 W.L.R. 144; 117
  S.J. 32; [1973] 1 All E.R. 160; [1972] F.S.R. 557 150
Hodge Clemco Ltd v. Airblast Ltd [1995] F.S.R. 806, Ch D 34, 54
Hodgkinson & Corby Ltd v. Wards Mobility Services, Ltd
  [1994] 1 W.L.R. 1564; [1995] F.S.R. 169; 14 Tr.L.R. 79; *The
  Times*, August 3, 1994; *The Independent*, October 17, 1994 (CS),
  Ch D 22, 23, 54, 142, 150, 151, 242, 244
Holly Hobbie Trade Mark, Re. See American Greetings Corp.'s
  Application, Re.
Home Box Office Inc. v. Channel 5 Home Box Office Ltd [1982]
  F.S.R. 449 ....:............................ 71
Hommel v. Gebrüder Bauer & Co.; In the Matter of the Trade
  Mark "Haematogen" (1904) 21 R.P.C. 576 93
Hopkinson's Trade Mark, Re [1892] 2 Ch. 116 114
Houtwipper (Case C-293/93) [1994] E.C.R. I-4249 177
Hubbuck v. Wilkinson [1899] 1 Q.B. 86, CA 45
Hudson's Trade Marks (1886) 3 R.P.C. 155, CA............... 113, 119
Hyper Hyper Ltd v. Hyper Active Ltd (unreported 1982, Lexis). 50
Hyper Hyper Ltd v. Hyper Active Ltd (unreported 1985, Lexis). 50

IHT Internationale Heiztechnik v. Ideal Standard (Case C-9/93)
  [1994] E.C.R. I-2789; [1994] 3 C.M.L.R. 857; [1998] F.S.R. 59;
  Financial Times, June 28, 1994; *The Times*, July 7, 1994, ECJ 142,
                                                                185, 218
IX Trade Mark (Case R4/1998-2) OHIM O.J. 10/98, 1059,
  Second Board of Appeal 132
Ide Line Aktiebolag v. Philips Electronics NV [1997] E.T.M.R.
  377 .... 130, 140, 155, 162
Imperial Tobacco [1915] 2 Ch. 27; [1915] 32 R.P.C. 40 177
Imperial Tobacco Co. of India v. Bonman [1924] A.C. 755 185
Imperial Tobacco v. De Pasquali [1918] R.P.C. 185............... 240
Imperial Group v. Philip Morris & Co. [1982] F.S.R. 72; [1982]
  Com.L.R. 95, CA; affirming [1980] F.S.R. 146 234
Inescourt (1928) 46 R.P.C. 13 181
Interlego EG's Trade Mark Applications [1998] R.P.C. 69; 20(8)
  I.P.D. 20079, Ch D....................................... 112, 159, 244
International News Service v. Associated Press 248 U.S. 215
  (1918).. 44
Irving's Yeast-Vite Ltd v. F.A. Horsenail (1934) 51 R.P.C. 110 194, 196,
                                                          198, 199, 240, 241
Isola Ltd's application (1922) 39 R.P.C. 171...................... 183

Jackson Co.'s Trade Mark (Kokoko), In the Matter of (1888) 6
  R.P.C. 80 .... 89, 91, 97
Jaleel's Application O/221/98 (cannot trace)..................... 151
James's Trade Mark, Re (1886) 33 Ch.D. 392, CA 116, 144, 146, 158, 221
Jarvard. See Kundry SA's Application.......................... 100, 103
Jean'Heurs SA Application No. 7117 ("ODEON") 234
JERYL LYNN Trade Mark; sub nom. Merck & Co. Inc. v.

SmithKline Beecham plc [1999] R.P.C. 491; *The Times*, December 18, 1998, Ch D 131, 234
Jian Tools for Sales Inc. v. Roderick Manhattan Group [1995] F.S.R. 924, Ch D 48
Joburgers ("McDonald's Case, The") 1997 (1) S.A. 1 60 et seq.,. 79, 80
John Robert Powers School Inc. v. Denyse Bernadette Tessensohn [1995] F.S.R. 947...................................... 45
Jois & Jo. *See* GTR Group's Application
Joseph Crosfield & Sons Limited (PERFECTION) [1910] 1 Ch. 130, CA 111, 112, 120, 122, 125, 127

Kabushiki Kaisha Yakult Honsha v. Danone Nederland BV [1998] E.T.M.R. 465... 155
Kali, Board of Appeal Decision R147/1998-2, March 4, 1999..... 105
Kaye v. Robertson [1991] F.S.R. 62, *The Times*, March 21, 1990, CA... 219
Kent County Council v. Price (1993) 12 Tr. L.R. 137; 158 L.G.Rev. 78, DC 16, 17
Kiku Trade Mark [1977] F.S.R. 246....................................... 96
Kimberley-Clark Ltd v. Fort Sterling Ltd [1997] F.S.R. 877; 20(7) I.P.D. 20066, Ch D.. 42, 51, 52, 195
Kodak (1898) 15 R.P.C. 105.. 81, 93
Kodak Trade Mark [1990] F.S.R. 49 219
Kogan v. Koala Dundee Pty Ltd (1988) 83 A.L.R. 187 (Fed. Court of Australia) 53
Kokoko. *See* In the Matter of Jackson Co.'s Trade Mark
Kundry SA's Application; Opposition by the President and Fellows of Harvard College [1998] E.T.M.R. 178, TMR......... 103

LRC v. Lilla Edets Sales Company [1972] F.S.R. 479; [1973] R.P.C. 560.. 52
LASTING PERFORMANCE Trade Mark (Case R 34/1998-3), OHIM O.J. 11/98, 1157... 133
Leather Cloth Co. v. American Leather Cloth Co. [1865] 11 H.L.C. 523; HL... 113, 182, 193
Lego System A/S v. Lego M. Lemelstrich [1983] F.S.R. 155, Pat Ct..................................... 23, 33, 43, 49, 50, 81
Lettuce Entertain You Enterprises Inc. v. Lauren Sabin Soll & Grants Investment Ltd [1979] E.I.P.R. 321...................... 71
Levy v. Walker (1879) 10 Ch.D. 436................................. 241
Lidl Stiftung's Application/Opposition by Procter & Gamble SRIS 0/059/99, February 26, 1999 100
Linotype Company Ltd for a Trade Mark (No. 2) (Tachytype), In the Matter of the Application of the (1900) 17 R.P.C. 380... 93
Liverpool Electric Cable Company Limited's Application (LIVERPOOL CABLES) (1929) 46 R.P.C. 99, CA....... 122, 124, 125
LONG POIT. *See* Artistic Upholstery Limited v. Art Form Limited
Lorimar Productions v. Sterling Clothing 1981 (3) S.A. 1129 76

Louise & Co. Ltd v. Gainsborough (1903) 20 R.P.C. 61 .... 116, 118
Lynstad v. Annabast Products Limited [1975] F.S.R. 488 ...... 214, 219

M'Andrew v. Bassett (1864) 4 De G.J. & Sm. 380 64
McCulloch v. Lewis A. May (1947) 65 R.P.C. 58 23
McDonald's Corp USA and McDonald's Restaurants Denmark
   A/S v. Pedersen [1997] E.T.M.R. 151 .... 59, 60
McDonald's Corp. v. Dieter Rahmer, April 30, 1998, noted at
   (1999) 30 I.I.C. 326 80
McDonald's Corp. v. McDonald's Corp. Ltd and Chang [1997]
   F.S.R. 760 75
McDonald's/McBagels [1987] E.I.P.R. D-108 60
McDonalds v. Burger King [1986] F.S.R. 45 245
McDowell's Application, Re (1926) 43 R.P.C. 313 .... 141, 191
MacMillan Magazines v. RCN Publishing Co. Ltd [1998[F.S.R.
   9; 20(9) I.P.D. 20089, Ch D 246
McNeil-P.C.C. v. Bristol-Myers Squibb 19 USPQ 2d 1525 (1991). 247
Macy's Trade Mark [1989] R.P.C. 546 71
MAGNOLIA Metal Company's Trade-Marks [1897] 2 Ch. 371,
   CA 117, 119
Mail Newspapers Ltd. v. Insert Media (No. 2) [1988] 2 All E.R.
   420 142
Marca Mode v. Adidas AG & Adidas Benelux BV [1999]
   E.T.M.R. 791 232
Marcos Balé y Hnos' Application, In the Matter of (1947) 65
   R.P.C. 17 97
Marcus Publishing plc v. Hutton-Wild Communications Ltd
   [1990] R.P.C. 576; The Times, October 31, 1989, CA 49
Mars GB Ltd v. Cadbury Ltd [1987] R.P.C. 387 .... 208, 244
Martin Luther King Jnr., Ctr. for Social Change Inc. v.
   American Heritage Prods Inc. 296 S.E. 2d 697 (Ga. 1982) 215
Masson Seeley & Co. v. Embossotype Mfg Co. (1924) 41 R.P.C.
   160 45
Matthew Gloag & Son Ltd. v. Welsh Distillers Ltd (No. 2)
   [1998] F.S.R. 718; 21(6) I.P.D. 21063; The Times, February 27,
   1998, Ch D 43, 45, 54
Maxim's v. Dye [1977] 1 W.L.R. 1155 121 S.J. 727; [1978] 2 All
   E.R. 55; [1977] F.S.R. 364; [1977] 2 C.M.L.R. 410 73
MAXIMA Trade Mark (Case 51/1998-1), September 30, 1998,
   First Board of Appeal (unreported) 133
Mecklermedia Corp v. D.C. Congress Gesellschaft mbH [1997]
   3 W.L.R. 479; [1997] F.S.R. 627; [1997] INfo T.L.R. 132; [1997]
   Masons C.L.R. 20; 20(4) I.P.D. 20042; The Times, March 27,
   1997, Ch D 50
Mercury Communication Ltd v. Mercury Interactive (UK)
   [1995] F.S.R. 850, Ch D 141
Metric Resources v. Leasemetrix Ltd [1979] F.S.R. 571 .... 48, 74
Midas International Corp. v. Midas Auto Care Ltd, unreported
   November 27, 1987, Malaysia 76

Midland Bank Trust Co. v. Green [1980] A.C. 513; 125 S.J. 33, HL; reversing [1979] 3 W.L.R. 167; 123 S.J. 388; [1979] 3 All E.R. 28; 39 P. & C.R. 265, CA; reversing (1978) 3 W.L.R. 149; 121 S.J. 794; [1978] 3 All E.R. 555 196
Midler v. Ford Motor Co. 849 F. 2d 460 (9th Cir. 1988)........... 215
Millington v. Fox (1838) 3 My. & Cr. 338 .... 113, 193
Mirage Studios v. Counter-Feat Clothing Ltd [1991] F.S.R. 145 38, 194
Mitchell's Trade-Mark, Re (1877) 7 Ch.D. 36 114
Mogul Steamship Co. Ltd v. McGregor, Gow & Co. [1892] A.C. 25 36
Molyslip Trade Mark [1978] R.P.C. 211, TMR 187
Montana Wines v. Villa Maria Wines [1985] R.P.C. 400, High Ct of New Zealand 199
Moore's Modern Methods Application (1919) 36 R.P.C. 6 159
Moorgate Tobacco Co. Ltd v. Philip Morris Ltd (No. 2) (1984) 56 C.L.R. 414, High Ct of Australia 142
Moosehead & Whitbread, Re [1991] 4 C.M.L.R. 391 xi
Morny Ltd. v. Ball & Rogers (1975) [1978] F.S.R. 91 39
Mothercare UK v. Penguin Books [1988] R.P.C. 113, CA 244
My Kinda Bones Ltd (t/a Chicago Rib Shack) v. Dr Pepper's Stove Co. Ltd (t/a Dr Pepper's Manhattan Rib Shack) [1984] F.S.R. 289 71

Namlooze Vennootschap Fabriek van Chocolade en Suikerwerken J C Klene & Co.'s Application (1923) 40 R.P.C. 103 183
National Cash Register Company for the Registration of a Trade Mark, In the Matter of Applications by (1917) 34 R.P.C. 273 120
National Galvanizers Ltd to Register a Trade Mark, In the Matter of an Application by (1920) 37 R.P.C. 202 120
NATURALS Trade Mark (Case 39/1998-2), November 22, 1998, Second Board of Appeal (unreported) 133
NEEDLETIP Trade Mark [1973] R.P.C. 113 125
NETMEETING Trade Mark (Case R 26/1998/3) OHIM O.J. 3/ 99, 517, Third Board of Appeal 132
News Group Newspapers v. Rocket Record Co. Ltd ("PAGE THREE") [1981] F.S.R. 89 202
Newton Chambers & Co. Ltd v. Neptune Waterproof Paper Co. Ltd (1935) 32 R.P.C. 399 195
Newton Chambers v. Neptune [1935] R.P.C. 399 241
Nice and Safe Attitude Ltd v. Piers Flook (t/a Slaam! Clothing Co.) [1997] F.S.R. 14; 19(4) I.P.D. 8, HC 39
Nicholson & Sons Ltd's Application (1931) 48 R.P.C. 227, CA 113, 114
Northern & Shell v. Condé Nast & National Magazine Distributors Ltd [1995] R.P.C. 117; [1995] Tr.L.R. 263; *The Independent*, February 13, 1995 (CS), Ch D 191, 234
NORTHROP. *See* Northrop Ltd v. Texteam Blackburn Ltd
NUTRITIVE Trade Mark [1998] R.P.C. 621, TMR 129

Oasis Stores Ltd's Trade Mark Application [1998] R.P.C. 631,
  TMR.. 225, 257
ODEON. *See* Jean'Heurs S.A. Application.
Oertli AG v. Bowman (London) Ltd (No. 3) [1959] R.P.C. 1,
  HL; affirming [1957] R.P.C. 388; [1957] C.L.Y. 3549, CA;
  reversing [1956] R.P.C. 282; [1956] C.L.Y. 8805 .... 70, 71, 181
Office Cleaning Services Ltd v. Westminster Window and
  General Cleaners Ltd (1946) 63 R.P.C. 39 21
One in a Million case, The. *See* British Telecommunications plc
  and others v. One in a Million Ltd and others
Optima, OHIM Board of Appeal Decision R94/1998-2, February
  11, 1999 105
ORANGE Trade Mark (Case R 7/97-3) OHIM O.J. 5/98, 605,
  Third Board of Appeal.. 132
Origins Natural Resources Inc. v. Origin Clothing Ltd [1995]
  F.S.R. 280, Ch D 34, 206, 207, 223
Orkin Exterminating Co. Ltd v. Pestco of Canada Ltd [1985] 19
  D.L.R. (4th) 90 (Canada) 48, 76, 81
ORLWOOLA Trade Mark (1909) 26 R.P.C. 283, CA 117
Orr Ewing v. Registrar of Trade-Marks (1879) 4 App. Cas. 479,
  HL.. 114
Otokoyama v. Wine of Japan Import 50 U.S.P.Q. 2d. 1626
  (1999).. 103
Overdrive Ltd v. Wells Fargo Bank (unreported 1982, Lexis) 50

Pacific Dunlop v. Hogan (1989) 87 A.L.R. 14 (Fed. Court of
  Australia) 53
PAGE THREE. *See* News Group Newspapers v. Rocket Record
  Co. Ltd
PALMOLIVE TM (1932) 49 R.P.C. 269............................. 183
Parfums Christian Dior SA v. Evora BV (Case C-337/95) [1998]
  R.P.C. 166; [1998] E.T.M.R. 26, ECJ; [1997] E.T.M.R. 323,
  AGO 53, 142, 181, 238, 255
Parker-Knoll Ltd v. Knoll International Ltd; *sub nom.* Parker-
  Knoll and Parker-Knoll (Textiles) v. Knoll International
  Britain (Furniture and Textiles); [1962] R.P.C. 265, HL;
  affirming [1961] R.P.C. 346, CA; reversing [1961] R.P.C. 31;
  [1961] C.L.Y. 8875 .... 29, 243
Parker-Knoll Ltd v. Knoll Overseas Ltd [1985] F.S.R. 349 242
PARTNER WITH THE BEST [1998] E.T.M.R. 679,
  Bundesgerichtshof (Ger) 106
Paton Calvert Cordon Bleu Trade Mark [1996] R.P.C. 94, TMR.. 99
Penn v. Lord Baltimore (1750) 1 Ves. Sen. 444 74
Penney (J.C.) Co. v. Punjabi Nick [1979] F.S.R. 26, Sup Ct of
  Hong Kong 75
Pentagon Stationers Ltd v. Pentagon Business Systems Ltd
  (unreported 1985, Lexis) 52
Perry v. Truefitt (1842) 49 E.R. 749; 6 Beav. 66.................. 36, 193

Peter Waterman Ltd v. CBS UK Ltd [1993] E.M.L.R. 27 . 48, 50, 60, 74
Phelps v. McDonald 99 U.S. 298 (1878) 74
Philippart v. William Whitely Ltd and In the Matter of
  Philippart's Trade Mark (Diabolo) (1908) 94, 95
Philips Electronics NV v. Remington Consumer Products, May
  5, 1999, CA; [1998] R.P.C. 283; [1998] E.T.M.R. 124; 21(3)
  I.P.D. 21023; *The Times*, February 2, 1998, Pat Ct .. 80, 111, 126, 128,
            130, 131, 133, 134, 135, 140, 146, 147, 148, 151, 153,
            154, 155, 156, 157, 159, 160, 161, 162, 163, 164, 165,
                 166, 168, 206, 208, 209, 231, 232, 244, 249
Planned Parenthood v. Bucci 42 USPQ 2d 1430 (SDNY 1997).... 252
Poiret v. Jules Poiret Ltd and Nash (1920) 37 R.P.C. 177 64, 68, 69, 71
Polaclip TM [1999] R.P.C. 282 233
Politechnika Ipari Szovertkezet v. Dallas Print Transfers Ltd
  [1982] F.S.R. 529 150
POLYESTRA [1968] G.R.U.R. 694, BGH 233
Pompadour Laboratories v. Fraser [1966] R.P.C. 7 .... 201, 203, 242
PORTALTO Trade Mark [1967] F.S.R. 395; [1967] R.P.C. 617..... 94
Powell v. The Birmingham Vinegar Brewery Company Ltd
  ("the Yorkshire Relish Case") (1897) 14 R.P.C. 720, HL; (1896)
  13 R.P.C. 235.. 118, 141, 191
Powell's Trade-Mark [1893] 2 Ch. 388, CA 118
Prairie flower case, The. *See* Cope v. Evans
Procter & Gamble Co.'s "Soap Tablet" Trade Mark Application
  [1998] R.P.C. 710, TMR.. 131, 151
Procter & Gamble's Trade Mark Application [1999] R.P.C. 673,
  [1999] E.T.M.R. 375........................... 14, 129, 131, 166, 232
Procter & Gamble's Application ("Baby-Dri") [1999] E.T.M.R.
  240... 104, 105
Profitmaker Trade Mark, Re [1994] R.P.C. 613, Ch D 235
Prorace v. le Brasseur (1927) 44 R.P.C. 73 177
Pub Squash Case, The. *See* Cadbury Schweppes Pty Ltd v. Pub
  Squash Co Pty Ltd
PUSSY GALORE Trade Mark [1967] F.S.R. 279; [1967] R.P.C.
  265.. 186

Qualitex v. Jacobson Products 131 L Ed 2d 248 (1995)......... 147, 158

Radiation (1930) 47 R.P.C. 37....................................... 182
Ramsay v. Nichol (1939) V.L.R. 330................................. 76
Reckitt & Colman Products Ltd v. Borden Inc. [1990] 1 All E.R.
  873; 134 S.J. 784; [1990] R.P.C. 341, HL; affirming [1988]
  F.S.R. 601; 8 Tr L.R. 97, CA 21, 35, 38, 39, 141, 194
Red Star case, The. *See* Société Anonyme des Verreries de
  l'Etoile Trade Mark
Reddaway v. Banham [1896] A.C. 199; (1896) 13 R.P.C. 218..... 21, 22,
                                                             34, 37, 193
Registered Trade Mark of David Gestetner, Re [1907] 2 Ch. 478. 115

Registrar of Trade Marks v. W. & G. Du Cros, Ltd [1913] A.C. 624, HL 120, 167, 232
Revlon Inc. v. Cripps & Lee Ltd (1979) 124 S.J. 184; [1980] F.S.R. 85 .... 40, 182
Richards v. Butcher (1890) 7 R.P.C. 288 241
Rijn Staal Trade Mark [1991] R.P.C. 400 96
Robineau v. Charbonnel [1876] W.N. 160 65
Robinson v. Finlay (1877) 9 Ch.D. 487 183
Roho's Application O/169/98 .... 152, 154, 163, 166
Rotheram and Son's Trade Mark, Re (1878) 11 Ch.D. 250; 49 L.J. Ch. 511, CA 88, 89
Royal Baking Powder Co. v. Wright, Crossley & Co. (1901) 18 R.P.C. 95 36

SDS Biotech UK v. Power Agrichemicals [1995] F.S.R. 787, Ch D 34, 54
Sabel BV v. Puma American Coy's Application No. 773, 098 for the Registration of a Trade Mark, In the Matter of AG; Rudolf Dassler Sport (Case C-251/95) [1998] R.P.C. 199; [1998] E.T.M.R. 1, ECJ; [1997] E.T.M.R. 283, AGO 102, 106, 206, 207, 257
Sanitas Company's Trade Mark, In the Matter of the (1887) 4 R.P.C. 533 90
Sarl RWS Ltd. v. Getten and Sté Translations [1999] E.T.M.R. 258 105
Scandecor Development AB v. Scandecor Marketing AB [1999] F.S.R. 26; [1998] F.S.R. 500 .... 71, 141, 239, 243
Schulke & Mayr UK Ltd v. Alkapharm UK Ltd (unreported 1995, Lexis) 54
Searle & Co. v. Budson Pharmaceutical Corporation 715 F.2d 837, 220 USPQ 496 (CA 3, 1983) 247
Selecta, Board of Appeal Decision R104/1998-3, February 11, 1999 105
Seville v. Constance (1954) 71 R.P.C. 146 44
Shell-Mex & BP and ALADDIN Industries v. R & W Holmes (1937) 54 R.P.C. 287 184
Sheraton Corp. of America v. Sheraton Motels Ltd [1964] R.P.C. 202 .... 69, 71
Sherry Case, The. See Vine Products Ltd v. Mackenzie & Co. Ltd
Shredded Wheat Co. Ltd v. Kellogg Co. of Great Britain Ltd (1939) 57 R.P.C. 137 154
Silhouette International Schmied GmbH & Co KG v. Hartlauer Handelsgesellschaft mbH [1998] 2 C.M.L.R. 953, ECJ, [1998] F.S.R. 474 .... 40, 128, 205, 232, 233
Singer Manufacturing Co. v. Loog (1880) 18 Ch.D. 395, CA ... 112, 193
Slenderella Systems v. Hawkins 1959 (1) S.A. 519 76
Smith Hayden (1946) 63 R.P.C. 97 14
Smith, Kline and French Laboratories Ltd v. Sterling-Winthrop

Group Ltd; *sub nom* Smith, Kline & French Laboratories' Applications, Re [1975] 1 W.L.R. 914; 119 S.J. 422; [1975] 2 All E.R. 578; [1975] F.S.R. 298; [1976] R.P.C. 511, HL; reversing [1974] 1 W.L.R. 861; 118 S.J. 441; [1974] 2 All E.R. 826; [1974] F.S.R. 455, CA; reversing [1973] 1 W.L.R. 1534; 117 S.J. 648; [1974] 1 All E.R. 529; [1973] F.S.R. 333; [1974] R.P.C. 91 124
Smitsvonk N.V.'s Application for a Trade Mark, In the Matter of (1954) 72 R.P.C. 117 .... 94, 95, 96
Sobrefina SA's Trade Mark Application [1974] R.P.C. 672 144, 158, 159
Société Anonyme des Anciens Etablissements Panhard et Levassor v. Manhard-Levassor Motor Company Ltd [1901] 2 Ch. 513; (1901) 18 R.P.C. 405 .... 25, 26, 29, 65, 66, 68, 69, 71, 73
Société Anonyme des Verreries de l'Etoile Trade Mark ("the Red Star" case) (1894) 11 R.P.C. 142 .... 89, 97, 106
Société Comptoir de l'Industrie Cotonnière Etablissements Boussac v. Alexander's Department Stores 299 F.2d 33 USPQ 475 (CA 2, 1962) 247
Société le Ferment's Application (Lactobacilline) (1912) 29 R.P.C. 497, CA 93, 94
Solibrisa. *See* Marcos Balé y Hnos' Application, In the Matter of (1974) 65 R.P.C. 17
SOLIO case, The. *See* Eastman Photographic Materials Company's Application
Something Special in the Air [1997] E.I.P.R. D 303 233
Sony KK v. Saray Electronics (London) [1983] F.S.R. 302, CA 42
Southern v. How (1618) Croke's Reports (Jac. 1) 468; Popham's Reports 143; Bridgman J. 125; 2 Rolle 5; 2 Rolle 21 .... 192, 193
Southorn v. Reynolds (1865) 12 L.T. 75 185
Spalding (AG) & Bros. v. Gamage (A.W.) (1915) 32 R.P.C. 273 . 21, 22, 35, 37, 38, 39, 40, 41, 67, 68, 70, 72, 193, 194, 238
Star Industrial Co. v. Yap Swee Kor (t/a New Star Industrial Co.) [1976] F.S.R. 256, PC 72, 73
Sté Felix the Cat Productions Inc. v. Sté Polygram [1999] E.T.M.R. 370 102
Stephens (Aeilyton), ex p. (1876) 3 Ch.D. 659; 46 L.J. Ch. 46 ... 86, 114
Stone (J.B.) & Co. Ltd v. Steelace Manufacturing Co. Ltd (1928) 45 R.P.C. 127 .... 206, 241
Stringfellow v. McCain Foods (GB) (1984) 128 S.J. 701; 81 L.S. Gaz. 2464; [1984] R.P.C. 501, CA; reversing [1984] F.S.R. 199 .. 52
Supreme Grand Lodge of the Ancient and Mystical Order Rosae Crucis Inc., Application No: 2051417 in the name of (1999) 28 C.I.P.A. 152 180
Supreme Shrine of the Order of the White Shrine of Jerusalem, ex p. 109 USPO 248 (Comm'r Pats. 1956) 180
Swizzels Matlow Ltd's "Chewy Sweet" Trade Mark Application [1998] R.P.C. 244, TMR 129, 144, 152, 163
Swizzels Matlow Ltd's "Love Heart" Application O/155/98 152
Sykes v. Sykes (1824) 3 B. & C. 541 193

Taittinger SA v. Allbev Ltd [1994] 4 All E.R. 75; [1993] F.S.R. 641; 12 Tr.L.R. 165; *The Times*, June 28, 1993; *The Guardian*, June 28, 1993; *The Independent*, June 30, 1993, CA; reversing [1992] F.S.R. 647; *The Times*, February 11, 1993; *The Independent*, February 11, 1993; *The Guardian*, February 12, 1993 .... 42, 51, 52
Talbot's Trade Mark, In the Matter of (1894) 11 R.P.C. 77 90
Tallerman v. Dowsing Radiant Heat Ltd [1900] 1 Ch. 1 .... 44, 45
TARANTELLA TMs, Re (1910) 27 R.P.C. 573 183
Teacher v. Levy (1905) 23 R.P.C. 117 39
Ten-Ichi Co. v. Jancar Ltd [1990] F.S.R. 151 75
Teofani & Co. Ltd v. Teofani (1913) 30 R.P.C. 110 195
Tie Rack plc v. Tie Rack Stores (Pty) Ltd 1989 (4) S.A. 427 ..... 62, 76
TORQ-SET. See American Coy's Application No. 773, 098 for the Registration of a Trade Mark, In the Matter of.
Torstein Ropeid's Application, Re (1986) A.I.P.C. 90–342......... 97
Tot Toys Ltd v. Mitchell [1993] I.N.Z.L.R. 325 .... 150, 151
TRAVELPRO Trade Mark, Re [1997] R.P.C. 864, TMR 181, 234
Trebor Bassett Ltd v. The Football Association [1997] F.S.R. 211; 19(12) I.P.D. 11, Ch D 206, 208, 249
Triangle Publications Inc. v. Rohrlich, 167 F. 2d 969 (2d. Cir, 1948) 71
Two Pesos Inc. v. Taco Cabana Inc. 505 U.S. 763, 120 L Ed 2d 615, 112 S Ct 2753 .... 166, 167
Ty Nant Spring Water Ltd's Trade Mark Application, July 12, 1999, Appointed Person, unreported 128
Tyco Industries v. Lego Systems 5 USPQ 2d 1023 (1987)......... 247

UBM Group Ltd v. Lankester Dibben Steels Ltd (unreported 1981, Lexis) 50
UNEEDA Trade-Mark, Re [1901] 1 Ch. 550 117
UNIS. See Union Nationale Inter-Syndicale des Marques Collectives to register trade marks, In the matter of an application by.
USA Detergent Inc.'s Application (XTRA) [1998] E.T.M.R. 562... 105
Unidoor Ltd v. Marks & Spencer plc [198] R.P.C. 275............ 245
Unilever v. Johnson Wax [1989] F.S.R. 583 (citator gives 145).... 8
Unilever's (Striped Toothpaste) Trade Mark Application [1980] F.S.R. 280 .... 128, 139, 154
Union Nationale Inter-Syndicale des Marques Collectives, Re an application by ("UNIS") [1922] 2 Ch. 653; (1922) 39 R.P.C. 97 .... 178, 187
United Biscuits (UK) Ltd v. Asda Stores Ltd [1997] R.P.C. 513; 20(5) I.P.D. 20043, Ch D.. 14, 33
United States Playing Card Company's Application [1908] 1 C. 197 159

Universal Agencies (London) Ltd v. Paul Swolf [1959] R.P.C. 247. 150

Van Duzer's Trade Mark and Leaf's Trade Mark (1887) 4 R.P.C. 31, CA. 90, 113, 115, 118, 121
Van Zeller v. Mason, Cattley & Co. (1907) 25 R.P.C. 37 183
Van Zuylen Bros v. Hag AG (Hag I) (Case 192/73) [1974] E.C.R. 731; [1974] 2 C.M.L.R. 127; [1974] F.S.R. 511, European Court. xi
Vaseline case (1902) 19 R.P.C. 342. 8
Verband Sozialer Wettbewerb v. Clinique Laboratories, ("Clinique") (Case C-315/92) [1994] E.C.R. I-317, ECJ 5th Chamber 104
Verschure & Zoon's Application (1905) 22 R.P.C. 568 96
Victoria's Secret v. Edgars Stores 1994 (3) S.A. 739 76
Vignier's Trade Mark (Monobrut) (1889) 6 R.P.C. 490 91
Vine Products Ltd v. Mackenzie & Co. Ltd (No. 2) ("the Sherry case") [1969] R.P.C. 1; [1967] F.S.R. 402 .... 29, 185
Vodafone Group plc v. Orange Personal Communications Services Ltd [1997] F.S.R. 34; [1997] E.M.L.R. 84; [1997] Info T.L.R. 8; 19(10) I.P.D. 8; *The Times*, August 31, 1996, Ch D 246

Wacker-Chemie GmbH's Application, Re [1957] R.P.C. 278 96
Wackers TM [1999] R.P.C. 453 234
Wackers Trade Mark [1999] R.P.C. 453 71
Wagamama Ltd v. City Centre Restaurants [1995] F.S.R. 713, Ch D 102, 141, 179, 206, 207
Walker (John) & Sons Ltd v. Ost (Henry) & Co. Ltd [1970] 1 W.L.R. 917; 114 S.J. 417; [1970] 2 All E.R. 106; [1970] F.S.R. 63; [1970] R.P.C. 489. 23
Warschauer (1925) 43 R.P.C. 46 181
Warsteiner Brauerie Haus Application [1999] E.T.M.R. 225 106
WATERFORD Trade Mark (Ireland) [1984] F.S.R. 390, Supreme Ct of Ireland. 124
Waterman v. Ayres; In the Matter of Waterman's Trade Mark (1888) 5 R.P.C. 368, CA 90
WELDED MESH, Court of Appeal, May 5, 1999 (transcript).. 149, 150
WELDMESH Trade Mark [1966] F.S.R. 65; [1966] R.P.C. 220, CA; affirming [1965] R.P.C. 590. .... 123, 150
WHAT A DAY [1998] E.I.P.R. N 203 233
WHIRLPOOL Trade Mark, Re [1997] F.S.R. 90, Sup Ct (India)... 48
White v. Mellin [1895] A.C. 154. 36
Wickes Plc's Trade Mark Application [1998] R.P.C. 698, TMR 130, 151
Wienerwald Holding AG v. Kwan, Wong, Tan and Fong [1979] F.S.R. 381, High Ct of Hong Kong. 75
William Edge & Sons Ltd v. William Nicholls Ltd [1911] A.C. 693; (1911) 28 R.P.C. 582 .... 21, 156
William Grant v. Glen Catrine Bonded Warehouse [1995] S.L.T. 936. .... 182, 183

Wilts Utd Dairies Ltd v. Thomas Robinson Sons and Co Ltd (1958) R.P.C. 94, CA; affirming [1957] R.P.C. 220; [1957] C.L.Y. 1988.. 40
Windsurfing Chiemsee Produktions und Vertriebs GmbH v. Boots und Segelzubehör Walter Huber and Franz Attenberger (Cases 108 and 109/97) [1999] E.T.M.R. 585 .. 107, 129, 170, 232, 233, 252
Wrigley's LIGHT GREEN Trade Mark (Case R 122/1998-3) OHIM O.J. 4/99, 605, Third Board of Appeal................ 132, 148
WSC Windsurfing Chiemsee Produktions und Vertriebs GmbH v. Boots und Segelzubehör Walter Huber, Case C-108/97, May 5, 1998 (unreported)............................... 129

Yakult's Application O/269/98................................... 141, 152
YELLOW Trade Mark (Case R 169-1998-3) January 22, 1999 Third Board of Appeal (unreported)........................... 132
YES Trade Mark, Re [1998] E.T.M.R. 386, Bundespatentgericht (Ger) 105
Yomeishu Seizo v. Sinma Medical Products [1994] F.S.R. 278, High Court, Singapore.. 98
YORK Trade Mark [1984] R.P.C. 231, HL...... 124, 125, 127, 148, 149
York Trailer Holdings v. Registrar of Trade Marks [1982] 1 All E.R. 257; 125 S.J. 97; [1982] F.S.R. 111, HL...................... 233
Yorkshire Copper Works v. Registrar of Trade Marks; *sub nom.* Yorkshire Copper Works' Application, Re; *sub nom.* Re Yorkshire Copper Works' Application [1954] 1 W.L.R. 554; 98 S.J. 211; [1954] 1 All E.R. 540; 71 R.P.C. 150, HL; affirming (1952) 70 R.P.C. 1; [1952] C.L.Y. 3672, CA; affirming (1952) 69 R.P.C. 207; [196–52] C.L.Y. 3493 124
Yorkshire Copper Works Limited's Application for a Trade Mark. *See* Yorkshire Copper Works v. Registrar of Trade Marks.
Yorkshire Relish Case, The. *See* Powell v. The Birmingham Vinegar Brewery Company Ltd.
Young v. Grierson Oldham [1924] R.P.C. 548 240

Zoppas Trade Mark [1965] R.P.C. 381 181

Table of U.K. Statutes

1862	Merchandise Marks Act (25 & 26 Vict., c.48) .... viii, 112		1905	Trade Marks Act (5 Edw. 7, c.15) .... vii, 95, 111, 118, 120, 121, 123, 124, 125, 177, 183, 194, 195, 205
1873	Supreme Court of Judicature Act (36 & 37 Vict., c.66). . . 37			s.3. . . . . 118, 119, 194, 195
1875–1938	Trade Marks Registration Acts 112, 134			s.9. . . . . 93, 119
1875	Trade-Marks Registration Act (38 & 39 Vict., c.91) . . . . . . vii, 4, 5, 86, 87, 112, 113, 114, 144, 191,194			(3) 93
				(4) 93
				(5) 115
				s.11. 121
	s.1. 112			s.19. 121
	s.2. 113			s.39. . . . . 194, 195, 196, 199
	s.3. 113			s.41. 194
	s.6. 5			s.44. 120, 195
	s.10. . . . . 87, 88, 113, 114, 144			s.62. 187
			1911	Merchandise Marks Act (1 & 2 Geo. 5, c.31) 177
1876	Trade-Marks Registration Amendment Act (39 & 40 Vict., c.33). . . . . vii, 114, 194		1919	Trade Marks Act (9 & 10 Geo. 5, c.79) . . vii, 93, 120, 121, 177, 187
				s.1. 120
1877	Trade Marks Registration Extension Act (c.37) . . . . . . vii, 194			s.2. . . . . 121, 122
				s.3. 121
1883–1888	Trade Marks Acts. 95, 118			s.4. 120
	s.64(1)(d) 117			s.7. 121
	(e) 117			s.12. 177
1883	Patents, Designs and Trade Marks Act (46 & 47 Vict., c.57) . . . . vii, 87, 90, 91, 114, 115, 194			Sched.2. 177
			1922	Law of Property Amendment Act 196
			1925	Law of Property Act (15 & 16 Geo. 5, c.20) 196
	s.64. 87		1937	Trade Marks (Amendment) Act (1 Edw. 8 & 1 Geo. 6, c.49) vii, viii, ix, 196
	(1) 114			
	(c) 90, 114		1938	Trade Marks Act (1 & 2 Geo. 6, c.22) . . . . vii–x, 93, 99, 100, 101, 111, 122, 123, 124, 125, 182, 196, 199, 205, 206, 217, 219, 221, 223, 234, 241, 244, 248
1887	Margarine Act (50 & 51 Vict) . . 67			
1887	Merchandise Marks Act (50 & 51 Vict., c.28) . . . . vii, 116, 117			
1883	Patents, Designs and Trade Marks Act (46 & 47 Vict., c.57) 91, 92, 93, 116, 194			
				s.1. 122
				s.2. 114
	s.10. 116			s.4. . . . . 196, 199, 204
	s.10(d)–(e) 87, 91			(1) 196, 197, 198, 199, 200, 201, 202, 203, 241
	s.64(e). 92			
	s.72. 89			(a) 197, 198, 200, 202, 203, 204, 208, 241
1890	Partnership Act (53 & 54 Vict., c.39)			
				(b) 197, 198, 199, 200, 201, 202, 203, 204, 208, 241, 242
	s.1. 182			
1891	Merchandise Marks Act (54 & 55 Vict., c.15) 177			
1891	Stamp Act (54 & 55 Vict., c.39) . 66			(3) 198, 200
	s.59(1). 66			(a) 234, 241
1894	Merchandise Marks (Prosecutions) Act (57 & 58 Vict., c.19) 177			(4) 185
				s.5(2) 199
				s.8. . . . . 241, 243
1905–1938	Trade Marks Acts. 98			(b) 202

1938	Trade Marks Act (1 & 2 Geo. 6, c.22)—*cont.*		1994	Trade Marks Act (c.26)—*cont.*	
	s.9.	95, 99, 124		(1)	129, 131, 132, 135, 151, 220
	(1)	122		(a)	101, 129, 130, 131, 132, 134, 135, 234
	(d)	93, 99		(b)	111, 112, 129, 130, 131, 132, 134, 135, 147, 151, 220
	(2)	122			
	s.10.	93, 124			
	(1)	123		(c)	100, 101, 129, 131, 132, 135, 147, 151
	(2)	123, 201			
	s.11	94		(d)	129, 131, 132, 135, 147, 151
	s.12(2)	185, 205			
	s.15	100		(2)	129, 130, 131, 132, 160, 162, 168, 170
	s.27	237			
	s.28	180, 197		(a)–(c)	160
	(2)	181, 186		(3)	159
	(6)	218		(a)	159, 160
	s.29(1)(b)	186		s.5	237
	s.37(1)	186		(3)	204, 225, 257, 258, 259
	s.63	183, 184, 186		(4)(a)	204
	s.68	234, 236		(5)	239
	(1)	124, 191, 196, 199, 235, 241		s.7	185, 205
	(2)	237, 241		s.9	205, 206, 208, 238, 250
1949	Registered Designs Act 12, 13 & 14 Geo. 6, c.88)			(1)–(3)	205
				(1)	205, 206, 234
	s.7(6)	161		(2)	205, 206
1952	Defamation Act (15 & 16 Geo. 6 & 1 Eliz. 2, c.66)			s.10	34, 201, 205, 206, 208, 209, 216, 222, 237, 238, 248, 250
	s.3	36		(1)–(3)	179
1956	Copyright Act (4 & 5 Eliz. 2, c.74) s.10	159		(1)	205, 206, 208, 210, 223, 238, 239, 246, 249
1968	Trade Descriptions Act (c.29)	ix, 16			
1972	Trade Descriptions Act (c.34)	P3		(2)	205, 206, 207, 208, 210, 224, 238, 239, 246, 249
1976	Restrictive Trade Practices Act (c.34)	176			
	s.28 Sched.3 para. 4	176		(3)	52, 206, 208, 209, 210, 224, 238, 239, 246, 251, 252
1980					
1984	Trade Marks (Amendment) Act (c.19)	x, 196, 217		(4)	201, 237
				(5)	205, 237
1986	Patents, Designs and Marks Act (c.39)	x, 196, 217, 236		(6)	21, 34, 195, 205, 209, 238, 239, 245, 246, 247, 248, 256
1988	Copyright, Designs and Patterns Act (c.48)	x, 217		s.11	34, 205, 206, 223, 238, 250, 256
	s.16(3)	164		(1)	185, 205, 239
	s.51	159		(2)	168, 209, 223, 239, 248, 249, 250
	s.85(1)(a)	220			
	(b)	220		(a)	21
	(c)	220		(b)	103, 208, 209, 248
	s.236	159		(3)	205, 239
	s.300	16		s.12	205, 238
1994	Trade Marks Act (c.26)	vii–x, xii, 9, 10, 16, 17, 33, 100, 101, 112, 123, 125, 129, 140, 141, 143, 145, 146, 148, 159, 160, 173, 174, 179, 180, 187, 188, 204, 206, 208, 217, 218, 221, 234, 236, 237, 239, 240, 247		s.13	238
				s.23(4)	174
				s.30	181
				s.31	181
				s.46	103, 181
				(1)(c)	103
	ss 1–4	100		(d)	239
	s.1	205, 249		(4)	103
	(1)	101, 111, 112, 129, 130, 131, 132, 133, 134, 135, 145		s.47	103
				(1)	103, 220
				(6)	239
	s.2	238		s.49	173
	(2)	52		(1)	173
	s.3	129, 130		s.56	78, 226
				(2)	48

1994	Trade Marks Act (c.26)—*cont.*		1994	Trade Marks Act (c.26)—*cont.*	
	s.60	181		para. 4	179
	s.70	206		para. 11	179
	s.92	17		para. 12	179
	s.103 (1)	237		para. 14	181
	(2)	237	1995	Olympic Symbol etc. (Protection) Act (c.32)	184
	Sched. 1	173			
	para. 2	173	1998	Competition Act (c.41)	176
	para. 12(6)	181	1998	Human Rights Act (c.42)	227
	Sched. 2 para. 2	179			

Table of U.K. Statutory Instruments

Trade Marks Rules 1875–1877 87
Trade Marks Rules 1883. 89
    r.15. 88
Trade Marks Rules 1890
    r.15. 88, 90
Trade Marks Rules 1897 r.2 (d) 90
Trade Marks Rules 1994 (S.I. 1994 No. 2583) 180
    r.11 129
    r.13 (8) 180
Olympic Symbol, etc. (Protection) Act Commencement Order 1995 (S.I. 1995 No. 2472) 184
Olympic Association Right (Infringement Proceedings) Regulations 1995 (S.I. 1995 No. 3325) 184

Table of Foreign National Legislation

1962	Benelux Trademark Act.......	140
1974	Australian Trade Practices Act s.52....................	53
1995	Australian Trade Marks Act ...	176
	s.169....................	176
1996	Australian Sydney 2000 Games (Indicia and Images) Protection Act	184
1992	French Intellectual Property Code...................	155
	Arts 171–4	179
	Art. 175	179
1963	Irish Trade Marks Act s.18.....................	124
1995	Portuguese Code of Industrial Property, Law 16/95 Art. L715-2..............	179
1963	South African Trade Marks Act 62 s.36.....................	61
1993	South African Marks Act 194..	61
	s.35.....................	78, 79
1946	United States "Lanham Act" U.S.C.A. para. 1054s.4	180
	s.43(c)....................	247
	s.1125(c)	252
	United States Restatement Third	
	comment b...............	167
	comment c...............	167

Table of European Legislation

Directives
First Council Directive to approximate the laws of Member States relating to trade marks 89/104 [1989] O.J. L40/1 .... ix, xiii, 100, 112, 125, 127, 139, 140, 141, 144, 155, 161, 170, 192, 210, 217, 231
Art. 2 .... 112, 125, 126, 128, 129, 132, 134, 135
Art. 3 .... 125, 128, 129, 134, 139
Art. 3(1) 127
   (a) 126, 127, 128, 129, 132, 135
   (b) 112, 126, 127, 128, 129, 132, 135
   (c) 127, 128, 129, 132, 135, 252, 253
   (d) 127, 128, 129, 132, 135
   (e) 128, 129, 132
   (3) 127, 129, 132, 135, 253
Art. 4 205
   (4) 204
Arts 5–7 255
Art. 5 .... 205, 254
   (1) 205, 206, 209, 210, 254
   (a) 254, 255
   (b) 207, 232, 254
   (2) 206, 209, 210, 254
   (5) 209, 250, 254
Art. 6 .... 205, 210, 250, 255, 256
   (1) 21, 209
   (b) 253
   (c) 255, 256
   (2) 205
Art. 7 .... 205, 255, 256
   (1) 233
   (2) 210, 255
Recital 3 204
Recital 6 105
Recital 7 .... 126, 128, 237
Recital 9 204
Recital 10 .... 207, 208, 209

Council Directive 93/98 harmonising the term of protection of copyright and certain related rights [1993] O.J. L290/9
   Recital 9 140
Council Directive 97/55 amending Directive 84/450 concerning misleading advertising so as to include comparative advertising [1997] O.J. L290/18 239

Regulations
Community Trade Mark Regulation 40/94 [1994] O.J. L11/1 .... ix, 112, 127, 155, 205, 210, 231
Art. 1(a) 105
Art. 4 .... 112, 132
Art. 7 132
Art. 7(1) 105
   (a) 132
   (b) 105, 112, 132, 133
   (c) 132
   (d) 132
   (e) 132, 133
   (e)–(j) 132
   (2) 105
   (3) 105, 107, 132
Art. 14 205
Art. 64 179
   (1) 173
Arts 91–101 205
Art. 93 134
Art. 94 134
Art. 97 205

Table of International Conventions, Treaties, Agreements and Declarations

Convention at The Hague Revision
   Conference, 1925
      Art. 6bis 77
European Convention on Human Rights and Fundamental Freedoms, 1950 .... 227, 228
      Art. 8 227
      Art. 10 228
European Economic Area Agreement, 1992 Annex XVII 192
Madrid Protocol, 1989 6
Paris Convention for the Protection of
   Industrial Property, 1983 .... xi, 77
      Arts 1–12 .... 22, 125
      Art. 6bis 78, 79, 80, 226
      Art. 6quinquies 125
      Art. 6quinquies A(1) 125, 126
      Art. 6quinquies B 125
      Art. 6septies 181
      Art. 10bis 21, 22, 30, 79

Paris Convention for the Protection of Industrial Property, 1983—*cont.*
      Art. 10bis(1) 209
      Art. 10bis(2) 209
      Art. 10bis(3) 209
      Art. 19 125
Revision Conference of Lisbon, 1958. . 77
Treaty of Rome, 1957 x
WTO's Agreement on Trade Related Aspects of Intellectual Property, 1994 (TRIPS) 22, 30, 78, 125, 226
      para. (3) 22
      para. (2).1 22
      Art. 2(1) 125
      Art. 8(2) 107
      Art. 15 128
      Art. 16(2) 78, 226
      Art. 16(3) 78, 226

1. The Brand Owner's View

Liz Cratchley

The Brand Owner's View

Introduction

I intend in this chapter to look at various aspects of trade mark selection, protection and maintenance and at the differences that have taken place over the last 100 or so years. Although 20 years of my working life were spent in the trade marks department of one of the largest brand owners in the world, the views expressed here are my own and not those of Unilever.

While some things are clearly different from what they were 100 years ago, some things remain the same. "I had big ideas of some sort of name—I did not know what—but it was going to be such a marvel, and when I saw it written down in cold ink—names that you could register and fight for, names that did not describe the article, that were neither geographical nor descriptive, did not refer to quality, and got over all the obstacles that the Trade Marks Law has very properly put in front of us—none of them appealed to me."[1] So said William Hesketh Lever in the 1870s when trying to find a trade mark for his new wrapped soap that would eventually be called SUNLIGHT. How many of us have not had the experience of talking to a client and advising him that of all the marks he had selected, the only ones that were protectable were the very ones he did not like?

Selection and Clearance of Trade Marks

In 1875 when W.H. Lever wanted a distinctive trade mark he called on "the best trade-mark and patent agent in Liverpool, W.P. Thompson, to ask for a suitable trade mark".[2] Not only would it be unusual these days to ask your patent or trade mark agent for a suitable trade mark, it would be even more unusual for the agent to be able to do what W.P. Thompson did which was to write down half a dozen *suitable* names, without apparently doing any searching at all.

Crowded trade mark registers have made the selection and clearance of trade marks not only difficult but incredibly time-consuming and this had led to the proliferation of brand creation agencies. The current need for pan-European or world-wide brands has increased the difficulty of selecting and clearing them; the

---

[1] W.H. Lever quoted in C. Wilson, The History of Unilever (Cassell & Company Limited 1954).
[2] *Ibid.*

brands, of course, have to be pronounceable in every major language and must not mean anything unpleasant or inappropriate in any language used in a country where the brand will be used. Even with the best brand creation agency and with a bucket of money, the process is lengthy and frustrating for the brand owner. When all the marks invented by the brand creation agency have turned out to be difficult or impossible and certainly time-consuming to clear, even today a brand owner may turn to his in-house or outside trade mark adviser and say in desperation, "Well you invent one for us".

Have trade marks themselves changed in the last 100 years? Some guidance is given in David Tatham's article entitled "Times Past"[3] in which he reviews the first Trade Mark Journals, that is, those published between May 3 and December 30, 1876. These were the first trade marks published under the Trade Marks Registration Act 1875; since the 1875 Act did not permit the registration of words unless the marks in question had been used before the passing of the Act, most of the marks advertised in these journals are device marks of one kind or another. Not only are these marks registered for goods which are unknown to us today, such as "horse blister" and "metal corset busks", they are, for the most part, very ornate marks including lots of descriptive material which we would not attempt to register today, and which would not be used. Some marks which were advertised in 1896 we would recognise today, for example, GUINNESS stout, STONES dry ginger wine. But clearly few marks are as long-lasting as these; who today knows of ROWLAND'S KALYDOR which was used for removing "eruptions, sunburns and freckles" from the skin?

Another interesting article providing insights into the development of trade marks over the years is "The Changing Face of Trademarks—An Australian Experience" by Andros Chrysiliou.[4] This article shows some advertisements from the 1930s which are interesting in their own right but, more importantly, makes the point that trademarks have always had secondary functions to the primary function of indicating origin. Certainly in the 1930s they were used to indicate quality but in later years the marketing function has come to dominate the nature of trade marks. For marketing reasons, descriptive trade marks are more popular than invented ones since they tell the consumer what the product is or what it does without the need to educate the consumer. Certainly from my own experience, marketing personnel are now more likely to want to use unregistrable trade marks than good, registrable invented words that seems to have been the case in the past. David Tatham's article[5] does, however, quote registrations of words such as MASTERPIECE

---

[3] *Trademark World*, October 1992.
[4] *Trademark World*, April 1990.
[5] See note 3.

and INSTANTANEOUS which not even today's marketeers would dare propose.

As I have already stated, the clearance of marks today is much more difficult than it used to be due to the crowded registers and the need for clearance on a multi-country basis. When the first marks were advertised in 1876, they had hardly any difficulty getting past the relative grounds hurdle since the 1875 Act was the first Trade Marks Act in the United Kingdom. Although section 6 of the Act stated that the Registrar "shall not . . . register in respect of the same goods or classes of goods a trade-mark identical with one which is already registered with respect to such goods or classes of goods, . . . nor a trade-mark which is so nearly resembling a trade-mark already on the register as to be calculated to deceive",[6] at least for the first few years the number of marks on the register was not very great. Thus, W.H. Lever, when he had considered the list of suitable marks prepared by W.P. Thompson for several days, reversed his original view and decided that SUNLIGHT was just the one he was looking for, rushed off the Liverpool to ask Thompson to register it at once. He was "all of a tremble to have it registered, for fear somebody else had got it".[7] Fortunately no one had, and the rest is history.

Even 30 years ago, the clearance of trade marks was not so difficult as it is today. One searched, found that the mark was not available or was going to encounter difficulties and therefore rejected the possibility of using the mark. A second or third possible mark was likely to be found to be available. Today, if a mark looks even remotely possible it will be pursued since any other mark selected will be likely to encounter the same kind of difficulties. If an identical, conflicting mark is found in a number of countries, the first question to be asked is "Is it in use?" and the second is "Do we know who owns it?". If the answer to the first question is "no" and the answer to the second is "yes", then an approach can be made to the owner to see if he is prepared to sell his registrations. In some circumstances, if the answer to the first question is "yes", an approach will still be made although the financial implications are likely to be much greater!

If the marks found in the searches are not identical, but sufficiently similar to cause problems, the same kind of procedure can be followed but in this case it is more important to find out if the marks are being used and, if so, on what goods or services. It may be possible to come to same arrangement with the owner short of outright assignment, if the conflicting marks are of interest only for dissimilar goods or services. Such negotiations inevitably take time, particularly if there is no established line of communication between

---

[6] It is of interest to note that the 1875 Act hyphenated the word "trade-mark"; today I believe the only country to do this is Canada.
[7] See note 1.

the two brand owning companies involved, so inevitably it is taking longer and longer to clear marks for use on a pan-country basis. Marketing people always want a mark to be available immediately, if not sooner, so that it is essential for brand owners today to keep their trade mark advisers informed of their new product developments—something which was not perhaps so vital 30 or more years ago.

Filing Programmes

In 1876 when Lever rushed off to Liverpool to get his trade mark agent to register SUNLIGHT, there was no thought in his mind that his competitors might find out what he was up to before he launched his new soap. Today one of the conflicts which a brand owner has to resolve is that between filing early to ensure that the rights obtained are his but letting his competitors know what he is doing, and delaying filing so that his competitors will remain in ignorance but taking the risk that someone else will have applied to register the trade mark. In my own view, the conflict can only be resolved by filing early.

However, in the case of some particularly paranoid brand owners or where the project involved is very secret, an application with a wide specification of goods can be filed so as to try and disguise the actual goods or services on which the brand will be used; today a multi-class application is useful since this makes the "disguise" more effective. An application filed for goods in Classes 3 and 29 could be used for shampoo or margarine, and it is for the competitor to try and find out which are the real goods of interest. Another possibility is to file in the name of an "unknown" subsidiary which may not be immediately recognised by a competitor as being associated with the brand owner. However, these ruses lead to extra work, extra expense and should, in my view, be avoided if possible.

The next question is to decide in which countries to file. Clearly if the brand owner's only business interests are in the United Kingdom, then a local application is all that is needed. But if his interests are likely to be wider than that, should the application be filed in all countries at once, or should a "rolling" programme of filing be adopted where applications are filed first in the most important countries while others are left till later? Obviously, in many cases it is a question of expense and it may not be economically possible to file in all the countries of interest at the same time. In such cases, the brand owner needs to think even more carefully about the system he is going to use for filing: the Community Trade Mark (CTM), the Madrid Protocol relating to international arrangements and so on—the cheaper the system then the more countries he can cover at the beginning of the operation—this must be the more effective strategy in the end.

It was the custom among brand owners more than 30 years ago, if a brand was needed internationally, to adopt a rolling programme since it was always extremely unlikely that the product or service would be launched in all the countries of interest within the space of only one or two years. This had the advantage that the cost was spread out over several, and in some cases many, years but it did in the end turn out to have disadvantages. Competition became ever fiercer in the 1960s to 1990s and filing in some countries first led to the brand owner's competitor seeing what the brand owner was doing; if the product was successful, the competitor himself could then file for the same mark in the countries where the brand owner had not yet filed. Of course, if the brand owner's product was unsuccessful, then he had saved some money by not filing in all countries at once.

Thus in the 1960s and after, many brand owners adopted the policy of filing internationally for a new brand name since this at least prevented competitors—either international competitors or purely local ones—from delaying product launches, causing litigation and so on by filing applications to register the same brand. This policy had the disadvantage that it was expensive; competitors also began to feel that this method of proceeding was not of any real benefit to them and consequently in the later 1990s reason began to prevail. Brand owners now identify the countries of priority to them for a particular mark and file in those countries; if these applications proceed and the product is a success, they then file in a second tranche of countries in which they are interested. This is a matter of the economic cycle; sooner or later the world may go into recession and then competition will become even fiercer and a brand owner will have to take all possible steps to ensure that his position is secure with respect to that of his competitors. In such a time, the strategy may again be followed in which applications are filed in all possible countries of interest just to ensure that the competition cannot steal a march on the brand owner.

It goes without saying that a brand owner should know if and where his products are likely to be counterfeited; if the products are subject to counterfeiting then the countries where these are likely to originate will be included in the first tranche of countries where applications are filed.

There are other difficulties for the brand owner to consider. He has an old registration of a mark which is going to be used on a new product which did not exist at the date of the registration. If COMFORT is registered for "detergents and preparations for laundry use", will the registration cover "fabric conditioners" which were unknown when the registration was first obtained? What does the brand owner do? Does he hope that the old registration covers the new goods on which he intends to use the mark? In my view, a fresh application should always be filed to be on the safe side.

What about the specification of goods or services? In my experience brand owners have always filed for very wide specifications of goods or services except in countries such as the

USA and Canada where "normal commercial terms" or proof of use prior to filing was required. This often results in the brand owners getting a wider specification than they are entitled to and can have the result that the registration can be invalidated for non-use. Specific terms in specifications of goods can also be more helpful than general terms. I can remember the case of *Unilever v. Johnson*[8] when Unilever was suing Johnson for using the trade mark LIFEGUARD. One of the questions which was considered at length was whether the term "detergents" in Unilever's specification of goods covered the toilet cleaner on which Johnson Wax were using the trade mark. Whitford J. asked one of the witnesses in the case: "If your wife asked you to go and buy some detergent, would she expect you to return with some LIFEGUARD toilet cleaner?" The answer was "no". One lesson to be learned from that case was that brand owners should be more careful about what they file their applications for—specifications should be more precise. Of course, the specification of goods should not be so precise as to put the registration in jeopardy. All brand owners would hope to avoid the situation which occurred in the nineteenth century when Cheseborough Manufacturing Co. filed an application for VASELINE in the United Kingdom for goods which included the word "vaseline".[9] To use your brand name in a generic fashion in the specification of goods of your trade mark application must be the height of folly.

Another question for the brand owner to consider is for what marks he files. The word mark alone? In any special script he is using? Packaging? One certain thing is that under the 1994 Act, brand owners whose products are the subject to the attentions of "look-alikes" are filing many more applications, at least in the United Kingdom, to cover all aspects of the products and its packaging in order to combat these attentions.

Relative Grounds

In this section I would like to deal with what are now called "relative grounds" and which arise when there is a conflict between marks during the prosecution of an application and/or during any opposition phase.

One of the most time-consuming and irritating relative grounds of objection occurred in the United Kingdom in the 1970s when "danger to public health" objections were raised by the Trade Marks Registry during the prosecution of an application. This objection arose due to Parliament's concern, specifically, about the possible confusion between SUNDROPS bleach and SUNDROPS fruit juice. Following the resultant publicity, the UK Trade Marks Registry made

---

[8] [1989] F.S.R. 583.
[9] (1902) 19 R.P.C. 342.

a point of cross-searching certain goods with others even though they were not at all similar. Therefore, detergents and other Class 3 goods were always cross-searched with Class 30 goods and if an identical mark was found this would lead to an objection under relative grounds. The whole point of the SUNDROPS controversy was that the public might be confused and drink the bleach instead of the fruit juice. However, the practice of the Trade Marks Registry did nothing to prevent *use* of the "conflicting marks"; it merely prevented registration of the later mark. There was always the possibility of overcoming the objection by limiting the specification of goods of the later mark to "none being in liquid form" since it was thought by the powers that be that goods in solid form were not so likely to be confused. But if the goods on which the later mark was used were liquid then it was obviously not possible to do this.

In the case with which I am most familiar, such a limitation was not possible since JIF scouring cream was a liquid, as was JIF lemon juice. A considerable amount of time was spent trying to prove that even if you did put JIF scouring cream in your gin and tonic instead of JIF lemon, you would come to no great harm. All to no avail. However, eventually wiser counsels prevailed since it was realised that a great amount of the Trade Mark Registry's time and that of their clients was being spent on these objections while the public were still free to drink SUNDROPS bleach.

Under the 1938 Act, one was able to deal with some objections on relative grounds raised during prosecution of the application by means of notice or consent. The brand owner always regarded notice as being more acceptable than consent since in the case of notice nothing was required from the potential competitor. In some instances it was difficult to persuade the Trade Marks Registry that a consent would overcome the relative grounds objection but all this has changed; under the 1994 Act, if a consent is provided, the Registry will deem it to have overcome the relative grounds objection. The State will not act as a "nanny" to brand owners; if the owner of a conflicting mark is prepared to give a consent, the later mark will proceed so that it is up to the brand owner to ensure that he does not give consent inappropriately.

Some brand owners were very exercised by the requirement of consent in the 1970s and 1980s after the line of cases in the European Court of Justice concerning the doctrine of "common origin". Clearly, common origin between two marks can arise due to assignment of one mark from one concern to another, but does the giving of consent mean that the two marks have a common origin? The concern was that giving a consent in the United Kingdom to the registration of a similar mark would lead to "common origin" between the two marks and therefore prevent any objection being raised to the registration or use of the second mark in any other country of the E.U. Similar fears were felt about revocation. In the 1970s and 1980s, if a revocation application was filed against one of a company's marks in one country of the E.U. then even if no grounds for contesting the revocation were available and the company would have liked to cancel the mark, the fear was always there that this too might lead to a "common origin" arising between the two marks. This might result in goods bearing the other mark being freely sold in countries of the E.U. where the mark the subject of the revocation application was in use due to the doctrine of common origin.

After *Hag II*,[10] both of these fears died a not untimely death. But for a time when they were a worry to brand owners they did consume time which could have been more beneficially spent, and also led to lengthy disputes which could have been avoided.

The practice in the United Kingdom relating to objections on relative grounds has changed; it is now much easier to speak to someone in authority at the Trade Marks Registry and to get some help and guidance. In the 1960s it was necessary to apply for, and attend, a Hearing before one could speak to someone at a high level at the Registry. I am sure that many in the profession can confirm that they have spent hours preparing for a Hearing on the basis of several citations of earlier marks, when on opening the proceedings the Hearing Officer immediately waived earlier objections. This did not bring the Registry into good repute and was, yet again, a waste of time and money and something which the brand owners found difficult to understand.

As far as relative grounds in opposition proceedings are concerned there has been a change in practice as a result of legislation rather than any change in the outlook of the respective brand owners or any independent change in the practice of the Trade Marks Registry. Prior to the 1994 Act, oppositions were scarce and were mostly settled long before the evidence stages were completed. However, this was largely achieved by the grant of almost indefinite extensions of time and therefore opposition proceedings were very lengthy. Now, with the set periods for each stage of the procedure and the little chance of extensions of time, oppositions are filed more as a matter of course and have to be settled much later in the procedure. The proposed cooling off period is to be welcomed since this may give the brand owners a chance to settle things before too much time and expense has been incurred.

One matter which has exercised brand owners for some time is whether a compulsory search should be done by the Trade Marks Registry as part of the prosecution procedure. Many brand owners have felt that this is a waste of time and money since they always search before filing and thus the search done by the Registry is a duplication of effort. The 1994 Act guarantees the continuance of the search until 2004 at which time the procedure will be reviewed.

Now that the U.K. Trade Marks Registry completes the process of examining and advertising marks more expeditiously, the need for an official search becomes even more questionable. In the past, when we

---

[10] *CNL-Sucal v. Hag* [1990] E.C.R.-I 3711.

heard a great deal about the "purity" of the U.K. Trade Marks Register it was possible to make out a case for having an official search. Now that U.K. applications are published before the end of any priority period of a potentially conflicting mark, and before any cited CTM applications have been registered, the purity of the U.K. Register must be in doubt. It becomes more and more doubtful whether the official search serves any useful purpose. We may therefore see a time in the early part of the twenty-first century when the official search is done away with after more than 125 years of its existence.

Management of brands

Since the inclusion of brand valuations on balance sheets became more common, the importance of brands has been increasingly realised—and not just by those companies which do include brand values on their balance sheets. Still, however, some companies do not give their brands the attention they deserve. "Brands are valuable assets which have a massive impact on the way you run your business. No one would hand a £12.5bn asset to a 23-year-old in the marketing department—but many companies that aspire to global reach do just that with their brands."[11] So what should brand owners be doing now that they did not do perhaps 50 years ago? Perhaps four items are the most important:

(i) House name or individual brands
(ii) Global or local brands
(iii) Ownership of brands
(iv) Brand extension

(i) House Names or Individual Brands

Some companies like Coca-Cola and Sony use their corporate brands while others, like Unilever, do not use the house name but use individual brands for individual products. One advantage of using separate brands is that if something goes drastically wrong with one product, the whole range of the company's goods is not affected. If Perrier had been marketing a range of products under the PERRIER name when it was discovered that their mineral water contained impurities, the sales of these other brands might have been affected in an equally detrimental fashion. On the other hand, with a well-known global house mark, the pressure to find new names is reduced or eliminated and the cachet attached to the house mark by its existing products and services can be extended easily to a new product in a similar category.

---

[11] Mr Perrier of Interbrand quoted in the *Financial Times* of October 22, 1998, "Perspective: Managing Global Brands".

For various reasons it may be preferable to have a series of global brands rather than merely using the single house name. This may occur where the products are in different categories, for example, who would want to buy a margarine having the same brand name as a lavatory cleaner? Differences may be desirable for other reasons; Campbell discovered that to use the brand so familiar from Campbell's soup on a spaghetti sauce was not a good thing since the consumers thought that the spaghetti sauce would be thin like soup. Nestlé own the BUITONI brand of Italian food products but did not, at one time, use the name Nestlé on the products. It was thought likely that this was because consumers saw the BUITONI brand as Italian and would not have liked to see that it belonged to a Swiss multi-national. Now, however, the Nestlé name does appear on the BUITONI products.

None of these factors seems to me to have changed in the course of the last century. Unilever has always used brand names rather than a house name while companies like Coca-Cola or Hoover have always used their house names, with or without the addition of sub-brand names.

(ii) Global or Local Brands?

Clearly there are cost-savings to be made if brands are global and the packaging is virtually the same wherever the product is sold. The same advertising can be used in many countries and the sources of manufacture can be reduced. This has led to some attempt in recent years to try and standardise the use of brands. For example, Mars MARATHON chocolate in the United Kingdom became SNICKERS in the interests of standardisation. Similarly the US company Frito-Lay tries to use its LAY brand on its potato crisps in each country except where it acquires an existing strong brand, such as WALKERS in the United Kingdom. Unilever uses JIF as a name for its scouring cream in the United Kingdom and elsewhere but in some countries CIF is used instead—for example, where JIF is difficult to pronounce. Elsewhere VISS is used to avoid third party rights. To try to standardise such a variety of brands even in Europe would be difficult since all the brands have been on the market for a long period and have built up brand equity. JIF, CIF and VISS are only standardised in so far as their packaging is concerned. There must be many more such examples.

Some products may be more difficult to standardise than others; foodstuffs, for example. Most countries have their own tastes and their own particular local food products so that it may not be possible to standardise brands across the globe. Clear exceptions are McDonalds hamburgers, and some brands for ice cream and snacks which are universal.

Until the advent of the Common Market, it was thought convenient to have a global brand but not a complete disaster if this could not be obtained. In the current climate, a company doing business in the E.U. will want a common brand at least for that area. This makes the search for new brands even more difficult since there can be no "holes" in the coverage.

(iii) Ownership of Brands

The trend in the last 20 years or so has been to concentrate ownership of the brands in one single company which is easy if the brand owner is only one company but rather more difficult if the brand owner is a multi-national since it may have a legacy of brands owned by different companies within the group in various countries. It has been realised that if the ownership of brands is concentrated in one company, it is possible to license other companies in the group to use the brands and thus to gain a royalty income. The trend is now towards centralised ownership of brands. This may not necessarily be by the holding company, but may be by a specially constituted company whose sole function is to own the brands and to collect royalties from their use.

A further advantage of one company owning all the brands, is that if a part of the company is sold, no brands are inadvertently sold with it. While this may seem a far-fetched advantage, I am aware of instances where this has happened.

(iv) Brand Extensions

Some companies have used the brand extension idea for a very long time. One example is Colgate-Palmolive with its range of AJAX cleaning products. Unilever on the other hand took over 70 years to extend its SUNLIGHT brand from a soap to a dishwash liquid.

There are clear advantages in extending a brand to other similar products; the products must usually be similar although Disney has managed to extend the brand to a vast range of merchandise. If a brand name is familiar, a consumer will be more like to notice a new product with the same brand and therefore give consideration to buying the product. Today when it has been discovered that consumers spend on average 12 seconds from the time the supermarket shelf is approached to the time an item is placed in the trolley[12] and that they examine only 1.2 brands on average, this must be a great advantage. How different from the pre-supermarket days when one went to the counter in Sainsbury's and asked for a particular product.

However, care must to taken that the extension does not threaten the benefits of the original product. For example, Carnation considered extending its name FRISKIES used on dog food to LADY

---

[12] B.E. Kahn, *Mastering Marketing: Brand Strategies and Consumer Behaviour* (*Financial Times*).

FRISKIES contraceptive dog food until this was found to adversely affect sales of FRISKIES.[13]

Enforcement

One of the, probably apocryphal, tales I was told when I joined my first firm was of the Smith Hayden[14] case in which the owners of the trade mark HOVIS opposed the registration of OVAX for bread improvers. Hovis lost because the court held that there was no reasonable likelihood of deception and confusion between the two marks. The Managing Director of Hovis was alleged to have said when leaving the court after the judgment: "Well, that will teach them to infringe our trade mark." Such an attitude to litigation, if it ever existed, must be rare today.

Infringement actions in whatever jurisdiction are generally to be avoided. They are more or less expensive but will inevitably take up a good deal of management time and in these days of pressure on head-counts in brand-owning companies, this is to be avoided. It is often thought that multi-nationals have no difficulty with meeting the cost of litigation but things are usually arranged so that the brand in question has to meet the cost of litigation out of its own budget. If the brand is a small one—in multi-national terms—then litigation will be as out of the question for the large company as it is for the small or medium sized company.

In recent years the look-alikes debate has come to the public's attention; an attempt was made to include a clause against look-alikes in the Trade Marks Bill of 1994 but this was rejected. It was said at the time that the new Trade Marks Act would enable a much wider range of marks to be registered so that a trade mark infringement action against a look-alike could be taken rather than an action for passing-off. The recent case where Procter & Gamble's application to register packaging was rejected in the High Court[15] appears to give the lie to this. The brave stand of United Biscuits in the PENGUIN case[16] was helpful, but nothing has happened in the last few years to encourage brand owners to take on their major customers in the courts.

Despite the reluctance to litigate, there is one area where litigation has to be embarked upon. This is in the area of counterfeiting. Counterfeiting has always been a problem but probably until after the second world war, counterfeiters did not export their goods in any quantity from the place of manufacture but only sold locally. Counterfeiting began to assume enormous proportions in the 1970s and it shows no sign of declining. The most obvious counterfeit

---

[13] See note 12.
[14] (1946) 63 R.P.C. 97.
[15] *Re Procter & Gamble's Trade Mark Application* [1999] E.T.M.R. 375.
[16] *United Biscuits (UK) Ltd v. Asda Stores Ltd* [1997] R.P.C. 513.

products to come to the attention of the average consumer in the United Kingdom are counterfeit watches, perfumes, and clothing which can not only be purchased there but also in holiday destinations such as Singapore, Hong Kong and Turkey where the purchase of counterfeit goods is regarded almost as part of the holiday activities.

It is not only "luxury" goods that are counterfeited: counterfeit detergent has been sold in the United Kingdom as has counterfeit liquor. The Far and Middle East are hot spots for counterfeit toiletries, foods such as tea, as well as the usual luxury goods. If a brand owner finds that his goods are being counterfeited, he should realise that he has to take action or lose his market altogether. In Nigeria, one brand owner took no action against counterfeiters and eventually could not sell any of his own products in that market and had to regard it as closed to him.

Counterfeiters can copy products very quickly, including those specifically designed to prevent them being copied. SUNSILK shampoo which was the target of many counterfeiters in the Middle East and in Taiwan in the 1970s was redesigned to prevent the packaging being copied so easily. Although it took the brand owners 18 months to design the new packaging, it only took the counterfeiters 12 months to copy it. Holograms have also been put on packaging to try as help the consumer recognise the genuine product. Procter & Gamble put a hologram on their TIDE detergent in the Middle East but it was not long before the counterfeiters had also included a hologram on the counterfeit product.

It is helpful for brand owners to join an association like the Anti-Counterfeiting Group (see later) which enables them to share experiences with other brand owners and to learn from each other's experience. Anti-counterfeiting strategy can cost huge sums of money—but if it is not done and the whole market is lost—it must be worth the expense.

Associations of Brand Owners

Brand owners, being by their nature concerned about competition and competitors, are often reluctant to combine into associations. Of course their trade mark advisers join the various professional associations but this is not quite the same as the brand owning company itself becoming a member of an organisation where it will inevitably meet other, competitive, brand owners. The instances which I know of where companies have joined together have usually occurred, at least initially, to combat specific issues and I am aware of three such organisations:

(i) The Trade Marks Patents and Designs Federation (TMPDF)

This organisation was formed after the first world war by a number of brand owners who wanted to lobby against the proposed Empire

Trade Mark. The fight was successful since the Empire Trade Mark has disappeared without trace. Initially the Federation was called the Trade Mark Federation (TMF) but in 1920 it was constituted as the TMPDF after it had been realised by the brand owners that it could have uses beyond the Empire Trade Mark, concerning itself with trade mark matters in general. Today the Federation handles trade mark issues by means of its Trade Marks Committee and its Council. Over the last nearly 80 years of its life the Federation has dealt with a great number of trade mark issues from the point of view of its members, the brand owners. There are few issues on which the members of the Federation have been unable to come to a common view—one being the look-alikes debate. Some members of the Federation are not troubled by look-alikes and yet others see no harm in them and therefore the Federation has had to sit on the fence on this issue.

The major issue with which the Federation is dealing at the time of writing is the issue of parallel imports and exhaustion of rights. In this instance the members of the Federation have agreed that they are opposed to international exhaustion and therefore have been able to put their weight on this side of the debate.

(ii) Anti-Counterfeiting Group (ACG)

This organisation was formed in 1980 by a group of brand owning companies who thought that the growing problem of counterfeiting might be dealt with more effectively if the brand owners spoke with one voice and had an organisation where they could exchange views and information. As a consequence of activity by the ACG and others, the criminal offence of fraudulent use of a trade mark was re-introduced into the Copyright Designs and Patents Act 1988, section 300.[17] Until this time, the various enforcement agencies had to use other pieces of legislation such as the Trade Descriptions Act 1968 to try to stem the tide of counterfeit products manufactured in or being imported into the United Kingdom. Even when this piece of legislation was on the statute book there were problems since the level of the fines imposed tended to be rather low and the use of disclaimers in the case of *Kent County Council v. Price*[18] led to further difficulties. In that case, the seller of the counterfeits put notices reading "Brand Copy" on his stall and also told customers that the garments he was selling were copies. He was acquitted.

As a result of further activity by the ACG and others, the Trade Marks Act 1994 contains useful anti-counterfeiting provisions; these replace the offence of fraudulent use of a trade mark introduced by the Copyright, Designs and Patents Act 1988. The 1994 Act also

---

[17] For a fuller account, see A. Worsdall and A. Clark, *Anti-Counterfeiting: A Practical Guide* (1998, Jordan Publishing Limited.)
[18] (1993) 12 Tr. L.R. 137b DC.

imposes a duty on local authorities to enforce these provisions. Section 92 of the Act defines the primary offences in term of infringement instead of requiring an intention to cause loss to another or an intention that the goods should be taken as connected in the course of trade with the brand owner. This has dealt with the problem of disclaimers in *Price*.

Sub-groups within the ACG reflect the interests of various industry sectors and enable those sectors to discuss problems with others in the same industry sector. Those industries such as footwear and clothing which have done this, find it extremely useful. Nonetheless there are still other sectors where the brand owners are not prepared to meet together in an industry grouping and prefer to soldier on alone.

(iii) British Brands Group (BBG)

This organisation is another which was formed to meet a particular need: that of combating look-alikes. The group was originally called the British Producers and Brand Owners Group and was set up during the passage of the Trade Marks Bill through Parliament in 1994 in the hope that a clause could be inserted in the Bill to deal with the problem of look-alikes. The activity of the group certainly raised the profile of the look-alikes problem in the press, coinciding as it did with the launch of Virgin Cola which Coca-Cola thought bore more than a passing resemblance to their Coca-Cola pack design.

Even though no clause to deal with the look-alikes problem was eventually included in the Trade Marks Act 1994, the Trade and Industry Minister stated in the House of Commons at the time that "even though we are firmly in favour of robust competition, some of the examples of look-alike products do seem to be close to the boundary between what is fair in business and what is not. I would therefore like to warn the producers of these goods . . . if they continue to sail close to the wind, there will undoubtedly be pressure on the government and, as I have said, we would look at the matter again." The BBG has therefore continued to exert pressure on the government to take action to deal with this problem which brand owners believe continues unabated.

Recently, the BBG has taken up cudgels in another debate of concern to brand owners: that of international exhaustion. Time will tell if the BBG is successful in this regard.

The Future for Brands

The decline and fall of manufacturers' brands have been forecast for some time. It was forecast as long ago as 1963[19] that with rising

---

[19] R. Brech, *Britain 1984: Unilever's Forecast* (1963, Darton, Longman & Todd Ltd.)

standards of living, advertising would have to change from what was thought to be "cuffing and shouting" to something more subtle. It was also thought that "with the developments of supermarkets and 'own brands' retailing, the manufacturer will find it more difficult to keep his own name before the public." In 1989, Frank Hone[20] forecast that new brands in the United States would decline and fall in the 1990s due to the increasing cost of new product introduction, the rise in the failure of new products and the rise of retailer power. Hone's view was contested by a number of name creation experts;[21] several of them thought that while no manufacturer would launch a new brand if it could successfully extend an existing brand, new brands were by no means a thing of the past. Various reasons were cited: consumers' liking and demand for ever greater variety; the need for new pan-European and global brands rather than purely national ones; development of brands by newly industrialised countries; generation of new brands by new industries such as the computer industry.

I have not noticed a decline in the introduction of new brands in the last 10 years. The U.K. Trade Marks Registry is receiving record numbers of applications, notwithstanding the existence of the Community Trade Mark Office in Alicante. What percentage of these applications are for extensions of old brands has not been assessed, but I cannot believe that there are more applications for extensions or existing brands being filed than for totally new brands. Despite all the difficulties involved in creating, protecting and maintaining brands, brand owning companies will, I believe, continue to develop new brands at the same or at a greater rate than in the past; the important thing is that these brands should be managed effectively so that at the start of the twenty-second century there will be new, strong, global brands to talk about in addition to those we know so well today.

---

[20] *Trademark World*, October 1989: "The Decline and Fall of New Brands in the US".
[21] *Trademark World*, October 1989.

2. Leading Cases in Passing Off

Christopher Morcom Q.C.

Leading Cases in Passing Off

Introduction

The term "leading case" is not necessarily confined to decisions of the House of Lords. The House of Lords has, on a number of occasions, defined and redefined the tort of passing off.[1] Generally speaking these decisions have, on a proper analysis, done little more than to affirm, on each occasion, the basic requirements of the tort, although they may also have served to remind us of its flexibility. But there are many other cases which may reasonably be described as leading cases; they not only emphasise the flexibility of the tort, but point the way to other kinds of conduct which are within its scope, even if this is not clear from the House of Lords decisions themselves. Such decisions are important, because they do demonstrate that British law may in fact comply with the requirements of Article 10bis of the Paris Convention for the Protection of Industrial Property to a greater extent than has sometimes been suggested.

Article 10bis of the Paris Convention

Artical 10bis of the Paris Convention, entitled "Unfair Competition", is in terms which have recently[2] become more familiar:

(1) The countries of the Union are bound to assure to nationals of such countries effective protection against unfair competition.
(2) Any act of competition contrary to honest practices in industrial or commercial matters constitutes an act of unfair competition.
(3) The following in particular are prohibited:
   1. all acts of such a nature as to create confusion by any means whatsoever with the establishment, the goods, or the industrial or commercial activities, of a competitor;
   2. false allegations in the course of trade of such a nature as to discredit the establishment, the goods, or the industrial or commercial activities, of a competitor;

---

[1] See *e.g. Reddaway v. Banham* [1896] A.C. 199; (1896) 13 R.P.C. 218; *William Edge & Sons Ltd. v. William Nicholls Ltd.* [1911] A.C. 693; (1911) 28 R.P.C. 582; *Spalding (AG) v. Gamage* (1915) 32 R.P.C. 273; *Office Cleaning Services Ltd. v. Westminster Window and General Cleaners Ltd.* (1946) 63 R.P.C. 39; *Erven Warnink B.V. v. Townend (J) & Sons (Hull) Ltd.* [1979] A.C. 731; [1980] R.P.C. 31; *Reckitt & Colman Products Ltd. v. Borden Inc.* [1990] R.P.C. 340.

[2] See ss. 10(6) and 11(2)(a) of the Trade Marks Act 1994 and Art. 6.1 of the First Council Directive 89/104.

3. Indications or allegations the use of which in the course of trade is liable to mislead the public as to the nature, the manufacturing process, the characteristics, the suitability for their purpose, or the quantity, of the goods.

It should be noted that the provisions of the TRIPS Agreement (Trade Related Aspects of Intellectual Property Rights)[3] re-impose the obligations of Members of the Paris Convention, to comply, *inter alia*, with Articles 1 to 12 of the Convention. It seems clear from the words 'in particular' that paragraph (3) is intended to be non-exhaustive. So other practices than those specified, and which are contrary to honest practices in industrial or commercial matters, may fall within the definition of unfair competition in paragraph (2). Even paragraph (2).1 is broader than the accepted definition of passing off, which requires a misrepresentation. It has been said that the essence of passing off is deception[4]; if that is so, then if mere "confusion" is proved, there would not be passing off.[5] In order to see to what extent the law of passing off does meet the United Kingdom's obligations, and to determine how much further the tort may be applicable, some leading cases will be examined.

Decisions Applying the Law Outside the Traditional Form of Passing Off

Traditionally the principle of passing off was stated[6] to be that "nobody has any right to represent his goods as the goods of anybody else". However even in that case it seemed clear that the list of different kinds of passing off was not regarded as closed. It was only a few years later, in *Spalding v. Gamage*,[7] that the selling of inferior quality goods of the plaintiff as the plaintiff's superior quality goods was held to be passing off. Some years later, a series of important decisions applied the law to cases in which what the defendant was doing was, in essence, trading on the reputation of the plaintiff but not actually representing that his goods were the plaintiff's goods or even goods connected with the plaintiff. The leading case in this area was that of Danckwerts J. (as he then was) in *J. Bollinger v. Costa Brava Wine Company Ltd*,[8] the "Spanish Champagne" case. The case is of particular interest because the defendant had previously been acquitted of an offence under the Merchandise Marks Acts. The judge was satisfied on the evidence that a substantial proportion of the public were likely to be misled

---

[3] Art. 2. The Agreement is administered by the World Trade Organisation (formerly GATT.)
[4] As was pointed out recently by Jacob J. in *Hodgkinson & Corby Ltd. v. Wards Mobility Service Ltd.* [1995] F.S.R. 169 at 175.
[5] See *e.g. HFC Bank Plc v. Midland Bank Plc* (Lloyd J.) [2000] F.S.R. 176, ChD.
[6] *e.g.* by Lord Halsbury L.C. in *Reddaway v. Banham*, note 1 above, (1896) 13 R.P.C. at 224.
[7] See note 1 above.
[8] [1961] R.P.C. 116.

by the description "Spanish Champagne" applied to a wine which was not Champagne. This decision has been applied in a number of other cases, including the "Scotch whisky" case,[9] and was finally approved and applied by the House of Lords in the "Advocaat" case.[10]

Another result of the development of the law[11] was that, after early suggestions that an action for passing off could only succeed if there was some common field of activity in which (however remotely) the parties were engaged,[12] it was finally made clear that there was no such requirement as a rule of law, even if it remained the position that it might be more difficult to establish a case of passing off where the defendant was trading in a completely different field. A leading decision which confirmed this point was that of Falconer J. in *Lego System A/S v. Lego M. Lemelstrich*.[13]

In subsequent decision the courts have on several occasions demonstrated that the list of categories of passing off is indeed not closed. Two particular examples will suffice. The first case is *Bristol Conservatories Ltd. v. Conservatories Custom Built Ltd.*,[14] a decision of the Court of Appeal. The plaintiff designed and manufactured ornamental conservatories, and the defendant was a competitor. The plaintiff's case was not that the defendant was copying the plaintiff's conservatories. Such a claim might well have met with the same kind of problems as those encountered by the plaintiff in *Hodgkinson & Corby v. Wards Mobility*.[15] The plaintiff's case was based on the conduct of the defendant's sales representatives, who had been showing to potential customers, as a sample of their products and workmanship, a portfolio of photographs which were in fact photographs of the plaintiff's conservatories. The defendant applied to strike out the statement of claim as disclosing no reasonable cause of action, and succeeded at first instance. The Court of Appeal reversed the decision. In the court's view, on the case as pleaded, the defendant was seeking, by a misrepresentation, to induce customers to purchase conservatories from them in order to obtain a conservatory from the same commercial source which had designed and manufactured those shown in the photographs. If instead, the defendant's conservatories were supplied, that was passing off. The court made it clear that it did not consider that there was any reason to hold that the House of Lords in *Warnink* expressly or by

---

[9] *Walker (John) & Sons Ltd. v. Ost (Henry) & Co. Ltd* [1970] R.P.C. 489.
[10] *Warnink*, above, note 1.
[11] Comprehensively reviewed in another chapter, see Carty, p.33.
[12] e.g. *McCulloch v. Lewis A. May* (1947) 65 R.P.C. 58.
[13] [1983] F.S.R. 155. See also the clear explanation of the position by Russell L.J. (as he then was) in *Annabel's (Berkeley Square) Ltd. v. G. Schock (trading as Annabel's Escort Agency)* [1972] R.P.C. 838, 844.
[14] [1989] R.P.C. 455.
[15] See note 4 above. It is to be noted that in that case Jacob J. accepted that, as a matter of law, when the court is concerned with the appearance of the article itself, if the ingredients of passing off are made out, there is no policy exception by way of defence, and the defendant must always do enough to avoid deception to escape liability.

implication ruled that the tort of passing off, outside the extended form approved and established by the decision, should be limited to the classic form of a trader representing his own goods as the goods of somebody else. Ralph Gibson L.J. cited an important passage from Lord Diplock's speech in *Warnink*[16]:

> Nevertheless, the increasing recognition by Parliament of the need for more rigorous standards of commercial honesty is a factor which should not be overlooked by a judge confronted by the choice whether or not to extend by analogy, in circumstances in which it has not previously been applied, a principle which has been applied in previous cases where the circumstances, although different, have some features in common with those of the case which he has to decide. Where over a period of years there can be discerned a steady trend in legislation which reflects the view of successive Parliaments as to what the public interest demands in a particular field of law, development of the common law and that part of the same field which has been left to it ought to proceed upon a parallel rather than a diverging course.

The second case is *Associated Newspapers plc v. Insert Media Ltd.*,[17] which concerned the practice of inserting advertising materials into newspapers. The plaintiff published two national newspapers, one a daily and the other a Sunday edition which included a colour magazine. As well as selling advertising space in its publications the plaintiff sold the right to insert loose advertising material between the pages of the magazine; it was expected that this would be extended to include insertion of advertising material into the newspapers themselves. The defendant, which was in the business of insert advertising, proposed, without the plaintiff's knowledge, to arrange for its own advertising material to be inserted between the pages of the plaintiff's publications, through the retail newsagents, prior to delivery of the newspapers to the customers. The defendant was willing, if necessary, to have printed on the inserts a statement of disclaimer disassociating them from the plaintiff. The plaintiff brought a *quia timet* action for passing off. Mummery J. granted a permanent injunction restraining the defendant from inserting unauthorised advertising material into the plaintiff's publications, whether or not the inserts bore a disclaimer. He held that the introduction of unauthorised material between the pages of a publication of the plaintiff, without consent, constituted a misrepresentation that the publication, so altered, was that of the plaintiff, and that the inserts were connected or associated with the plaintiff and their publication, and that such misrepresentation

---

[16] [1980] A.C. 731 at 743B.
[17] [1990] 1 W.L.R. 900 (Mummery J.); [1991] 1 W.L.R. 571, CA.

constituted passing off. He held that the offered disclaimer would not be discernible at the point of sale and that, even if read later, it might suggest collaboration with the plaintiff; it would in any event be insufficient to nullify the misrepresentation. He made the following observations, in effect applying the views of Lord Diplock in *Advocaat*:

> It is important, both in the evaluation of the facts and in the formulation and application of the law, never to lose sight of the legal and economic basis of the action for passing off. That tort has been developed for the protection of the property which exists not in a particular name, mark or style, but in an established business, commercial or professional reputation or goodwill. Those terms embrace the enjoyment of custom and business connection, popularity and good name, and, indeed, all that attracts favour and business to a particular concern and to the goods and services which it supplies. That form of property may be damaged in a number of ways by a wide variety of factual misrepresentations.

The decision was upheld by the Court of Appeal, which did not in any way criticise the judge's observations, which form a useful guide in applying the law when the subject of a claim is a new type of passing off.

The "One in a Million" case

What the cases mentioned above show is that the tort of passing off remains flexible, despite many attempts to define its scope in what might, at first sight, seem comparatively narrow terms. The recent decision of the Court of Appeal in *British Telecommunications plc and others v. One in a Million Ltd. and others*[18] is another example. The case involved the practice which has become known as "domain name grabbing" on the Internet. It provides an opportunity to examine some previous decisions of the courts in other areas, in particular cases concerning the unauthorised registration of company names which are similar to established names in the market. Before looking at the *One in a Million* decision, it is instructive to refer to some of the earlier cases.

Many years ago, Farwell J. delivered a potentially far reaching decision in a case in which a defendant had registered an English company under a name which was virtually identical to the material part of the plaintiff's corporate name.[19] The case is of particular interest because the French plaintiff company, which manufactured

---

[18] [1999] F.S.R. 1, affirming decision at first instance reported at [1998] F.S.R. 158.
[19] *La Société Anonyme des Anciens Établissements Panhard et Levassor v. Panhard-Levassor Motor Company Ltd.* [1901] 2 Ch. 513; (1901) 18 R.P.C. 405.

and sold the once famous Panhard motor cars, had no place of business in England, although its motor cars had sometimes been imported by purchasers abroad. Neither had the defendant traded in this country. The object of those responsible appears to have been to exclude the plaintiff from the country and to prevent them from interfering with some other company which was not a party to the action. The judge's view was clear. He said:

> This appears to me to be a plain case. The Plaintiff's are a well-known firm of manufacturers of motor cars. Their reputation on the evidence has for some years been, I may say, European—including in that term England. Their reputation has certainly extended to England for several years. Although until last December they had no agency in England, and did not sell, so far as I see, directly to England, they sold indirectly in the sense that a company bought their cars and imported them into England, and individuals went over to Paris and bought cars there and imported them into England, so that England was one of their markets.
> ... I should have thought that it was plain that in a case such as I have stated this Court would certainly interfere to protect a foreign trader who has a market in England, in the way I have specified, from having the benefit of his name annexed by a trader here in England who assumes that name without any sort of justification.

In the result, Farwell J. granted an injunction not only to restrain the company and the other defendants, who were responsible for forming the company, from using the name of *Panhard* or *Levassor*, but also to restrain the individual defendants from allowing the defendant company to remain registered under its existing name or any other title or description including the names of *Panhard* and *Levassor* or either of them. This case differs from the *One in a Million* case and the other decisions mentioned hereafter, because the plaintiff was a foreign company without a place of business in this country.[20] However its significance lies in its treatment of persons who, without any proper justification, seek to register a company name which is intentionally similar to another well known name or trade mark.

In more recent years other cases have been decided in which judges have adopted a similarly robust approach to the practice of registering company names for improper purposes. It seems to have become fashionable to use such means as a way of obtaining money

---

[20] This decision seems to have been almost ignored in some of the "foreign plaintiff" cases, most notably the decision of the Court of Appeal in the "Budweiser" case, *Anheuser-Busch Inc. v. Budejovicky Budvar NP* [1984] F.S.R. 413, but its correctness has never previously been doubted. Now it seems to have been given new life as a result of the decision of the Court of Appeal in *One in a Million*.

from the rightful owners of the names concerned. Notable examples include the cases of *Glaxo plc v. Glaxowellcome Ltd.*,[21] in which Lightman J. ordered the defendant to change its name, holding that the defendants' conduct was a dishonest scheme to appropriate the goodwill of the plaintiff and to extort a substantial sum as the price for not damaging the plaintiffs' goodwill. He went well beyond the traditional view of passing off in saying:

> The court will not countenance any such pre-emptive strike of registering companies with names where others have the goodwill in those names and the registering party then demanding a price for changing the names. It is an abuse of the system of registration of company names. The right to choose the name with which a company is registered is not given for that purpose.

A similar approach was adopted by Laddie J. in *Direct Line Group Ltd. v. Direct Line Estate Agency Ltd.*,[22] another case in which a company was established with a view to either selling the company to the plaintiffs or to a third party. Again the defendant had not traded, but that fact did not dissuade the judge from granting an injunction.

The *One in a Million* case did not involve company names; as already mentioned, the case concerned the growing practice of registering Internet domain names which are similar to, or include, the names or trade marks of well known companies. Although the medium concerned is new, the principles are not new. Such cases are in essence analogous to the company name cases. It is instructive to refer to some passages from the judgment of Aldous L.J., with which judgment the other two Lords Justices agreed. He set out the history and development of the tort of passing off at some length. After considering the speech of Lord Diplock in the *Warnink* case,[23] and referring to the characteristics of the tort of passing off as set out by Lord Diplock, Aldous L.J. said:

> His five characteristics were those he identified in 1980 from previously decided cases, but I do not believe that he was thereby confining for ever the cause of action to every detail of such characteristics, as to do so would prevent the common law from evolving to meet changes in methods of trade and communication as it had in the past.

On the cases before him, Aldous L.J. approached the matter on the basis that the courts will always prevent traders from being

---

[21] [1996] F.S.R. 388.
[22] [1997] F.S.R. 374.
[23] *Warnink*, above, note 1.

equipped with or equipping others with instruments of fraud, citing a number of decisions supporting that view. One of the best examples was the decision of the Supreme Court of New South Wales in *Fletcher Challenge Ltd. v. Fletcher Challenge Pty. Ltd.*,[24] in which the defendant was restrained, notwithstanding the offer of an undertaking not to trade without making it clear that it was not associated with the plaintiff. He said:

> If it be the intention of the defendant to appropriate the goodwill of another or enable others to do so, I can see no reason why the court should not infer that it will happen, even if there is a possibility that such an appropriation would not take place. If, taking all the circumstances into account the court should conclude that the name was produced to enable passing-off, is adapted to be used for passing-off and, if used, is likely to be fraudulently used, an injunction will be appropriate . . .
>
> It follows that a court will intervene by way of injunction in passing-off cases in three types of case. First, where there is passing-off established or it is threatened. Second, where the defendant is a joint tortfeasor with another in passing-off either actual or threatened. Third, where the defendant has equipped himself with or intends to equip another with an instrument of fraud. This third type is probably mere *quia timet* action.

After reviewing the facts, Aldous L.J. concluded:

> In my view there was clear evidence of systematic registration by the appellants of well-known trade names as blocking registrations and a threat to sell them to others. No doubt the primary purpose of registration was to block registration by the owner of the goodwill. There was, according to Mr Wilson[25] nothing unlawful in doing that. The truth is different. The registration only blocks registration of the identical domain name and therefore does not act as a block to registration of a domain name that can be used by the owner of the goodwill in the name. The purpose of the so-called blocking registration was to extract money from the owners of the goodwill in the name chosen. Its ability to do so was in the main dependent upon the threat, expressed or implied, that the appellants would exploit the goodwill by either trading under the name or equipping another with the name so he could do so.

In his conclusions on the passing off issue, Aldous L.J. held that the mere registration of a domain name containing a well-known name or mark amounted in itself to the making of a misrepresentation to

---

[24] [1982] F.S.R. 1.
[25] Alastair Wilson Q.C., leading counsel for the appellants.

persons who consult the register of domain names; further, that the purpose of the appellants was to threaten use and disposal sometimes explicitly and on other occasions implicitly, and that the judge had been right to grant *quia timet* relief to prevent the threat becoming reality. He held, in addition, that the domain names concerned were instruments of fraud.

Conclusion

Although the conclusions of the Court of Appeal in the *One in a Million* case were based on the principles laid down by the House of Lords and already mentioned, it is possible to detect a broader approach to any kind of commercial conduct which involves dishonest or unfair trading. Aldous L.J. emphasised the flexibility of the common law and the need to allow it to evolve to meet changes in methods of trade and communication, reflecting the remarks of Lord Diplock cited by Ralph Gibson L.J. in *Bristol Conservatories*.[26] Thus the emphasis is very much on the importance of maintaining rigorous standards of commercial honesty.

Lord Morris of Borth-y-Gest once referred[27] to "the straightforward principle that trading must not only be honest but must not even unintentionally be unfair". A few years later Cross J. (as he then was) observed[28]:

> If I may say so without impertinence I entirely agree with the decision in the *Spanish Champagne* case—but as I see it it uncovered a piece of common law or equity which had till then escaped notice—for in such a case there is not, in any ordinary sense, any representation that the goods of the defendant are the goods of the plaintiffs, and evidence that no-one has been confused or deceived in that way is quite beside the mark. In truth the decision went far beyond the well-trodden paths of passing off into the unmapped area of "unfair trading" or "unlawful competition".

In outlawing the practice of domain name grabbing in the *One in a Million* case, and in applying the long standing decision in *Panhard-Levassor* and the more recent decisions in company name cases, and applying in a flexible manner the principles of the *Warnink* case and the *Spanish Champagne* line of cases which preceded it, the Court of Appeal has made a valuable contribution to the maintenance of honest commercial practices. There may still be some way to go, but

---

[26] Note 13, above.
[27] See *Parker-Knoll Ltd. v. Knoll International Ltd.* [1962] R.P.C. 265 at 278.
[28] In *Vine Products Ltd. v. Mackenzie & Co. Ltd.* [1969] R.P.C. 1 (the "Sherry") case, at 23, with reference to the "Spanish Champagne" case, *Bollinger v. Costa Brava Wine Co. Ltd.* [1961] R.P.C. 116.

it can be seen that the law of passing off is now another step nearer to proper compliance with the unfair competition provisions of Article 10bis of the Paris Convention, and the United Kingdom's obligations under those provisions, now re-affirmed by the TRIPS Agreement.

3. The Development of Passing Off in the Twentieth Century

Hazel Carty

The Development of Passing Off in the Twentieth Century

Aim

Few texts deal adequately with the tort of passing off and many judgments, being at the interlocutory stage, consider its basis and potential in only a cursory manner. This being so, it is interesting in itself to chart the expansion of this "protean" tort[1] which has grown in line with new techniques of marketing and persuasion, "to meet changing conditions and practices in trade".[2] Yet, as this paper will attempt to show, it is in fact vital that the role of the tort be discussed as we enter the twenty-first century. The courts need to decide whether the tort remains a useful but limited misrepresentation action or develops into an action against "unfair competition" or "misappropriation". The conclusion of this writer is that without a reasoned debate as to the rationale of the tort it is in danger of being fashioned into an undue constraint on the competitive process.

Continued Importance

Of course the debate would be academic if the tort itself had been overtaken by the registered trade mark system. Indeed, some predicted its role would decline after the Trade Marks Act 1994, with its extensions to statutory trade mark protection. However the high number of reported cases reveals the continued importance of the tort of passing off at the end of the 20th century.

Obviously some of its importance lies in its parallel application to statutory trade mark protection. Sometimes this has merely a tag-on quality, an almost automatic addition to a statutory claim. However, the tort has a far more important function than that, even where the issue concerns a registrable mark. Get up and advertising themes may change during the life span of a given brand, this brand upgrading being perceived in the trade as necessary to "boost awareness".[3] Thus, the plaintiff may have failed to register a new mark or a variation of an existing mark. Again, the tort of passing off provides a more fluid, less technical protection even for those

---

[1] Lord Diplock in *Erven Warnink BV v. Townend (J) & Sons (Hull) Ltd* (Advocaat) [1979] A.C. 731 at 740.
[2] Falconer J. in *Lego Systems A/S v. Lego M Lemelstrich Ltd* [1983] F.S.R. 155 at 186.
[3] As was the case in *United Biscuits (UK) Ltd v. Asda Ltd* [1997] R.P.C. 513.

marks that are registered. Thus the tort does not protect according to registration for a particular class of goods or services nor is it subject to the "mark for mark" rule of registered marks, whereby the court assesses the way the defendant uses the mark, discounting external matter.[4] Moreover, the tort does not contain specific defences as found under the registered system.[5]

However, as the century has worn on it has become apparent that the real importance of the tort of passing off lies in the fact that it is not simply a parallel protection to the registered scheme. It is a tort of misrepresentation that has a life and importance of its own. The misrepresentation does not have to emanate from a mark as such.[6] Lord Scarman in *Cadbury Schweppes Pty Ltd v. Pub Squash Co Pty Ltd*[7] (*Pub Squash*) acknowledged that the actionable misrepresentation in the tort could involve descriptive material other than trade names or get up "such as slogans or visual images which radio, television or newspaper advertising campaigns can lead the market to associate with the plaintiff's product, provided always that such descriptive material has become part of the goodwill of the product". The test for this is whether "the product has derived from the advertising a distinctive character which the market recognises".

As we leave the twentieth century, the debate over passing off and its "proper" limits centres on attempts to use the tort beyond the scope of the registered system. Given the fluid nature of the action such attempts sometimes disguise what are in fact actions for "unfair competition" or "misappropriation" (or both, as the concepts are obviously related) . So there are actions brought where the nub of the allegation against the defendant is that they have gained an "unfair" competitive advantage by misrepresentation or misdescription alone. Thus in *SDS Biotech UK v. Power Agrichemicals*[8] and *Hodge Clemco Ltd v. Airblast Ltd*[9] the real complaint was that the plaintiffs had complied with government regulations, while the defendant had not, though they wrongly indicated that they had. Again, other plaintiffs attempt to use the tort to protect the promotional or advertising function of what they perceive to be a useful commercial magnet. That magnet may be a trade mark or more generally an "image" they have created for their product or business. Here, "dilution" is often alleged. The danger behind this

---

[4] Jacob J. in *Origins Natural Resources Inc v. Origin Clothing Ltd* [1995] F.S.R. 280 at 284, re Trade Marks Act 1994, s. 10.
[5] See in particular Trade Marks Act 1994, ss. 10(6) and 11.
[6] There are nineteenth century *dicta* that paved the way for this wider scope of the tort. Thus Lord Herschell in *Reddaway v. Banham* [1896] A.C. 199, 211, commented "I am unable to see why a man should be allowed *in this way more than any other* to deceive purchasers into the belief that they are getting what they are not and thus to filch the business of a rival." [emphasis added]
[7] [1981] R.P.C. 429 at 490.
[8] [1995] F.S.R. 797, Aldous J. (The case was in fact decided in 1989.)
[9] [1995] F.S.R. 806, Jacob J.

process is that it no longer focuses on misrepresentation but rather pleads for protection against misappropriation of commercial success.

Perceived Rationale

To comment on the progress of the tort in the 20th century it is necessary to establish its rationale. What emerges is that this is in line with the traditional rationale of trade mark law generally: to protect source and quality information passing between trader and consumer. Thus the tort protects against harm to "deserving" plaintiffs where it is in the public interest that this should happen. By preventing misrepresentations as to source and quality of the goods and services offered to the public, the tort polices the information on which consumer choice will be made. However, commercial misrepresentations are not sufficient as such to allow private actions by competitors (though the State has a role here).[10] As Lord Scarman noted in *Pub Squash*[11]: "competition is safeguarded by the necessity for the plaintiff to prove that he has built up an intangible property right". Thus the tort protects the trader who is particularly damaged by that misrepresentation where the effect is to encourage efficient market choices.

This rationale can be gleaned from the landmark passing off cases (reviewed in more detail later) that span the century. In 1915 the House of Lords in *Spalding v. Gamage*[12] emphasised the basis of the tort in misrepresentation and its role in the protection of the plaintiff's goodwill. In 1979 in *Warnink (Erven) BV v. Townend & Sons Ltd*, the *Advocaat* case, Lord Diplock extended the misrepresentations applicable to the tort by reference to the fact that "[Parliament has] progressively intervened in the interests of consumers" given that is what "the public interest demands".[13] The same emphasis is found in two of the leading passing off cases in the last decade of this century: in *Reckitt & Colman Ltd v. Borden Inc*,[14] the Jif Lemon case, Lord Oliver commented that: "the essence the action for passing off is a deceit practised upon the public" while Millett L.J. in *Harrods Ltd v. Harrodian School*[15] noted that:

---

[10] Naresh, "Passing Off, Goodwill and False Advertising" [1986] C.L.J. 97 at 120: "...a legal rule that discourages misrepresentations may encourage other forms of socially undesirable behaviour to such a degree that the cure it achieves is worse than the original illness. It is this very danger that has caused the common law, in the past, to be extremely cautious about allowing commercial misrepresentations to be controlled through the mechanisms of private actions brought by competitors".
[11] [1981] R.P.C. 429 at 490.
[12] (1915) 32 R.P.C. 273.
[13] [1979] A.C. 731 at 742–3.
[14] [1990] R.P.C. 340.
[15] [1996] R.P.C. 697.

to date the law has not sought to protect the value of the brand name as such, but the value of the goodwill which it generates; and it insists on proof of confusion to justify its intervention.

The rationale is mirrored in the framework of the tort, often referred to as "the classic trinity": that is, the need for misrepresentation, goodwill and damage. The tort arises where there is customer reliance, based on a misrepresentation of the defendant, harming the goodwill of the plaintiff.

The Nineteenth Century Beginnings of the Tort

Passing off is a tort of comparatively recent origin: the term was first used in the head note of a case reported in 1842.[16] It emerged from deceit[17] and originally required fraud to be proved. However, its key features began to be formalised at the end of the nineteenth century, as did the key features of malicious falsehood and deceit itself, the other misrepresentation economic torts. What is interesting about all three is that at about the start of the twentieth century all had limits placed on them by the House of Lords.[18] This concern to limit liability even where there has been confusion and inaccuracies caused by a competitor was still apparent in the late 1970s in the Advocaat case. So Lord Diplock noted[19]:

> ...in an economic system which has relied on competition to keep down prices and to improve products, there may be practical reasons why it should have been the policy of the common law not to run the risk of hampering competition by providing civil remedies to everyone competing in the market who has suffered damage to his business goodwill in consequence of inaccurate statements of whatever kind that may be made by rival traders about their own wares.

Thus in *Derry v. Peek*,[20] the House of Lords established that the tort of deceit required proof of fraud while in *White v. Mellin*[21] and *Royal Baking Powder Co v. Wright, Crossley & Co*[22] the House of Lords established that special damage and malice were necessary ingredients in the tort of malicious falsehood.[23]

---

[16] *Perry v. Truefitt* (1842) 49 E.R. 749.
[17] See Morison, "Unfair Competition and Passing Off" (1956) 2 Sydney Law Rev. 50 at 54.
[18] This is in line generally with a policy at this time to limit the role of the courts in refereeing the competitive process, as evidenced in *Allen v. Flood* [1898] A.C. 1 and *Mogul Steamship Co Ltd v. McGregor, Gow & Co* [1892] A.C. 25.
[19] [1979] A.C. 731 at 742.
[20] (1889) 14 App. Cas. 377.
[21] [1895] A.C. 154.
[22] (1901) 18 R.P.C. 95. See especially the judgment of Lord Davey at p. 99.
[23] Though what malice meant was still doubtful – see Lord Herschell in *White v. Mellin* [1895] A.C. 154 at 160. The requirement of special damage was modified by the Defamation Act 1952, s. 3.

With passing off different limiting mechanisms were employed, due to the way in which the tort had arisen, a product of equity and the common law. Although the common law had required fraud for the tort, equity focused not on the defendant's intention but on the effect of the misrepresentation so an injunction might be granted to restrain a practice that was calculated to deceive, though there was no proof of an intention to deceive. After the Judicature Act 1873, fraud was no longer an essential element in passing off [24] which left passing off as a strict liability tort, based on misrepresentation. The fact that intentional harm was not required gave the tort wider potential scope than any of the other economic torts but necessitated an exposition of the tort's limits. That it was based on misrepresentation was accepted and provided some framework. This was noted in *Reddaway v. Banham*[25] which provides the classic discussion of the tort at the end of the nineteenth century.[26] However, it was still not clear what the nature of the interest being protected was. The Court of Appeal in *Reddaway v. Banham*,[27] appeared content to focus on "interference with trade".[28]

The Tort enters the Twentieth Century: *Spalding v. Gamage*

In 1915, the modern framework of the tort was provided in *Spalding v. Gamage* by Lord Parker, who noted that there was "considerable diversity of opinion as to the nature of the right, the invasion of which is the subject of what are known as passing off actions".[29] Rather than protect the plaintiff's trade in a general sense, or his mark as such, the tort protects a right to "goodwill" (a property right) against misrepresentation. This goodwill only exists "so long as the mark is distinctive of his goods in the eyes of the public or a class of the public". Subsequently, the accepted definition of goodwill

---

[24] Though the presence of fraud leads to a loosening of the requirements of the classic trinity, especially the need to show likely harm to goodwill. The most recent example of this are a series of cases involving "scams" to gain financial advantage by registering a famous name and demanding that the "legitimate" owner pay for its return. Thus attempts to extort money by registering famous names as company names and domain names were all held in the late 1990s to constitute passing off (or rather threatened passing off, sufficient for an interlocutory injunction). *Direct Line Group Ltd v. Direct Line Estate Agency Ltd* [1997] F.S.R. 374; *Glaxo plc v. Glaxo-Wellcome Ltd* [1996] F.S.R. 388, Lightman J.; *British Telecommunications plc v. One in a Million Ltd* [1999] R.P.C. 1., CA.
[25] (1896) 13 R.P.C. 218 at 224.
[26] And was in itself a radical decision, accepting the concept of "secondary meaning" whereby a descriptive term can become distinctive of the plaintiff.
[27] Commented on by Lord Herschell (1896) 13 R.P.C. 218 at 227.
[28] However it is clear that Lord Herschell at least was aware of the need for greater precision, doubting whether the trade mark itself could be property.
[29] (1915) 32 R.P.C. 273 at 284. Though most agreed it was a right of property, Lord Parker asked the obvious question—property in what?

was identified as that contained in Lord Macnaghten's speech in *CIR v. Muller & Co's Margarine Ltd*[30]:

> [Goodwill] is the benefit and advantage of the good name, reputation and connection of a business. It is the attractive force that brings in business.

By denying property in the name, mark or get up that the plaintiff uses the way was open for the action to extend beyond the deceptive use of trade names.

The modern theoretical basis of the tort and its limiting principles were thereby established. Control mechanisms were spelled out—misrepresentation and the need to show potential harm to existing goodwill (though it was clear from *Spalding v. Gamage* itself that there may be more than one actionable misrepresentation relevant to the tort). The two link in the need to show damage—the misrepresentation must be "calculated to injure" the plaintiff's business or goodwill and must cause or be likely to cause such damage. In essence, the misrepresentation must have been relied upon.[31] Reliance is the cement between the misrepresentation and the harm to goodwill—without reliance there is no material misrepresentation. Interestingly, though Lord Diplock suggested a more complex definition of the tort in *Advocaat*, subsequently the courts have applied the analysis provided by this classic trinity.[32]

It is important, as will be underlined in this paper, that the classic trinity is adhered to if a coherent development of the tort is to be maintained and an action for "unfair competition" or "misappropriation" rejected. Moreover, this coherence requires a precise application of the three ingredients of the tort. The concept of misrepresentation is not synonymous with the notion of confusion *per se*. Misrepresentation requires deception and reliance.[33] Nor is

---

[30] [1901] A.C. 217 at 223.

[31] Despite the views of Brown-Wilkinson V.-C. in *Mirage Studios v. Counter-Feat Clothing* [1991] F.S.R. 145, it is submitted that the better and accepted view is that expressed by Laddie J. in *Elvis Presley Trade Marks* [1997] R.P.C. 543 that reliance is necessary. This follows the line of cases on product simulation where the courts have stressed that without reliance on the misrepresentation there is no protection: so in *British American Glass Co Ltd v. Winton Products (Blackpool) Ltd* [1962] R.P.C. 230 the plaintiffs complained when the defendants copied the shape of their novelty ornamental glass dogs. Pennycuick J. denied redress: "...a member of the public buying an ornamental trinket of this nature is concerned only with what it looks like and is unlikely to care by whom it is made".

[32] Lord Oliver in *Reckitt & Colman Products v. Borden Inc* [1990] R.P.C. 340, HL; *Consorzio del Prosciutto di Parma v. Marks and Spencer plc* [1991] R.P.C. 351, CA (where Nourse L.J. commented that the speeches of Lords Diplock and Fraser do not give the same degree of assistance in analysis and decision as the classical trinity); *Harrods v. Harrodian School Ltd* [1996] R.P.C. 697, CA.

[33] *Barnsley Brewery Co Ltd v. RBNB* [1997] F.S.R. 462, Robert Walker J. at p. 467: "there must be deception, whether intentional or unintentional. If there is no deception, mere confusion or the likelihood of confusion is not sufficient to give a cause of action". Indeed, the Court of Appeal in *Bristol Conservatories Ltd v. Conservatories Custom Built Ltd* [1989] R.P.C. 455 noted that there may be passing off without confusion.

goodwill synonymous with mere commercial reputation—it requires customer connection with the product.[34]

Development of the Tort in the Twentieth Century
The Growth of Relevant Misrepresentations

In *Morny Ltd v. Bull & Rogers*,[35] Goulding J. remarked that the passing off action goes beyond simple representation "into a field of greater refinement and subtlety". The expansion of the number of misrepresentations relevant to the tort reflects this. In charting this development it is apparent that all the types of misrepresentation that have been accepted so far are either source or quality misrepresentations, mirroring the classic function of trade marks.

Of course it would be neat and satisfying if it were possible to chart a chronological development of the tort but in fact the extensions to be discussed have arisen in a haphazard fashion, not always easy to date (*Spalding v. Gamage* itself accepted a variation on the classic form of misrepresentation). In part this is no doubt because the majority of passing off cases are completed at the interlocutory stage and there may well be underlying judicial disapproval of the defendant's actions that has led to unacknowledged extensions. Thus it is interesting to note that *Spalding v. Gamage* was pre-empted by the judgment of Swinfen-Eady J. in *Teacher v. Levy*.[36] There the plaintiff distillers of Scotch whisky successfully brought an action in passing off against the defendant pub owners who had been supplying customers with the plaintiff's ordinary quality whisky when they had demanded the plaintiff's special quality whisky. Fraud was involved which no doubt led to the lack of discussion as to the proper scope of the tort, except for the conclusion of the judge that the plaintiffs had established that inferior whisky had been "passed off" by the defendants as the superior product.

The classic misrepresentation for the tort remains source misrepresentation, pure and simple. So even in 1990, Lord Oliver in *Reckitt & Colman Products v. Borden Inc* summarised the general proposition contained in the tort as "no one may pass off his goods as those of another". However the tort has clearly developed over the century to include more exotic types of misrepresentation: as Lord Diplock noted in *Advocaat*,[37] the decision in *Spalding v. Gamage* recognised that misrepresenting one's own goods as the goods of

---

[34] Walker J. in *Nice and Safe Attitude Ltd v. Piers Flook* [1997] F.S.R. 18 underlines his preference for goodwill over reputation as he rightly points out reputation devoid of commercial goodwill is insufficient. Yet the courts, including the Court of Appeal, sometimes appear to equate these concepts – see Nourse L.J. in *Consorzio del Prosciutto di Parma v. Marks and Spencer plc* [1991] R.P.C. 351.
[35] [1978] F.S.R. 91 at 92.
[36] (1905) 23 R.P.C. 117.
[37] [1979] A.C. 731 at 741.

another was not a separate genus of actionable wrong but a particular species of wrong included in a wider genus.

Three categories of extension in this area can be discerned: misdescription of the plaintiffs' products; connection misrepresentation and product misdescription. All of course must damage the plaintiff's goodwill in order to be actionable.

(i) Misdescription of the Plaintiffs' Products

In *Spalding v. Gamage*, the House of Lords accepted that a misrepresentation as to the quality of the plaintiff's goods would be a relevant misrepresentation for the tort. There the defendant had obtained the plaintiffs' old, discarded stock of footballs (which had been sold to waste rubber merchants) and advertised them for sale as the plaintiffs' new, improved product. This form of actionable misrepresentation is particularly useful in combatting a black market in the plaintiffs' discarded or poor quality products.[38]

Where the alleged misrepresentation concerns the quality of the plaintiffs' products, it is necessary for the plaintiff to distinguish the different categories of his products for the court. This is particularly so where the defendant's representation as to a particular category/quality is implied. The plaintiff succeeded in doing this in *Wilts Utd Dairies Ltd v. Thomas Robinson Sons and Co Ltd*[39] where the defendant was selling out of date stock of the plaintiff's product (the indication of age would only have been obvious to those in the trade). The court held they were selling old goods as new and that the plaintiff's goodwill was in fresh milk. However, plaintiffs at times attempt to stretch the concept of quality misdescription too far and the courts are aware of this, particularly where no fraud is alleged and where attempts are made to circumvent other intellectual property rights. Thus the plaintiff failed to convince the court of separate categories in *Harris v. Warren and Phillips*.[40] The defendants, copyright owners of the plaintiff composer's early work, re-published the earlier work when the plaintiff's later compositions became popular. She alleged that the defendant wished to deceive the public into believing that this was a recent composition. However she failed to show the court that there existed two classes of product (early, inferior compositions; new, superior compositions), of differing quality.

Though this addition to actionable misrepresentations was an advance, it flows easily from the classic protection against source

---

[38] Goods emanating from the grey market may also fall foul of the tort: see *Colgate-Palmolive Ltd v. Markwell Finance Ltd* [1989] R.P.C. 497. There is, of course, a need to show a misrepresentation as to quality: which the plaintiffs were unable to do in another parallel import case, *Revlon Inc v. Cripps & Lee Ltd* [1980] F.S.R. 85, Dillon J. In *Silhouette International Schmied GmbH & Co KG v. Hartlauer Handelsgesellschaft mbH* [1998] F.S.R. 474 the E.C.J. addressed the question of exhaustion of rights for goods from outside the E.C.
[39] [1958] R.P.C. 94, CA.
[40] (1918) 35 R.P.C. 217.

misrepresentation. This form of misdescription (unlike product misdescription, discussed below) also involves source misrepresentation as it is the quality of the plaintiff's product that is being called into question. As Naresh explains, of *Spalding v. Gamage,*:

> ...failure to stop the defendant would have damaged the plaintiff's reputation as a supplier of footballs in exactly the same way as this reputation would have been damaged if the defendant had misrepresented its own inferior footballs as coming from the plaintiff . . . source-goodwill can be threatened even by a misrepresentation purely as to quality.[41]

It is hardly surprising, therefore, that this extension is consistent with the rationale of the tort: the protection of trader and customer alike.

(ii) Connection Misrepresentation

Again, this extension is a variation on source misrepresentation: an allegation by the defendant that his business or goods are in some way connected to the plaintiff. This form of actionable misrepresentation has been accepted since the start of the century: so in *Ewing v. Buttercup Margarine*,[42] liability rested on a connection misrepresentation, leading people to conclude that the defendants were in some way "mixed up with" the plaintiffs and was acknowledged by Lord Diplock in *Advocaat*.[43]

Unlike the classic case of passing off, this actionable misrepresentation does not necessarily involve a representation as to source. Rather, the effect of the misrepresentation is that customers/consumers may believe that the plaintiff has sanctioned the standard of the product concerned or authorised the activities of the defendant in some way. Exactly what constitutes a "connection" sufficient for the tort is unclear, as was highlighted by the differing views of Millett L.J. and Sir Michael Kerr in *Harrods v. Harrodian School*.[44] For Millett L.J., a perception that the plaintiffs had sponsored or given financial support to the defendants would not be a relevant connection for the tort. Sir Michael Kerr, on the other hand, asserted that "some assumed or even philanthropic connection" linking the plaintiffs to the defendants' business would appear to be sufficient.[45] This wider definition of "connection" is supported by the views of

---

[41] Naresh, above, at 117.
[42] (1917) 34 R.P.C. 232 at 237.
[43] *"Spalding* v *Gamage* led the way to recognition by judges of other species of the same genus, as where...a false suggestion the defendants that their businesses were connected with one another would damage the reputation and thus the goodwill of the plaintiffs' business".
[44] [1996] R.P.C. 697.
[45] [1996] R.P.C. 697 at 721.

Laddie J. in *Kimberley-Clark Ltd v. Fort Sterling Ltd*[46] where confusion that the plaintiffs' were "in some way behind" the defendants' promotion was held sufficient.

It may be that the precise nature of a link, sufficient to constitute a connection misrepresentation does not need defining. The connection misrepresentation must be such that reliance and consequent damage to goodwill is likely. With this in mind, the extension is in keeping with the rationale of passing off provided the courts apply the classic trinity in full—where the connection misrepresentation is relied upon and causes harm (or likely harm) to the plaintiff's customer connection then both deserving traders and the public interest are being served by applying the tort.

The ability to allege passing off, based on this form of misrepresentation, is an extremely useful weapon against those whom a plaintiff perceives to be free-riding on his success. This is especially so where the alleged connection misrepresentation is implied or vague. The courts may be willing to provide interlocutory protection especially where a well-known or "household" name is involved. Thus in *Sony v. Saray*,[47] the plaintiffs sold their consumer electronic goods through a network of carefully chosen authorised dealers, trained in the maintenance and repair of Sony equipment. The plaintiffs' advertising stressed this fact. The defendants dealt in Sony goods but were not authorised dealers (and there was evidence of a bad reputation). The Court of Appeal found there to be an implied misrepresentation that the defendants were authorised dealers, leading the public to expect that they were entitled to the full back-up of the manufacturers.

Yet the fact that it is an extremely useful weapon in an attempt to prevent misappropriation of commercial success underlines the need for caution in its application. The courts have accepted the fact that there is public awareness of merchandising, licensing and diversification. They have also (rightly) rejected the need to show a "common field of activity" between the plaintiff and defendant traders. Given these two facts, this allegation (of connection misrepresentation) is obviously particularly useful where the plaintiff seeks to protect the promotional or advertising magnetism of a product or an image surrounding a product.[48] What the courts need to be careful about (and where there will be renewed attempts to break down their resistance) is the possibility of providing protection against what may be termed "confusion dilution".[49] Here, though confusion is present, connecting the plaintiff in some way with the defendant, no damage to goodwill is clearly identified. Rather, the fact that the defendant has caused a mistaken connection to be made between his and the plaintiff's product appears sufficient for liability.

---

[46] [1997] F.S.R. 877 at 883.
[47] [1983] F.S.R. 30, CA.
[48] This was the real issue in *Taittinger SA v. Allbev Ltd* [1993] F.S.R. 641.
[49] Carty, "Dilution and Passing Off: Cause for Concern" (1996) 112 L.Q.R. 632 at 646–648.

If this argument is accepted, then connection misrepresentations become actionable *per se* and the need to show goodwill and damage is replaced by an action that in fact protects the name or mark in itself (a prospect rejected by Lord Herschell 100 years ago).

The nature of the classic trinity is such that merely to claim that the public have been confused into assuming some sort of connection between the defendant and the plaintiff cannot be sufficient to provide relief in passing off. The connection misrepresentation must have been relied upon in some way and must have harmed the plaintiff's goodwill in some way. If the mere fact of connection confusion is sufficient then misappropriation has indeed crept into the tort. In essence, this links into the extensions achieved in the types of damage recognised by the courts in this tort, more of which later. There are shades of just such a process in the judgment of Falconer J. in *Lego System A/S v. Lego M Lemelstrich Ltd*.[50] He accepted that the mark Lego had become distinctive of the plaintiffs and extended beyond the actual field of their activity in toys and construction kits. The defendants were restrained from using the mark on garden equipment even though there was no allegation of injurious association or diversion of sales. Rather, the fact that the plaintiffs was a "household name" appeared to provide justification for protection.

(iii) Product Misdescription

This third category of misrepresentation presents the most radical extension to the classic form of passing off. The category does not involve source misrepresentation nor does it involve a misdescription of the *plaintiff's* goods. Rather, protection is afforded where the defendant has misdescribed the product he is selling and that harms the goodwill of the plaintiff. The shift in the tort here is from source misrepresentation to product misrepresentation. In such cases, if the courts do not link the misrepresentation/misdescription to the plaintiff's goodwill the passing off action is in danger of becoming an unfair competition action.

The first group of cases on product misdescriptions that may constitute passing off centre on what is often termed "inverse passing off". Here the plaintiffs' complaint is that the defendant is claiming the plaintiffs' goods are his goods or that the plaintiffs' quality is his quality (whether by means of examples, commendations or testimonials).[51] To claim a high quality product which in fact emanates from the plaintiff as an indication of the quality of your own products or services is likely (like the classic

---

[50] [1983] F.S.R. 155.
[51] Laddie J. in *Matthew Gloag & Son Ltd v. Welsh Distillers Ltd* [1998] F.S.R. 718 at 724, described the typical inverse passing off case thus: "the defendants falsely represented that the plaintiffs' goods or tests carried out on or qualities possessed by the plaintiffs' goods were his goods or tests carried out on or qualities possessed by them."

case of passing off) to harm both plaintiff (through diversion of custom) and consumer alike (through product misinformation).

English[52] courts have been reluctant to accept inverse passing off. In *Tallerman v. Dowsing Radiant Heat Ltd*,[53] though the defendant falsely claimed testimonials which in fact referred to the plaintiffs' product, the claim failed as there was no representation that the product was the plaintiffs. Part of the reluctance to provide protection in such a case no doubt resulted from the fact that the process of misrepresentation was the exact opposite of the classic case.[54] But in part there would appear to have been a fear that the tort should not allow the plaintiff to claim a protected right of property in the product in question—that misdescription alone should not be sufficient.

However, such fears are unfounded (as *Advocaat* demonstrated) *provided* the classic trinity is applied.[55] Indeed, there have been examples throughout the century of successful actions based on what are in reality allegations of inverse passing off. So in *Copydex Ltd v. Noso Products Ltd*[56] the plaintiffs' adhesive product had been (anonymously) the subject of a successful television demonstration. The defendants were liable[57] for wrongly advertising their rival adhesive as the one "seen on television". Provided there is a misrepresentation that is relied upon and causes harm to the plaintiffs' customer connection, then passing off can apply and misappropriation as such is not the key to liability.[58] This would appear to have been at least implicitly accepted by the Court of Appeal in *Bristol Conservatories Ltd v. Conservatories Custom Built Ltd*.[59] The defendants' salesmen showed their prospective customers a portfolio of photographs of conservatories built by the plaintiffs, as if they were samples of their own work. The Court of Appeal refused the defendant's action to strike out the plaintiffs' claim in passing off and though the court would not determine the precise limits of the tort in such an action, it held that the cases cited by the defendant,

---

[52] *cf.* the Court of Session in *Henderson v. Munroe* (1905) 13 S.L.T. 57.
[53] [1900] 1 Ch. 1.
[54] This was noted in *Cambridge University Press v. University Tutorial Press* (1928) 45 R.P.C. 335, Maugham J. Here, the defendants advertised their edition of a text as "the prescribed edition", though in fact it was the plaintiffs who had been given permission to supply the prescribed edition. The judge, though critical of the defendants, held that they were not liable as they were no representing that their product was the plaintiffs'.
[55] Hence *Serville v. Constance* (1954) 71 R.P.C. 146 (Harman J.) is correctly decided: the plaintiff boxer was the champion of Trinidad. When he came to England to fight, he found that the defendant boxer had fought in England for some time, falsely billed as the champion of Trinidad. There was no passing off as there was no goodwill in England.
[56] (1952) 69 R.P.C. 38, Vaisey J.; though it has to be noted that he was unsure whether this was an instance of passing off or whether it could have been malicious falsehood.
[57] Though an injunction was deemed proper, the defendants in fact gave an undertaking instead.
[58] As it was in reality in *International News Service v. Associated Press* 248 U.S. 215 (1918): see the dissenting judgment of Brandeis J.
[59] [1989] R.P.C. 455.

including *Tallerman v. Dowsing Radiant Heat Ltd*,[60] were not authority binding on the court. Thus it is not surprising that the Court of Appeal of the Republic of Singapore in *John Robert Powers School Inc v. Denyse Bernadette Tessensohn*[61] saw *Bristol Conservatories* as an example of inverse passing off. Indeed, Laddie J. in *Matthew Gloag & Son Ltd v. Welsh Distilleries Ltd*[62] accepted the legitimacy of an allegation of inverse passing off.

The second group of cases where product misdescription can amount to passing off involves liability for incorrectly claiming product equivalence between your product and the plaintiffs'. This is product misrepresentation, which though linked to the plaintiff alone has obvious affinities to the *Advocaat* liability that emerged in the 1970s (see below). An injunction was granted on this basis in *Masson Seeley & Co v. Embossotype Mfg Co*[63] because of the defendants':

> ... deliberate and concerted attempt ... to find a market for their own goods which differed materially from the goods supplied by the plaintiff company, by means of conduct calculated and intended to induce people to believe that the goods offered by them were, contrary to fact, the same as the goods supplied by the plaintiff company.

In *Combe International Ltd v. Scholl (UK) Ltd*,[64] the plaintiffs had successfully marketed shoe insoles to alleviate foot odour with heavy emphasis in their marketing on their use of "activated" charcoal. Fox J. found that the defendants had highlighted the fact their new anti-odour insole contained charcoal (though not in fact "activated" charcoal, which was more effective) in order to suggest that the product was the same as the plaintiffs. The defendants had also created a product that was "strikingly similar" in appearance and in packaging. If such equivalence is being wrongly claimed then again the rationale for passing off protection applies: the plaintiff is damaged (by the public perception of equivalence to inferior goods) and it is in the public interest to protect consumer information. Of course, "mere puffs" and comparisons lacking specific content will not be sufficient, as is also the case in malicious falsehood.[65]

This protection against wrongful assertion of equivalence to a superior product was extended[66] in *Advocaat* to misdescription concerning a distinctive product rather than a distinctive plaintiff.

---

[60] [1900] 1 Ch. 1.
[61] [1995] F.S.R. 947, and see *Gloag* [1998] F.S.R. 718.
[62] [1998] F.S.R. 718 at 724.
[63] (1924) 41 R.P.C. 160 at 165, Tomlin J.
[64] [1980] R.P.C. 1, Fox J.
[65] For malicious falsehood see *Hubbuck v. Wilkinson* [1899] 1 Q.B. 86, CA. This was accepted for passing off by Michael Wheeler Q.C. in *Coopervision Inc v. Aspect Contact Lenses Ltd* (1987), Lexis.
[66] In the *Chocosuisse* case, Laddie J. lists the differences between the classic and the extended form, see [1998] R.P.C. 117 at 125–6.

Starting with the "drinks" cases,[67] by the late 1970s product misrepresentation was accepted as an evil in its own right, the plaintiff not having to show that he was uniquely affected. Clearly the tort could move in this direction once product misdescription had been identified as an actionable misrepresentation, though the nature of the goodwill had also to expand to cover not only source goodwill but also goodwill in the product.[68]

Advocaat, therefore, though seen as radical, in fact built on the extensions that had gone before. The plaintiffs had goodwill *in the product* (as did other "genuine" producers) and this was likely to be damaged both by reduced sales and by the reputation of the product being debased through the defendants' misrepresentation. The action is not protecting the name as such.[69] Nor did the case take the tort into the field of trade misdescriptions *per se*: mere false advertising or labelling would not have been sufficient. In *Advocaat*, the plaintiffs were thus deserving parties and the public interest in information concerning the product was involved.

For those who wish to keep the tort within manageable and acceptable bounds there are two dangers in this area of actionable misrepresentation. The first danger arises from the extended concept of goodwill. Unless in such cases, the courts still require that the plaintiff to show *his own* customer connection in the product in question we move uncomfortably close to an action for unfair competition or misappropriation of an attractive name (see below). The second danger lies in the scope of a "product" that plaintiffs might seek to protect. To keep the boundaries of the tort clear, the courts must demand that the plaintiff show he is protecting a separate and clearly defined class of goods, a point acknowledged by Lord Diplock in *Advocaat*[70] and in line with cases on misdescription of the plaintiffs' products (see above).

---

[67] Lord Diplock acknowledged that this "extended form of passing off" was first recognised and applied by Danckwerts J. in *Bollinger v. Costa Brava Wine Co* [1960] R.P.C. 16. For a discussion of the other drinks cases, see Wadlow *The Law of Passing Off* (2nd ed, 1995), 29–30.
[68] Walton, "A Pervasive But Often Not Explicitly Characterised Aspect of Passing Off" 87 E.I.P.R. 159 at 162: "it is clear that the offence [in Advocaat] is no more than a generalisation of the more individual case of the *Combe v. Scholl* type, and the gist of the offence consists in misrepresenting that the defendant is selling goods which are the plaintiff's goods in the sense only that they are an equivalent".
[69] Even though Lord Scarman falls into this loose terminology in *Pub Squash* [1981] R.P.C. 429 at 489: "the Advocaat case is all about a name. But Lord Fraser did not, any more than did Lord Diplock, limit the principle to the misappropriation of a name."
[70] Lord Diplock stated in *Advocaat* [1979] A.C. 731 at 747: ". . . so if one can define with reasonable precision the type of product that has acquired the reputation, one can identify the members of the class entitled to share in the goodwill". For Laddie J. in *Chocosuisse Union des Fabricants Suisses de Chocolat v. Cadbury Ltd* [1998] R.P.C. 117, there must be a "defined class of goods with a distinctive reputation". He was willing to accept that it is the public perception of special qualities that is important, even though there is no real qualitative difference in fact between the plaintiffs and defendant products. Here he accepted the "designation" Swiss Chocolate had a bearing on consumer choice. The Court of Appeal upheld his decision on passing off: *The Times*, March 15, 1999.

The Attack on Goodwill

The twentieth century has also seen attempts to expand the concept of the interest being protected by the tort. Of course, as has been shown, *Advocaat* saw a clear refocusing of goodwill to include product goodwill as well as source goodwill. But this development was in line with the perceived rationale of the tort. *Advocaat* involved the recognition that the tort of passing off could protect the goodwill generated for the plaintiffs' business *by a product*, even though the plaintiff did not have an exclusive right to produce that product: "it is the reputation that type of product itself has gained in the market by reason of its recognisable and distinctive qualities that has generated the relevant goodwill".[71] To be consistent with the rationale of the tort, the plaintiff must be able to show his own goodwill in the product—he should only be able to use the tort to maintain his interest in the goodwill of the product he sells.[72] For this reason, it is alarming that Laddie J. in *Chocosuisse Union des Fabricants Suisses de Chocolat v. Cadbury Ltd*[73] indicated that, provided the product has attracted goodwill, the trader might not need to have built up his own reputation in the product. If this is right, we thereby lose sight of the need for a "deserving" plaintiff and end by protecting the product or rather its name as such. However, as has been argued above, *Advocaat* demands the plaintiff be protecting his own goodwill in the product.

There have, of course, been direct attacks on the concept of goodwill from those who argue that reputation alone should be sufficient—whether derived from an international reputation or derived from pre-launch publicity or promotion. In neither case can the plaintiffs show customer connection in this country as they have yet to commence trading here but they have argued for protection based on their reputation or public awareness of their proposed commercial activity.

Such an argument in fact replaces the need to show goodwill with a concept of misappropriation of commercial magnetism (either actual or potential). As such, the claims for passing off protection should be rejected. Yet there are judges who are sympathetic to such plaintiffs, particularly where a dim view is taken of the defendants' conduct. There have been plaintiffs who lack goodwill who have been afforded protection on the basis that "some businesses are... truly international in character and reputation and the reputation and goodwill attaching to them cannot in fact help being

---

[71] *Advocaat* [1979] A.C. 731 at 747, Lord Diplock.
[72] This was clearly the view of Lord Diplock in *Advocaat* and see Wadlow, *Passing Off*, above, p. 136.
[73] [1998] R.P.C. 117 at 125. The defendant appealed to the Court of Appeal which upheld Laddie J.'s decision on passing off, but held that the trade association had no *locus standi* to sue: *The Times* March 15, 1999.

international also".[74] Though the majority of cases (such as *Alain Bernadin et Cie v. Pavilion Properties Ltd*;[75] *Athlete's Foot Marketing Associates Inc v. Cobra Sports Ltd*[76] and *Anheuser-Busch Inc v. Budejovicky Budvar*[77]) still accept the need to show real trading goodwill the point is still arguable, at least for interlocutory purposes.[78] So Browne-Wilkinson V.-C. in *Pete Waterman Ltd v. CBS UK Ltd*[79] commented:

> . . . in my view the law will fail if it does not try to meet the challenge thrown out by trading patterns which cross national and jurisdictional boundaries due to a change in technical achievement.

Similarly, inconsistency and uncertainty applies to the position of those who rely on pre-launch publicity to claim goodwill. The argument proposed by such plaintiffs is that the expenditure on advertising and the stimulation of customer interest creates a demand even before the product is on the market. This demand (in effect the expenditure on marketing), the argument continues, should be equated to goodwill and should be protected against those who "misappropriate" it, prior to the launch. So in *BBC v. Talbot Motor Co Ltd*[80] the defendants were prevented from using the name "Carfax" for their car spares business because of the extensive pre-launch publicity undertaken by the BBC for their proposed Carfax traffic information system. And in *Elida Gibbs v. Colgate-Palmolive Ltd*[81] the defendants, Colgate-Palmolive, were prevented from pre-empting the public launch (after trade advertising and expenditure) of the plaintiffs' new toothpaste, promoted on a tree theme, by advertising, also on a tree theme, a product they as yet did not intend to market in the United Kingdom.

However both these cases reveal the pitfalls of deciding a case on the basis of "fairness", rather than on the classic trinity. The BBC never *in fact* launched their "Carfax" service and Colgate-Palmolive were understandably aggrieved by the Elida Gibbs tree theme, as they had themselves been using just such a theme to promote their

---

[74] *Baskin-Robbins Ice Cream Co v. Gutman* [1976] F.S.R. 545. Similar views are found in the judgment of Templeman J. in *Globelegance v. Sarkissian* [1973] E.S.R. 461 (he found the contrary view a "straitjacket") and Megarry V.-C. in *Metric Resources v. Leasemetric* [1979] F.S.R. 571.
[75] [1967] R.P.C. 581, followed in *Amway Corp v. Eurway International Ltd* [1974] R.P.C. 82.
[76] [1980] R.P.C. 343.
[77] [1984] F.S.R. 413.
[78] And has met with increasing acceptance in the Commonwealth: see *e.g. Orkin Exterminating Co Ltd v. Pestco of Canada Ltd* [1985] 19 D.L.R. (4th) 90 (Canada); *Conagra Inc v. McCain Foods (Australia) Pty Ltd* Fed Court of Australia [1992] 23 I.P.R. 193; *Re Whirlpool Trade Mark* [1997] F.S.R. 906 (High Court of India). There is also an expansive view of goodwill in *Jian Tools v. Roderick Manhattan Group* [1995] F.S.R. 924, Knox J. Of course, s.56 (2) of the Trade Marks Act 1994 provides some protection for "well-known" marks, but no damages are available.
[79] [1993] E.M.L.R.27 at 51.
[80] [1981] F.S.R. 228, Megarry V.-C.
[81] [1983] F.S.R. 95, Goulding J.

continental products. The defendants thus alleged that the plaintiffs were misappropriating *their* idea and acting contrary to "the proper moral conduct operated by international companies"![82]

Though the need to show goodwill rather than reputation was stressed by Court of Appeal in *Anheuser-Busch*,[83] there are still *dicta* that leave the matter open, where pre-launch publicity is concerned. So Staughton L.J. noted in *Marcus Publishing plc v. Hutton-Wild Communications Ltd*[84]:

> it may be . . . that it is now possible to create goodwill for a future product by lavish hospitality or advertising of some other kind and that a competitor ought not to be allowed to appropriate to himself goodwill so engendered.

Where protection is provided on the basis of reputation or advertising expenditure, the courts appear to be prepared to protect on the basis of "name goodwill" rather than source or product goodwill. This criticism applies with equal force to a more insidious attack on goodwill that has been apparent increasingly in the last two decades or so of the 20th century. This indirect attack on goodwill has been undertaken by slipping new heads of damage into passing off litigation. By seeking to enlarge the heads of damage in the tort, the plaintiffs are in reality trying to re-shape or avoid the need for goodwill at all.

Increased Heads of Damage and the Spectre of Misappropriation

The standard heads of damage in a passing off action are diversion of custom and devaluation of reputation. Both clearly attack the plaintiff's goodwill. Of course there may be other heads of damage consistent with the likelihood of harm to goodwill but the more speculative they are, the more wary a court should be to validate them.

The problem for the tort in the latter part of the 20th century has been the acceptance in interlocutory actions of what are often purely speculative or even notional allegations of harm. Thus "loss of control of reputation" and "restriction on expansion potential" have been accepted as heads of damage in their own right by some judges and are now routinely alleged, though most frequently as additional heads of damage to the established pair above. So one of the reasons

---

[82] [1983] F.S.R. at 95.
[83] Both parties claimed the right to use the name Budweiser for their beer. The plaintiffs' beer was unavailable to the English public at this time but it was known to a substantial number of people in England by reputation alone. Confusion might have arisen, therefore, when the defendants' beer was marketed here, but no cause of action in passing off arose.
[84] [1990] R.P.C. 576 at 585, CA. An injunction was refused on the facts.

for awarding the injunction in *Lego v. Lego M Lemelstrich*[85] was the lack of control over the quality of the defendants' products. Falconer J. commented:"it seems to me that the inability of the plaintiffs to control such use must involve a real risk of injury to their reputation". The Court of Appeal in the *Harrods* case appeared to accept "loss of control" as a legitimate head of damage,[86] while Jacob J. in *Mecklermedia Corp v. D.C. Congress Gesellschaft mbH*[87] accepted that the potential harm to the plaintiffs (in a connection misrepresentation case) was that "to a significant extent" the plaintiffs' reputation was in the hands of the defendants.

And of course the stablemate of these heads of damage is the allegation of harm through "dilution". This was the real basis of *Lego*.[88] The theory behind the concept of dilution harm "is based on the fact that the more widely a symbol is used, the less effective it will be for any one user".[89] Like loss of control and expansion restriction,[90] the theory of dilution undermines the role played by goodwill in the tort, as anti-dilution protection focuses on the name or image in itself, without regard to the public interest. Pure dilution (that is, an allegation of "a lessening of the capacity to distinguish", without any confusion) has yet to be accepted, given misrepresentation has to be established. However, "confusion dilution" and liability for connection misrepresentation *per se* has guided some courts in their decision to award interlocutory injunctions. In such cases, the plaintiff has apparently succeeded on an allegation of a connection misrepresentation without any obvious or provable harm to goodwill. Falconer J., the judge in *Lego*, allowed dilution claims in a series of connection confusion cases in the early 1980s.[91] Dilution was also accepted as a head of damage by Blackburne J. in *Dalgety Spillers Foods Ltd v. Food Brokers Ltd;*[92] Aldous J. in *Direct Line Insurance v. Lotus Leisure Group Ltd,*[93] and Knox J. in *All Weather Sports Activities Ltd v. All Weather Sports (UK) Ltd.*[94]

---

[85] [1983] F.S.R. 155.
[86] [1996] R.P.C 697. Millett L.J., while rejecting on the facts that there was a misrepresentation, accepted the reasoning of the *Lego* case that "the danger in such a case is that the plaintiff loses control over his own reputation" (at 715). Sir Michael Kerr (dissenting on the facts), equates a connection misrepresentation with the loss of distinctiveness and loss of control (at 724.)
[87] [1997] F.S.R. 627 at 633.
[88] Browne-Wilkinson V.-C. in *Pete Waterman v. CBS* [1993] E.M.L.R. 27 stated that "loss of exclusivity" had constituted sufficient damage to justify relief in *Lego*.
[89] Brown, "Advertising and the Public Interest" (1940) 57 Yale L.J. 1191. The theory of dilution was proposed by Schechter in "The Rational Basis of Trade-Mark Protection" (1927) 40 Harv.L. Rev 813.
[90] *Direct Line Insurance v. Lotus Leisure Group Ltd* (1993); *All Weather Sports Activities v. All Weather Sports UK* (1987); *Hyper Hyper Ltd v. Hyper Active Ltd* (1985), all available in Lexis.
[91] Apart from *Lego* all are reported in Lexis: *UBM Group v. Lankester Dibben Steels Ltd* (1981); *Overdrive Ltd v. Wells Fargo Bank* (1982); *Hyper Hyper Ltd v. Hyper Active Ltd* (1982).
[92] [1994] F.S.R. 504.
[93] Unreported 1993, Lexis.
[94] Unreported 1987, Lexis. He accepted the plaintiffs' allegation that the use of the same name by the defendant would harm the name's "unique association" with the plaintiff (though he refused to award an injunction).

Most significantly, the Court of Appeal in *Taittinger SA v. Allbev Ltd*[95] appeared to accept dilution as a legitimate head of damage in passing off. There, champagne producers attacked the use of the word "champagne" in the name of the defendants' non-alcoholic drink, "Elderflower Champagne". Pleaded as a connection misrepresentation case, the real issue was the use of the name in itself and its advertising and marketing pull. This being so, it is not surprising that all three members of the Court of Appeal highlighted this aspect of the case: the threat of dilution.[96] Indeed, Sir Thomas Bingham M.R. remarked:

> "any product which is not champagne but is allowed to describe itself as such must inevitably, in my view, erode the singularity and exclusiveness of the description Champagne [and cause damage] of an insidious[97] but serious kind."

Regrettably, the subsequent Court of Appeal decision in *Harrods Ltd v. The Harrodian School*,[98] where dilution was raised as a secondary allegation,[99] has not clarified the situation. Millett L.J. was obviously unhappy with the wider implications of *Taittinger* and stressed that the tort protects the trading activity behind the name, not the name itself. Yet he only referred to Peter Gibson L.J.'s judgment from that case and classified *Taittinger* as a case of dilution through "generification" of a famous name (where the mark becomes descriptive of the product itself). On this basis *Taittinger* could not apply to *Harrods*.[1] But unfortunately it is not possible to discount the *dicta* in *Taittinger* on such a neat and narrow basis—the concept of dilution is not so limited nor was its discussion in *Taittinger*.[2] The plaintiffs in *Taittinger* were seeking to prevent the use of their name on any other product.

Thus we leave the twentieth century with the impression of conflict within the Court of Appeal on the issue of dilution—an impression reinforced by the strong dissenting judgment of Sir Michael Kerr in *Harrods*. He specifically referred to debasement or dilution of reputation as a result of the defendant's action as a relevant head of

---

[95] [1993] F.S.R. 641.
[96] [1993] F.S.R. 641. Peter Gibson L.J. stressed the "blurring or erosion of the uniqueness that now attaches to the word champagne" (at 669). Mann L.J. accepted that the plaintiffs' case was "that the word champagne has an exclusiveness which is impaired if it is used in relation to a product... which is neither champagne nor associated with or connected to the businesses which produce champagne" (at 673.)
[97] Laddie J. uses this word in *Kimberley-Clark Ltd v. Fort Sterling Ltd* [1997] F.S.R. 877 at 890.
[98] [1996] R.P.C. 697.
[99] The plaintiffs alleged that the defendant was seeking to attract to his school the "aura of excellence" attached to the name Harrods.
[1] There was obviously no such threat of generification in *Harrods*—the plaintiffs could not possibly allege that the defendants' use of the word "Harrodian" would lead to the name Harrods becoming a generic term for all luxury shops.
[2] *Taittinger* was not concerned with generification—the use of the name "Elderflower Champagne" for a non-alcoholic drink did not threaten generification, given it is far removed from sparkling white wine.

damage in the tort of passing off and cited the wide *dicta* on dilution from all three members of the Court of Appeal in *Taittinger*. It is hardly surprising, therefore, that it continues to be alleged in actions for passing off and that there is judicial sympathy for such a claim.[3] So Laddie J. in *Chocosuisse Union des Fabricants Suisses de Chocolat v. Cadbury Ltd*[4] noted "[if confusion is present] it must follow that the exclusivity of the designation Swiss chocolate must suffer and that will damage the plaintiffs . . . the damage will be insidious". Indeed, he asserted that in the *Advocaat* form of passing off, "it is mainly reduction of the distinctiveness of the descriptive term which is relied on as relevant damage".[5]

In reality these extended heads of damage should be backed by clear evidence of possible harm. Thus the plaintiff should be required to show an active intention to diversify[6] or probable harm through lack of control over his name/image or likely reduction in distinctiveness, with consequent harm to his customer connection. With a typical case of passing off, traditional damage will be assumed. However for the less typical examples, the courts should require "clear and cogent proof" of actual damage or proof that the real likelihood of damage was "substantial".[7] Without such an approach, these new heads of damage simply focus on injury to commercial magnetism or potential, assuming harm whenever there is a connection misrepresentation. Misappropriation is the concern behind these allegations—undermining as they do the need to show goodwill. Indeed, where courts focus on dilution there is a subtle change in the analysis of the type of damage relevant to the tort. Traditionally the focus has been on the plaintiffs' loss: diversion of sales or injurious association, reducing the marketability of the products in question. However with dilution claims, the courts focus on the "misappropriated" gain made by the defendant. This was the case with Sir Thomas Bingham M.R. in *Taittinger SA v. Allbev* where he asserted that the defendants were "cashing in" on the reputation of champagne and more recently with Laddie J. in *Kimberley-Clark Ltd v. Fort Sterling Ltd*[8] where he felt that the court should protect not only against diversion of sales but also "from the more insidious

---

[3] And of course the inclusion of a dilution claim in the Trade Mark Act 1994, s.10(3), although the Act does not directly affect the law relating to passing off: see s.2 (2). It must be noted, however, that "dilution" is something of a weasel word, sometimes used as if synonymous for diversion of trade or injurious association: see *e.g.* Aldous J. in *Bomford Turner Ltd v. Turner* unreported 1992, Lexis.
[4] [1998] R.P.C. 117 at 143. The main part of Laddie J's judgment was upheld by the Court of Appeal: *The Times*, March 15, 1999.
[5] [1998] R.P.C. 117 at 127.
[6] As was evident in *Alfred Dunhill Ltd v. Sunoptic SA* [1979] F.S.R. 337, C.A., and see *LRC v. Lilla Edets* [1973] R.P.C. 560.
[7] See the analysis in *Stringfellow v. McCain* [1984] R.P.C. 501, CA. and see Judge Baker Q.C. who rejected an application for an interlocutory injunction in *Pentagon Stationers Ltd v. Pentagon Business Systems Ltd*, unreported, 1985, Lexis, because the plaintiff's claim was "simply that the defendants are trading in an area into which the plaintiffs hope to expand".
[8] [1997] F.S.R. 877 at 890.

long-term commercial damage which will be caused by his competitor strengthening his own position by taking the benefit of the owner's mark and reputation".

Conclusion

Given the growth in the range of actionable misrepresentations, it is somewhat flat to summarise the tort of passing off at the end of the twentieth century in the general proposition "no man may pass off his goods as those of another". Despite extensions to the tort, however, the courts have adhered to the framework of the classic trinity. Yet the inter-linked structure of that trinity is under attack by those who seek protection against misappropriation or unfair competition.

With the tension in existing case law, the direct attack on goodwill will continue where international and pre-launch reputations are concerned. However, it is the backdoor attack on goodwill that will provide the stiffest test for the resolve of the courts. Should unprovable allegations/assertions of damage become standard in the tort, then confusion dilution will have transformed the tort and removed the need to show a misrepresentation that has been relied upon. Ultimately this could lead to automatic protection against use of another's name or mark or character and even a right to publicity, to prevent trading on someone else's reputation.[9] The rationale of the tort would then be the prevention of misappropriation, to protect the persuasive effect of an image or aura surrounding a product rather than the information content of the message. Whether this shift is justified is an issue for trade mark law generally.[10]

There will also be continued attempts to dress up mere misdescriptions[11] as examples of passing off. In such cases, it is clear that the plaintiffs are concerned about the unfair advantage gained by a defendant, rather than with direct harm to their goodwill. So in

---

[9] In Australia, misappropriation of licensing or merchandising potential has been accepted as a head of damage in the tort: *Henderson v. Radio Corp Pty Ltd* [1969] R.P.C. 218, where the court in effect granted the ballroom dancers a "publicity right". In *Hogan v. Koala Dundee Pty Ltd* and *Pacific Dunlop v. Hogan* (1988) 83 A.L.R. 187, (Fed. Court of Australia) and (1989) 87 A.L.R. 14 (Fed. Court of Australia) respectively it was held that the creator of a fictional film character—Crocodile Dundee—could prevent manufacturers "misappropriating" the value of the character. In many ways this is the aim of the brand owners who seek to prevent own-brand-lookalikes.

[10] This debate has been characterised by Advocate-General Jacobs in *Parfums Christian Dior SA v. Evora BV* [1998] R.P.C. 166 at 180–1, as the debate between those who support the origin/quality function of trade marks and those who see the "modern" function as including protection for their investment and advertising function. Some protection for the "image" of a mark appears to have been accepted by the E.C.J. in *Parfums Christian Dior SA v. Evora BV* [1998] R.P.C. 166 and in *Frits Loendersloot v. George Ballantine & Son Ltd* [1998] 1 C.M.L.R. 1015, though the guidance of such protection is sketchy as yet. See Gagliardi, "Protection of Trade Marks: The New Regime" [1998] E.I.P.R. 364.

[11] Of course s.52 of the Australian Trade Practices Act 1974 provides consumers and traders alike with an action against traders who engage in misleading or deceptive conduct.

SDS Biotech UK v. Power Agrichemicals[12] the real concern of the plaintiffs was that the defendants were wrongly claiming MAFF approval for their pesticide (a rival of the plaintiffs' product). Again, in Matthew Gloag & Son Ltd v. Welsh Distilleries Ltd,[13] Laddie J. refused to strike out an unusual action for passing off, given the defendants were "misleading the public for the purpose of advancing their business". There, Scotch whisky (with the consent of the producer in question) was flavoured with herbs and sold by the defendants as "Welsh Whisky". The plaintiffs, as Scotch whisky producers, alleged that this was some sort of inverse passing off through product misdescription. The claim was that defendants were "diluting" the reputation of Scotch whisky by using its quality to sell their own product—that they were "wrongly generating a goodwill in Welsh whisky on the back of what is, in fact, Scotch whisky".[14]

There are thus tensions and uncertainties within the tort of passing off. For those who applaud the decision to keep the misrepresentation economic torts within bounds at end of the 19th century and wish to see this process continue into the 21st century, the key decision of the 20th century is *Pub Squash*. There, Lord Scarman stressed that the tort is concerned with misrepresentation and not merely misappropriation of a trade value or "unfair trading". So when the plaintiffs opened up the market for a "macho" soft drink, they could not allege passing off against the defendants using the same idea and advertising theme. Competition should not be stifled and the way to ensure that is to keep to the classic trinity.[15] In particular, he stressed that a defendant does no wrong by entering a market created by another and there competing with its creator. These sentiments have been echoed most recently by Jacob J. in *Hodgkinson & Corby Ltd v. Wards Mobility Ltd*:[16]

> there is no tort of copying. There is no tort of taking a man's market or customers. Neither the market nor the customers are the plaintiff's to own

The same judge has stressed[17] that mere misdescription is not sufficient for the tort, for "passing off involves not only a false representation but a false representation related to the plaintiffs'

---

[12] [1995] F.S.R. 797 (in fact decided in 1989), Aldous J. See also *Hodge Clemco Ltd v. Airblast Ltd* [1995] F.S.R. 806.
[13] [1998] F.S.R. 718 at 724.
[14] [1998] F.S.R. 718 at 724. They further alleged (without the slightest evidence) that the defendants, having gained this reputation could then promote the sales of any spirit which they choose to sell under the name Welsh whisky!
[15] Lord Scarman, *Pub Squash* [1981] R.P.C. 429 at 496.
[16] [1995] FSR 169 at 174–175. He goes on to state "at the heart of passing off lies deception or its likelihood . . . never has the tort shown even a slight tendency to stray beyond cases of deception. Were it to do so it would enter the field of honest competition, declared unlawful for some reason other than deceptiveness. Why there should be any such reason I cannot imagine. It would serve only to stifle competition".
[17] *Schulke & Mayr UK Ltd v. Alkapharm UK Ltd*, [1999] F.S.R. 161.

procuct or goodwill, not any free-standing representation". Above all, the courts in the new century need to be careful that any further extensions to the tort of passing off do not allow powerful corporations to use their financial muscle to the detriment of what may ultimately prove to be genuine commercial competition.[18]

---

[18] Paraphrasing Russell L.J. in *Dunhill v. Sunoptic SA* [1979] F.S.R. 337, 368, CA.

4. The Foreign Trade Mark Owner's Experience: An Absence of Goodwill?

Norma Dawson

The Foreign Trade Mark Owner's Experience: An Absence of Goodwill?

1. Pasadena, 1937

In 1937, in Pasadena, California, Maurice and Richard McDonald opened the first McDonald's restaurant. Two years later, about 50 miles further east at San Bernardino, the brothers opened a second restaurant incorporating what was to become an icon of the twentieth century—two neon-lit golden arches jutting through the roof of the building, representing the first letter of their surname. These hamburger restaurants were successful on a local basis only until the 1950s when Ray Kroc, a salesman, offered to sell their concept as a franchise, an increasingly popular means of rapid territorial expansion of business reputation. The McDonald's Corporation was formed in 1955 and within six years Kroc had licensed over 200 McDonald's restaurants in the United States and bought the brothers out for US$2.7 million.[1] Ten years later, the company began to franchise the McDonald's concept and brands on an international basis and today there are some 25,000 McDonald's restaurants throughout 115 countries.[2] A central strength of the franchise operation is a battery of well-known trade marks: the golden arches logo, McDONALD'S, BIG MAC, and a range of other marks incorporating "Mc" or "Mac"—McCHICKEN, McPIZZA, MACFRIES and so on, all supported by an annual advertising budget of $1.5 billion.[3] The McDonald's brand has been judged one of the strongest brands in the world and, valued at over US$25 billion, it is one of the most valuable. McDonald's is one of a growing number of global brands, so-called because a largely consistent brand proposition and product formulation are used on a global basis: the brandowner's aspiration is for the mark to become a household word in every language. International and global branding only became widespread in the twentieth century in consequence of a number of factors which favour globalised trade[4] and contribute to the success of brand-building across frontiers, for example, the

---

[1] Morgan, *The Symbols of America* (1987).
[2] "The Burger that ate the World", *The Independent*, June 10, 1999.
[3] See *McDonald's Corp USA and McDonald's Restaurants Denmark A/S v. Pedersen* [1997] E.T.M.R. 151.
[4] Levitt, "The Globalization of Markets", *Harvard Business Review*, May/June 1983. Other factors may militate against global branding: language or cultural factors, legal difficulties, the fact that a brand may be differently positioned or at different stages of development in different markets; corporate structures also bear on the feasibility of global branding.

convergence of lifestyles, the emergence of systems of mass and instantaneous communication, the mobility of consumers, and the homogenising effect of technological development.

> The changes in the second half of the twentieth century are far more fundamental than those in [the] nineteenth century . . . . They have produced worldwide marks, worldwide goodwill and brought separate markets into competition with the other. Radio and television with their attendant advertising cross national frontiers. Electronic communication via satellite produces virtually instant communication between all markets. . . . This has led to the development of the international reputation in certain names, particularly in the service fields, for example Sheraton Hotels, Budget Rent A Car. A first division recording studio is catering to a market which treats crossing the Atlantic as an everyday incident . . . . an internationally famous hospital in Paris or Boston, Massachusetts draws its patients from worldwide.[5]

The rewards for successful global or international branding are significant: brand strength of this magnitude contributes to continued corporate independence and gives access to world events with immense advertising opportunities: only global brands are seen at Formula One Grand Prix races, World Cup matches or the Olympic Games.

> World class brands . . . aim to own a global forum of visibility which is sufficiently attractive that business partners, including governments, line up to join their club.[6]

But the cost is an ongoing commitment from brandowners to the protection and maintenance of the reputation of their trade marks throughout the world.[7]

II. JOHANNESBURG, 1992

George Sombonos was the managing director of Joburgers Drive-Inn Restaurant (Pty) Ltd ("Joburgers"), a South African company based in Johannesburg. He had been involved in the fast food business since 1968 and was the principal shareholder in Chicken Licken, a franchise operation with over 170 outlets in South Africa. In 1992, Sombonos decided that Joburgers would establish fast food restaurants using the trade marks McDonald's, Big Mac and the

---

[5] *Pete Waterman Ltd v. CBS UK* [1993] E.M.L.R. 27, Browne-Wilkinson V.-C.
[6] *Marketing Week*, September 7, 1990.
[7] McDonald's often pursue even small traders who imitate their marks: see *e.g. Pedersen*, above, note 3, and *McDonald's/McBagels* [1987] E.I.P.R. D-108.

golden arches logo. Accordingly, Joburgers applied to register these and other McDonald's trade marks in South Africa although they were in fact already registered but not used by the McDonald's Corporation. *The Sunday Times* for August 29, 1993 carried the following story:

> Big Macs may soon be eaten all over South Africa, but not because American hamburger giant McDonald's is entering the market . . . . Chicken Licken franchise owner Georger Sombonos plans to start his own national McDonald's hamburger chain.

McDonald's obtained an interim order restraining Joburgers from infringing the McDonald's trade marks and from passing off but Joburgers counterclaimed for expungement of the McDonald's marks on grounds of non-use.

At all relevant times McDonald's did not conduct any business in South Africa, probably because of the trade and political sanctions which had developed against the apartheid regime.[8] Where major brandowners choose, whether for political or commercial reasons, not to trade in markets where their trade marks are already known, this creates an opportunity for local traders like Joburgers to pre-empt the exploitation of the mark's reputation by the brandowner. One strategy to reduce the risk of pre-emption is to register trade marks before setting up business in a given territory as McDonald's had done in South Africa, but a registered trade mark is of course vulnerable to expungement from the register for non-use if it can be shown either that it was registered without any bona fide intention of using it or that, since registration, the mark has not been used for a continuous period of five years unless "special circumstances in the trade" can be relied upon to justify non-use.[9] McDonald's argued that it registered its marks in South Africa with a bona fide intention of using them and that any subsequent non-use could be explained on the basis of special circumstances in the trade, namely the trade sanctions against the South African government. Joburgers argued that at all material times McDonald's lacked bona fide intention to use its registered trade marks and pointed to the fact that during the period 1968–1985, McDonald's had secured registration of 52 marks, 27 of which included "McDonald" or "McDonald's", and that these registrations had occurred at roughly five-yearly intervals, some evidence of an attempt to circumvent the non-use provisions. Joburgers had a real prospect of establishing an absence of bona fide intention on the part of the McDonald's Corporation to use its

---

[8] See Webster, "The McDonald's Case: South Africa joins the Global Village"[1996] 86 T.M.R. 576 577. The case is reported at 1997 (1) S.A. 1.
[9] South Africa: Trade Marks Act 62 of 1963, s.36; this Act was replaced by the Trade Marks Act 194 of 1993 which came into force on May 1, 1995, after the application for expungement had been made.

registered marks and thus of succeeding in the application for expungement.

Could the law of passing off provide McDonald's with an effective alternative remedy in the event of their registered trade marks being expunged? It was likely that if Joburgers used the McDonald's trade marks in relation to fast food outlets, a substantial number of consumers would be deceived into believing that they were McDonald's franchisees. Any shortcomings in the products or service which Joburgers provided would be beyond the control of McDonald's and could cause significant damage to their reputation. The loss of an opportunity for business expansion by selecting a genuine McDonald's franchisee was an obvious second head of damage. Thus, proof of deception and likelihood of damage seemed a relatively straightforward task. Furthermore, to the untutored eye, the need for goodwill or reputation is unlikely to present any difficulty for the owner of one of the strongest and most valuable global brands. At this point, however, English law cast a long shadow across the McDonald's claim in passing off. As Kriegler J. of the Transvaal Provincial Division had pointed out in a similar case in 1989 involving the pre-emption of the Tie Rack mark in South Africa: "it has long since been accepted that we lean heavily on English authority in regard to the law of passing off".[10] The then current state of English law of passing off so far as it affected international reputation of a trade mark unsupported by actual trade in the forum was summed up in the 12th edition of *Kerly's Law of Trade Marks and Trade Names* published in 1986:

> Since an essential ingredient of passing off is damage . . . to goodwill, [the plaintiff] must show that he had . . . in this country not merely a reputation but also a goodwill capable of being damaged. Goodwill, however, is local: it is situated where the business is. Thus a foreign plaintiff may have a reputation in this country—from travellers on the one hand, or periodicals of international circulation, for instance, on the other—yet still fail in an action for passing off because he has here no business and so no goodwill. Such cases have not been uncommon in recent years, and have caused considerable difficulty.[11]

But the ninth edition of *Kerly* published some 20 years previously had stated: "if in fact the plaintiff has the necessary reputation in this country, it does not matter whether it was acquired by user here or in any other way".

Upon what basis could the authors of *Kerly* make these inconsistent assertions in 1966 and 1986, indicating a retrograde tendency in legal development clearly at odds with commercial and economic trends

---

[10] *Tie Rack plc v. Tie Rack Stores (Pty) Ltd* 1989 (4) S.A. 427 at 442.
[11] Para. 16–18.

in branding, and which strand of thought should the court adopt in *Joburgers*?

III. London and Dublin, 1901

1901 marked the end of the long Victorian era during which the rapid expansion of markets began. A revolution in communications was underway; wireless telegraphy was in its infancy and the Wright brothers' first aeroplane flight was just two years away. Consumerism and commercial communication were developing apace. Thorstein Veblen's *The Theory of the Leisure Class*, published in 1899, had identified the social significance of "conspicuous consumption" for the new century:

> The means of communication and the mobility of the population now expose the individual to the observation of many persons who have no other means of judging his reputability than the display of goods . . . . The only practicable means of impressing one's pecuniary ability on those unsympathetic observers of one's everyday life is an unremitting demonstration of ability to pay.[12]

In itself, the branding of goods could not support the practice of conspicuous consumption, but with the power of advertising harnessed to invest brands with meaning, trade marks were to become a major force in the twentieth century development of marketplace activity generally, including the practice of consumerism. By 1901 in the United States, the J Walter Thompson advertising agency already had some 800 clients and the figures for advertising expenditures and trade mark registrations were rising steeply on both sides of the Atlantic.[13] By that same year, almost 100,000 trade mark registrations had taken place in the United Kingdom since the Registry opened in 1876.

It was still the case in 1901 that for many goods or services, reputation could only be built up around a trade mark by means of actual sales somewhere within the jurisdiction but this was not universally so: brand reputation could develop on the strength of articles in newspapers or magazines circulating in a particular territory or because of greater consumer awareness engendered by increased travel. The issues posed by territorial spread of reputation ahead of actual sales had already been recognised by the courts on both sides of the Atlantic. In England, injunctions granted to prevent passing off have as a rule extended throughout the jurisdiction even

---

[12] 1899 (Unwin Books, London, 1970), 71.
[13] Ohmann, *Selling Culture* (1996), chap. 6.

where sales were conducted on a more localised basis.[14] Furthermore, the doctrine of honest concurrent user had been devised in the nineteenth century partly to address the problems caused by converging reputations within the same territory.[15] In the United States, a huge territory comprising many intra-state and inter-state markets, it was established early in the twentieth century that trade mark owners enjoyed common law protection against potentially deceptive use of their marks by other traders both within their actual geographical markets and beyond them where "advertising and reputation zones" had been established.[16] Holmes J. simplified the application of this principle by ruling that if a mark "is good in one part of the state, it is good in all",[17] but where the parties traded in different states and the plaintiff's reputation had not spread beyond the actual trading area, injunctions could be refused where a defendant acting in good faith and without notice of the plaintiff's mark operated outside that area.[18]

In England long before 1901, the Court of Chancery had indicated a willingness to protect the reputation of marks owned by foreign traders who conducted no English trade at all in the event of another trader usurping the mark's reputation in England. In *Collins Co v. Brown* and *Collins Co v. Cohen*, decided in 1857, Page-Wood V.-C. granted relief to an American tool manufacturer whose trade mark was being imitated in the English market.[19] Equitable intervention was justified on the basis of the auxiliary jurisdiction in aid of a legal right since such cases involved a fraud on the plaintiff actionable at law,[20] although in the exercise of the auxiliary jurisdiction the Court of Chancery did not require proof of actual fraud.[21] In the *Collins* cases, the Vice-Chancellor's view on the policy to be pursued in such cases in England and in "every civilised community" was clear: "fraud may be redressed in the country in which it is committed, whatever may be the country of the person who has been defrauded." Another potential basis for equitable intervention—the

---

[14] *Faulder & Co v. O G Rushton Ltd* (1903) 20 R.P.C. 477, *Brestian v. Try* [1958] R.P.C. 161, *Chelsea Man Menswear Ltd v. Chelsea Girl Ltd* [1987] R.P.C. 189. Cf. *Clock Ltd v. Clock House Hotel Ltd* (1936) 53 R.P.C. 269, where the injunction applied only to specific premises—such cases have been rare.
[15] See *GEC v. GE Co Ltd* [1972] 2 All E.R. 507 at 519.
[16] *Hanover Star Milling Co v. Metcalf* 240 U.S. 403 (1916).
[17] *Hanover*, p. 426.
[18] See Comment, "Territorial Protection of Trademarks" (1970) 65 Northwestern Univ L.R. 781 and "Developments in the Law—Trademarks" (1955) 68 Harvard L.R. 857.
[19] (1857) 3 K. & J. 423 and 428 respectively. One defendant, Brown, also exported marked goods to other countries where the plaintiff company did conduct trade.
[20] *Farina v. Silverlock* (1856) 6 De G.M. & G. 214.
[21] The equity jurisdiction was sometimes justified on the basis that, in the absence of actual fraud, the Court of Chancery restrained what would have constituted a fraud if the defendant, now on notice, were to continue his activities: *M'Andrew v. Bassett* (1864) 4 De G.J. & Sm. 380; *Edge & Sons Ltd v. Gallon & Son* (1900) 17 R.P.C. 537, *Grant (t/a Globe Furnishing Co) v. Leavitt* (1901) 18 R.P.C. 361, 364; *Poiret v. Jules Poiret Ltd and Nash* (1920) 37 R.P.C. 177, 183. See also Wadlow, *The Law of Passing Off* (1995), para. 1. 12, and Morison, "Unfair Competition and Passing Off" (1956) 2 Sydney L.R. 50, 54.

protection of property in a trade mark—was rejected by the Vice-Chancellor in the *Collins* cases although it was asserted in several cases a decade later by Lord Westbury L.C. as if to put the equity jurisdiction on a more secure theoretical basis than the prevention of unconscionable market behaviour or a consideration of competing equities.[22]

There the matter rested until 1901.[23] In that year, the reputation for motor cars made by the French firm, Panhard et Levassor, already extended throughout Europe including England even though fragmentation of patent rights prevented them from selling their products directly on the English market. Another company licensed by the British patentee bought Panhard cars in France and imported them into England while individuals also bought and imported Panhard cars into England. When a group of traders for no good reason adopted the name Panhard-Levassor Motor Company in England, the French company's application for an injunction was met with the argument that the defendants had not interfered with the plaintiffs' trade in England. Farwell J. found it "a plain case": "the conclusion I have come to is that . . . the defendant company has the fraudulent intention of annexing the benefit of the plaintiffs' name."[24] He advanced two bases of liability: first, relying on *Collins Co v. Brown*, the fraudulent nature of the defendant's conduct and secondly, interference with the plaintiffs' interest in the English market. From an intervention during counsel's argument, it appears that he considered that trade reputation provided a proprietary basis for equitable relief whether or not the plaintiffs had a market, directly or indirectly, in England, and although he concluded that "England was one of their markets" albeit indirectly, this was not a basis of jurisdiction. A month earlier, the Irish Master of the Rolls had granted an injunction restraining the unauthorised use in Ireland of "Globe Furnishing Company", the well-known name of a Liverpool furniture business. The latter firm advertised its business in English newspapers and magazines circulating in Ireland. Porter M.R. granted an injunction to restrain a calculated attempt to pre-empt the plaintiff's use of its mark in Ireland.[25]

Thus, in 1901 in England and in Ireland, deceptive use of foreign traders' marks was clearly considered actionable and there is no suggestion in *Panhard* or *Globe Furnishing* that the enactment of the Judicature and Trade Mark Registration Acts in the 1870s had altered the theoretical basis of the action for passing off or affected its availability in such cases: on the contrary, *Collins* was expressly

---

[22] See *e.g. Edelsten v. Edelsten* (1863) 1 De G. J. & S. 185.
[23] The briefly reported case of *Robineau v. Charbonnel* [1876] W.N. 160 turned on the issue of likelihood of damage occurring on the facts of the case and does not appear to be inconsistent with *Collins*.
[24] *La Société Anonyme des Anciens Établissements Panhard et Levassor v. Panhard-Levassor Motor Co* (1901) 18 R.P.C. 405 at 408–9.
[25] *Grant*, above, note 21.

followed in *Panhard* and counsel for the plaintiff in *Globe Furnishing* asserted that "the authorities go the length of extending the principle even to the case of a business carried on [by the plaintiff] in a foreign country", a view not contested by counsel for the defendant or by the court.[26]

Lurking in the 1901 reports is the famous stamp duty case, *Commissioners of Inland Revenue v. Muller & Co's Margarine Ltd*,[27] which will thicken our plot at a later stage. It concerned the tax liability of a purchaser under an agreement to sell a wholesale margarine business in Gildehaus, Germany. Under the contract, the vendor agreed to transfer the premises at Gildehaus along with plant, machinery, patents, trade marks and the business goodwill. The purchaser would be exempt from duty only if it could be established that the contract was for the sale of property "locally situate out of the United Kingdom".[28] The Inland Revenue accepted that all of the property in question was locally situate outside the United Kingdom with the exception of the business goodwill. In the House of Lords, six of the seven judges decided that on the facts of the case and for the purpose of the Stamp Act 1891, the goodwill was "locally situate out of the United Kingdom".[29] Lord Davey, for example, stated that the question whether goodwill can have any local situation could more accurately be expressed as "whether the goodwill . . . comprised in this contract has a locality for the purpose of the Stamp Act".[30] Lord Macnaghten commented:

> No doubt, where the reputation of a business is very widely spread . . . it may be difficult to localise goodwill. But here, I think, there is no difficulty . . . Moreover, under the Stamp Act of 1891 we are not required to define the local situation of the goodwill. We have only to determine whether it is or is not situate out of the United Kingdom.[31]

Although Lord Macnaghten's remarks quoted above were potentially highly relevant to the issue of the legal protection of international reputation in territories where a plaintiff has not yet begun to use its well-known mark, they have been forgotten while another passage from his speech has assumed totemic significance in the English law of passing off.

> What is goodwill? It is a thing very easy to describe, very difficult to define. It is the benefit and advantage of the good

---

[26] Counsel for the defendant argued that locality went to the issue of deception, not jurisdiction.
[27] [1901] A.C. 217.
[28] Stamp Act 1891, s. 59 (1).
[29] Lord Halsbury held that goodwill has no local situation: p. 239.
[30] *Muller*, p. 226. See also Lord James, p. 228, Lord Brampton, p. 232, and Lord Robertson, p. 233.
[31] *Muller*, p. 224.

name, reputation, and connection of a business. It is the attractive force which brings in custom. It is the one thing which distinguishes an old-established business from a new business at its first start. The goodwill of a business must emanate from a particular centre or source. However widely extended or diffused its influence may be, goodwill is nothing unless it has power of attraction sufficient to bring customers home to the source from which it emanates .... I think that if there is one attribute common to all cases of goodwill it is the attribute of locality.[32]

This analysis was intended to answer the Revenue case that goodwill generally has no local situation at all and so could never be exempt from duty, and its authority was immediately qualified by Lord Macnaghten when he said that "where the reputation of a business is very widely spread... it may be difficult to localise goodwill". Lord Lindley agreed that goodwill must always have some local situation and went on to say that "such business may be carried on in one place or country or in several, and if in several there *may* be several businesses, each having a goodwill of its own."[33] In the end, *Muller* was found to be a case where, in the words of Lord Robertson, "the goodwill of [the] business begins and ends abroad" and attracted no stamp duty liability, hardly a surprising result for a wholesale business for the sale of margarine, a relatively new product,[34] conducted in a small way in Germany. The fact that the vendor entered into a covenant not to engage in the same trade within 50 miles of the premises sold was some indication of the limited reach of the business.

The *Muller* case was to be made relevant to this discussion by a 1915 House of Lords ruling on passing off, *AG Spalding & Bros v. AW Gamage Ltd* where Lord Parker accepted one strand of equity trade mark jurisprudence, that the action for passing off had a proprietary basis, but ruled that the property protected by the action is not the trade mark itself but the "business or goodwill likely to be injured by the misrepresentation".[35] As a result of this development, Lord Macnaghten's remarks about the nature of goodwill would become relevant as the courts embraced and applied the property theory of passing off.

---

[32] *Muller*, pp. 223–4.
[33] *Muller*, p. 235. Italics added.
[34] "Margarine" and its longer form "oleomargarine" were coined around 1873. The Margarine Act 1887 was passed to prevent the sale of butter substitutes (margarine) as "butter".
[35] (1915) 32 R.P.C. 273, 284. Wadlow comments that "goodwill was not identified as the basis of the action until the present century, and that was after a hiatus of over 30 years during which hardly any judge suggested passing-off defended property rights at all": above, note 21, para. 1.05.

IV. Lowestoft, circa 1907

Although Paul Poiret, a celebrated French fashion designer, never paid for a single advertisement, within a few years of establishing his own fashion house in Paris he enjoyed a reputation which extended far and wide, including across the English Channel. So it was that in 1909, Mrs Asquith, wife of the British Prime Minister, invited Poiret to exhibit his creations at a show in 10, Downing Street, provoking the hostility of the English press and fashion industry. Press comment ran to 285 articles in 160 papers denouncing her lack of judgment in giving a foreigner such an opportunity to enhance his international reputation. Even the mannequins were brought from France to model his gowns. Poiret gowns were supplied direct to private customers and for theatrical revues in England, and by 1914 his trade in England constituted 20 per cent of total turnover. He had, however, no place of business in England. On the outbreak of war, he was called up for military service and his business was suspended. An Englishman, Nash, assumed the name of Jules Poiret and set up business in London as a dressmaker and theatrical costumier but Paul Poiret was unable to take any action to prevent the use of the Poiret name until the war ended.

The decision in *Poiret v. Jules Poiret Ltd and Nash*[36] took place after the landmark ruling in *Spalding v. Gamage*, but Lawrence J. made no reference to it or any other authority. Counsel for the plaintiff relied on the decisions in *Collins Co v. Brown and Panhard*, specifically alleging fraud. A number of instances of actual confusion were established in evidence. It was also proved that Poiret was an uncommon name even in France, which raised the question why Nash should have adopted it:

> The defendant's account as to how he came to choose the name of "Poiret" is that he is fond of sailing; that about seven years prior to 1914 he was staying at Lowestoft for the purpose of enjoying the recreation of sailing; that whilst there he met a Frenchman in the bar of the hotel whose name was Poiret; that he asked him to come sailing with him, and that they spent a fortnight together . . . . Nash said that he did not ascertain the Christian name but thought it was Henri. He also said he did not get to know from what part of France he came . . . but on parting, he promised to write to the defendant, Nash, the defendant, Nash, not having given him his address. I decline altogether to accept this story, and notwithstanding the attempt which was made to bolster it up by the evidence of the witness, Stigles, who stated that . . . he recognised [the defendant] as the man who used to walk about the quay with an oilskin over one arm and his head turned slightly to the right and asked him,

---

[36] *Poiret*, above, note 21.

Nash, what had become of the foreigner whom he had once seen talking to him in French on the quay.[37]

It is bad enough to pinch a fellow's trade name or mark while he is at the Front fighting with Allied forces, without also insulting the court's intelligence by explaining one's conduct in such a far-fetched way. As Lawrence J. said, "such a story . . . needs no comment". The unmistakeable "Lowestoft tendency" which permeates trade mark law generally is nowhere more in evidence than in the area under consideration. While bad faith in itself gives rise to no cause of action, it is a relevant factor in the broader legal and economic analysis. To begin with, deliberate pre-emption of a well-known mark indicates that the defendant considers that the mark possesses, in Lord Macnaghten's words, "the attractive force which brings in custom". Further, the unrestrained annexation of the reputation of a well-known trade mark has potentially far-reaching consequences in the marketplace: not only consumers may be affected by dishonest trading. Thus, when one Henderson proposed to build and run a Sheraton Motel at Prestwick Airport without the consent of the internationally renowned Sheraton Hotel group which had then no English or Scottish operation, many other local firms, builders and suppliers, approached him with a view to being associated with the enterprise. Their involvement was only prevented when the Sheraton Corporation of America obtained an interlocutory injunction restraining Henderson's use of "Sheraton".[38] Counsel for the Sheraton Corporation, relying on *Poiret*, argued that case law established that foreign traders were entitled to protect their reputation and goodwill even though the goodwill related to a business outside the United Kingdom. Opposing counsel did not challenge this view but argued that on the facts the plaintiffs would suffer no damage from Henderson's activities. Buckley J. disagreed, finding that exposure of reputation and goodwill to risk as a result of consumer deception and pre-emption of an opportunity for business expansion were relevant heads of damage.

In light of the decisions in *Collins, Panhard, Globe Furnishing, Poiret* and *Sheraton*, it would seem that refusal *as a matter of law* to restrain pre-emption of a well-known mark would require some principled and convincing justification.

V. London, 1967

The owners of the Crazy Horse Saloon, a Parisian nightclub opened in 1951, were justifiably aggrieved when another company decided in

---

[37] *Poiret*, p. 186.
[38] *Sheraton Corp of America v. Sheraton Motels Ltd* [1964] R.P.C. 202. An interlocutory injunction was granted. The court was unimpressed by Henderson's explanation that he chose "Sheraton" because he operated from an office in Sheraton Street, London: the address in question had been destroyed by enemy action in 1944.

1967 to appropriate some of their international reputation by opening a "Crazy Horse Saloon" in London, advertising it as "Crazy Horse comes to London". In the legal proceedings which ensued, Pennycuick J. considered that "it is perfectly clear that the defendant . . . has chosen the identical name . . . with the sole purpose of 'cashing in' on the [plaintiff's] reputation".[39] However, he concluded "with considerable reluctance" that in the absence of user of the name "Crazy Horse Saloon" by the plaintiffs in the jurisdiction, they had failed to establish any protectable goodwill. He reasoned that the foundation of the action for passing off is the protection of goodwill, that Lord Macnaghten's statement in *Muller* that goodwill has the "attribute of locality", supported by a statement of Jenkins L.J. in the 1957 case, *Oertli AG v. Bowman (London) Ltd*,[40] referring to "user in this country", required the plaintiff to establish trading activities within the jurisdiction, and that the earlier cases on this point were consistent with this view.

His first point, that the foundation of the action for passing off is the protection of goodwill, overlooks the fact that this was an *ex post facto* justification for judicial intervention in cases of piracy of an established trade mark. Even accepting that it has become, since *Spalding*, the acknowledged basis of the action, *Spalding* leaves considerable scope for interpreting "goodwill" broadly so as to provide a remedy for dishonest trading practices considered actionable before 1915. In general terms, the decision in *Spalding* is seen as having opened up the action for passing off, making it available in new situations. Indeed, the House of Lords in *Spalding* itself held that the action lay even though the defendants in that case had not actually sold goods before the writ was issued and no actual passing off had occurred. The tort was complete when they advertised their goods for sale.[41] Morison comments that:

> With the decision in *Spalding's case* the way was opened up for the escape of the tort from the confines of the typical commercial situation which gave it its name . . . . And the desirability of such a broad approach to the tort of passing off seems evident. . . because of the public interest in the control of misrepresentation in the economic process.[42]

It is therefore ironic to find that where there is passing off *in fact*, the action for passing off cannot lie because the plaintiff has not traded in the forum. This is the effect of the *Crazy Horse* decision.

So far as the relevance of geographical location of goodwill is concerned, we have seen that the House of Lords in *Muller* recognised that goodwill could spread beyond the frontiers of one

---

[39] *Alain Bernardin et Cie v. Pavilion Properties Ltd* [1967] R.P.C. 581, 588.
[40] [1957] R.P.C. 388; the House of Lords' decision is reported at [1959] R.P.C. 1.
[41] *Spalding*, above, note 35.
[42] Morison, above, note 21, p. 57.

jurisdiction although on the facts of the case goodwill was confined to Germany. *Muller* provides no authority for the decision in *Crazy Horse*. This is also true of *Oertli* which concerned the competing rights of a Swiss trade mark owner and its British licensee to protect the mark in the English market. There was user of the mark in England. The issue, whether this actual "user in this country" had rendered the mark distinctive of the parent company and its products or of the licensee's products, was resolved in favour of the licensee. Thus, when Jenkins L.J. referred to "user in this country", he was describing a state of affairs which did exist rather than commenting on its absence. *Oertli*, like the recent *Scandecor* case,[43] was a case of disputed ownership of actual goodwill rather than a dispute about its very existence.

This leaves the question of the consistency of earlier cases with Pennycuick J.'s finding that some trading activity beyond mere advertisement must be conducted in the forum before an action for passing off will lie. He pointed out that in *Poiret* and in *Sheraton*, the trade mark owners had a trading presence of sorts in the jurisdiction; only on a strained construction might the same be said of *Panhard* which was not cited in *Crazy Horse*. Yet, in none of these was trading presence part of the *ratio decidendi* and all of the earlier cases are entirely consistent with the opposite view—the view advanced in the ninth edition of *Kerly* in 1966—that user in the jurisdiction is not necessary provided that reputation exists.

It has been said that "a concept is what it does".[44] The *Crazy Horse* conception of goodwill territorially limited to countries where the plaintiff is engaged in trading activities, confers on other traders a right of deception and pre-emption in those countries where the plaintiff's mark enjoys only reputation. No convincing justification for such an outcome emerges from Pennycuick J.'s judgment.

VI. London and Dublin, 1976

Despite being at odds with previous policy, principle and precedent, *Crazy Horse* has had a significant impact on the issue of pre-emption of well-known trade marks throughout the last three decades of the twentieth century.[45] Wadlow suggests that its impact has been legendary rather than real[46] because subsequent courts have found within Pennycuick J.'s reasoning an easy means of circumventing it

---

[43] [1999] F.S.R. 26.
[44] *Triangle Publications Inc v. Rohrlich*, 167 F. 2d 969, 982 (2d. Cir, 1948), Frank J.
[45] *Globelegance BV v. Sarkissian* [1974] R.P.C. 603; *Amway v. Eurway* [1974] R.P.C. 82; *Athlete's Foot Marketing Associates Inc v. Cobra Sports Ltd* [1980] R.P.C. 343; *Lettuce Entertain You Enterprises Inc v. Lauren Sabin Soll & Grunts Investment Ltd* [1979] E.I.P.R. 321; *Home Box Office Inc v. Channel 5 Home Box Office Ltd* [1982] F.S.R. 449; *My Kinda Bones Ltd v. Dr Pepper's Stove Co Ltd* [1984] F.S.R. 289; *Macy's Trade Mark* [1989] R.P.C. 546; *Harrods Ltd v. Harrods (Buenos Aires) Ltd* [1999] F.S.R. 187 and *Wackers Trade Mark* [1999] R.P.C. 453.
[46] Wadlow, above, note 21.

by fastening upon the slightest evidence of trading presence within the jurisdiction. Some plaintiffs, however, like the owners of the Crazy Horse Saloon, have left English courts bewildered by their reluctance to suppress deliberate deception.[47] Under the line of authority which developed after *Crazy Horse*, trade marks are protected not on the basis of very substantial international reputation but because the evidence is just sufficient to establish an actual trading presence in the United Kingdom. In this way, we find *Poiret*, *Panhard* and other pre-1967 cases being transformed from authority for a rule protecting trade reputation into authority for an often-used exception to a rule exposing trade reputation to predators. The game of "find the customer" was articulated by Walton J. in *Athlete's Foot Marketing v. Cobra Sports*:

> This will normally shortly be expressed by saying that he does not carry on any trade in that particular country . . . but the inwardness of it will be that he has no customers in that country; no people who buy his goods or make use of his services . . . there,[48]

but no clear principles have emerged as to the basis upon which the customer requirement has been satisfied in particular cases:

> . . . the question, to which no very clear answer emerges from the authorities, is what form of activity on the part of the plaintiff is required before it can be said that he has a "business" here to which goodwill can attach.[49]

Despite these difficulties, in 1976 a degree of entrenchment was provided for the *Crazy Horse* principle. In *Star Industrial Co v. Yap Kwee Kor*, an appeal to the Privy Council from the Singapore Court of Appeal, at issue were the plaintiff's rights to prevent the defendant's use in Singapore of a trade mark similar to one for which the plaintiff had established a reputation in that territory. The plaintiff, a Hong Kong company, had ceased trading in Singapore and had no intention of resuming trade there. It was therefore not a case of the defendant pre-empting a well-known mark in a new market. Further, the plaintiff was guilty of significant delay in commencing proceedings. The Privy Council held that the plaintiff had no protectable goodwill in Singapore. Lord Diplock, referring to *Spalding* and *Muller*, commented that "goodwill is local in character and divisible; if the business is carried on in several countries a separate goodwill attaches to it in each."[50] This statement not only goes much

---

[47] See Morcom, "Passing off Actions by Foreign Traders" [1997] E.I.P.R. 321 and [1980] E.I.P.R. 169.
[48] *Athlete's Foot*, above, p. 350.
[49] *Anheuser-Busch Inc v. Budejovicky Budvar* [1984] F.S.R. 413 at 465, Oliver L.J.
[50] [1976] F.S.R. 256.

further than *Muller*, it is also inconsistent with Lord Macnaghten's view that localising goodwill might be difficult in specific cases. Nevertheless it provides considerable support for *Crazy Horse*, although Lord Diplock did not refer to it or to other similar cases. The only other support for *Crazy Horse* in a superior court was in a case involving disputed rights to use the well-known mark-cum-geographical indication, Budweiser, under a market-splitting arrangement. *Crazy Horse* provided a convenient basis for denying relief to a plaintiff perceived as undeserving, the Court of Appeal making an effort to exclude the operation of the trading presence exception.[51]

Lord Diplock's view of the strictly territorial nature of goodwill provoked a swift reaction in the courts in London and Dublin, also recorded in the law reports for 1976. The pre-emption of the internationally-renowned Baskin-Robbins ice cream trade marks prompted this from Graham J. in the English High Court, finding for the plaintiffs:

> Some businesses are . . . to a greater or lesser extent truly international in character and the reputation and goodwill attaching to them cannot in fact help being international also. Some national boundaries such as, for example, those between members of the E.E.C. are in this respect becoming ill-defined and uncertain as modern travel and Community rules make the world grow smaller . . . [In *Star Industrial*] it would be impossible to hold that the goodwill of a business [in Singapore] must be confined to the strict legal boundaries of that city and could not extend some few hundred yards across the bridge over the Johore Straits to the bank on the other side in West Malaysia. It must surely be a question of fact in each case . . . .[52]

Graham J. would return to his theme a year later when granting an injunction restraining the use of "Maxim's", the name of a world-famous Paris restaurant, for a restaurant in Norwich,[53] and his attack on the *Crazy Horse* principle was later continued by two senior Chancery judges, Megarry V.-C. and Browne-Wilkinson V.-C. The former, mocking the "high authority" of *Star Industrial* which was in fact decided *per incuriam*, *Panhard* not having been cited, commented:

> [Counsel] was unable to give any satisfactory explanation why there must be a separate goodwill for each country . . . . For instance, if a French clothing company established a chain of shops on the French side of the Channel, and the excellence of their products . . . attracted English customers by the boatload,

---

[51] *Anheuser-Busch*, above.
[52] *Baskin-Robbins Ice Cream Co v. Gutman* [1976] F.S.R. 545.
[53] *Maxim's v. Dye* [1977] 1 W.L.R. 1155 at 1159–60.

so that the French company's name became a household name in southern England, nevertheless anybody might with impunity set up a rival business in England under the trading name of the French company, and would be able to prevent the French company from trading here under their name. I found that surprising. . . .[54]

And in *Pete Waterman v. CBS UK*, Browne-Wilkinson V.-C. criticised *Crazy Horse* in terms of policy:

> In my view, the law will fail if it does not try to meet the challenges thrown up by trading patterns which cross national and international boundaries due to a change in technical achievement. . .

in terms of principle:

> The essence of a claim in passing off is that the defendant is interfering with the goodwill of the plaintiff. The essence of the goodwill is the ability to attract customers and potential customers to do business with the owner of the goodwill . . . . Only if English law refuses to recognise the existence of rights locally situate abroad, should the English courts refuse to protect such rights. But English law is not so chauvinistic; it does recognise and protect rights which are locally situate abroad . . .[55]

and finally in terms of precedent: "down to the decision in the *Crazy Horse case* . . . in 1967 there was nothing in the authorities inconsistent with that view."[56] Even Walton J. who followed *Crazy Horse* in a case involving non-deliberate pre-emption of the Athlete's Foot trade mark for sports shoes wavered over the boundaries of the principle:

> . . . no trader can complain of passing off as against him in any territory—*and it will usually be defined by national boundaries, although it is well conceivable in the modern world that it will not*—in which he has no customers.[57]

In 1976 in Dublin, the Irish Supreme Court had to address a case of deliberate pre-emption of the C&A mark. The C&A company had over 60 stores in the United Kingdom including one in Belfast, but

---

[54] *Metric Resources Corp v. Leasemetrix Ltd* [1979] F.S.R. 571.
[55] Equity acts *in personam*: *Penn v. Lord Baltimore* (1750) 1 Ves. Sen. 444, *Ewing v. Orr-Ewing* (1883) 9 App. Cas. 34; *Phelps v. McDonald* 99 U.S. 298 (1878): "where the parties are before a court of equity, it is immaterial that the *res* of controversy is beyond the jurisdiction".
[56] *Pete Waterman*, above, note 5.
[57] *Athlete's Foot*, above, note 45, p. 350. Italics added.

had none in the Irish Republic. The trade mark was nonetheless very well known south of the border because of television and print advertising accessible in the Republic and because many people regularly travelled to Belfast on shopping excursions. When two Irish businessmen adopted "C&A" for their retail drapery business in Waterford, no honest motive could be suggested. Their actions were likely to cause deception and hinder further business expansion by C&A across the border. Finlay P., President of the High Court, regarded the matter as one of policy: "I can see no sound reason why the Court should absolve itself from the responsibility to prevent deception and . . . dishonest trading."[58] The Supreme Court agreed but insisted, disapproving *Crazy Horse*, that the plaintiffs had goodwill in the jurisdiction; as Henchy J. famously said, "goodwill does not necessarily stop at a frontier".[59] Kenny J. pressed a modernist perspective:

> I suspect that the idea that some of the goodwill must be acquired by user or trading in this country where it is sought to protect it comes from the days when television and radio were unknown and when international trade in domestic goods was not as extensive as it is today. It is not an appropriate rule for this age. . . .[60]

The desire for a rule fit for contemporary market conditions has also been expressed in other jurisdictions. In the Hong Kong High Court, for example, Sears J. stated in 1990:

> . . . this is an evolving field of law, and . . . a court must respond to the changes which have occurred in international communications. The large number of tourists crossing . . . national boundaries; the speed and efficiency of modern technology which causes business reputation to be more widely spread and recognised than in the past. . . . This, in view of the proximity of Hong Kong to other such major international centres as Singapore, Tokyo, Bangkok and Kuala Lumpur raises a matter of some importance.[61]

To advocate the abandonment of the *Crazy Horse* principle on the basis that the social and economic context has altered so radically since the 1960s that it is no longer an appropriate rule is to overlook the fact that in 1857 the Court of Chancery indicated that a policy of

---

[58] *C&A Modes and C&A Ireland v. C&A (Waterford) Ltd* [1976] I.R. 198 at 207.
[59] *C&A*, p. 212.
[60] *C&A*, p. 214.
[61] *Ten-Ichi Co v. Jancar Ltd* [1990] F.S.R. 151 at 154. See also *McDonald's Corp v. McDonald's Corp Ltd and Chang* [1997] F.S.R. 760 (Jamaica), and *Wienerwald Holding AG v. Kwan, Wong, Tan and Fong* [1979] F.S.R. 381 and *JC Penney Co v. Punjabi Nick* [1979] F.S.R. 26. Wadlow, above, note 21, paras. 2.43 *et seq.*, provides an overview of the law relating to foreign plaintiffs in other jurisdictions.

legal intervention to prevent piracy in this country of the international reputation of foreign traders' marks was a legitimate expectation in every civilised community. It has to be admitted, however, that contextual changes have resulted in many more well-known marks requiring the protection which *Crazy Horse* denies them. To the extent that the Irish Supreme Court took the view that *Crazy Horse* was wrong in principle, a view adopted by the courts in India,[62] Canada[63] and Australia,[64] this would appear to be more consistent with pre-1967 authority. Nevertheless, Canadian and Australian courts have suggested that the geographical separation of England from foreign plaintiffs by the English Channel and the Atlantic Ocean contributed to the development of a protectionist approach weighted towards local enterprise, and that this, combined with the fact that television was in its infancy in the 1960s, explains the harshness of the *Crazy Horse* principle.[65] But perhaps historical and geographical considerations combine more subtly. Could it be that *Collins* decided in 1857, reflects the confidence of an expansionist British economy at the hub of a huge imperial market whilst *Crazy Horse* more accurately reflects the protectionism of a post-imperial, pre-European mood in Britain? And could the political and economic isolation of the South African market in the apartheid era explain why the South African courts became enthusiastic advocates of the *Crazy Horse* doctrine?

VII. Johannesburg, 1995

A number of jurisdictions receptive to the English law of passing off[66] accepted the *Crazy Horse* doctrine and required evidence not only of reputation but of some degree of business activity. In the South Africa of the apartheid era, trade sanctions had the effect that evidence of trading presence in the jurisdiction was unlikely to be available.[67] Judicial condonation of the pre-emption by a local trader of the global mark Tie Rack, for example, was summed up in the phrase "no goodwill, no attractive force",[68] a complete subversion of commercial reality.

The freedom of nation states to address in isolation the issue of pre-emption of well-known marks was challenged as long ago as

---

[62] *Calvin Klein Inc v. International Apparel* [1995] F.S.R. 515.
[63] *Orkin Exterminating Co v. Pestco Co of Canada* (1985) 50 O.R. (2d) 726.
[64] *Conagra Inc v. McCain Foods* (1992) 23 I.P.R. 193 at 223; *Ramsay v. Nichol* (1939) V.L.R. 330.
[65] See *e.g. Orkin* and *Conagra*, above.
[66] New Zealand: *Esanda Ltd v. Esanda Finance Ltd* [1984] 2 N.Z.L.R. 748; *Midas International Corp v. Midas Auto Care Ltd*, unreported November 27, 1987, Malaysia: *Dun & Bradstreet (Singapore) Pte Ltd v. Dun & Bradstreet (Malaysia) Sdn Bhd* [1994] 1 M.L.J. 32 and *Compagnie Generale des Eaux v. Compagnie Generale des Eaux Sdn Bhd* [1997] F.S.R. 610.
[67] *Slenderella Systems v. Hawkins* 1959 (1) S.A. 519; *Tie Rack plc v. Tie Rack Stores (Pty)* 1989 (4) S.A. 427; *Lorimar Productions v. Sterling Clothing* 1981 (3) S.A. 1129, and *Victoria's Secret v. Edgars Stores* 1994 (3) S.A. 739.
[68] *Tie Rack*, above, note 10, p.445.

1925 when members of the Paris Convention for the Protection of Industrial Property of 1883 adopted Article 6*bis* of the Convention at The Hague Revision Conference.

> The countries of the Union undertake . . . to refuse or to cancel the registration and to prohibit the use of a trademark which constitutes a reproduction, imitation or translation, liable to create confusion, of a mark considered by the competent authority of the country of registration or use to be well known in that country as being already the mark of a person entitled to the benefits of the present Convention and used for identical or similar goods.

As one commentator has observed:

> The 1925 Hague Revision Conference acknowledged for the first time in an international treaty the fact that frontiers and national boundaries are only political divisions and geographical accidents incapable of affecting commercial reality.[69]

Yet questions have always remained about the precise scope of Article 6*bis* in particular, whether a requirement of actual use of a mark within the jurisdiction is compatible with it? In *Joburgers*, the Appellate Division considered that the common law of passing off as laid down in *Crazy Horse* and *Tie Rack* does not comply with Article 6*bis*, but Bodenhausen's *Guide to the Application of the Paris Convention* challenges such a view:

> The Revision Conference of Lisbon in 1958 rejected a proposal according to which use of a well-known mark in the country in which its protection is claimed would *not* be necessary for such protection. This means that a member State is not obliged to protect well-known trademarks which have not been used on its territory, but it will be free to do so.[70]

This is further confirmed by the fact that a WIPO Committee of Experts on Well-Known Marks established in 1995 has recognised the uncertainty surrounding this point and recommended clarification. The WIPO view is that whatever Article 6*bis* may have been intended to mean, it should be interpreted in such a way that well-known marks are protected regardless of registration *or use*. The view of the International Bureau of WIPO is that whatever Article 6*bis* may have been intended to mean, in order to make it

---

[69] Rangel-Ortiz, "Well-Known Trademarks under International Treaties—Part I", *Trademark World*, February 1997, p. 15.
[70] (1968), 91.

"meaningful", it should be interpreted in such a way that well-known marks are protected regardless of registration *or use*.[71]

The establishment of the Committee of Experts signals a fresh international effort to clarify and strengthen Article 6*bis* as part of globalised legal policy on the protection of well-known marks generally. It was set up in the wake of the WTO's Agreement on Trade Related Aspects of Intellectual Property (TRIPS), which endorsed Article 6*bis* of the Paris Convention and enlarged its operation, for example, by extending it to service marks.[72] Even before the Committee of Experts began its work, legislative changes had been made at national level to enhance the protection of well-known marks in response to global economic forces, as states have realised that respect for foreign well-known marks has become a *de facto* if not a *de jure* condition of engagement in international trade. Section 56 of the United Kingdom Trade Marks Act 1994, for example, confers a statutory right on the owners of foreign trade marks which are not registered or used in the jurisdiction to sue for an injunction to restrain confusing use of the mark on similar products, and in South Africa, section 35 of the Trade Marks Act 194 of 1993 which came into force on May 1, 1995 has the same effect. On the strength of section 35, McDonald's added an application for interdict restraining the use of their well-known mark to its other claim against Joburgers. The Witwatersrand Local Division found that "McDonald's" was not well-known in South Africa, dismissed the McDonald's claims, and ordered the expungement of the McDonald's trade marks from the register. Against the background of a threat that the U.S. Department of Commerce would list South Africa on its Section 301 Watch List of countries with inadequate intellectual property protection,[73] the case proceeded to the Appellate Division which reversed the findings of the lower court and laid down a number of general principles relating to "well-known marks".

Joburgers argued that to qualify for the exceptional protection of section 35, the McDonald's marks must be shown to have a reputation which was (a) more widespread and (b) more profound than the reputation which gives rise to an action for passing off. The court ruled that a mark need not be well-known to all sectors of the population but only to the relevant sector, in this case, potential franchisees and potential consumers of McDonald's products among the more affluent groups of society. The court also rejected a qualitative test of the knowledge which renders a mark well-known:

---

[71] *Memorandum prepared by the International Bureau* for the Committee of Experts on Well-Known Marks, WIPO, WKM/CE/I/2, para. 27. The proceedings of the Committee of Experts can be found in: WIPO, WKM/CE/I, November 13–6, 1995; WKM/CE/II, October 28–31, 1996; and WKM/CE/III, October 20–3, 1997.

[72] TRIPS 1994, Article 16(2) and (3). See generally Blakeney, *A Concise Guide to the TRIPS Agreement* (1996), 60–5.

[73] See Webster, above, note 8, p. 576.

"the important practical question is not whether a few people know the mark well but rather whether sufficient persons know it well enough to entitle it to protection against deception or confusion". Rejecting the use of fixed percentages as a means of measuring public knowledge of the mark, the court held that it was sufficient if a substantial number of persons in the relevant sector knew of the mark.

> The legislature intended to extend the protection of a passing off action to foreign businessmen who did not have a business or enjoy a goodwill inside the country, provided their marks were well-known in the Republic. It seems logical to accept that the degree of knowledge of the marks that is required would be similar to that protected in the existing law of passing off. The concept of a substantial number of persons is well established. It provides a practical and flexible criterion which is consistent with the terms of the statute. No feasible alternative has been suggested.[74]

In reaching its decision on the facts of the case, the court considered evidence of McDonald's annual turnover, international advertising and marketing campaigns including sponsorship of the Olympic Games, and the spillover effect of such advertising, numerous requests from South Africans for McDonald's franchises, evidence of actual deception, and the conduct of the defendants who had quite openly announced their intention to pre-empt the plaintiffs' use of "McDonald's".

It is a curious but welcome twist that South Africa in moving away from the *Crazy Horse* approach has adopted a flexible standard of reputation—known to a substantial number of persons in the relevant sector of the population—whilst in some States where enhanced protection for well-known marks has long been available as a means of preventing unfair competition,[75] mark-owners have had to establish higher standards of reputation based upon fixed percentages of the population. Some legal systems further refine this by reference to two distinct groups, well-known and famous marks.[76] The WIPO Committee of Experts has grappled with the various national approaches to reputation and published a set of guidelines

---

[74] *Joburgers*, above, note 8, p.21, Grosskopf J.A. The court also rejected a narrow interpretation of what it is that has to be well-known, ruling that only the mark itself need be well-known, and not the nationality, domicile or place of business of the owner, nor the fact that the relevant country is a Convention country. The narrower interpretation, adopted by the court of first instance, would have made s.35 a dead letter.
[75] The relationship between Art 6*bis* and Art 10*bis* (unfair competition) of the Paris Convention has been raised in the WIPO Committee of Experts: see WKM/CE/III/3, para. 42.
[76] See Kur, "Well-Known Marks, Highly Renowned Marks, and Marks Having a (High) Reputation—What's It All About?" (1992) 23 I.I.C. 218, Blakeney, "Well-Known Marks" [1994] E.I.P.R. 481, Mostert, "Well-Known and Famous Marks: Is Harmony Possible in the Global Village?" [1996] T.M.R. 103.

in 1999 which, while not binding at this stage, may have considerable persuasive impact. Significantly, these follow the *Joburgers* approach on the quantitative aspect of reputation.[77]

An agenda for the twenty-first century has emerged in relation to well-known marks. How can reputation be measured and to what standard? What weight should be given to national lists or registers of well-known marks, such as the *The Journal of Japanese Well-Known Marks* (1998)? At what stage in the proceedings must a mark be shown to have achieved well-known status?[78] What types of mark attract this exceptional protection?[79] What should be the impact of the defendant's bad faith on the outcome of the case?[80] And when should well-known marks be protected against use on dissimilar products? The *Joburgers* decision leads the way in avoiding what Rangel-Ortiz has described as "strict and fastidious rules which limit the possibility of providing a just and fair solution"[81] to these issues. A flexible approach which gives due weight to bad faith and actual deception and which incorporates a willingness at least to assume jurisdiction in all cases is most likely to achieve maximum equity in cases of pre-emption of well-known marks.

VIII. The Future: The Spectre Less Troubling

> The brand has travelled a long way this century: from the mark of a local product to a global corporate symbol. It has been the brainchild of our era of mass communications.[82]

In 1857 in *Collins*, Page-Wood V.-C. anticipated Article 6*bis* of the Paris Convention when he rejected any territorial limits upon trade mark rights predicated upon an analogy with copyright and patents. Rights stemming from marketplace communication were bound to transcend national frontiers and advertised brands no less than brands which have been purchased and experienced exert the attractive force which brings in custom and create in the consumer's mind a predisposition to buy. In ignoring the effect of "mere" reputation, *Crazy Horse* has sometimes been justified on the basis that the mark-owner cannot prove damage to goodwill.

> One important limitation on the right of a trader to restrain another is that he must show invasion of the intangible right of

---

[77] The WIPO Assemblies adopted these policies in a non-binding resolution: WIPO press release, PR/99/192, September 29, 1999.
[78] See *McDonald's Corp v. Dieter Rahmer*, April 30, 1998, noted at (1999) 30 I.I.C. 326.
[79] See *Philips Electronics BV v. Remington Consumer Products* [1998] R.P.C. 283, comments of Jacob J. concerning shape marks under Art 6*bis*.
[80] See WIPO, WKM/CE/III/2, paras 4.14–5.
[81] "Well-Known Trademarks under International Treaties—Part II", March 1997, 31.
[82] Macrae, *World Class Brands* (1991).

property described as goodwill *which can only exist [in this jurisdiction] when attached to a business having some connection with this country.*[83]

Or to put it another way, to succeed in a passing off action, one must establish goodwill; to establish goodwill, one must succeed in a passing off action. The circularity of this approach only thinly disguises the choice which courts must make between the interests of local traders and those of international traders whose activities do not yet extend to the forum of the litigation although their brand reputation does. While it is true that in other commercial contexts, the concept of goodwill appears to have had positive effects in the shaping of trade mark policy, facilitating for example the development in English law of an action for trade mark dilution[84] and a law of geographical indications,[85] none of these "goodwill outcomes", positive or negative, was inevitable. At every stage, the courts have been required to balance the interests of those involved in trade mark law's eternal triangle described here by Lord Diplock:

> A right of property of this character calls for an accommodation between the conflicting interests of the owner of the monopoly, of the general public . . ., and of other traders.[86]

Crazy Horse represented a choice in favour of local traders and reflected a desire not to stifle competition but it condoned consumer deception within the local market and protected a local business which could never expand into foreign markets because of the superior reputation of the well-known mark. It isolated markets in an era of ever-increasing global trade while also jeopardising international brand reputation, undermining the expenditures which underpinned it. It was a choice which Pennycuick J. understandably regretted. *Crazy Horse* has now been overwhelmed by the tide of international legal policy which runs in favour of choosing to protect the interests of foreign traders in such cases, on the basis that, as Morden J.A. put it in the Ontario Court of Appeal:

> The spectre of [a trader] having a monopoly in . . . its name and distinctive logo, even though it is not now carrying on business here, is considerably less troubling than the deceptive use of its name and symbol by another.[87]

---

[83] *Dominion Rent a Car v. Budget Rent a Car* [1987] 2 N.Z.L.R. 395 at 421, Somers J.
[84] See *e.g. Kodak* (1898) 15 R.P.C. 105 and *Lego* [1983] F.S.R.155.
[85] See the line of cases from *Bollinger v. Costa Brava Wine* [1959] 3 All E.R. 800 to *Chocosuisse Union des Fabricants Suisses de Chocolat v. Cadbury* [1998] R.P.C. 117.
[86] *GEC*, above, note 15, p. 519.
[87] *Orkin*, above, note 63, p. 742.

5. Foreign-language Words as Trade Marks

Ellen Gredley

Foreign-language Words as Trade Marks

Foreign-language marks have distinct advantages: they can disguise an otherwise banal product name, their exotic nature can enhance a brand's image, and they can offer astute brand owners a chance to circumvent strict registrability criteria and avoid liability for infringement. No English trade marks statute has ever made specific provision for marks in languages other than English, which have always been subject to the same legal principles as any others. Nevertheless, they are in fundamental ways unlike other marks and the special problems they create have exercised the minds of trade mark examiners and judges from the earliest days of the registration system. They have also presented the courts with some of their most difficult decisions. A mark's "foreignness" can become a critical issue at several stages: initially at application for registration, and subsequently during opposition, cancellation or infringement proceedings, when confusing similarity is being considered. Although the English courts have never developed an explicitly named "doctrine of foreign equivalents" of the kind found in United States trade mark law,[1] similar principles are discernible in English law.

By the beginning of the twentieth century, the arguments for and against the registration of foreign-language words had been well aired and the guidelines relatively well established, even if at times controversial and difficult to apply. An article in the *Solicitors' Journal* in 1900, questioning the decision in the *Savonol* case, observed tartly:

> all a trader need do, if he wishes to lay a ground for claiming— we do not say, of course successfully claiming—a monopoly in a foreign word, even though it be current in his trade, is to register that word with the termination "ol" affixed thereto as a trade mark—"vinol" for wine, and "Eau-de-Colognol" for perfume...[2]

Acknowledgements: Quotations from U.K. Trade Marks Registry documents are Crown copyright and are used with permission.
The author thanks Ian Reid for assistance in searching the archives of the British Library.
[1] Under this doctrine, words from common modern languages are translated into English to determine whether the mark is generic, descriptive or confusingly similar to a pre-existing mark. The doctrine is applied flexibly, with regard to the circumstances of each case. *Restatement of the Law: Unfair Competition*. American Law Institute, 1995, s.14. McCarthy on *Trademarks and Unfair Competition* (4th ed,) s.11.34.
[2] (1900) 44 *Solicitors' Journal* 548–9. *J.C. & J.Field v. Wagel Syndicate: In the Matter of Trade Mark No.96,997 (Savonol)* (1900) 17 R.P.C. 266.

Writing in 1905, reviewing English and North American case law, James Love Hopkins remarked that with regard to words and phrases from modern foreign languages, the "topic has been fruitful of conflicting holdings. It is not settled what character of words so taken will be sustained as valid trademarks."[3] The situation in respect of marks from the dead languages was alleged to be more certain; although many words, such as "Eureka" and "Excelsior" had been accepted as valid marks, Hopkins noted that a "descriptive word from a dead language cannot be other than a generic term when used as a mark for goods".[4]

Laying Down the Guidelines for the Twentieth Century

The Statutory Context: 1875–1888

Despite the popularity and widespread use of word marks, new marks consisting solely of words were not registrable under the 1875 Act.[5] Composite marks comprising words and other elements such as signatures or devices were admissible, but there was no statutory protection for the word-mark as such, which was left to take its chances at common law and in equity.[6] Long before the introduction of the registration system, owners of marks containing terms in foreign languages or scripts could in certain circumstances prevent their use by trade rivals.[7] Registration of foreign words under the 1875 Act was in many instances a straightforward matter: some were accepted in their capacity as names of individuals or firms presented in a distinctive manner, or as signatures; while others were allowed on to the Register under the provision which admitted "special and

---

[3] J. Love Hopkins, *The Law of Trademarks, Tradenames and Unfair Competition* (2nd ed, 1905, Chicago, Callaghan), 115.
[4] *ibid.* p. 114. The situation was in fact less clear cut than Hopkins implied.
[5] *Ex parte Stephens (Aeilyton)* (1876) 3 Ch.D. 659; 46 L.J. Ch. 46. By coincidence, "Aeilyton" derived from the Greek $\dot{α}εί$ and $λυτόν$ meaning "always soluble". The applicant sought to register it in respect of inks. *cf. In re Barrow's Trade-Marks* (1877), 5 Ch. D. 353, CA, allowing registration of strings of letters used as trade marks before the Act.
[6] For the development of early passing off cases see C. Wadlow, *The Law of Passing-off* (2nd ed. Sweet & Maxwell, 1995) p. 9 *et seq.*
[7] See *e.g. Gout v. Aleploglu* (1833) 6 Beav. 69n; 49 E.R. 750; 5 Leg. Obs. 495. At issue was the Turkish word "Pessendede", said to mean "warranted", which was part of a composite mark also containing the maker's initials, a crescent and a sprig. The defendant was restrained *inter alia* from making or selling watches marked with the word "Pessendede" in Turkish characters. As Turkish was not officially written in Roman script until 1929, the characters were presumably in the former Arabic script. The reported details are sketchy and, although the Vice-Chancellor is said to have held that the plaintiff had the exclusive right to designate his goods by means of the Turkish characters, the case appears to have involved fraud on the part of the defendant. Later cases include *Broadhurst v. Barlow* [1872] W.N. 212, in which the plaintiffs obtained an injunction restraining the defendants from branding their cloth with Turkish, Armenian or Greek words meaning "exactly 12 yards"; and *Cope v. Evans* ("the prairie flower" case) (1872) L.R. 18 Eq. 138, involving an unsuccessful "infringement" claim in respect of the mark "Flor Fina Prairie Superior Tabac", used for cigars.

distinctive words" used as trade marks before the passing of the Act.[8]

The 1883 Act increased the number of purely word marks that might be registered by admitting a "fancy word or words not in common use".[9] This new provision was unfortunately so narrowly interpreted by both Registry and Courts that it was said to have become practically inoperative and was widely criticised.[10] Nonetheless, it led to a line of judicial decisions which helped formulate principles for handling foreign words. The Report of Lord Herschell's Committee in 1888 touched on the issue of foreign-language marks, expressing the view that:

> There can be no objection to permitting the registration of an invented word not to be found in the vocabulary of our own or any other country,

but as a matter of policy

> ...where any English word would be rejected as not entitled to registration, no person ought to be permitted to register its translation into any other language.[11]

Following the Herschell Report the statutory position changed and from 1888 onwards a mark could be registered if it consisted of or contained "an invented word or words" or "a word or words having no reference to the character or quality of the goods, and not being a geographical name".[12]

The Registry and the Rules

Soon after the passing of the 1875 Act the Registry began to develop its own guidelines for dealing with the problems raised by foreign-language terms, which meant that in practice these were subjected to special scrutiny.[13] Although only minor players in a wider drama,

---

[8] Trade Marks Registration Act 1875, s. 10. See *e.g. The Bodega Company and Rivière v. Owens (2) (Bodega)*(1890) 7 R.P.C. 31 (C.A.): the plaintiffs had used "Bodega" (the Spanish word for "wine-store" or "wine-shop") for seven years prior to 1875. "La Flor de Margaretta" was registered in 1876 as a trade mark for cigars, having been in use before the 1875 Act: *Benedictus v. Sullivan Powell & Co.* (1895) 12 R.P.C. 25. "Frigi Domo" (assumed to be a contraction of "frigida domo") was registered for horticultural protective cloth in 1878 after 20 years' prior use: *In the Matter of Edginton's Trade Mark* (1889) 6 R.P.C. 513.
[9] Patents, Designs and Trade Marks Act 1883, s. 64.
[10] D.M. Kerly, *The Law of Trade-marks, Trade-name and Merchandise Marks.* (Sweet & Maxwell 1894), 140ff.
[11] Herschell Report, 1888, Command Paper C. 5350 (1888), p. xi. Lord Herschell's Committee was appointed by the Board of Trade to conduct a wide-ranging enquiry into the running of the Patent Office and the registration of trade marks.
[12] Patents, Designs and Trade Marks Act 1888, s. 10(d–e)(amending 1883 Act, s. 64). The *Solio* case (discussed below) finally established that categories (d) and (e) were to be treated as distinct and separate.
[13] The Trade Marks Rules 1875–1877 made no mention of marks in foreign languages. All applications, however, were to be made in English: Registry Instruction no. 2 (1877).

early cases on foreign-language marks shed interesting light on the conflicts between the Registry, the Courts and trade mark applicants, as all struggled to come to terms with new and developing criteria for registrability.

Between 1875 and 1898, several significant cases involving foreign-language marks tested and clarified first the regulatory powers of the Registry with regard to non-Roman scripts and characters and, ultimately, the interpretation of key sections of the Acts of 1883–88 concerning criteria for registration of word marks. The crucial issue was whether all foreign-language words should be treated as identical to the corresponding English forms, and it is evident from the early case law that the Registry feared trade mark applicants would use foreign-language terms to secure exclusive rights in words that named or described goods. Some judges and commentators supported the Registrar's initial hard line, on the ground that allowing one trader to register descriptive words from modern foreign languages, simply because they were not readily understood by the population in general, would lead to unacceptable restrictions on the freedom of other traders, who might subsequently wish to import goods into England under the names by which they were known in the countries of origin.[14] Many applicants, on the other hand, argued that the question of registration should be decided on purely English considerations, in particular by reference to the comprehension of the ordinary Englishman.[15] Nineteenth-century case law shows not only an appreciation by the judiciary of the importance of trade to the British Empire, but an acute awareness of the conflict between freedom of trade and the protection of marks which could, within the English market, distinguish a particular trader's goods.

Foreign Characters and Scripts: Registrability and Confusing Similarity

In 1880 the Court of Appeal held that the word "Tod" written in Arabic characters qualified under section 10 of the 1875 Act as a "distinctive device".[16] The mark had initially been refused registration, despite fifteen years' use as a trade mark on dial plates of watches, the Registrar stating that he was acting in accordance with an office rule laid down by the Commissioners of Patents forbidding the acceptance of applications for marks written in foreign characters. The rule applied only to words in foreign

---

[14] See *e.g. Davis v. Stribolt; In the Matter of Davis, Bergendahl & Co's Trade Marks* (1889) 6 R.P.C. 207 at 212.
[15] *ibid.* at 210.
[16] *Re Rotheram and Son's Trade Mark.* (1878) 11 Ch. D. 250; 49 L.J. Ch. 511. (CA). In this case the mark was used on watches made in Coventry and supplied to Messrs. Tod, Müller & Co of Alexandria. The word "Tod" was said to mean "high mountain" in Arabic and the mark was in fact a pun.

characters, not to foreign words as such, and had been introduced for practical purposes, to avoid dealing with terms which could not be understood in the Registrar's office.[17] The Vice-Chancellor's dismissal of the Registrar's complaints was upheld by the Court of Appeal. The language and intent of the Act was plain: the Commissioners' refusal to register "any trade mark which is not expressed in English words or letters, or intelligible to the English public" was *ultra vires* and the applicants were entitled to their registration.[18] Presumably as a result of *Rotheram*, the Trade Marks Rules 1883 included an explicit provision on the translation and transliteration of foreign characters.[19]

In 1896 the Court of Appeal upheld the right of the Registrar not to accept without disclaimer a device mark including Burmese characters meaning "The Golden Fan Brand" because the mark conflicted with other registered marks consisting of or including the device of a fan.[20] As required by Rule 15 of the Trade Mark Rules 1890, the applicants had endorsed their application with a note explaining the translation of the Burmese characters.[21] In upholding the Comptroller, Lindley LJ offered some interesting comments on foreign words. Referring to the Burmese characters as "hieroglyphics", he stated as an important matter of principle:

> ...it does not matter what the language is nor what the hieroglyphics are, if the meaning of the hieroglyphics or the meaning of the foreign language is a mere verbal description of a mark already on the Register. If you have got a mark on the Register, applicable to cotton goods, of a golden fan, you cannot have another mark called "Golden fan" in any language or in any hieroglyphics.[22]

In response to the argument that the Burmese characters would not mislead or deceive and should therefore be registered, Lopes L.J.

---

[17] It was, however, regular practice for the Registry to accept for publication device marks including non-Roman scripts. See for example Trade Marks Journal No. 2, May 10, 1876, p. 40: Brocksopp Sons & Co's trade mark for tea, comprising Chinese script and a picture of a man carrying a tea chest. The early Trade Marks Journals have many such examples, for which no translations or transliterations are given.
[18] *Rotheram* (1878) 49 L.J. Ch. 511, at 513.
[19] Rule 15 of the Trade Mark Rules 1883 reads, "Wherever a mark consists of or includes words printed in other than Roman character, there shall be given at the foot or on the back of each representation a translation of such words, signed by the applicant or his agent." That this Rule was included in the wake of *Rotheram* is implied by L.B. Sebastian, *The Law of Trade Marks* (2nd ed, 1884, Stevens & Sons), at p. 344.
[20] *In the Matter of Dewhurst's Application (Golden Fan)* (1896) 13 R.P.C. 288: refused under section 72 of the 1888 Act, which forbade the registration of deceptively similar marks. The application was in respect of cotton thread for sewing, crochet and embroidery and consent had been obtained from the owners of four other cited marks. A request for registration with a limitation of the use of the Burmese characters to goods exported to Burma was also refused.
[21] Trade Marks Rules 1890, rule 15, (identical to Rule 15 of the 1883 Rules).
[22] *Ibid*. The Court relied on the earlier "Red Star" case: *La Société Anonyme des Verreries de l'Etoile Trade Mark* (1894) 11 R.P.C. 142. On a similar point, see also *In the Matter of the Jackson Co's Trade Mark (Kokoko)* (1888) 6 R.P.C. 80.

pointed out the difficulty of drawing the line with regard to the deceptiveness in general of foreign-language marks:

> What would be said with regard to French: what would be said with regard to German: what would be said with regard to Welsh? In point of fact, we should have to go to the length, if we pushed that matter to its logical conclusion, of holding that words being in any foreign language would be sufficient to rebut the probability of deception. In my opinion that cannot be done.[23]

In 1897, Rule 15 of the Trade Marks Rules 1890 was repealed and a new version substituted, which included a requirement for transliteration of words in other than Roman characters.[24] By 1898, applications were regularly being advertised in the Trade Marks Journals accompanied by notes on transliteration and translation of non-Roman characters in marks.

Words: fancy, invented, descriptive

The "fancy word" criterion introduced by the 1883 Act led to many casualties in the race for registration and during the 1880s several foreign-language marks were either refused registration or expunged from the Register *inter alia* on the grounds that they were not "fancy words not in common use", that is, they did not pass the test laid down by the Court of Appeal that a fancy word must be obviously non-descriptive when used as a trade mark for the goods in question.[25] In 1889 the marks "Boköl" and "Bokøl", registered for preparations of malt containing alcohol, were ordered to be struck off. As Swedish and Norwegian terms for a particular kind of beer they could not qualify as "fancy words" under the 1883 Act.[26] During the proceedings it was conceded that had the words been French, German or Italian terms for beer, they would not originally

---

[23] Lopes L.J. in *Golden Fan* at p. 297.
[24] Trade Marks Rules 1897, r. 2(d): "When a trade-mark contains a word or words in other than Roman characters, there shall be endorsed on the application... a sufficient transliteration and translation to the satisfaction of the Comptroller of each of such words... Where a trade-mark contains a word or words in a language other than English, the Comptroller may ask for an exact translation thereof, and if he so requires such translations shall be endorsed and signed as aforesaid."
[25] *Van Duzer's Trade Mark* (1887) 4 R.P.C. 31, CA; *Waterman v. Ayres; In the Matter of Waterman's Trade Mark* (1888) 5 R.P.C. 368, CA. Various phrases were used by the Lords Justices, including "obviously meaningless as applied to the article in question" and "cannot have reference to any description or designation of where the article is made or of what its character is". Among the casualties were the Latin derivative "Emolliolorum" and the word "Sanitas"; *In the Matter of Talbot's Trade Mark* (1894) 11 R.P.C. 77; and *In the Matter of the Sanitas Company's Trade Mark* (1887) 4 R.P.C. 533. "Sanitas" was said to be known to everybody as a result of Lord Beaconsfield's (*i.e.* Disraeli's) quotation "Sanitas, sanitas et omnia sanitas" (a punning variant of the Biblical "Vanitas vanitatum, et omnia vanitas").
[26] *Davis v. Stribolt; In the Matter of Davis, Bergendahl & Co's Trade Marks* (1889) 6 R.P.C. 207; 1883 Act, s. 64(1)(c).

have been registered.[27] The proprietors argued unsuccessfully that their case should be distinguished on the grounds that the Scandinavian languages were less well known in England and that the words would not be understood by the ordinary Englishman. Chitty J. was unable to accept the proposition that "every word is a fancy word because it is unknown to the average Englishman"; further, "there are many good English words descriptive of articles which are unknown to an average Englishman, taking rather a high standard."[28] Cautiously limiting himself to the European languages,[29] he held that in respect of "an article produced in a foreign country and imported into England where it was previously unknown and without a name, the word used in that foreign country as the common term to describe or denote the article is not a fancy word within the meaning of the Act".[30] As a matter of policy, in the interests of free and fair trading, "Boköl" was treated as generic or descriptive of the product, although the word may well have been completely obscure to the general English public. In contrast, "Oomoo" alleged to be an Australian Aboriginal word meaning "choice" or "select" was accepted under the 1883 Act; not only was it meaningless in England when used with reference to wines and spirits, but it was not the actual name of the goods in the language concerned.[31]

Despite the changes in the law effected by the 1888 Act, it was evident that the Registry and the courts were adopting an illiberal and restrictive approach to the interpretation of section 10 (d) and (e).[32] In 1898 the House of Lords tackled head-on the problems generated by the new criteria for registrability and in so doing incidentally set down principles for the registration of foreign-language words which were to endure well into the latter half of the twentieth century. In 1895 a second application for registration of the word "Solio" for photographic printing paper met with objections from the Comptroller, chiefly on the grounds that the word had

---

[27] See also *Vignier's Trade Mark (Monobrut)* (1889) 6 R.P.C. 490. "Monobrut" (from the Greek μόνος ["only", "sole"] and the French "brut"), registered for wines, was ordered to be removed from the Register: the word was descriptive, and had been accepted by the public as signifying "very dry".

[28] *Davis v. Stribolt*, at 212.

[29] "European" evidently meant languages written in Roman characters, such as French, German, Scandinavian. See also Lindley L.J. in *Dewhurst's Application* (1896) 13 R.P.C. 288 at 294.

[30] *Davis v. Stribolt*, at 212.

[31] *In the Matter of Burgoyne's Trade Mark* (1889) 6 R.P.C. 227. cf. *In the Matter of the Jackson Co's Trade Mark (Kokoko)* (1888) 6 R.P.C. 80 in which "Kokoko" an onomatopoeic word used by the Chippeway Indians of North America to signify the cry of an owl was refused registration in respect of cotton goods primarily because the device of an owl was common to the trade.

[32] See for example *Farbenfabriken Co's Application* [1894] 1 Ch. 645; 11 R.P.C. 84, in which "Somatose" (from the Greek σῶμα meaning "body") was refused registration by the Court of Appeal in respect of meat products. In contrast the Court of Appeal had allowed "Mazawattee", *Densham's TM* [1895] 2 Ch. 176; 12 R.P.C. 75 and 271 (a compound of the Hindustani Maza meaning "luscious, taste, relish" and the Sinhalese Wattee meaning "garden") in respect of tea, holding that the word had no direct reference to character or quality.

reference to the quality of the goods.[33] Although clearly not descriptive of the goods in question, the word was alleged to suggest, because of a perceived resemblance to the Latin word "sol", the operation of sunlight on the photographic medium.[34] In due course the case reached the House of Lords, where their Lordships took the opportunity to discuss in detail the provisions of the 1888 Act. Reversing the Court of Appeal, they accepted "Solio" both as an "invented word' and a word which did not refer to the character or quality of the goods concerned, registrable therefore under either head. In explaining the nature of invented words Lord Herschell stated:

> It may no doubt sometimes be difficult to determine whether a word is an invented word or not . . . I do not think that a foreign word is an invented word, simply because it has not been current in our language. At the same time I am not prepared to go so far as to say that a combination of words from foreign languages so little known in this country, that it would suggest no meaning except to a few scholars, might not be regarded as an invented word.[35]

Concurring, Lord Macnaghten stated:

> If it is an invented word—if it is "new and freshly coined" . . . it seems to me there is no objection that it may be traced to a foreign source, or that it may contain a covert and skilful allusion to the character or quality of the goods.[36]

Solio established that foreign-language words (classical or modern) might qualify as invented, although they did not fall within this category merely because they were not current in the English language; nor were they barred from registration simply because they alluded to the character or quality of goods. Kerly notes that after *Solio* the Registry relaxed its former hard line and habitually accepted as "invented" words with very little inventive character, albeit with frequent requirement of disclaimers.[37] "Savonol" (from the French "savon" meaning "soap") was confirmed as an invented word and allowed to remain on the Register in respect of soaps and detergents.[38] The fact that the French word "savon" was widely used in the trade for soap did not adversely affect the outcome, though

---

[33] *Eastman Photographic Materials Company's Application (Solio)* (1898) 15 R.P.C. 476, HL.
[34] Thus falling foul of s. 64(e) of the 1888 Act. "Solio" means "throne" in Spanish and is the ablative form of the Latin "solium" meaning a seat or bathtub. The connection, if any, with the "bath" used in photographic development escaped the attention of the Court.
[35] *Solio* at 485.
[36] *Solio* at 486.
[37] F.G. Underhay, *Kerly on Trade Marks* (5th ed, 1923, Sweet & Maxwell), at 166.
[38] *J.C. & J. Field v. Wagel Syndicate Ld, and In the Matter of Trade Mark No. 96,997 ("Savonol")*. (1900) 17 R.P.C. 266.

the decision was criticised.[39] "Tachytype" (from the Greek ταχύς [tachus] meaning "fast" and τύπος [tupos] meaning "impression") was permitted registration in respect of typographical composing and casting machines. Relying on *Solio*, Cozens-Hardy J. deemed it an invented word; further he doubted "whether anybody not being a scholar more or less would have the faintest conception of what the word meant".[40] In contrast, the mark "Haematogen" (for a proprietary medicine designed to encourage formation of red corpuscles in blood) was not permitted to remain on the Register.[41] The word was derived from the Greek αἷμα [haima] (meaning "blood") and was not invented; it was an old German word, known in England by 1893, by which time it had become extensively used by physiologists. Accordingly, as the application had been made in 1899, it failed the test of invention for adoption as a trade mark for the proprietor's goods.[42]

After *Solio:* The Statutory Context 1905–1938

Section 9 of the 1905 Act (registrable trade marks) modified certain passages in the Act of 1888. Giving statutory sanction to *Solio*, it retained the provision on "invented words",[43] but replaced "word or words having no reference to the character or quality of the goods and not being a geographical name" with "word or words having no *direct* reference . . . and not being *according to its ordinary signification* a geographic name or a surname".[44] This significantly increased the pool of words available for registration.[45]

The Acts of 1919 and 1938 added nothing which in principle significantly affected the registration of foreign-language words, although the division of the Register by the 1919 Act made it possible for marks which had been in *bona fide* use as trade marks for not less than two years to be registered in Part B. Thus, owners of foreign-language marks which met the formal requirements could insist on their registration. Section 10 of the Trade Marks Act 1938 abandoned the requirement of two years' *bona fide* use as a trade mark and freed the Registrar from the compulsion to register. The changes, together with the more lenient Part B test of "capability to

---

[39] (1900) 44 *Solicitors' Journal* 548.
[40] *In the Matter of the Application of the Linotype Company Ld for a Trade Mark (No. 2) (Tachytype)* (1900) 17 R.P.C. 380 at 385.
[41] *Hommel v. Gebrüder Bauer & Co; In the Matter of the Trade Mark "Haematogen"* (1904) 21 R.P.C. 576.
[42] The issue of date of invention also arose in *La Société le Ferment's Application (Lactobacilline)* (1912) 29 R.P.C. 497, CA, where it was said that the word need not be newly invented at the time of application. Nor need the applicant be the actual inventor: see *Tachytype* (1900) 17 R.P.C. 380 and *Kodak* (1903) 20 R.P.C. 337.
[43] s. 9(3).
[44] Trade Marks Act 1905, s. 9(4). Additions are given here in italics. This provision was retained in the 1938 Act: s. 9(1)(d).
[45] *Kerly on Trade Marks* (5th ed, 1923) *above*, p. 10.

distinguish" meant that Part B "became largely used for new marks, refused for Part A but near the borderline of registrability".[46] Consequently some foreign-language marks refused for Part A found their way on to the Part B Register.

After *Solio:* Case Law Under The Acts Of 1905–1938

Throughout this period *Solio* remained a leading authority on marks derived from foreign languages. Foreign words continued to be registered, though foreign place names were generally unacceptable and foreign surnames presented particular problems.[47] Key cases restated the long-standing difficulties of policy faced by the Registry and Courts in applying the statutory criteria to non-English terms and reiterated principles laid down in the late nineteenth century.

Many foreign language marks (and constructs from one or more languages) qualified as invented words, including "Parlograph", for sound recording and reproducing apparatus[48]; "Lactobacilline" for lactic acid ferments[49] and "Portalto" for wines, liqueurs and spirits.[50] Amongst those not accepted as invented were "Cyclostyle" for rotary pens,[51] "Diabolo" for tops for a children's game,[52] "Smitsvonk" for electric spark producing apparatus[53] and "Magnetophon", for sound recording apparatus.[54]

Words rejected as "invented" might nevertheless qualify as having "no direct reference to character or quality". Kerly notes the difficulty in discerning any definite principle in the relatively few cases involving the issue of "direct reference". Many attractive trade marks are in some degree laudatory or descriptive and the perennial problem is "to decide whether that reference is a direct reference: one that seriously affects the word's capacity for distinguishing goods from a particular source, as distinct from the sort of reference

---

[46] *Kerly's Law of Trade Marks and Trade Names* (12th ed, Sweet & Maxwell, London, 1986), para. 8–73.
[47] Foreign surnames and geographic names are excluded from this discussion primarily for reasons of space; arguably, they are best considered with surnames and geographic names generally.
[48] *In the Matter of an Application by Carl Lindstroem Aktiengesellschaft for Registration of a Trade Mark* (1914) 31 R.P.C. 261. ("Parlograph" derived from the French "parler" and the Greek $\gamma\rho\alpha\phi\epsilon\iota\nu$, literally "speak-write")
[49] *La Société le Ferment's Application* (1912) 81 L.J. Ch. 724; (1912) 29 R.P.C. 497, CA.
[50] *Portalto Trade Mark* [1967] R.P.C. 617. Said to be an Anglo-Portuguese hybrid. Although invented, and accepted as having no direct reference, registration was refused under s. 11 of the 1938 Act as likely to cause confusion if used other than on certified port wine.
[51] *In re Gestetner's Trade Mark* [1907] 2 Ch. 748; 748; (1908) 25 R.P.C. 156 (C.A). The mark derived from the Greek and Latin nouns $\kappa\acute{\upsilon}\kappa\lambda o\varsigma$ and "stilus" meaning "wheel-pen". It was removed from the Register.
[52] *Phillipart v. William Whitely Ld and In the Matter of Phillipart's Trade Mark (Diabolo)* (1908) 25 R.P.C. 565.
[53] *In the Matter of Smitsvonk N.V.'s Application for a Trade Mark* (1954) 72 R.P.C. 117.
[54] *Allgemeine Elektricitats A.G.'s Application* [1957] R.P.C. 127. In contrast to "Lactobacilline" "Magnetophone" and "Magneto-phonograph" were known dictionary words; held descriptive of the goods.

that can be found only as an academic exercise."[55] When the mark in question is in a foreign language, the difficulty is compounded and in many such cases the "ordinary Englishman' is brought centre-stage.

Foreign-language Marks and the "Ordinary Englishman"

Diabolo, a trade mark infringement action and counterclaim for rectification, was one of the earliest cases involving foreign-language words heard under the provisions of the 1905 Act. The plaintiffs had revived an old game involving a spinning top held by a string between two sticks and had marketed it under the name "Diabolo", which had been registered for tops.[56] The game had been known in England and on the Continent under names such as "The Devil on Two Sticks", "Le Diable" and "Le Jeu de Diable". Parker J. found that the word was not invented: it was merely a well-established variant for the ordinary Italian word "diavolo", very close to the English word "diabolical", and presumably selected in order to suggest that the revived game was identical to the old one. The "ordinary Englishman" would inevitably conclude that it contained a reference to the devil. Further, it was suggestive of the character of the goods: those in France or England acquainted with the old game would identify the "Diabolo" tops as those used therein. He concluded that:

> ...the word "Diabolo" is no more registrable for a double coned top than the word "Cricket" is registrable for a set of stumps ... there was never a time at which 'Diabolo' could have been registered for tops under the Act of 1905.[57]

"Smitsvonk", a combination of the common Dutch surname "Smits" and "vonk" the Dutch word for spark, was refused registration in Part A for electric spark-producing apparatus. The word was inherently non-distinctive under section 9 of the 1938 Act, qualifying neither as an invented word nor a word with no direct reference. In stating his reasons for refusal, Hearing Officer Whyman commented:

> ...it has long been a recognised principle in dealing with applications for the registration of trade marks that the

---

[55] *Kerly's Law of Trade Marks and Trade Names* (12th ed, Sweet & Maxwell, London, 1986), at p. 88. See also *Aphrodisia Trade Mark* [1977] F.S.R. 133 in which the Irish court stated: "Trade mark law is concerned with the impression which a mark makes on the public generally and not on those of them who are classical scholars or historians... the best approach is to look at dictionaries in common use and not at five-volume works which are rarely consulted".
[56] The mark was registered in 1905 under the provisions of the Acts of 1883–88.
[57] *Diabolo* at 572. The Court also doubted whether the mark had ever been used as a trade mark, being simply the name of the revived game.

considerations as regards registrability that apply to an English word apply also to any foreign equivalent thereof.[58]

On this point the Hearing Officer cited Lord Herschell's Report of 1888, and the leading cases *Boköl* and *Solio*. Applying these principles, "Smitsvonk" was in effect treated as equivalent to "Smith-spark" or "Smiths-spark" and regarded as inherently non-distinctive.[59] On appeal, Lloyd-Jacob J. upheld the Hearing Officer in respect of the application for Part A:

> ...the fact that these two words are derived from the Dutch language cannot be expected to imply that they will convey no meaning in the British market...[60]

Nevertheless, considering the mark as a whole, he permitted it to proceed to Part B, as capable of acquiring a distinctive character. Although some section of the trading community might recognise the descriptiveness of the mark, its "potentiality of descriptiveness" was not such as to cause it to be incapable of distinguishing.[61] In due course, the issue of its distinctive character would be determined by persons engaged in the relevant trade.

In 1977 the Irish Supreme Court specifically addressed the issue of "direct reference".[62] The applicant had unsuccessfully sought registration of "Kiku" (meaning "chrysanthemum" in Japanese) as a mark for perfumes and cosmetics and was granted permission to appeal to the Supreme Court on a precise question of law: "whether when a word for which registration as a trade mark is sought is one in a foreign language the Controller and the Court must treat the application as one for the registration of the corresponding English or Irish word."

Conceding that the name of a flower or plant ought not to be registered in connection with perfumes or soaps, O'Higgins C.J. held that the word "Kiku" denoted nothing to those unacquainted with Japanese:

> In order that its meaning can be conveyed it has to be translated, which means another word has to be used to convey its

---

[58] *Smitsvonk* at 118.
[59] "Smits" was also said to be not uncommon as a surname in England.
[60] *Smitsvonk* at 120; *cf.* the earlier case *Verschure & Zoon's Application* (1905) 22 R.P.C. 568, where the Court felt that "not many people in England" were familiar with the Dutch language.
[61] *cf. Wacker-Chemie* [1957] R.P.C. 278, where a combination of a "not uncommon" foreign surname and the German word for "chemistry" was treated as equivalent to "Wacker Chemicals" and refused registration for chemical products both in Parts A and B. *cf.* also *Rijn Staal* [1990] R.P.C. 400, where the mark "Rijn Staal" was treated as equivalent to "Rhine Steel" and refused for chemical products used in steel production in Parts A and B. These cases of course also contained surnominal and geographic elements.
[62] *Kiku Trade Mark* [1977] F.S.R. 246.

meaning. This seems to me to be the very antithesis of 'direct reference'. . . .[63]

The Court's answer to the specific question was "No". The primary consideration was the foreign word's meaning to ordinary persons living in Ireland and the Court clearly believed that to such persons Japanese was a completely unknown language.[64]

Deceptive Similarity and the Foreign Market

Although the crucial test for deception or confusion is normally limited to the United Kingdom, in cases where the goods are destined for export, the pool of persons likely to be deceived may be enlarged to include foreign purchasers unfamiliar with the English language as well as those in England engaged in the relevant trade.[65] The law in this area is not entirely clear and has been described by Kerly as "open".[66]

The makers of "Eno's Fruit Salts" prevented the registration of "Salina de Frutas Evans", arguing successfully that the words "Fruit Salt" and "Eno's Fruit Salt" and their equivalents in foreign languages were well-known throughout the world as denoting their product.[67] On the other hand, in *Solibrisa*, consideration of the effect of the mark on those engaged in the export trade in the United Kingdom was paramount.[68] The applicant's mark (from the Spanish "sol y brisa", meaning "sun and breeze") would not be confused (even through imperfect recollection) with the opponent's "Summer Breeze", though both were used on textile goods exported to Argentina. Little weight was given to the opponent's claim that the marks might seem to Spanish speakers phonetically similar. Similarly, in *Hassan El-Madi's Application*, which also involved textile goods for the export market, it was held on appeal that there was no likelihood of confusion or deception in the export market in the United Kingdom (either among English-speaking or Arabic-speaking people involved in the textile trade) between the applicant's representation in Arabic script of the words "The Flying Carpet" and the opponent's prior registration in similar script of the Arabic words

---

[63] *ibid.* at 249.
[64] Had the application been for a word closer to the English-language term, for example "crisantemo" (the Spanish, Portuguese and Italian equivalents), the decision might have been more difficult. An interesting contrast is provided by the Australian case *Re Torstein Ropeid's Application* (1986) A.I.P.C. 90–342, where the Icelandic word "Lopi" was refused registration for wool because it was the actual name of the product. Little weight was attached to the fact that Icelandic was virtually unknown in Australia.
[65] As in *Golden Fan* (1896) and *Kokoko* (1888).
[66] *Kerly's Law of Trade Marks and Trade Names* (12th ed., Sweet & Maxwell, London, 1986), para. 10–10. See also *Red Star* [1894] 3 Ch. 26; 11 R.P.C. 142, CA.
[67] In the Matter of an Application by Evans Sons Lescher and Webb Ltd for the Registration of a Trade Mark (1934) 51 R.P.C. 423. Eno's had a number of registrations including "Fruit Salt" and "Sal de Fruta".
[68] *In the Matter of Marcos Balé y Hnos' Application* (1947) 65 R.P.C. 17.

meaning "Rider of the Wind".⁶⁹ In the complex *Al Bassam* case, where the Court needed expert advice on the translation of the mark, its ability to distinguish was considered by reference to the position in the United Kingdom only, and in this context it qualified for Part B.⁷⁰

Registry Practice under the Acts of 1905–1938

All Trade Marks Rules issued under the Acts of 1905–1938 stipulated that applications for trade marks containing a word or words in characters other than Roman should, unless the Registry otherwise directed, be accompanied by sufficient transliteration or translation and additionally should state the language to which the words belong. Where the mark contained a word or words in languages other than English, the Registrar had discretion to ask for an exact translation, together with the name of the language.⁷¹ The concern of the Registry to inform both the general public and other mark owners is apparent from an internal memorandum dated 1934:

> Up to the present we have generally refrained from making such a requirement with regard to words in Roman characters, but in some cases it would appear very desirable that the public should know what the words mean. For example, a registered owner of a mark consisting of the word 'Bear' would be unlikely to know all the foreign equivalents of that word and consequently might pass unnoticed the advertisement of a mark containing prominently the word 'Bear' in, say, Italian or Norwegian, if the translation were not advertised. Further, in the case of foreign words having a semi-descriptive meaning and for which there is a disclaimer, a translation of such words would throw light on the reason for the disclaimer. There is an additional advantage in the fact that the translations will automatically find their way into the Indexes (including the public index).⁷²

Practice on this point was determined by the language and the meaning of the words in relation to the goods concerned. The same memorandum noted that "generally speaking, words in French or German will not need translation, but it may well be otherwise with regard to (*e.g.*) Italian or Spanish or other lesser known languages." Further Registry notes from the 1940s and 1950s indicate that

---

⁶⁹ (1954) 71 R.P.C. 281; 348, CA. Applicant's mark transliterated was "Bissat-el-Rih" and opponent's mark transliterated was "Rakeb-el-Rih". Both marks also included devices respectively of a flying carpet and a trumpet-blowing angel. "El-Rih" was said to mean "air" or "wind".
⁷⁰ *Al Bassam Trade Mark* [1994] R.P.C. 315; [1995] R.P.C. 511, CA.
⁷¹ In *Yomeishu Seizo v. Sinma Medical Products* [1991] F.S.R. 278, HC (Singapore), inaccuracy in translation led to an allegation that the registration was obtained by fraud on the Registry. Mandarin characters claimed to be meaningless were in fact descriptive.
⁷² Foreign Words in Roman Characters on Marks, 1934. (Internal Registry Memorandum).

decisions on the need for translation were taken on a case-by-case basis, though transliterations and translations were automatically required for marks comprising characters from languages such as Chinese, Japanese, Russian, Arabic and Indian dialects.

Registry practice on registrability of foreign-language words under the 1938 Act was incorporated in work manuals, which were made publicly available in 1989. There would be no objection under section 9(1)(d) to Latin or classical Greek terms that might be meaningful for the goods, unless the words or phrases were well-known "as a matter of general knowledge".[73] The Registry would also overlook the meaning of "obscure" laudatory or descriptive terms in modern foreign languages such as Tibetan, unless the meaning of the word had been drawn to the attention of the purchasing public and had consequently become well-known. Noting that *Solio* remained "the keystone of trade mark law with regard to invention", the Manual included foreign equivalents of English words amongst its list of examples of what did *not* constitute "invented words".[74] Words in remote foreign languages (Tibetan was again cited as an example) might qualify as invented, but this would not apply to words in languages commonly encountered in the United Kingdom, such as Western European or Indian. Although *Parlograph* gave authority for treating hybrids of terms from foreign languages as "invented", the Registry offered the French "bon" as a good example of a well-known foreign word whose familiarity disentitled it to registration in compounds such as "Bontoy" for toys or "Bonchocs" for chocolates.[75] Many examples in the Manual involved French, which was assumed to be the most familiar modern foreign language in the United Kingdom, and these illustrate both the flexibility of the approach taken and the difficulty of laying down hard and fast rules. Some French words had for many years been part of the English language;[76] others occupied a more indeterminate position.[77] "Au Printemps" was refused registration for clothing as non-distinctive under section 9 of the 1938 Act.[78] The phrase did not qualify as invented and had direct reference to the character of the goods. Even those with a "basic understanding of the French language" would recognise the mark as descriptive of clothing intended for wear in the spring.[79] The mark was also unacceptable prima facie for Part B, as it was common practice for traders in the United Kingdom and France to use French words in advertising clothing for sale in the United Kingdom.

The Registry continued to be guided by *Golden Fan* as giving

---

[73] *Trade Marks Registry Work Manual*, Department of Trade and Industry, 1989, para. 9–179.
[74] *ibid.* para. 9–70.
[75] *ibid.* para. 9–72.
[76] e.g. "Cordon Bleu": *Paton Calvert Cordon Bleu Trade Mark* [1996] R.P.C. 94 (Registry).
[77] See e.g. the treatment of "Toujours", "Avenir" and "Prochain(e)"; *Registry Work Manual*, 1992, chap. 20.
[78] *Au Printemps Trade Mark* [1990] R.P.C. 518. (Registry).
[79] *ibid.* at 520.

judicial support to the view that foreign words and their English equivalents could be confusingly similar.[80] On the other hand, the *Golden Fan* rule was not applied rigidly and there would be conflict only if the foreign equivalent was reasonably close visually and phonetically.[81] Thus, the proprietor of the mark "Always" failed in opposing registration of the Italian and Spanish terms "Sempre" and "Siempre" (each with a device).[82] The words had "no direct reference to the character or quality of the goods" and the applicant's marks were easily distinguishable aurally and visually from the opponent's. The Registry was not persuaded by the opponent's argument that an increasing number of United Kingdom residents are familiar with Italian and Spanish and would therefore be confused. Objection, however, would be taken when the meaning of the foreign word was very well known, despite the absence of visual or phonetic similarity.[83] Similarly, the "idea" of the mark would be taken into account, so that the silhouette of a black cat and the phrase "Chat Noir" would most likely have been judged confusingly similar. Where the foreign word was the name of the goods, as in "Kretek", the Indonesian word for a type of cigarette, the mark was unregistrable. The most celebrated case involving section 15 of the Act, which dealt with marks which had after registration become the name or description of an article or substance, saw the removal from the Register of the mark "Daiquiri Rum". Originally registered for rum, the word "Daiquiri" was found to have become generic for a type of cocktail.[84]

Foreign Language Marks and the 1994 Act

By the time the 1994 Act came into force, a long line of Registry and judicial decisions meant that guidelines on the treatment of foreign-language marks under the 1938 Act were well established. These obviously had to be reviewed in the context of a new Act constructed within a pan-European framework.[85] As with all previous statutes, no specific mention is made in the 1994 Act of foreign language marks, which are subject to the general criteria for registrability.[86] Problems with the registration of foreign-language

---

[80] *Registry Work Manual*, 1992, chap. 10, para. 10–54.
[81] For example, the German term "Engel" would normally be too close to "Angel", whereas the German term "Dom" would not be in conflict with "Cathedral".
[82] *Lidl Stiftung's Application/Opposition by Proctor & Gamble*: SRIS O/059/99, Feb 26, 1999, (class 5 goods). The matter was subject to the 1938 Act but was heard in 1999 and is indicative of current Registry thinking: a similar viewpoint was put forward in the *Jarvard* case (below note 94).
[83] As in the case of "Oui" and "Yes".
[84] *Daiquiri Rum Trade Mark* [1969] R.P.C. 600, HL; Daiquiri was the name of a mining town in Cuba.
[85] The Act was designed to implement European Council Directive 89/104 approximating the trade mark law of Member States of the European Community.
[86] Primarily, ss. 1–4.

words will often occur in respect of section 3(1)(c) which forbids registration of marks which "consist exclusively" of signs or indications that describe or characterise products or services.[87] All foreign-language marks are scrutinised accordingly. Distinctiveness acquired through use in trade may overcome these objections and the Registry clearly accepts the principle that if an English descriptive word can acquire distinctiveness, the same applies in the case of a foreign descriptive term. Although the Act does not refer explicitly to generic terms, these are regarded as incapable of distinguishing goods or services, thus incapable of functioning as trade marks and therefore unregistrable under sections 1(1) and 3(1)(a). The most difficult decisions will involve generic terms from languages which are relatively or wholly unknown in the United Kingdom.

Registry practice under the 1994 Act is guided by whether the relevant language is well-known amongst residents of the United Kingdom and whether the application is for goods or services. For this purpose, languages are loosely categorised as "Well Known", "Less Well Known", "Languages of Ethnic Minorities" and "Native Languages other than English".[88] French, German, Italian and Spanish are considered likely to be well-known to a reasonable (and increasing) number of United Kingdom residents, and are objected to in respect of goods if the English equivalent would be the subject of an objection under section 3(1)(c). A more liberal approach towards distinctiveness, however, means that "Au Printemps", refused for clothing under the 1938 Act, would be unlikely to meet with objection under the 1994 Act. With respect to international services, objection is taken to descriptive words from foreign languages that would be excluded from registration by section 3(1)(c); and the same applies to services in conjunction with which foreign-language terms are commonly used (for example, French for restaurant services). For local services, more latitude is given and foreign language names are generally acceptable.

The list of less well-known languages is illustrative, including at the present time Dutch, Swedish, Portuguese, Czech, Russian and Japanese. For goods, no objection is taken unless the country has a reputation for any of the goods covered by the application. Thus "Kiku" would presumably pass muster under the 1994 Act, whereas "Rijn Staal" would not.[89] Objection is made to foreign descriptive words only for international services.

The languages of ethnic minorities category includes by way of example Chinese, Greek, Urdu, Gujerati and Arabic, some of which are spoken by sizeable minorities of United Kingdom residents. If the goods are destined for the ethnic market, the mark (either in original

---

[87] s. 3(1)(c) is subject to the proviso that registration may proceed if distinctiveness in use has been demonstrated before the date of application.
[88] *Trade Marks Registry Work Manual*, 1998, chap. 6, pp. 53–54.
[89] See notes 61, 62. "Rijn Staal" also involves a geographic element.

script or in transliteration) is treated in the same manner as for well-known languages. Objection is taken to words whose English equivalents would be open to objection under section 3(1)(c). Thus the old example "Aeilyton" would no doubt be accepted today for soluble inks destined for the general United Kingdom market. Services are treated in similar manner to goods, bearing in mind that some services are associated with particular languages, for example, healing or martial arts with Chinese, and certain words may therefore be recognised phonetically by United Kingdom residents, even if they do not speak the language concerned. Greek (and Cyrillic) letters appearing in trade marks are considered on their merits, though care is taken in respect of Greek letters used as symbols in mathematics, as these are regarded as non-distinctive for class 9 goods.

Marks in native languages other than English, such as Welsh and Gaelic, will be objected to where the country concerned has a reputation for the relevant goods or services or where these may be especially associated with a particular culture.

Perhaps as a sign of the changing times and the diminution of classics teaching in the United Kingdom, the Registry Manual no longer has separate sections devoted to classical languages and marks derived from Latin or classical Greek are subject to standard treatment. The Manual does offer guidelines for words such as "Aqua", "Futura", "Lux", "Magna," "Optima", "Prima" and "Ultro", though most of these are also current in Italian, Spanish or Portuguese.

There is relatively little authority on foreign-language words and the concept of "likelihood of confusion including the likelihood of association".[90] In the notorious *Wagamama* case, which involved a Japanese word, the fact that the word had no significance for the overwhelming majority of the population meant that imperfect recollection was more likely. Both parties were involved in comparatively inexpensive restaurant services and the defendant's "Rajamama" was found confusingly similar to the plaintiffs "Wagamama" mark.[91] Infringement by likelihood of mere association without confusion as to origin was rejected. The Registry and the U.K. Courts are now of course bound by the ruling of the European Court of Justice in *Sabel v. Puma*, where it was decided that "likelihood of association" serves to define the scope of "confusion" and should be interpreted globally, taking into account all relevant circumstances of the case, including the reputation of the original mark.[92]

---

[90] Trade Marks Act 1994, ss. 5(2) and 10(2).
[91] *Wagamama Ltd v. City Centre Restaurants* [1995] F.S.R. 713; "Wagamama" means wilfulness or selfishness in Japanese. "Rajamama" was a coined word.
[92] Case C-251/95, *Sabel v. Puma* judgment November 11, 1997; [1998] R.P.C. 199; [1998] E.T.M.R. 1. Nevertheless in *GTR Group's Application* [1999] E.T.M.R. 164, following ECJ guidelines, the mark "Jois & Jo" was held not confusingly similar to the opponent's well-known "Joy" mark for

A widened orbit of protection would logically mean that foreign-language equivalents are more likely to infringe.[93]

The *Jarvard* case raised the issue of potential confusion through pronunciation of a meaningless word.[94] The application by a Spanish company to register the word "Jarvard" for clothing was opposed by Harvard College which argued that the word "Jarvard" would be pronounced "Harvard" by Spanish speakers, and was therefore confusingly similar to its own registered marks. Hearing Officer Morgan accepted that in the Spanish language the two words were not easily distinguishable, but relied on "the English ear and eye" in finding that the mark was not likely to confuse. The crucial test was said to be "a likelihood of confusion on the part of the public in the United Kingdom".[95] Little weight was given to the opponent's argument that the British public was becoming increasingly sophisticated with regard to languages and that many people familiar with Spanish, assuming the mark was pronounced "Harvard", would infer a connection, especially as the clothing emanated from a Spanish company. The decision is interesting in that Spanish is listed in the Registry Work Manual as one of the "Well-Known" languages, although of course the word is not in the Spanish lexicon and the relevant public would probably be sufficiently sophisticated to recognise a case of brand copying and realise that the Spanish entrepreneur was "cashing-in" on the fame of the opponent.

There is at the time of writing no authority for the treatment of foreign-language marks which have been registered under the 1994 Act but which, as a result of changing linguistic and cultural conditions, have become non-distinctive. The 1994 Act makes provision under section 46 for revocation of registration, but this can occur only as a consequence of acts or inactivity of the proprietor.[96] Registrations may also be invalidated under section 47, though the owner of a descriptive foreign-language mark whose validity is attacked under section 47(1) may be able to withstand the challenge if it can be shown that the mark has acquired distinctiveness in use

---

perfumes. "Jois" and "Jo" had no dictionary meaning and were described as "fancy words". The later ruling of the ECJ in *Canon* appears to have increased the scope of protection of a well-known mark: Case C-39/97, *Canon Kabushiki Kaisha v. Metro-Goldwyn-Mayer Inc.* Judgment September 29, 1998: [1999] R.P.C. 117; F.S.R. 332; E.T.M.R. 1.

[93] "Opposites" may also be confusingly similar, as in the French case *Sté Felix the Cat Productions Inc. v. Sté Polygram* [1999] E.T.M.R. 370, in which "Felix the Cat" was infringed by "Felix le Souriceau". In addition to a common grammatical construction, there was conceptual similarity by means of contrast (cat/mouse).

[94] *Kundry SA's Application* [1998] E.T.M.R. 178. See also "Jois & Jo" [1999] E.T.M.R. 164, above note 92.

[95] *ibid.* at 185. The application was found to have been made in bad faith.

[96] s. 46(1)(c). Arguably an application to register a term denoting goods or services in another language is made in bad faith: s. 46(4). In the U.S. case *Otokoyama v. Wine of Japan Import* 50 U.S.P.Q. 2d. 1626 (1999) the Court of Appeals for the Second Circuit confirmed that the "bedrock principle" of trade mark law that no trader may acquire exclusive rights to generic terms extended to those in foreign languages. Evidence of refusal to register by the Japanese Patent Office was relevant to the defendant's claim that the plaintiff's application to the USPTO to register "Otokoyama" (a generic term in Japanese) for sake wine had been made in bad faith.

since registration. A defendant facing an infringement action through use of a descriptive foreign-language term may also have a good defence.[97] Those who adopt a descriptive foreign-language mark run the risk that there may be a change in the status of the foreign term that renders the mark vulnerable to removal from the Register.

The Community Trade Mark and the Language Problem

The problems arising from foreign-language marks, hitherto confined to national trade mark offices, now face Europe, and on a vastly increased scale. Issues similar to those first discussed in the nineteenth century confront the examiners of OHIM,[98] and the leading decisions emanate from the European Court of Justice. More than twenty languages, excluding dialects, are currently spoken within the European geographic area. There are at the time of writing eleven official languages of the European Union and five of these (English, French, German, Italian, Spanish) have been selected as official languages of OHIM. Further, there may be more than one official language within an individual Member State. Already the translation burden on OHIM is immense and the accompanying problems well documented.[99] Individual nations and regions have their own distinct linguistic, social and cultural practices and ethnic composition. Ethnic minorities can fluctuate, even within relatively short periods of time, with consequent changes in patterns of linguistic distribution and awareness. The same mark may well be registrable in some Member States but, because it is generic, descriptive, misleading or in some other way undesirable, not in others.[1] These difficulties will be intensified by the admission in the next few years of new Member States. Indeed the unitary nature of the Community Trade Mark may be threatened by the need to respect the languages of new Members, resulting in a CTM which has limited effect in parts of the European Union.[2]

The Community Trade Mark will not replace national registration systems, which will operate independently for as long as applicants

---

[97] Provided the use is in accordance with honest practices in industrial or commercial matters, the defendant should be able to claim the protection of s. 11(2)(b), which deals with cases where the use is to indicate kind, quality, quantity or various other characteristics of goods or services. This also touches on the thorny question whether use "in a trade mark sense" is a prerequisite for infringement.
[98] Office for Harmonization in the Internal Market (Trade Marks and Designs).
[99] See e.g. R. Kobia, "Reflections on the Effects of Future Enlargement of the E.U. on Industrial Property: The Case of Trade Marks" [1998] E.I.P.R. 183.
[1] The mark "Cotonelle" was permissible in France and Spain for toilet paper and tissues, but not in Italy: Case C-313/94 *Fratelli Graffione v. Fransa*, [1997] F.S.R. 538. See also "Clinique": Case C-315/92 *Verband Sozialer Wettbewerb v. Clinique Laboratoires* [1994] E.C.R. I-317; and "Baby-Dry": *Proctor & Gamble's Application* [1999] E.T.M.R. 240.
[2] For example, an existing CTM may be descriptive in the language of a new Member State. This possibility and proposals for dealing with the problem were outlined in papers issued by OHIM in November 1998 entitled Priorities for the OHIM in the Face of Enlargement.

wish, or are forced, to seek national protection for their marks. Although Member States must harmonise their trade mark law, they are free to decide on issues such as revocation and invalidity of marks and to what extent the use of a revoked mark may be prohibited.[3] They are also able to apply to trade marks any relevant national laws on consumer protection and unfair competition, provided their application is justifiable and the aim not achievable by alternative, less stringent, means.[4] Nevertheless, free movement of goods within the European Union is the overriding concern and the twin policies of free trade and free competition make it unacceptable that a term used as the name or necessary description of a product or service in the language of one Member State should be registered in another Member State. Hitherto, the willingness of the trade marks offices of Member States to register foreign descriptive terms has varied, though most appear to favour as the decisive criterion the perception of the relevant public in the jurisdiction where protection is sought.[5] As trade mark law is harmonized across the Union, consistency in the treatment of foreign-language words is essential. The existence of a registration in another country will be a persuasive, but not a deciding factor in assessing the suitability of a mark as a Community Trade Mark.[6]

Article 7.1 of the Community Trade Mark Regulation forbids the registration *inter alia* of marks which are non-distinctive or descriptive.[7] By virtue of Article 7.2, a mark unacceptable under Article 7.1 in one Member State is barred from registration as a Community Trade Mark.[8] OHIM examiners therefore have the unenviable task of checking applications for descriptiveness or

---

[3] Case C-313/94, *Fratelli Graffione v. Fransa (Cotonelle)* [1997] F.S.R. 538.
[4] *ibid.*; see also Directive 89/104, Recital 6.
[5] Reports of current practice can be found in AIPPI Annuaire 1996/VI, Réunion du Comité Exécutif, Vienna, 1997: *Rapports de Groupes Q 135: Protection D'expressions en Langue Etrangère Comme Marque*, Zurich: AIPPI, 1996. It has been suggested that since the "Active Line" decision: (Case No.I ZB 7/95, judgment June 19, 1997) it will be more difficult in Germany to register foreign descriptive words: [1998] 12(3) W.I.P.R. 80. See also *Yes Trade Mark* [1998] E.T.M.R. 386. An interesting contrast is provided by *Sarl RWS Ltd v. Getten and Sté Translations* [1999] E.T.M.R. 258, in which the Paris Cour d' Appel decided it was not necessary for the word "translations" to be held free for use in its English sense; its meaning in French (more like "transfer") differed from its meaning in English.
[6] See *e.g. Cosmedent Inc.'s Application* [1998] E.T.M.R. 658; *USA Detergents Inc.'s Application* [1998] E.T.M.R. 562 and *Procter & Gamble's Application* [1999] E.T.M.R. 240.
[7] There is no express prohibition on generic terms, but if a term is truly generic it cannot acquire distinctiveness, so this must be covered by Art 1(a). The OHIM Examination Guidelines, Section 8.3 refer to "wine" as a non-distinctive term barred by Art. 7.1.b. though "wine" is generic and could never on its own acquire secondary meaning in respect of wines.
[8] For example "Optima" (meaning "excellent" or "very good" in Portuguese) was devoid of distinctiveness for patient membrane oxygenators, OHIM Board of Appeal Decision R94/1998-2, February 11, 1999; cf "Selecta" R104/1998-3, February 11, 1999 and "Kali" R147/1998-2, March 4, 1999. An applicant putting forward evidence of acquired distinctiveness in respect of a word which is descriptive in one of the Community languages is required only to provide evidence relating to the territory where the language in question is spoken or understood: OHIM Examination Division, Practice Note, Evidence of Use under Art. 7(3) CTMR. Acquired Distinctiveness, March 1999.

"genericness" against all languages of the European Union.[9] The OHIM Examination Guidelines require examiners to consult standard dictionaries in all eleven official languages as well as specialist technical reference material. Unfortunately colloquialisms, neologisms, dialectal variants and obscene words will not necessarily be included in standard dictionaries and it is doubtful that OHIM examiners would be expected to extend their search into what they might regard as linguistic by-ways. It is, however, sometimes very difficult to draw a line between the unacceptably descriptive and the acceptably suggestive mark and an examiner needs to be alert to linguistic nuances and subtleties which cannot be detected simply from a dictionary. Further, like the cultural boundaries they mark, languages are naturally unstable and, despite attempts by some national governments to maintain linguistic purity by the exclusion of foreign terms, remain exposed to change and consequent indistinctness. Increasing and widespread use of the Internet is likely to favour the English language at the expense of others.[10] The experience gained by OHIM examiners should nevertheless lead to the creation of a substantial centralised database of terms and their meanings in all the languages of the Union; it is to be hoped that this will serve as a major reference tool and facilitate a co-ordinated approach to the treatment of foreign-language words.

Confusing similarity, including likelihood of association, will be tested chiefly at opposition stage and constant vigilance on the part of trade mark proprietors will be necessary to safeguard valuable rights. Following *Sabel v. Puma*, likelihood of confusion will be assessed by a global appreciation of the visual, aural or conceptual similarity of the marks.[11] According to the OHIM Examination Guidelines, word marks and figurative marks may have a similar impact on members of the public and may therefore be confusingly similar.[12] The fact that potentially conflicting marks in different languages convey the same meaning will not in itself be decisive; thus cases involving marks such as "Star", "Estrela", "Stebla" and "Etoile" must be considered on a case-by-case basis.[13] The Guidelines require reference to the "relevant public" and the "ordinary user" of the goods or services; whether, in the case of foreign-language marks, this should be the purchasing public for the goods or services in question, or those segments of the population familiar with the

---

[9] *USA Detergents Inc.'s Application (XTRA)* [1998] E.T.M.R. 562 is a good illustration of the linguistic detective work undertaken by the OHIM examiners.
[10] See for example the remarks made by the Bundesgerichtshof in *Partner With the Best* [1998] E.T.M.R. 679.
[11] Clearly enunciated, for example, in *Warsteiner Brauerie Haus Application* [1999] E.T.M.R. 225.
[12] Guidelines, section 7. These cite the example of "Red Star". The old English "Red Star" case, (1894) 11 R.P.C. 142, is pertinent and shows that problems remain constant, though times change.
[13] ECTA, *Community Trade Mark: Are You Ready?* Proceedings of the Conference in Cannes, 1995, (ECTA; 12), p. 122.

languages(s) concerned, is debatable.[14] Indications are, however, that the nature of the goods or services will be a determining factor, in particular whether they are intended for a specialist market or the public in general.[15] Apart from Greek, the official languages of current Member States are in Roman script. Comparisons between marks, already problematic across a range of same-script languages, will be made more difficult when the marks concerned contain non-Roman scripts.[16]

Conclusion

Foreign-language marks highlight conflicting areas of trade mark policy. On the one hand, arising from principles of international comity, is the policy that a term which denotes goods or services in the language of one country should not be registered as a trade mark in another country where a different language predominates.[17] Self-interest is also at stake here: were one country's generic or descriptive terms routinely appropriated and monopolised in another, the appropriators might find themselves on the receiving end of similar treatment. Free movement of goods under the product names and descriptions used in their country of origin would be jeopardised. On the other hand are the distinct but related issues of national independence and the capacity of a mark, within a defined territorial market, adequately to distinguish the goods of an individual undertaking, even if it is generic or descriptive elsewhere in the world. An excessively restrictive policy on foreign-language words places a heavy burden on trade mark registries and may also lead to the diminution of the pool of word-marks available to potential traders.

The United Kingdom Registry and Courts have tried to find a balance between these potentially conflicting principles, whilst

---

[14] In *Chevy*, the Advocate-General specifically addressed the issue of reputation in a multi-lingual territory (the Benelux), opining that "it is sufficient that a mark has a reputation in a substantial part of the Benelux territory, which may be part only of one of the Benelux countries. That is the sole method of recognising the cultural and linguistic differences which may exist within a Member State . . .": Case C-375/97 *General Motors Corporation v. Yplon SA*, opinion of A-G Jacobs, November 26, 1998.
[15] See OHIM Examination Division Practice Note, March 1999, Evidence of Use under Art. 7(3) CTMR, which discusses *inter alia* the public to which evidence of acquired distinctiveness must relate. In *Windsurfing Chiemsee Produktions v. Huber* [1999] E.T.M.R. 585 (a case involving geographic names) the relevant public was said by the ECJ to be persons in the trade and average consumers of the category of goods in the territory in respect of which registration is applied for.
[16] The difficulties of comparing marks in different characters is well known to industrial property offices in countries such as China, Japan and Korea, where different standards from those operating in Western countries may be applied. For good discussions of the pitfalls and problems see D.B. Kay, "Translating Chinese Character Marks" [1988] 1 I.P. Asia 3; and J. Kakinuki. "Topics in Japanese Trade Mark Law" [1994] E.I.P.R. 103.
[17] Arguably such a practice amounts to restraint of trade under Art. 8.2 of the TRIPS Agreement: AIPPI Resolution Q 135, April 1997. NAFTA, Art. 1708. 13 specifically prohibits registration of English, French or Spanish terms which generically designate goods or services.

maintaining a "clean" register which affords certainty to third parties. Since the registration system was introduced, policies have developed from an initial reluctance to accept word marks in characters other than Roman, to a flexible set of guidelines which attempt to consider changing linguistic and social circumstances, taking into account the degree of comprehension of the language within the United Kingdom, the types of goods or services in respect of which the mark is to be used, the relevant market (ethnic or general) and whether or not the typical consumer would be likely to stop and translate the foreign word into its English equivalent. In the last resort, distinctiveness in fact may overcome prima facie objections.

It is often said that increased communications and the spread of the Internet, as well as business and tourist travel, are leading to the development of a worldwide village, in which linguistic and cultural differences become of less obvious significance. The "ordinary Englishman" is giving way to the "global consumer". In a twenty-first century dominated by the politics of international trade and the dispute-resolution procedures of the World Trade Organisation, trade mark law will inevitably confront a wider, more diverse and increasingly sophisticated audience. In developing a view of the foreign-language mark to match the complexity of cultural and linguistic interrelationships this audience implies, trade mark practitioners will find one of their most substantial—and appropriately millennial—challenges.

6. Developments in Registrability: The Definition of a Trade Mark and its Relationship with the Requirement for Distinctiveness

Ruth Annand

Developments in Registrability: the Definition of a Trade Mark and its Relationship with the Requirement for Distinctiveness.[*]

The Problem

Section 1(1) of the Trade Marks Act 1994 defines a "trade mark" for the purposes of the Act as "any sign . . . which is capable of distinguishing the goods or services of one undertaking from those of other undertakings". Section 3(1)(b) of the 1994 Act prohibits the registration of trade marks which are devoid of any distinctive character. How are the two provisions reconciled?

In *Philips Electronics NV v. Remington Consumer Products*,[1] Jacob J. read section 1(1) into section 3(1)(b). The result was the "confusing"[2] proposition that a trade mark is invalid if it is: "A sign which is capable of distinguishing which is devoid of any distinctive character".[3] It is tempting to accuse Jacob J. of sophistry. However the judge's proposition exemplifies the historical tendency of the United Kingdom courts to define registered trade marks by reference to the conditions governing their registrability. Two factors in particular command that tendency. The first is the courts' perception that the grant of registration to a specific trade mark opens the floodgates to registration of all trade marks of that class. Undesirable monopolies must be avoided:

> Wealthy traders are habitually eager to enclose part of the great common of the English language and to exclude the general public of the present day and of the future from access to the inclosure.[4]

---

[*] The author thanks Marie Davies, University of Bristol, Peter Lawrence, U.K. Director of Trade Marks and Lochners, Solicitors, for their assistance in researching this essay. The views expressed are the writer's own.
[1] [1998] R.P.C. 283.
[2] Jacob J.'s description, *ibid.* at 299.
[3] *ibid.* at 299.
[4] Cozens Hardy M.R. in *Re Joseph Crosfield & Sons Limited* [1910] 1 Ch. 130, CA at 141, cited most recently by Jacob J. in *British Sugar plc v. James Robertson & Sons Ltd* [1996] R.P.C. 281 at 284. The Master of the Rolls was speaking in the context of three applications under the Trade Marks Act 1905 to register marks consisting of a laudatory epithet, a geographical name and a descriptive word respectively. However echoes of his words are equally detected in applications to register trade marks consisting of other signs. For example, in *Coca-Cola Trade Marks* [1986] R.P.C. 421, HL at 457, Lord Templeman said of the Coca-Cola Co.'s application under the Trade Marks Act 1938 to register the distinctive shape of their bottle: "This raises the spectre of a total and perpetual monopoly in containers and articles achieved by means of the Act of 1938". Again, in *Philips Electronics NV v. Remington Consumer Products*, above, note 1,

The second factor is the availability of the action for passing off[5] which provides alternative relief against misuse of a mark but only in so far as is necessary to prevent public deception in any particular case.[6]

Part I of this essay charts the development of the relationship between the definition of a trade mark and the requirement for distinctiveness from 1875 when registration started until immediately prior to the introduction of the 1994 Act. Sections 1(1) and 3(1)(b) of the 1994 Act derive from Articles 2 and 3(1)(b) of the First Council Directive to approximate the laws of the Member States relating to trade marks.[7] Part II seeks to ascertain the intended meaning of these criteria in the Directive. Part III considers United Kingdom decided cases on sections 1(1) and 3(1)(b) of the 1994 Act. It compares the relevant Trade Marks Registry practice with that of the Office for Harmonisation in the Internal Market (Trade Marks and Designs) under the Community Trade Mark Regulation.[8] Ultimately the Court of Justice of the European Communities must decide the true relationship between "capable of distinguishing" and "devoid of any distinctive character". Pending such guidance, Part IV reflects upon where United Kingdom trade marks law presently stands on the issue.

Part I: The trade marks registration Acts 1875 to 1938

Trade Marks Registration Act 1875

The Trade Marks Register was first set up in 1875.[9] Among the advantages it offered to registrants was that registration was prima

---

concerning the validity of an "existing" registration under the Trade Marks Act 1994 for the two dimensional representation of Philip's three-headed shaver face, Jacob J. at 299 saw the issue as: "the extent to which trade mark law, conferring a perpetual monopoly, can interfere with the freedom within the European Union of manufacturers to make an artefact of a desirable and good engineering design".

[5] *Re Joseph Crosfield & Sons Limited*, ibid. at 150–1, Farwell L.J.; *Dee Corporation plc and Others' Trade Mark Applications* [1990] R.P.C. 159, CA at 182, Slade L.J.; *Interlego AG's Trade Mark Applications* [1988] R.P.C. 69 at 106–7, Neuberger J.

[6] "[N]o man is entitled to represent his goods as being the goods of another man; and no man is permitted to use any mark, sign or symbol, device or other means, whereby, without making a direct false representation himself to a purchaser who purchases from him, he enables such a purchaser to tell a lie or to make a false representation to somebody else who is the ultimate customer." James L.J. in *Singer Manufacturing Co. v. Loog* (1880) 18 Ch.D. 395, CA at 412. The action for passing off has remained unaffected by successive Trade Marks Acts.

[7] Council Directive 89/104 [1989] O.J. L 40/1.

[8] Council Regulation 40/94 on the Community Trade Mark [1994] O.J. L 11/1. Arts 4 and 7(1)(b) of the CTMR are the equivalent to sections 1(1) and 3(1)(b) of the 1994 Act and Arts 2 and 3(1)(b) of the Directive.

[9] Trade Marks Registration Act 1875, s.1, in response to the demands of traders who were unable to obtain protection of their marks abroad unless they were registered in the country of origin. Earlier attempts had been made to establish a system of registration. However the Trade Marks Bill 1862 was vigorously opposed by W.M. Hindmarch Q.C. the leading trade mark lawyer of the day, and by the Attorney-General. Instead, a second Bill (drafted by Hindmarch) which dealt mainly with the criminal law was amended and became the Merchandise Marks Act 1862. *Report from the Select Committee on the Trade Marks Bill and Merchandise Marks Bill*, May 6, 1862, No. 212.

facie evidence of the proprietor's right to the exclusive use of the trade mark and became conclusive evidence of such right after five years.[10] Registration was designed to replace the action for infringement that had originated in the Court of Chancery and was based on a right of property in the trade mark.[11] Success in an infringement action depended on use.[12] It was established in *Hudson's Trade Marks*[13] that "new" trade marks[14] could be registered under the 1875 Act irrespective of use.

A major objective of the 1875 Act was to protect the public by making the Register a complete record of marks adopted. Vested rights could not be interfered with but new trade marks, that is, marks not in use before the commencement of the 1875 Act,[15] had to conform to a narrowly drawn list.[16] To this end "trade mark" was not defined as such[17] but by reference to one or more essential particulars that it must contain namely:[18]

> A name of an individual or firm printed, impressed, or woven in some particular and distinctive manner; or
> A written signature or copy of a written signature of an individual or firm; or
> A distinctive device, mark, heading, label, or ticket; . . .

---

[10] Subject to the goodwill in the business associated with the trade mark being retained; Trade Marks Registration Act 1875, s. 3.
[11] Equity regarded this as a logical development from the ruling in *Millington v. Fox* (1838) 3 My. & Cr. 338 that an injunction would lie to restrain non-fraudulent use of the plaintiff's marks; *Edelsten v. Edelsten* (1863) 1 De G.J. & S. 185; *Hall v. Barrows* (1863) 4 De G.J. & S. 150, *Leather Cloth Co. v. American Leather Cloth Co.* [1865] 11 H.L.C. 523, HL.
[12] "The cases to which I have referred (and there are others to the like effect) show that it was firmly established at the time when the Act of 1875 was passed that a trader acquired a right of property in a distinctive mark merely by using it upon or in connection with his goods irrespective of the length of such user and of the extent of his trade and that such right of property would be protected by an injunction restraining any other person from using the mark": Lawrence L.J. in *Nicholson & Sons Ld.'s Application* (1931) 48 R.P.C. 227, CA at 253. See also the response of W.M. Hindmarch Q.C. to question no. 2761 *Report from the Select Committee on the Trade Marks Bill and Merchandise Marks Bill*, above, note 9.
[13] (1886) 3 R.P.C. 155, CA.
[14] That is, a trade mark which complied with the first part of s. 10, Trade Marks Registration Act 1875, see below. S. 2, Trade Marks Registration Act 1875 provided that "registration of a trade-mark shall be deemed to be equivalent to public use of such mark."
[15] August 13, 1875.
[16] "In my opinion we must take it that, although the intention of the Act was to benefit traders—persons whose goods are known by a particular mark—by giving them, if they registered under the Act, this privilege, that they do not require to enter into evidence at all after five years, and during the five years they have *prima facie* evidence of their rights, the Act was also intended to protect the public, by having a register of marks so that they might know what it was that was protected by the trade marks adopted, and also by cutting down the numerous forms of words and other things, by the use of which traders tried to secure themselves exclusive rights". Cotton L.J. in *Van Duzer's Trade Mark and Leaf's Trade Mark* (1887) 4 R.P.C. 31, CA at 34.
[17] This lack of definition caused initial uncertainty over whether new marks had to be used before they could be registered under the 1875 Act. To lawyers of the day "trade mark" connoted a sign which was being used to denote a trader's goods. See *Hudson's Trade Marks*, above, note 13.
[18] s. 10, first part, Trade-Marks Registration Act 1875.

The concession for "old" marks not falling within the above was that:[19]

> Any special and distinctive word or words or combination of figures or letters used as a trade-mark before the passing of this Act may be registered as such under this Act.

"Distinctive" was not defined but it was accepted that old marks though prima facie non-distinctive could be registered on proof of having acquired a reputation in the market as denoting goods of the proprietor's manufacture or merchandise.[20]

The incentive for registering under the 1875 Act was that section 1 prohibited proceedings to prevent the infringement of any trade mark that could be but had not been registered by July 1, 1876.[21] Although 27,844 marks were entered on the register,[22] it became apparent that the list of registrable trade marks was unreasonably restrictive. No provision was made for the registration of old marks comprising a single letter.[23] More importantly, a mark which consisted solely of a word or words could not registered unless it had been used before the commencement of the 1875 Act. In *Ex parte Stephens*[24] the applicant was refused registration for the mark AEILYTON. Counsel failed to persuade Jessel M.R that since Longfellow in his poem described "Excelsior" as a device and "Excelsior" had long been used as trade mark for soap, AEILYTON qualified for registration not as a word but as a distinctive device.

1883 to 1905

The Patents, Designs and Trade Marks Act 1883 abandoned any semblance of a definition of "trade mark". Instead the essential particulars which a registrable trade mark had to consist of or contain were set out under the heading: "Conditions of registration of trade mark".[25] The most material alteration was that the list now included "a fancy word or fancy words not in common use".[26] The

---

[19] s. 10, second part, Trade Marks Registration Act 1875.
[20] *Re Hopkinson's Trade Mark* [1892] 2 Ch. 116; *Orr Ewing v. Registrar of Trade-Marks* (1879) 4 App.Cas. 479, HL at 500, Lord Blackburn; *Nicholson & Sons Ld.'s Application*, above, note 12 at 254, Lawrence L.J.
[21] The deadline was extended by subsequent Acts to July 1, 1878. The Trade Marks Registration Amendment Act 1876 extended s. 1 to the recovery of damages for infringement but made clear that the ban did not apply to an old mark which had been refused registration under the 1875 Act. The ban was continued by subsequent Acts in its 1876 form until the institution of proceedings for infringement of *any* unregistered trade mark was rendered impossible by s. 2 of the Trade Marks Act 1938.
[22] *Kerly's Law of Trade Marks and Trade Names* (6th ed, 1927), F. Underhay, p. 7.
[23] *Re Mitchell's Trade-Mark* (1877) 7 Ch.D. 36.
[24] (1876) 3 Ch.D. 659.
[25] Patents, Designs and Trade-Marks Act 1883, s. 64(1).
[26] *ibid*. s.64(1)(c): "A distinctive device, mark, brand, heading, label, ticket or fancy word or words not in common use". The term "brand" was apparently added to remove uncertainty under the 1875 Act as to whether old cigar marks burnt in the ends of cigar boxes were

new essential particular was intended to cure the defect exposed by the AEILYTON case.[27] Additional provision continued to be made for the registration of marks in use before August 13, 1875 and an amendment was introduced to cover the registration of old marks comprising a single letter or figure.[28]

In determining the scope of the new essential particular, "the Courts were almost driven to despair".[29] Eventually the Court of Appeal decided in *Van Duzer's and Leaf's Trade Mark*[30] that a fancy word or fancy words must be "obviously meaningless" in relation to the goods applied for. It was irrelevant that the word was distinctive in fact, that it had acquired a secondary meaning in the market for goods of the applicant; the single issue was: is it a fancy word— fancifulness being an inherent quality? The case concerned two applications to register under the 1883 Act the marks MELROSE and ELECTRIC for hair preparations and velvet and velveteen respectively. Neither mark was in use before August 13, 1875 but both marks were recognised by the trade as denoting the respective goods of the applicants. MELROSE was refused because of its geographical connotation. Evidence showing that customers were unlikely to believe that hair preparations were made in Melrose had to be ignored. ELECTRIC suggested a description of velvet and velveteen.

Although none of the judges in *Van Duzer and Leaf* was prepared to hold that no geographical name or descriptive word could ever achieve registration, their stringent approach meant that few words in practice did. Amongst the successful was BOVRIL for substances used as food or as ingredients in food,[31] MAZAWATTEE for tea[32] and OOMOO for wine.[33] The unsuccessful included APOLLINARIS for mineral water,[34] COMPACTUM for umbrellas,[35] TOWER for tea[36] and CYCLOSTYLE for stationery and duplicating apparatus.[37]

On February 24, 1887 a Committee was appointed under the chairmanship of Lord Herschell to conduct an inquiry into the

---

registrable: *Report of the Committee appointed by the Board of Trade to inquire into the Duties, Organisation and Arrangements of the Patent Office under the Patents, Designs and Trade Marks Act 1883, so far at it relates to Trade Marks and Designs*, 1888, C-5350, page XI and reply to question no. 2993 by the Comptroller, H.R. Lack. In *Alexander Pirie & Sons v. Goodall* [1892] 1 Ch. 35, CA, it was held that a watermark on paper did not constitute a brand.
[27] *Van Duzer's Trade Mark and Leaf's Trade Mark*, above, note 16 at 38, Lindley L.J.
[28] s. 64(3).
[29] *In the Matter of an Application of the Eastman Photographic Materials Company, Ld., for a Trade Mark* (1898) 15 R.P.C. 476, HL at 486, Lord Macnaghten.
[30] Above, note 16.
[31] *Re Trade-Mark "Bovril"* [1896] 2 Ch. 600, CA.
[32] *Re Densham's Trade-Mark* [1895] 2 Ch. 176, CA.
[33] *In the Matter of Burgoyne's Trade Mark* (1889) 6 R.P.C. 227.
[34] *Re Apollinaris Company's Trade-Marks* [1891] 2 Ch. 202, CA. APOLLINARIS was subsequently accepted for registration under s.9(5) of the Trade Marks Act 1905, see below, on proof of acquired distinctiveness through use, *Re "APOLLINARIS" Trade Mark* [1907] 2 Ch. 179.
[35] *In the Matter of Davis' Trade Marks* (1897) 14 R.P.C. 903.
[36] *The Great Tower Street Co. v. Smith* (1889) 6 R.P.C. 165.
[37] *Re Registered Trade Mark of David Gestetner* [1907] 2 Ch. 478.

operation of the 1883 Act so far as it related to trade marks and designs. In its report,[38] the Herschell Committee acknowledged that the most difficult question of law that had arisen under the Act was what should be regarded as a fancy word. While the Committee accepted that words are a most popular form of trade mark, it expressed the view that words descriptive of the character, quality or provenance of products ought to remain in the public domain:[39]

> It will be convenient to consider first *what words ought to be allowed as trade marks*.[40] There can be no objection to permitting the registration of an invented word not found in the vocabulary of our own or any other country. It seems to us further that existing words may with advantage be permitted as trade marks subject to limitations which at once suggest themselves. It is manifest that no one ought to be granted the exclusive use of a word descriptive of the quality or character of any goods. Such words of description are the property of all mankind, and it would not be right to allow any individual to monopolise them and exclude others from their use. Again geographical words, which can be regarded as descriptive of the place of manufacture or sale of the goods, are open to obvious objections. One manufacturer or merchant cannot properly be allowed to prevent all his competitors from attaching to their goods the name of the place of their manufacture or sale.[41]

Although the Committee was reporting on the "Conditions for registration of trade mark", its comments are more mindful of definition.

Following the recommendations of the Herschell Committee, the "Conditions of registration of trade mark" were amended by the Patents, Designs and Trade Marks Act 1888.[42] The reference to "fancy word or fancy words not in common use" was deleted and two new essential particulars were inserted in its place: "an invented word or

---

[38] *Report of the Committee appointed by the Board of Trade to inquire into the Duties, Organisation and Arrangements of the Patent Office under the Patents, Designs and Trade Marks Act 1883, so far as it relates to Trade Marks and Designs* above, note 26.
[39] The Herschell Committee applied their view on descriptive words to descriptive devices: "Registration, it appears, is sometimes sought of devices which are descriptive of the goods to which they are to be applied, *e.g.* a representation of a hinge to be applied to doors. We think these are not legitimate marks." *ibid.* page XII. See also *Re James's Trade Mark* (1886) 33 Ch.D. 392, CA, where Lindley L.J. considered (obiter) at p. 396 that a picture of a fish was not registrable for that particular type of fish. In *James* a two dimensional representation of dome shaped lead was held to have been validly registered for black lead. The Court of Appeal was persuaded by the fact that it could be used for lead of any shape. In *Louise & Co. Ld. v. Gainsborough* (1903) 20 R.P.C. 61, a mark consisting of a reproduction of Gainsborough's picture the "Duchess of Devonshire" was removed from the register because it had been in common use before the registration date.
[40] Author's own emphasis.
[41] Above, note 26 at page XI.
[42] s. 10, Patents, Designs and Trade Marks Act 1888.

invented words"[43] and "a word or words having no reference to the character or quality of the goods, and not being a geographical name".[44]

At first the courts reacted as if no change had occurred. In *Farbenfabriken's Application*,[45] the mark SOMATOSE was applied for in respect of a preparation made out of meat. The Court of Appeal held that the new provisions must be construed together so that an invented word could have no reference to the character or quality of the goods. SOMATOSE was descriptive of the character of the meat product because it was a combination of the Greek word "soma" meaning "body" and "tose" which was a common suffix.

The breakthrough came with the House of Lords decision in the *SOLIO* case.[46] Objection had been taken to the registration of SOLIO for photographic paper on the ground that "sun" or its equivalent "sol" was descriptive of the goods. Their Lordships ordered the Registrar to proceed with the application. SOLIO was an invented word and it made no difference that it could be traced to a foreign source or that it contained "a covert and skilful allusion to the character or quality of the goods".[47] The two particulars added by the 1888 Act were separate and distinct. In the wake of *SOLIO*, words demonstrating a minimum of invention were accepted for registration.[48] However the House of Lords had set certain limits. Invention was not achieved through the use of misspellings,[49] phonetic[50] or foreign [51] equivalents or combinations of ordinary words.[52]

The *SOLIO* case also had an effect on the interpretation of the particular "a word or words having no reference to the character or quality of the goods, and not being a geographical name". Lords Halsbury, Herschell and Macnaghten held that SOLIO had no reference to the character or quality of photographic paper, in effect overturning the Court of Appeal decision in *SOMATOSE*. In *Magnolia Metal Company's Trade-Marks*[53] the Court of Appeal made clear that a word should not be denied registration simply because some place in the world has been called by it. The exclusion of geographical names must be consistent with the popular meaning of terms unless there existed some local connection between the name and the goods in

---

[43] s. 64(1)(d), Patents, Designs and Trade Marks Acts 1883 to 1888.
[44] s. 64(1)(e), Patents, Designs and Trade Marks Acts 1883 to 1888.
[45] [1894] 1 Ch. 645, CA.
[46] *In the Matter of an Application of the Eastman Photographic Materials Co. Ld., for a Trade Mark*, above, note 29.
[47] Lord Macnaghten, *ibid.* at p. 486.
[48] The following examples are given in *Words as Trade Marks* (1900) 43 Sol. J. 548: PERFUMETTE for perfumes, ENAMELINE for blacking, GLAZO for creams and polishes for leather, FIREPROOFINE for fireproofing liquid.
[49] ORLWOOLA Trade Mark (1909) 26 R.P.C. 683, CA at 850 ("all wool").
[50] EANCO Trade Mark (1920) 37 R.P.C. 134 ("E and Co.").
[51] DIABOLO Trade Mark (1908) 25 R.P.C. 565.
[52] Re UNEEDA Trade-Mark [1901] 1 Ch. 550 ("You need a").
[53] [1897] 2 Ch. 371, CA.

question:[54] "'Monkey' is not proved to be a geographical name by showing merely that a small and by no means generally known island has been called by that name".[55] The objection to the registration of MAGNOLIA for metals on the ground that there were towns in America named Magnolia was dismissed.[56]

Despite the liberal interpretation given to the conditions of registration subsequent to *SOLIO*, the Acts of 1883 to 1888 proved insufficient to meet the needs of traders who continued to adopt marks outside the list of essential particulars. Even if such marks achieved total recognition in the market, they were unable to attain registration. As a consequence of the accommodation made for marks in use before August 13, 1875, new marks had to be distinctive irrespective of use, that is, inherently distinctive.[57] The essential particulars were excluding classes of de facto trade marks from registration not by condition but by definition.[58] In *Powell's Trade-Mark*[59] an application was made to expunge YORKSHIRE RELISH for sauces from the Register. The registration could not stand as a new mark even though the court accepted that no other trader could legally use the words in connection with sauces. Nor was the registration valid as an old mark. Use of "Yorkshire relish" before August 13, 1875 had not been use of the trade mark. Four years later, the monopoly in YORKSHIRE RELISH was established through an action for passing off.[60]

Trade Marks Act 1905

The Trade Marks Act 1905 adopted an entirely different strategy. Aimed at facilitating the registration of de facto marks, it started with the general and proceeded to the particular, not vice versa as previous Acts had done.[61]

"Mark" was defined widely to include "a device, brand, heading, label, ticket, name, signature, word, letter, numeral, or any combination thereof".[62] The intention was that no mark should be

---

[54] The example was given of APOLLINARIS for water from the Apollinaris spring, *ibid.* at 393.
[55] *ibid.* at 393, Rigby, L.J.
[56] However the registration of MAGNOLIA was declared invalid because at the time of application it had become known as the name of a variety of metal.
[57] See *Van Duzer's Trade Mark and Leaf's Trade Mark*, above, note 16 at 35, Cotton L.J. and *Louise & Co. Ld. v. Gainsborough*, above, note 39 at 67, Farwell J.
[58] D. M. Kerly and F. G. Underhay, *The Trade Marks Act 1905*, (1906), at p. 2. *Report and Special Report from the Select Committee on the Trade Marks Bill*, July 7 1905, reply of J. Fletcher Moulton K.C. (a draftsman of the Bill) to question no. 54: "I think one cause of the difficulties that have arisen is that our legislation has proceeded on the principle that a Trade Mark must come under one or other of a certain number of classes or else not be registrable, and they have sought, therefore, to limit those classes so that all Trade Marks in that class should be of such a character as to be registrable."
[59] [1893] 2 Ch. 388, CA.
[60] *Powell v. The Birmingham Vinegar Brewery Company, Ld.* (1897) 14 R.P.C. 720, HL.
[61] See the evidence of J. Fletcher Moulton KC, above, note 58.
[62] Trade Marks Act 1905, s. 3.

excluded from registration purely because of its form.[63] Next, "trade mark" was stated to mean "a mark used or proposed to be used upon or in connection with goods for the purpose of indicating that they are the goods of the proprietor of such trade mark by virtue of manufacture, selection, certification, dealing with, or offering for sale".[64] The intentions here were first to confirm the rule in *Hudson's* case[65] that an unused mark could be the subject of an application for registration and second to make clear that proprietorship of a trade mark was not limited to manufacturers of goods.[66] Finally "registrable trade mark" was described as one capable of registration under the Act[67] recognising that not all trade marks would individually qualify for registration.

In the event, regrettably, registrable trade marks were assessed by reference to a familiar list of essential particulars:[68]

(1) The name of a company, individual, or firm represented in a special or particular manner;
(2) The signature of the applicant for registration or some predecessor in his business;
(3) An invented word or invented words;
(4) A word or words having no direct reference to the character or quality of the goods, and not being according to its ordinary signification a geographical name or surname;
(5) Any other distinctive mark, but a name, signature, or word or words other than such as fall within the descriptions in the above paragraphs . . . shall not, except by order of the Board of Trade or the Court, be deemed a distinctive mark.

The fourth particular had been amended to incorporate the rulings in *SOLIO* and *MAGNOLIA* respectively. But it was the fifth particular that encapsulated the break with the previous law. Designed to ensure that "everything that ought to be on the Register can get on and the Courts will not be hampered by fears as to the effect of their decisions on other cases"[69] distinctiveness was to be judged in fact and not in law.

The Act stated that "distinctive" meant "adapted to distinguish the goods of the proprietor of the trade mark from those of other persons".[70] Further:

In determining whether a mark is so adapted, the tribunal may,

---

[63] Above, note 58, responses by J. Fletcher Moulton K.C. to question nos. 33 and 34.
[64] Trade Marks Act 1905, s. 3.
[65] Above, note 13.
[66] Above, note 58, responses by J. Fletcher Moulton K.C. to question nos. 36 to 40.
[67] Trade Marks Act 1905, s. 3.
[68] Trade Marks Act 1905, s. 9.
[69] Above, note 58, response by J. Fletcher Moulton K.C. to question no. 80. Fletcher Moulton recalled arguing the *SOLIO* case: " . . . a long list of words was produced, as to which it was said: 'If you allow Solio you must allow this, that and the other.'"
[70] Trade Marks Act 1905, s. 9.

in the case of a trade mark in actual use, take into consideration the extent to which such user has rendered such trade mark in fact distinctive for the goods . . .[71]

That direction covered not only particular (5) but also the continued provision for marks in use before August 13, 1875.[72] The direction signified that use after 1875 could have the same effect as use before 1875. Any mark that operated in the market to denote the goods of its proprietor was registrable under the 1905 Act, regardless of inherent distinguishing quality.

Contemporary writers doubted whether the courts would allow the 1905 Act to fulfil its purpose.[73] Their scepticism proved true. In *Joseph Crosfield's Application*[74] the Court of Appeal denied registration to PERFECTION for soap. The evidence established that PERFECTION denoted the applicant's soap to a large number of persons.[75] Moreover it was accepted that there is no "natural and innate antagonism between distinctive and descriptive as applied to words".[76] Nevertheless the court held that laudatory epithets must be kept free for other traders to use.[77] Such terms could not be "adapted" to distinguish the goods of one trader, however distinctive in fact an individual mark might be. Subsequently the rationale of the *PERFECTION* case was extended to two letter marks[78] and to the names of new articles.[79]

Trade Marks Act 1919

In 1919 a further attempt was made to enable the registration of de facto marks by dividing the Register into two parts, A and B.[80]

---

[71] *ibid.*
[72] *ibid*, proviso.
[73] L. Boyd Sebastian, *The Law of Trade Mark Registration under the Trade Marks Act, 1905*, (1906), at page iv; D.M. Kerly and F. G. Underhay, *The Trade Marks Act 1905*, (1906), at page 5.
[74] Above, note 4.
[75] It was acknowledged that a passing off action might lie, *ibid.* Cozens Hardy M.R. at p. 142.
[76] *ibid.*, Fletcher Moulton L.J. at pp. 145–6. Thus, for example CALIFORNIA SYRUP OF FIGS was admitted to registration on proof of factual distinctiveness, *Re California Fig Syrup Company* [1910] 1 Ch. 130, CA. Similarly NATIONAL was accepted for cash registers, *In the Matter of Applications by the National Cash Register Company for the Registration of a Trade Mark* (1917) 34 R.P.C. 273. Contrast *In the Matter of an Application by National Galvanizers Ld to Register a Trade Mark* (1920) 37 R.P.C. 202 where evidence of use was insufficient to support an application for NATIONAL in respect of metal hollow ware goods.
[77] Fletcher Moulton L.J. drew guidance from s. 44 of the 1905 Act providing a defence to infringement for bona fide descriptions of goods, *ibid*, at 148.
[78] *Registrar of Trade Marks v. W. & G. Du Cros, Ltd.* [1913] A.C. 624, HL. W & G unregistrable for motor vehicles despite strong evidence of distinctiveness in fact in the London area: ". . . the tribunal is not bound to allow registration even if the mark be in fact distinctive. A common law mark is still not necessarily registrable", Lord Parker of Waddington at 637.
[79] *Re Gramophone Company's Application* [1910] 2 Ch. 423; GRAMOPHONE was distinctive among the trade but the only word by which the article was known.
[80] Trade Marks Act 1919, s. 1. *In the Matter of an Application by Egg Products Ld. for a Trade Mark* (1922) 39 R.P.C. 155. A lesser degree of protection was afforded to Part B marks under s. 4 of the 1919 Act. Registration in Part B could never be conclusive evidence of the right to exclusive use of the mark and it was a defence to infringement for the defendant to show that

Registrability in Part A continued to be governed by the essential particulars in the 1905 Act, [81] that is, by the standard of adaptability to distinguish. However marks claimed under particular (5) were no longer to be referred to the Board of Trade or the court but could be accepted by the Registrar upon evidence of their distinctiveness.[82] Registrability in Part B appeared to depend solely on a requirement for two years prior bona fide use.[83] Provided that requirement was met, registration had to be granted unless the Registrar was not satisfied that the mark was capable of distinguishing[84] or the mark offended against other provisions of the 1905 Act.[85] The application of the essential particulars in the 1905 Act was expressly excluded for Part B marks [86] emphasising that while discretion might exist to refuse registration of de facto marks in Part A,[87] no such discretion existed in relation to Part B.

Cases prior to the 1905 Act had used the phrase "capable of distinguishing" to refer to a mark's inherent distinctiveness.[88] As a result, the courts had some difficulty in differentiating between "adapted to distinguish" for registration in Part A and "capable of distinguishing" for registration in Part B. In *Davis's Trade Mark*,[89] Lord Hanworth M.R. thought the latter referred to a mark's ability to become distinctive in the future through appropriate use.[90] Sargant L.J. explained the phrase negatively:

> . . . for registration in Part B of a mark in actual use for two years it is not necessary for the applicant to prove that the mark has actually become distinctive. It is sufficient for him to satisfy the Registrar that it is not incapable of becoming distinctive.[91]

On either view, Davis's mark USTIKON was registrable in Part B in respect of rubber soles for boots and shoes. But the Court of Appeal as it had done earlier in *PERFECTION* added that certain classes of marks such as laudatory epithets and descriptions were incapable of becoming distinctive and therefore of registration even in Part B.[92]

---

its use was not calculated to deceive or to cause confusion.
[81] "The principal Act", *ibid*.
[82] Trade Marks Act 1919, s. 7.
[83] Trade Marks Act 1919, s. 2.
[84] As Lord Hanworth M.R. pointed out in *In the Matter of Davis's Trade Mark* (1927) 44 R.P.C. 412, CA at p. 422: ". . . if it is established that they have been used for two years for the purpose of indicating that they are the goods of the proprietor, it would almost seem to follow that such a mark is capable of distinguishing the goods of the applicant".
[85] ss. 11 and 19 of the 1905 Act, preventing the registration of deceptive and conflicting marks.
[86] Trade Marks Act 1919, s. 3.
[87] See *PERFECTION*, above, note 4, Cozens-Hardy M.R. at 141 and Farwell L.J. at 152, and W. & G. above, note 78.
[88] For example, *Van Duzer's Trade Mark and Leaf's Trade Mark*, above, note 16, Cotton L.J. at 35.
[89] Above, note 84.
[90] *ibid.* at 423, see also Lawrence L.J. at 427.
[91] *ibid.* at 426.
[92] *ibid.* Lord Hanworth M.R. at 423, Sargant L.J. at 425 and Lawrence L.J. at 427.

Those remarks proved fatal to the intention of the 1919 Act. *Liverpool Electric Cable Company Limited's Application*[93] concerned applications for LIVERPOOL CABLES in Parts A and B of the Register in respect of electric cables. The evidence established that the mark was 100 per cent distinctive in fact. Romer J. held that the mark was not only capable of distinguishing for Part B but also adapted to distinguish for Part A. The Court of Appeal decided that the mark was registrable in neither Part. Non-fanciful geographical names belonged to the *PERFECTION* classes of unregistrable marks. LIVERPOOL CABLES should be refused in Part A by virtue of the Registrar's discretion. In order for a mark to be capable of distinguishing within Part B: "... it has not merely to be capable in fact, but it must also be capable in law".[94] The names of commercial centres like "Liverpool" were incapable of distinguishing in law. LIVERPOOL CABLES was subsequently confirmed by the House of Lords in *A. Bailey & Co., Ltd. v. Clark Son & Morland, Ltd.*[95] although that case involved only an application in Part A of the Register.

Trade Marks Act 1938

The division of the Register into Parts A and B was carried through into the 1938 Act.[96] The essential particulars were retained for Part A[97] but the exception for old marks was omitted.[98] "Distinctiveness" for Part A meant "adapted to distinguish" and the tribunal was directed to take into account the extent to which:

(a) the trade mark is inherently adapted to distinguish . . .; and
(b) by reason of the use of the trade mark or of any other circumstances, the trade mark is in fact adapted to distinguish . . . .[99]

The Goschen Committee had reported in 1934 a demand by British traders to relax the conditions for registration in Part B.[1] While that Committee recommended the abolition of the two years user qualification, it advised retention of the test of "capable of distinguishing" subject to a provision (modelled on Part A) that account should be taken of a mark's factual distinctiveness.[2]

---

[93] (1929) 46 R.P.C. 99, CA.
[94] *ibid.* Lord Hanworth M.R. at p. 118. It was necessary to give "capable of distinguishing" such an interpretation to circumvent the Registrar's lack of discretion under s. 2 of the 1919 Act where a mark had been used bona fide for a minimum of two years and was shown to be distinctive in fact.
[95] (1938) 55 R.P.C. 253, HL.
[96] Trade Marks Act 1938, s. 1.
[97] Trade Marks Act 1938, s. 9(1).
[98] That is, marks in use before August 13, 1875. See, *Departmental Committee on the Law and Practice relating to Trade Marks. Report. (Goschen Committee)*, Cmnd 4568 (1934), para. 50.
[99] Trade Marks Act 1938, s. 9(2).
[1] Above, note 98, para. 57. British traders were disadvantaged because they could not obtain registration abroad unless their marks were registered in the country of origin; see note 9.
[2] *ibid.* paras 58–62.

Following those recommendations, the 1938 Act provided that the sole criterion for registration in Part B was a mark's capacity to distinguish[3] having regard to the extend to which:

(a) the mark is inherently capable of distinguishing . . .; and
(b) by reason of the use of the trade mark or of any other circumstances, the trade mark is in fact capable of distinguishing . . .[4]

The Registrar's discretion under the 1905 Act to refuse registration in Part A had been extended by the 1938 Act to cover also Part B.

The approximation of the definitions of distinctiveness did little to elucidate the difference between the criteria for registration in Parts A and B.[5] In *WELDMESH Trade Mark*,[6] Lloyd-Jacob J. thought it not unreasonable:

> . . . to regard the two expressions "adapted to distinguish" and "capable of distinguishing" as being deliberately chosen to direct the particular enquiry aright, the former emphasising that it is because of the presence of a sufficient distinguishing characteristic in the mark itself that distinctiveness is to be expected to result whatever the type and scale of the user and thus secure an estimation of a positive quality in the mark; and the second that, in spite of the absence of a sufficient distinguishing characteristic in the mark itself, distinctiveness can be acquired by appropriate user, thereby overcoming a negative quality in the mark."[7]

WELDMESH was directly descriptive but 100 per cent distinctive of the applicant's goods steel wire mesh. The Court of Appeal confirmed Lloyd-Jacob J.'s view that the mark was acceptable for registration in Part B.[8] Both the first instance and appeal decisions suggested that under the 1938 Act de facto marks were at least registrable in Part B.[9]

---

[3] Trade Marks Act 1938, s. 10(1). New marks therefore became registrable in Part B.
[4] Trade Marks Act 1938, s. 10(2).
[5] The Mathys Committee noted that: "... the difference between the criteria for the two parts of the register is incomprehensible even to those immersed in trade mark law and practice". The Mathys Report recommended the abolition of the two parts of the Register. Henceforth there should be a single Register with the test for registrability combining the essential particulars and the definition of capable of distinguishing in s. 10(1) and (2) of the 1938 Act. That proposal was never implemented although the two parts of the Register were merged by the Trade Marks Act 1994. *British Trade Mark Law and Practice, Report of the Committee to Examine British Trade Mark Law and Practice*, Cmnd. 5601 (1974).
[6] [1965] R.P.C. 590.
[7] *ibid.* at 595.
[8] [1966] R.P.C. 220, CA.
[9] *ibid.* at 227, Wilmer J.: "In my judgement the legislature must have intended to draw a distinction between that which is 'inherently capable of distinguishing' and that which is inherently 'adapted to distinguish'. . . . I have no doubt that proof of 100 per cent distinctiveness is conclusive to show that the mark here in question is 'inherently capable of distinguishing' . . .; and at 228, Harman L.J.: "the goods (sic.—mark) were 'capable' of

However by 1984[10] it had become clear that *LIVERPOOL CABLES* was still good law.[11] An application had been made to register YORK in respect of trailers. The House of Lords accepted that the mark was 100 per cent distinctive of the applicant's goods. The question of law on appeal was whether such factual distinctiveness entitled the applicant to registration in Part B.[12] Their Lordships answered no. Registration in Part B required the tribunal to consider the extent to which a mark was "inherently capable of distinguishing". Those words meant "capable in law of distinguishing", the relevant law being that no trader could obtain a monopoly in certain words of which laudatory epithets and some geographical names were examples.[13]

The definition of "mark" was also carried forward from the 1905 Act to the 1938 Act.[14] Despite the lack of express mention colour combinations were held to fall within that definition.[15] However resort in the so-called interest of free competition was again had to class exclusion when the courts were confronted with applications to register the distinctive shape of the COCA-COLA bottle: "A bottle is a container not a mark".[16]

---

distinctiveness. This has been proved by the event. It has come about by the events which have happened and these prove inherent capability."

[10] *YORK Trade Mark* [1984] R.P.C. 231, HL.

[11] *LIVERPOOL CABLES* had been approved by the House of Lords in *Yorkshire Copper Works Limited's Application for a Trade Mark* (1953) 71 R.P.C. 150 but counsel for the applicant had conceded that if registration in Part A was refused, registration in Part B must also be refused.

[12] Above, note 10 at p. 251.

[13] *ibid*. Lord Wilberforce at p. 254 with whom the other Law Lords concurred. It is unclear whether Lord Wilberforce decided that YORK should be refused pursuant to the Registrar's discretion or as a matter of law; *Kerly's Law of Trade Marks and Trade Names* (12th ed, 1986), T.A. Blanco White and R. Jacob (eds), 8–74. YORK was not followed by the Supreme Court of Ireland in *Waterford Trade Mark (Ireland)* [1984] F.S.R. 390: " . . . many English decisions in this area of trade mark law, particularly with regard to geographical words, have been more confusing than enlightening and, for that reason, I have found difficulty in following them.", O'Higgins C.J. at 394. In the majority's view, the direction for the tribunal to consider inherent capacity to distinguish was necessary to accommodate unused marks which only became registrable in Part B by virtue of s. 10 of the 1938 Act (s. 18 of the Irish Trade Marks Act 1963). A mark in use before application in Part B could rely on either inherent distinctiveness *or* factual distinctiveness or a combination of both. WATERFORD was 100 per cent factually distinctive of crystal glassware and could be registered in Part B. See Dawson, "The Waterford Case in Ireland: Geographical Names as Trade Marks" [1985] E.I.P.R. 21.

[14] Trade Marks Act 1938, s. 68(1). The meaning of "trade mark" although not dissimilar to the 1905 Act definition was amended chiefly to take on board the registered user system introduced by the 1938 Act. There was no definition of "registrable trade mark" in the 1938 Act but s. 9 and 10 were included in that part of the 1938 Act entitled "Registrability and validity of registration".

[15] *Smith, Kline and French Laboratories Ltd v. Sterling-Winthrop Group Ltd.* [1976] R.P.C. 511, HL.

[16] *Coca-Cola Trade Marks*, above, note 4, Lord Templeman at 457. See Franzosi, "What is a trade mark?—a challenge to the House of Lords" [1987] 3 E.I.P.R. 63, The Mathys Committee recommended the express exclusion from registration as trade marks of colour, the shape of goods or their packaging, sounds and smells, above, note 5 at para. 64.

Conclusion

Immediately prior to the introduction of the 1994 Act, the Pickwickian[17] position was that some marks were unregistrable even though 100 per cent distinctive in fact. That position had come about because the courts were able to limit what a trade mark was for the purposes of the Acts in effect through application of the essential particulars:[18]

> The history of the Acts for regulating the registration of trade marks is the history of a continued struggle on the part of the mercantile community to bring about a state of law suited to their practical requirements, of repeated attempts on the part of the Legislature to comply with those requirements, and of a succession of discoveries of the failure of the language employed, when submitted to judicial decision, to carry out the objects arrived at.[19]

Part II: The Trade Marks Harmonisation Directive 1988

Articles 2 and 3 of the Directive[20] follow Article 6*quinquies* of the Paris Convention.[21] Article 6*quinquies*A(1) states the principle[22] that a trade mark registered in one Contracting Party shall be accepted for filing and protected in other Contracting Parties subject to the grounds for refusal listed in Article 6*quinquies*B. The principle concerns only the signs of which a trade mark is composed. Contracting Parties are free to deny registration to signs which are not trade marks according to their domestic law.[23]

---

[17] *In the Matter of an Application by Hans Lauritzen for the Registration of a Trade Mark* (1931) 48 R.P.C. 392, Eve J. at 397.
[18] A mark had to be inherently distinctive to contain or consist of an essential particular *(PERFECTION)*. After the division of the Register a mark had to be inherently distinctive to qualify even for Part B *(LIVERPOOL CABLES, YORK)*. It followed that a mark, which could never be registered in Part A (however long it was used) because it lacked inherent distinctiveness, was also unregistrable in Part B. The definition of "mark" in the 1905 Act (repeated in the 1938 Act) was a synthesis of the essential particulars in the Acts of 1883 to 1888 *(COCA-COLA)*.
[19] *The Law of Trade Mark Registration under the Trade Marks Act 1905*, above, note 73 at p. iii.
[20] Above, note 7.
[21] Paris Convention for the Protection of Industrial Property, 1883.
[22] Known as "telle quelle". The United Kingdom has never considered itself bound by telle quelle; *Re Carter Medicine Company's Trade Mark* (1892) 9 R.P.C. 401; *NEEDLETIP Trade Mark* [1973] R.P.C. 113. A fashionable argument is that international conventions are directly effective in the United Kingdom through Community law. The argument for present purposes would run that the Community was competent to conclude the Agreement on Trade-Related Aspects of Intellectual Property Rights (TRIPS) in the field of harmonisation of trade marks and Art. 2(1) of TRIPS obliges Members to comply with Arts 1–12 and 19 of the Paris Convention (*Re The Uruguay Round Treaties, Opinion 1/94* [1994] E.C.R. I-5267, ECJ and Council Decision 94/800/E.C. of December 22, 1994 [1994] O.J. L 336/1). See *Azrak-Hamway International Inc's Licence of Right (Design and Copyright) Application* [1997] R.P.C. 134 and *COFFEEMIX Trade Mark* [1998] R.P.C. 17.
[23] See further G. H. C. Bodenhausen, *Guide to the Paris Convention* (1968).

Article 2 of the Directive reflects the principle of Article 6*quinquies*A(1). It states that no type of sign is automatically excluded from registration as a trade mark and is similarly an enabling provision:

> A trade mark may consist of any sign capable of being represented graphically, particularly words, including personal names, designs, letters, numerals, the shape of goods or of their packaging, provided that such signs are capable of distinguishing the goods or services of one undertaking from those of other undertakings.

The right within Article 6*quinquies*A(1) to declare unregistrable a sign that does not qualify as a trade mark under Community law is subsequently claimed as an absolute ground for refusal in Article 3(1)(a) of the Directive.

Article 2 of the Directive is said to contain three requirements which must be satisfied before a sign can constitute a trade mark for the purposes of Article 3(1)(a).[24] First there must be a sign. Second the sign must be capable of graphic representation. Third the sign must be capable of distinguishing. If such a third requirement exists, the tribunals of Member States are given a mechanism for excluding signs on policy grounds not stated in the Directive. An alternative view is that the words "provided that such signs are capable of distinguishing" are a statement of general principle and set the standard of distinctiveness which an individual mark must display on examination as to the absolute ground for refusal in Article 3(1)(b).

Support for the latter interpretation is found in Recital 7 of the Preamble to the Directive:

> ...whereas...it is necessary to list *examples of signs* which may constitute a trade mark, provided that such signs are capable of distinguishing the goods or services of one undertaking from those of other undertakings; whereas the grounds for refusal...concerning *the trade mark itself*, for example, the *absence of any distinctive character* ... are to be listed *in an exhaustive manner*...,[25]

in the Minutes of the Council Meeting at which the Directive was adopted:

> Re Article 3(1)(b)
> The Council and the Commission consider that a trade mark is

---

[24] See, for example, *AD2000 Trade Mark* [1997] R.P.C. 168 at 173, Hobbs Q.C. and *Philips Electronics NV v. Remington Consumer Products*, above, note 1, Jacob J. at 298–9.
[25] Author's emphasis.

devoid of any distinctive character if it is not capable of distinguishing the goods or services of one undertaking from those of other undertakings,[26]

and in the *travaux préparatoires* surrounding the introduction of the Community Trade Mark Regulation[27] and the Directive:

> ...not only words and pictorial presentations should be admitted to registration as marks, but also letters, numbers, colour combinations, as well as shapes of articles or their packaging. *Instead of excluding any of these categories from registration* or making their registration dependent on special requirements, *the criterion for registration* should be an examination as to *whether the mark applied for* is by its nature inherently distinctive or has acquired distinctiveness as a result of its use in the course of trade,[28]

Furthermore the structure of the Directive itself indicates that an objection on absolute grounds should not be taken under Article 3(1)(a) where the issue is whether a sign is capable of distinguishing. The reasons are twofold.

First, a proviso to Article 3(1) applies to Article 3(1)(b), (c) and (d) but not to Article 3(1)(a). Article 3(1)(b) provides an absolute ground for refusal where a mark is devoid of any distinctive character; (c) where a mark consists exclusively of descriptive indications; and (d) where a mark consists exclusively of indications common to the trade. The proviso is contained in Article 3(3) and states that registration shall not be refused under (1)(b), (c) or (d) where a mark is proved to have acquired a distinctive character through use. The proviso in Article 3(3) was deliberately inserted to avoid the *PERFECTION/YORK/COCA-COLA* situations of some marks being unregistrable even though 100 per cent distinctive in fact.[29] If a sign can be denied registration under Article 3(1)(a) on the ground it is incapable of distinguishing and, therefore, not a trade mark (that is, incapable in law of distinguishing) then the intention of the legislation is frustrated.

Second, although the shape of goods or of their packaging is mentioned in the list of signs of which a trade mark can comprise, Article 3(1)(e) excepts certain shapes which are necessary for effective competition namely:

---

[26] *Joint Statements by the Council and the Commission of the European Communities entered in the minutes of the Council meeting, on the first Council Directive approximating the laws of the Member States on trade marks adopted on 21 December 1988,* OHIM O.J. 5/96 607.
[27] Above, note 8.
[28] *Memorandum on the creation of an EEC trade mark,* adopted by the Commission July 6, 1976, Bull. E.C. suppl. 8/76, para. 72; author's emphasis.
[29] *Memorandum on the creation of an EEC trade mark,* above, note 28 at para. 85.

signs which consist exclusively of:
- the shape which results from the nature of the goods themselves, or
- the shape of goods which is necessary to obtain a technical result, or
- the shape which gives substantial value to the goods;

Signs that fall within Article 3(1)(e) are unregistrable because they cannot constitute trade marks according to Community law.[30] Article 3(1)(e) derogates from Article 2. Derogation is construed narrowly in Community law.[31] If it is possible to object to a shape application under Article 3(1)(a) on the ground that it is incapable of distinguishing, additional policy considerations may enter into the equation[32] and a Community rule of interpretation is breached. Moreover the absolute grounds for refusal of registration in Article 3 of the Directive are stated in Recital 7 to be exhaustive.

Conclusion

The words "provided that such signs are capable of distinguishing" in Article 2 of the Directive either present an additional hurdle to registration or state the general principle that a specific mark shall be refused registration under Article 3(1)(b)–(d) if it is not capable of distinguishing. Argument favours the latter view[33] so that objection can only be taken under Article 3(1)(a) where what is applied for is not a sign[34] or is a sign which is incapable of graphic representation.[35]

---

[30] This was much clearer in the original draft legislation for the Community trade mark. A similar provision to Art. 2 of the Directive was immediately followed by an exclusion from registration as European trade marks of: "shapes which are dictated by the goods themselves or affect their essential value or result in a technical effect". That exclusion was in turn followed by the absolute grounds for refusal. *Proposed European Trade Mark, Preliminary Draft of a Convention for a European Trade Mark*, DTI, 1973, Arts 8 and 11.
[31] See most recently, Case C-335/96 *Silhouette International Schmied GmbH & Co KG v. Hartlauer Handelsgesellschaft mbH*, [1998] 2 C.M.L.R. 953, ECJ.
[32] See B. Strowel, "Benelux: A Guide to the Validity of Three-dimensional Trade Marks in Europe" [1995] 3 E.I.P.R. 154. J. Bornkamm "Harmonising Trade Mark Law in Europe" [1999] I.P.Q. 3, 283.
[33] The latter view is further supported by TRIPS, Art. 15. The Article begins: "Any sign . . . capable of distinguishing the goods or services of one undertaking from those of other undertakings, shall be capable of constituting a trademark." It is clear that this is intended to be a *general* statement (not a requirement to a sign being a trade mark) that a *specific* mark shall be distinctive because the Article continues: "Where signs are not inherently capable of distinguishing . . ., Members may make registrability depend on distinctiveness acquired through use." Further Members may make visual perceptibility a condition to registration, *c.f.* the requirement for graphic representation in Art. 3(1)(a) of the Directive. And see above, note 22.
[34] In *Philips Electronics NV v. Remington Consumer Products*, above, note 1 at 298, Jacob J. thought that a sign was "anything which can convey information". On that view a feature which the consumer could not see at the point of sale might not be a "sign", see *Unilever's (Striped Toothpaste) Trade Mark Application* [1980] F.S.R. 280 criticised in P. Prescott "Trade Marks Invisible at Point of Sale" [1990] E.I.P.R. 241, and *Bostick Ltd v. Sellotape GB Ltd* [1994] R.P.C. 556.
[35] *Ty Nant Spring Water Ltd's Trade Mark Application*, [2000] R.P.C. 55, Appointed Person. An objection under s. 3(1)(a) is only appropriate where a sign is incapable of graphic

Part III: Decisions under the Trade Marks Act 1994, U.K. and Community Office Practices compared

The United Kingdom tribunals are presently demonstrating how to return under the 1994 Act to the proposition that a mark must be capable in law of distinguishing. The problem of the relationship between sections 1(1) and 3[36] is clearly appreciated including the lack of discretion under section 3(1)(b), (c) and (d) to refuse registration of a factually distinctive mark.[37]

British Sugar plc v. James Robertson & Sons Ltd[38] was the first case in which the relationship arose for consideration. Jacob J. thought that "capable of distinguishing" in section 1(1) added nothing to the absolute grounds for refusal at least in so far as section 3(1)(b), (c) and (d) were concerned: "If a mark on its face is non-distinctive . . . but is shown to have a distinctive character in fact then it must be *capable of distinguishing*."[39] However the judge continued that some signs cannot in practice be registered[40] and reprimanded the Registrar for accepting TREAT on evidence of five years' use.[41] He dismissed as unhelpful survey evidence showing 60 per cent consumer awareness of the TREAT product and held that British Sugar's extensive use of TREAT since the date of registration was insufficient to displace its laudatory meaning.[42] The TREAT registration was therefore invalid. Following *TREAT,* L'Oreal's application for NUTRITIVE was refused despite 12 years' use for skin care and hair products, high turnover and substantial advertising expenditure.[43]

The second attempt to clarify the relationship came in *AD2000*

---

representation not where a sign is so capable but is inadequately represented in the application. The latter attracts objection under r. 11 of the Trade Marks Rules 2000. For inadequate graphic representations see: *Swizzels Matlow Ltd's Trade Mark Application* [1998] R.P.C. 244—"chewy sweet on a stick" and Case R 1/1998-2 *DÉCLIC Trade Mark*, October 7, 1998, OHIM Second Board of Appeal (unreported)—sound mark inadequately represented in words.

[36] Implementing respectively Arts 2 and 3 of the Directive. 3(1)(a), (b), (c) and (d) of the 1994 Act correspond respectively to Art. 3(1)(a), (b), (c) and (d) of the Directive. The proviso to section 3(1) implements the first sentence of Art. 3(3). S. 3(2) implements Art. 3(1)(e).
[37] *EUROLAMB Trade Mark* [1997] R.P.C. 279 (Appointed Person), *Proctor and Gamble Limited's Trade Mark Applications* [1999] R.P.C. 673.
[38] [1996] R.P.C. 281, described as a "helpful" case by Robert Walker L.J. *Re Proctor and Gamble Limited*, above, note 37.
[39] *ibid.* at 305.
[40] Above, note 39.
[41] *ibid.* at 286.
[42] *ibid.* at 302–305. Contrast the Opinion of Advocate General Cosmas in Case C-108/97 *WSC Windsurfing Chiemsee Produktions—und Vertriebs GmbH v. Boots—und Segelzubehör Walter Huber*, 5 May 1998 (unreported) that as a rule of thumb anything above 50% recognition in the market place would be sufficient proof of acquired distinctiveness. The Court of Justice in *Windsurfing* [1999] E.T.M.R. 585 cautioned against use of fixed percentages in assessing factual distinctiveness. A mark would be registrable if a significant proportion of the relevant class of persons identify goods or services as originating from a particular undertaking because of the trade mark.
[43] *NUTRITIVE Trade Mark* [1998] R.P.C. 621 (Registry).

Trade Mark.[44] The applicant argued that the Registrar could not raise an objection under section 3(1)(b) unless he also raised an objection under section 3(1)(a). Hobbs Q.C. as Appointed Person, said that in order to be registrable under the 1994 Act a mark had to possess the qualities identified in section 1(1) and none of the defects identified in section 3. A sign met the requirements of section 1(1) if it was graphically represented and not incapable of distinguishing. A mark could be not incapable of distinguishing yet devoid of distinctive character. With respect that formulation is unhelpful. First, it is circular. Second, it begs the question identified in the beginning, whether a mark can be incapable of distinguishing yet distinctive. Third, it obscures the intention of the Directive. The mark applied for must be not incapable of distinguishing—not to qualify as a trade mark—but to avoid refusal of registration under section 3(1)(b) on the ground that it is devoid of any distinctive character.

In *Wickes Plc's Trade Mark Application*,[45] the Registrar appeared to recognise the circularity of *AD2000* by accepting that if the section 3(1)(b) objection to a three-dimensional booklet was overcome, the 3(1)(a) objection should be waived. He did not accept that the section 3(1)(a) objection was ill conceived in the first place.

Philips Electronics NV v. Remington Consumer Products[46] exposed the consequences of treating "capable of distinguishing" as a condition of registration. Jacob J. held on the one hand that the public associated the three-headed shaver face solely with Philips but on the other hand that the shape was incapable of distinguishing because it conveyed to the public how the shaver worked. His true reason for declaring the registration invalid was that no trader should be granted a monopoly in a good engineering design.[47] He dismissed counsel for Philips' argument that such matters of policy could only be raised, if at all, under section 3(2).[48]

Jacob J. further held that the shape was devoid of any distinctive character again because it conveyed to the public how the shaver worked. The link between *Philips* and the judge's earlier decision in *TREAT* now became clear. In *TREAT*, Jacob J. said that the question to be asked under section 3(1)(b) is whether the sign is likely to be taken (or, in the case of a sign in use, taken) by the public as a trade mark. In *Philips*, he posed exactly the same question under section 3(1)(a). In *TREAT*, Jacob J. held that the evidence was insufficient to displace the mark's primary laudatory meaning. In *Philips*, he held

---

[44] [1997] R.P.C. 168 (Appointed Person).
[45] [1998] R.P.C. 698 (Registry).
[46] Above, note 1. By contrast, the Stockholm District Court (Judge Göran Nilsson dissenting) upheld the validity of Philips' Swedish registration for the three-headed shaver face in *Ide Line Aktiebolag v. Philips Electronics NV* [1997] E.T.M.R. 377. Both the English and Swedish decisions have been appealed. The English appeal, was heard in May, the Swedish appeal was due shortly thereafter. For the English appeal, see below, at note 72.
[47] *ibid* at 297.
[48] *ibid* at 302.

Developments in Registrability

that the evidence was insufficient to displace the mark's functional meaning.

The fact of the matter is that Jacob J. is applying what is essentially the former Part A test of distinctiveness in order to determine registrability. Moreover, he is importing that test of distinctiveness into the definition of "trade mark" in order to exclude certain categories of sign from registration. The *TREAT* test of distinctiveness places an impossible burden of proof on all but applicants for inherently distinctive marks especially in a jurisdiction like the United Kingdom where survey evidence is so readily dismissed. Lip service is being paid to the proviso to section 3(1) and section 3(2) is being circumvented in relation to shapes.

Philips and *TREAT* were followed by Laddie J. in *JERYL LYNN TRADE MARK*.[49] Merck and Co. Inc's registration for JERYL LYNN in respect of medicinal and pharmaceutical preparations was declared invalid because it was the name of a particular strain of virus. Signs that perform an overwhelmingly descriptive or technical function are not capable of distinguishing within section 3(1)(a) of the 1994 Act.

The United Kingdom Registry has always regarded "capable of distinguishing" as a third requirement of section 1(1) particularly in relation to non-traditional marks. Nonetheless the registration of a three-dimensional mark, sound or smell was relatively easy to obtain provided the requirement for graphic representation was met. The test of prima facie registrability under section 3(1)(b)—(d) was as set out in *TORQ-SET*[50] for former Part B marks: whether the mark was an indication which other traders would legitimately wish to use in the normal course of business.

Following *TREAT* and *Philips*, the Registry applies the same considerations to objections under 3(1)(a)-(d). The question is whether what is applied for is likely to be taken by the public as a trade mark, not just what other traders will wish to use.[51] Recognising the asymmetry of such practice with the proviso to section 3(1), the *Work Manual* states that evidence is admissible to overcome an objection under section 3(1)(a).[52]

The result is confusion. Non-traditional marks are difficult to obtain and shapes are routinely objected to under section 3(1)(a) and (b) with or without a reference to section 3(2). In *Procter & Gamble Co.'s Trade Mark Application*,[53] an application for the "bone" shape of the applicant's soap was objected to on the ground that it was devoid of any distinctive character. Before dealing with the section 3(1)(b) objection, the Hearing Officer concluded that the shape was

---

[49] [1999] R.P.C. 491.
[50] *In the Matter of American Coy.'s Application No. 773,098 for the Registration of a Trade Mark* [1959] R.P.C. 344, 345.
[51] *Trade Marks Registry Work Manual*, Chap. 6 (1998).
[52] *ibid.* at 63.
[53] [1998] R.P.C. 10 (Registry).

not capable of distinguishing because it improved the user's grip on the soap when wet. That functional feature meant that the shape was unlikely to be regarded by the public as a trade mark. It is entirely unclear whether the Hearing Officer was raising a late 3(1)(a) objection or whether that conclusion formed part of his decision under 3(1)(b). No objection was taken to the application under section 3(2).

Further, a high standard of distinctiveness (essentially Part A) is being applied to applications for word marks so that, for example, FROOT LOOPS for cereals[54] and BONUS GOLD for investment account services[55] were both refused registration under section 3(1)(b) and (c).

By contrast, the practice emerging from the Office for Harmonisation in the Internal Market (Trade Marks and Designs) (OHIM) is consistent with the enabling purpose of Article 4 of the Community Trade Mark Regulation.[56] In *IX Trade Mark*,[57] the Second Board of Appeal held that Articles 4 and 7,[58] when read together, place the onus on the examiner to justify any objection made on absolute grounds.[59] Each application must be considered on its own merits. There was no "per se" rule excluding two letter marks from registration on the ground that they were lacking in distinctiveness.

In *NETMEETING Trade Mark*,[60] the Third Board of Appeal stressed that Article 7 of the Regulation must be interpreted properly taking into account, *inter alia*: first, that the proviso in Article 7(3) applies only to Article 7(1)(b), (c) and (d); and second, that Article 7(1)(a) (and Article 4) refer to "signs" whereas Article 7(1)(b), (c) and (d) refer to "trade marks" or signs within "trade marks". Similarly, the OHIM Examination Guidelines[61] caution examiners separately to itemise objections on absolute grounds because evidence of acquired distinctiveness through use can overcome objections raised under Article 7(1)(b)–(d) but not those arising under Article 7(1)(a), (e)–(j).

Whatever the type of mark applied for, distinctiveness objections are raised under Articles 7(1)(b)–(d) of the Regulation not under Article 7(1)(a). In *ORANGE Trade Mark*,[62] the Third Board of Appeal said that a colour can generally be protected as a Community trade mark under Article 4 but that an individual application may be

---

[54] [1998] R.P.C. 240 (Appointed Person).
[55] [1998] R.P.C. 859 (Appointed Person).
[56] Above, note 8.
[57] Case R 4/1998-2, OHIM O.J. 10/98, 1059 (Second Board of Appeal).
[58] Art. 4 of the Regulation is the equivalent of section 1(1) of the 1994 Act and Art. 2 of the Directive. Art. 7 of the Regulation contains the absolute grounds for refusal. Art. 7(1)(a)–(e) correspond to s. 3(1)(a)–(d) and (2) of the 1994 Act and Art. 3(1)(a)–(e) of the Directive. Art. 7(3) corresponds to the proviso to s. 3(1) in the 1994 Act and Art. 3(3) of the Directive.
[59] Contrast *EUROLAMB*, above, note 37 at p. 288 and *Procter & Gamble* above, note 37 at 13.
[60] Case R 26/1998-3, OHIM O.J. 3/99, 517 (Third Board of Appeal).
[61] OHIM O.J. 9/96, p 1324–1346 at 1330.
[62] Case R 7/97-3, OHIM O.J. 5/98, 641 (Third Board of Appeal). See also Case R 122/1998-3 *LIGHT GREEN Trade Mark*, OHIM O.J 4/99, 605 (Third Board of Appeal) and Case R 169-1998-3 *YELLOW Trade Mark*, January 22, 1999 Third Board of Appeal (unreported).

refused under Article 7(1)(b)–(d) because it is not distinctive. Communication No. 2/98 of the President of OHIM[63] makes the same point in relation to three-dimensional marks but explains that the examinations of a three-dimensional mark may additionally involve the grounds for refusal in Article 7(1)(e) of the Regulation.

The assessment of distinctiveness is acknowledged to be an inexact science. A balanced approach is adopted which involves a combination of objective and subjective elements when judging the overall impression of the mark as a whole. Relevant factors include the nature of the goods or services, the circumstances in which they reach the consumer, the level of awareness of the likely consumer and the interests of competitors.[64] Thus, for example, MAXIMA[65] and BLOODSTREAM[66] were allowed for medical and surgical apparatus because of the specialised nature of the market and LASTING PERFORMANCE[67] was accepted for soap but not for perfumes and cosmetics. In *NETMEETING Trade Mark*,[68] the Third Board of Appeal drew attention to the word "any" in Article 7(1)(b). "Devoid of *any* distinctive character" means that a mark can possess minimal distinctiveness but its scope of protection as compared to a highly distinctive mark (inherent or acquired) is accordingly less.[69]

Conclusion

The United Kingdom tribunals apply a high standard of distinctiveness to applications and import that condition of registrability into the definition of "trade mark" to exclude, in particular, descriptions and the shape of goods from being registered trade marks. OHIM takes a more balanced view of distinctiveness and interprets it only as a condition to the registrability of an individual mark.

Part IV: Assessment of the current U.K. position

In *Philips Electronics NV v. Remington Consumer Products*,[70] Jacob J. said of his finding that Philips' three-headed shaver face was incapable of distinguishing within section 1(1) of the 1994 Act: "I do

---

[63] April 8, 1998, OHIM O.J. 6/98, 701.
[64] Case 39/1998-2, *NATURALS Trade Mark*, November 22, 1998, Second Board of Appeal (unreported).
[65] Case 51/1998-1, *MAXIMA Trade Mark*, September 30, 1998, First Board of Appeal (unreported).
[66] Case R 33/1998-2, *BLOODSTREAM Trade Mark*, September 1998, Second Board of Appeal (unreported).
[67] Case R 34/1998-3, *LASTING PERFORMANCE Trade Mark*, OHIM O.J. 11/98, 1157 (Third Board of Appeal).
[68] Above, note 60.
[69] Case C-39/97, *Canon Kabushiki Kaisha v. Metro-Goldwyn-Mayer Inc.*, [1999] 1 C.M.L.R. 77, ECJ.
[70] Above, note 1.

not think in so holding I am resurrecting the old British law". The conclusions to be drawn from this essay indicate that the judge was mistaken in his thinking.

First, Part I demonstrates that under the trade marks (registration) Acts of 1875 to 1938, the courts used the requirement of distinctiveness to limit the meaning of registered trade marks in the so-called interests of free trade. The outcome of that strategy was that certain types of mark were excluded from registration by class. Second, while Part II argues that Article 2 of the Directive merely sets the standard of distinctiveness for the absolute grounds of refusal in Article 3, it acknowledges that Article 2 is susceptible of an interpretation which imposes a positive requirement for distinctiveness on the registrability of an individual mark. In the latter sense, the Directive has provided the United Kingdom courts with a vehicle to continue their former strategy of denying registration to marks by class unless or until the Court of Justice rules otherwise.

Third, Part III confirms that the United Kingdom tribunals regard "capable of distinguishing" in section 1(1) of the 1994 Act as a—if not the—primary requirement of registration. The combined effect of *TREAT* and *Philips* is not only that a high standard of distinctiveness is being applied under section 3(1)(b) but also that section 3(1)(a) is being used to declare some marks unregistrable on the ground that they are non-distinctive and cannot, therefore, constitute trade marks within section 1(1). In other words, an inherently non-distinctive mark is not a trade mark. To date, such policy has operated to exclude from registration under section 3(1)(a) technical or functional descriptions and the shapes of goods themselves.

Significant procedural improvements have been and are being made to the United Kingdom law and practice of trade marks. An aim is to render the United Kingdom a more attractive jurisdiction in which to register and litigate trade marks. But procedural efficiencies rank second when registrations are difficult and, thus, costly to obtain and the price of litigation to enforce exclusive rights is that the trade mark is declared invalid. A Community trade mark is generally easier to obtain, confers Community-wide protection and, provided the rules for international jurisdiction are met,[71] enables the proprietor to enforce trade mark rights in the United Kingdom through a differently situated Community trade mark court.

The United Kingdom should not be surprised when proprietors and their advisers increasingly choose the Community system for the protection of their trade marks.

---

[71] Arts 93 and 94 of the Community Trade Mark Regulation, above, note 8. See R. Annand and H. Norman, *Blackstone's Guide to the Community Trade Mark* (1998), chap. 7.

Postscript

On May 5, 1999 the English appeal in *Philips Electronics NV v. Remington Consumer Products Limited*[72] was heard by the Court of Appeal. The Court provisionally held that section 1(1) of the 1994 Act[73] imposes an initial condition on the registrability of an individual mark that must be satisfied in relation to the goods or services for which registration is sought. Since the proviso to section 3(1)[74] applies to section 3(1)(b)–(d)[75] but not to section 3(1)(a)[76] that condition must be met irrespective of use of the mark. The trade mark must itself possess features which enable it to distinguish the applicant's goods or services from those of other undertakings—or be "capable in law of distinguishing".

Turning to the registration in suit, the shape depicted in Philips' trade mark was nothing more than a pictorial description of the product. The shape of an article cannot be registered for goods of that shape unless it contains some addition to the shape of the article which has trade mark significance. To hold otherwise would enable a few traders to monopolise the best designs. Philips' trade mark was invalid because it was incapable of distinguishing electric shaves within the meaning of section 1(1).

Recognising that the appeal raised difficult questions of construction under the Directive, the Court of Appeal referred, *inter alia*, the following questions to the Court of Justice before giving final judgment[77]:

(i) Is there a category of marks which is not excluded from registration by Articles 3(1)(b)–(d) and Article 3(3) of the Council Directive 89/104/EEC ("the Directive") which is nonetheless excluded from registration by Article 3(1)(a) of the Directive (as being incapable of distinguishing the goods of the proprietor from those of other undertakings)?

(ii) Is the shape (or part of the shape) of an article (being the article in respect of which the sign is registered) only capable of distinguishing for the purposes of Article 2 if it contains some capricious addition (being an embellishment which has no functional purpose) to the shape of the article?

Pending the outcome of that reference, the provisional judgment of the Court of Appeal in *Philips v. Remington* is binding on lower tribunals. As regards the subject matter of this essay, the history of United Kingdom trade marks law has turned full circle.

---

[72] [1999] R.P.C. 809; [1999] E.T.M.R. 816.
[73] Art. 2, Directive.
[74] Art. 3(3), Directive.
[75] Art. 3(1)(b)–(d), Directive.
[76] Directive, Art. 3(1)(a)
[77] Case C–299/99 [1999] O.J. C 299/13.

7. Three-dimensional Trade Marks: Should the Directive Be Reshaped?

Robert Burrell
Huw Beverley Smith
Allison Coleman

Three-dimensional Trade Marks: Should The Directive Be Reshaped?

1. Introduction

Trade mark law has come to protect a diverse range of intangibles. The Directive approximating the laws of the E.U. Member States relating to trade marks,[1] both reflects and furthers this development by providing a broad and open-ended definition of what can be protected as a trade mark. As a result, a number of marks have now been registered which would not have been registrable under earlier trade marks legislation. Newly registrable marks include sound marks, olfactory marks, gesture marks, and the shape of goods and their packaging. In general the possibilities created by registrability of such marks have created considerable interest and speculation. However, it is the final category of three-dimensional[2] marks which has thus far proved to be the most controversial and the most problematic of the new types of mark.

The most obvious danger in allowing the registration of three-dimensional marks is that this may be too strong a form of protection, raising the "spectre of total and perpetual monopoly in containers and articles."[3] A related concern is that trade mark protection may begin to encroach on the proper sphere of designs law and, albeit to a lesser extent, patent law. Such concerns led the drafters of the Directive to introduce a special set of exceptions designed to keep trade mark protection for shapes within appropriate limits.[4] Courts in the United Kingdom and elsewhere in Europe have now begun to grapple with the scope of these exclusions. In addition, they have been forced to consider the extent to which policy considerations should be built into other parts of the test of registrability and, in particular, whether the test of distinctiveness ought to be applied in such a way as to prevent an applicant from monopolising product features which a competitor

---

Our thanks to Lionel Bently, Graeme Dinwoodie and John Philips.
[1] Council Directive 89/104; hereafter "the Directive."
[2] "Three-dimensional mark" is used here as a shorthand for marks consisting of the shape of goods or their packaging. Strictly speaking, however, three-dimensional marks were not excluded as such from registration under the 1938 Act. See, in particular, *Unilever Ltd's (Striped Toothpaste No. 2) Trade Marks* [1987] R.P.C. 13.
[3] See *Coca-Cola Trade Marks* [1986] R.P.C. 421 at 457, and see text below.
[4] Art. 3 of the Directive provides that the following shall not be registered or if registered shall be liable to declared invalid: (e) signs which consist exclusively of (i) the shape which results from the nature of the goods themselves, or (ii) the shape of goods which is necessarily to obtain a technical result, or (iii) the shape which gives substantial value to the goods.

may legitimately wish to copy. Thus far courts in the United Kingdom[5] and Sweden[6] have come to different conclusions and a reference to the ECJ is now imminent.[7] An analysis of the proper scope of trade mark protection for the shape of articles and containers is therefore timely. As will be seen, we believe that an understanding of the arguments that were historically used to block the registration of three-dimensional marks in the United Kingdom is vital to an appreciation of the difficulties likely to be faced in this area.[8] We argue that, by and large, courts in the United Kingdom are moving in the right direction, but that their decisions in this area have been at least partly based on unarticulated premises. The courts now need to move to a situation where they refer directly and consistently to policy considerations when interpreting the Directive and the 1994 Act—they need to adopt an overtly teleological approach.[9] However, we begin our analysis by considering why the drafters of the Directive thought it necessary to extend trade mark protection to shapes given the problems outlined above. This preliminary enquiry will allow us to juxtapose the difficulties created by trade mark protection for three-dimensional marks with the justifications for such protection.

2. Why Trade Mark Protection For Shapes Was Introduced

The decision to introduce trade mark protection for three-dimensional marks was influenced by a number of factors. One important practical reason was that a number of European countries already provided such protection.[10] Since the general approach of the Community is to harmonise rights up rather than down[11] an obvious way to proceed was to make such protection available throughout Europe. Moreover, those countries in Europe that had introduced trade mark protection for shapes had done so without any obvious dire consequence and this was also true of countries outside of

---

[5] *Philips Electronics NV v. Remington Consumer Products* [1998] R.P.C. 283; [1999] R.P.C. 809, CA.
[6] *Ide Line Aktiebolag v. Phillips Electronics NV* [1997] E.T.M.R. 377 (Stockholm District Court).
[7] See *Philips Electronics N.V. v. Remington Consumer Products Ltd* CA, note 5, above.
[8] It is important to stress that we have no desire to see a modern European trade mark system constrained by the historical peculiarities of U.K. trade mark law, but that does not mean that prior U.K. practice cannot throw light on important and difficult issues. See *Philips Electronics N.V. v. Remington Consumer Products Ltd* [1998] R.P.C. 283 at 299.
[9] *cf.* Dinwoodie "The Death of Ontology: A Teleological Approach to Trade Mark Law' (1999) 84 *Iowa L. Rev.* 61.
[10] See Tatham and Richards, *ECTA Guide to E.U. Trade Mark Legislation* (Sweet & Maxwell, London, 1998) for a concise and comprehensive survey. See also, Gielen and Strowel, "The Benelux Trademark Act: A Guide to Trademark Law in Europe" (1996) 86 T.M.R. 543; Gielen, "Three-Dimensional Marks in Europe" [1996] T.M.W. 31.
[11] See *e.g.* Council Directive 93/98 harmonising the term of protection of copyright and certain related rights, recital 9.

Europe where such protection was available, including the United States.[12]

A second, and more fundamental, reason for making such protection available is that consumers are said to have come to associate particular shaped goods and packaging with particular manufacturers. Everyday experience would suggest that this is at least true of a small number of very well-known products[13] and there are consumer surveys which suggest that at least some sections of the public are able to make the relevant connection even in the case of less well-known products.[14] More generally, there is a considerable body of postmodern scholarship which suggests that we can draw meaning from a huge array of signs in our "symbol rich" environment.[15] Once it is accepted that the public is capable of recognising a type of symbol as a badge of origin then it would seem to follow that symbols of that type should be registrable as trade marks, both so as to protect the consumer and the producer, but also for the sake of consistency.[16]

A further justification for the extension of trade mark protection to shapes relates to a perceived change in the function of trade marks, which the law should (at least presumptively) reflect. Traditionally, trade marks were seen as serving to indicate the source of goods, albeit an anonymous source[17] and courts in the United Kingdom have historically accorded this function most weight.[18] It is also frequently contended that trade marks further serve to provide an indication or guarantee of quality on which consumers can, in practice, rely; although consumers may be indifferent as to the product's precise origin, they may well seek an assurance that a

---

[12] From the perspective of the United Kingdom, allowing three-dimensional features to be registered as trade marks also made sense since some protection for shapes as trade marks was already available prior to 1994. In particular, traders were sometimes able to use the law of passing off to secure protection for the get-up of their products. See, e.g., *Edge & Sons Ltd. v. Nicolls & Sons Ltd* (1911) 28 R.P.C. 53; *Reckitt & Colman Products Ltd v. Borden Inc.* [1990] 1 W.L.R. 491. Given the expense and uncertainty associated with a passing off action, with the need to prove confusion and damage in each case, it hardly made sense to force a producer to rely on such an action by refusing registered trade mark protection. See *Mercury Communication Ltd v. Mercury Interactive (UK)* [1995] F. S.R. 850 at 863–4 per Laddie J., on the advantages of trade mark registration over a common law action.

[13] Perhaps the most obvious example being the Coca-Cola bottle: see *Coca-Cola Trade Marks* [1986] R.P.C. 421, and see also *Reckitt & Colman Products Ltd v. Borden Inc.*, above, where there was extremely strong evidence of the distinctiveness of the plaintiff's get-up.

[14] See, e.g. the evidence adduced in *Yakult's Application* O/269/98, note 64 below.

[15] See Dinwoodie, above, note 9.

[16] Also see *Reform of Trade Marks Law*, Cm 1203 (1990), paras 1, 2, 18: trade mark law should reflect the reality of the marketplace.

[17] See, for example, *Powell v. Birmingham Vinegar Brewery Co. Ltd.* (1896) 13 R.P.C. 235 at 250; *Re McDowell's Application* (1926) 43 R.P.C. 313 at 337.

[18] See *Wagamama Ltd v. City Centre Restaurants plc* [1995] F.S.R. 713 at 730; *Scandecor Development AB v. Scandecor Marketing AB* [1998] F.S.R. 500 at 519; *British Sugar plc v. James Robertson and Sons* [1996] R.P.C. 283 at 298 per Jacob J., going so far as to suggest that indication of origin is the sole purpose which permeates the Directive and the Trade Marks Act 1994.

product is of a certain quality.[19] Thus, the origin function, broadly construed, encompasses both the source of the product and its key qualities which allow it to be differentiated from rival products.[20]

More important, for our purposes, is the protection which is increasingly claimed for the value of a trade mark as an advertising or merchandising symbol.[21] Rather than being seen as an indication of origin, either in its strict sense, or in a broader sense encompassing quality guarantee or product differentiation functions, the mark is regarded as a silent salesman, triggering an association between the consumer and the goods or services and seeking to sell such goods or services, or, more controversially, seeking to sell itself. Such an approach does not rely on the notion of consumer confusion as to a product's source or quality but seeks to protect the mark's marketing power, thereby safeguarding investment in the promotion of a product,[22] and, as such, borders on protection against misappropriation.[23]

Whilst trade marks can be regarded as valuable assets which reach "across the counter"[24] to sell the goods, it does not follow that every feature of a product which helps sell the goods should be regarded as a trade mark. Indeed, those who wish to see trade mark protection extended beyond its traditional limits should be forced to explain the public policy goals and demands of justice that would be met by such an extension. Proponents of extended protection often base their claims on the fact that certain trade marks "have value",

---

[19] See, e.g. *S.A. CNL-Sucal NV v. HAG GF AG* [1990] 3 C.M.L.R. 571 at 583; *IHT Internationale Heiztechnik v. Ideal Standard* [1994] 3 C.M.L.R. 857 at 877; *Deutsche Renault AG v. Audi AG* [1995] 1 C.M.L.R. 461 at 475. Such a guarantee of quality is not, of course, an absolute legal guarantee, since the manufacturer is at liberty (albeit at its own risk) to vary the quality: see HAG above, at 583. *cf.* Parks, "'Naked' is Not a Four-Letter Word: Debunking the Myth of the 'Quality Control Requirement' in Trade Mark Licensing" (1992) 82 T.M.R. 531, in particular at pp. 535–45. See also Hanak, "The Quality Assurance Function of Trademarks" (1975) 65 T.M.R. 318; Akazaki "Source Theory and Guarantee Theory in Anglo-American Trade Mark Policy: A Critical Legal Study" (1990) 72 J.S.P.T.O. 255.
[20] See *Parfums Christian Dior SA v. Evora BV* [1998] R.P.C. 166 at 180 *per* Jacobs A.G., citing Cornish, *Intellectual Property* (3rd ed., 1996) at 529. See also, *Loendersloot v. Ballantine & Son Ltd.* [1988] F.S.R. 544, at 522–3; *Sabel BV v. Puma AG* [1998] R.P.C. 199 at 209.
[21] See Schechter, "The Rational Basis of Trademark Protection" (1927) 40 Harv. L. Rev. 813 and see also Martino, *Trademark Dilution* (OUP, Oxford, 1996) in particular at pp. 72–8.
[22] See *Parfums Christian Dior SA v. Evora BV* [1998] R.P.C. 166 at 180, Jacobs A.G. (*ibid.* at pp. 180–81) seems to adopt a rather narrow and somewhat sceptical view of the advertising or investment functions, stating that ". . . those functions seem to me to be merely derivatives of the origin function: there would be little purpose in advertising a mark if it were not for the function of that mark as an indicator of origin, distinguishing the trade mark owner's goods from those of his competitors. In my view, therefore, even if other facets of trade marks might require protection in certain circumstances, the court's emphasis on the origin function of trade marks was, and remains, an appropriate starting point for the interpretation of Community law relating to trade marks."
[23] See Kamperman Sanders, *Unfair Competition Law* (OUP, Oxford, 1997) at pp. 107–8. Such a doctrine has been rejected by the English courts: see *Hodgkinson & Corby v. Wards Mobility Ltd.* [1994] 1 W.L.R. 1564 at 1569; *Mail Newspapers Ltd. v. Insert Media (No. 2)* [1988] 2 All E.R. 420 at 424; *Harrods Ltd. v. Schwartz-Sackin & Co. Ltd* [1986] F.S.R. 490 at 494. See also *Moorgate Tobacco Co. Ltd. v. Philip Morris Ltd. (No. 2)* (1984) 56 C.L.R. 414 at 445, High Ct of Aus.
[24] See Schechter, note 21 above.

although such claims, in turn, often rest on the assumption that value = property, in itself "a massive exercise in question begging."[25] Nor is it enough to show that companies have often invested large sums of money on fostering a sign's selling power, since it still needs to be asked whether such investment should be encouraged and thus protected. While it may be appropriate to reward a manufacturer for maintaining a certain quality of goods, thereby protecting and enhancing the manufacturer's goodwill and, as a corollary, providing consumers with some form of assurance, it is not clear why investment in developing brand values should, as such, be protected. Moreover, even if such investment is deemed to be worthy of protection, it would seem to make more sense to employ a legal regime that has protection and encouragement of investment at its core, such as the design system, or, for that matter, a separate doctrine of misappropriation, rather than trying to secure protection of investment and advertising values through trade mark law.

Given the practical and theoretical problems of the advertising function of trade marks, and the apparent antipathy of the judiciary towards a move away from the origin function,[26] our analysis will proceed on the basis that trade mark protection for three-dimensional signs may be justified where such signs are capable of acting as a badge of origin, broadly defined. As will be seen, one of the difficulties with relying on an origin justification for trade mark protection for shapes is that even if consumers have come to recognise a certain shape as emanating from a particular source, it is by no means clear how they would react if a rival began to use the shape, given that both products are likely to be supported by a host of two-dimensional signs and other sources of information.

With this in mind, we will proceed to consider some of the objections to trade mark protection for product and packaging design. We will examine the provisions of the legislation which are designed to overcome these objections, how courts in Europe have interpreted these provisions and how courts might proceed in the future. We believe that such issues can be better understood in their historical context.

3. Historical Opposition and the 1994 Solution

Prior to the coming into force of the 1994 Act, the Trade Marks Registry had apparently refused applications for the shape of goods

---

[25] See Gordon, "On Owning Information: Intellectual Property and the Restitutionary Impulse" (1992) 78 Virg. L. Rev. 149 at 178, citing Lange, "Recognizing the Public Domain" (1981) 44 Law and Contemp. Prob 147 at 157. As Cohen famously noted, the argument is often circular where trade mark protection is purportedly based on economic value "when, as a matter of actual fact, the economic value of such a sales device depends upon the extent to which it is legally protected": "Transcendental Nonsense and the Functional Approach" (1935) 35 Colum. L. Rev. 809 at 815.
[26] See note 18, above and accompanying text.

and their containers ever since a Trade Mark Register was first established pursuant to the Trade Mark Registration Act 1875.[27] In *Coca-Cola's Trade Marks*[28] this practice was unanimously upheld by both the House of Lords and the Court of Appeal. Moreover, the Departmental Committees charged with reviewing trade mark law prior to the passage of the Directive had concluded that the definition of a mark should not be extended so as to include shapes or containers.[29] Thus, prior to the passage of the Directive, there was a formidable consensus of opinion in the United Kingdom that shapes and containers should not be registrable as trade marks. On closer inspection, it appears that there were three main objections to the registration of shapes as trade marks, namely: (1) shapes of goods and their packaging are incapable of acting as trade marks, that is to say, they cannot act as signs in the trade mark sense; (2) trade mark protection for shapes might lead to overly broad protection and might therefore "embarrass" other honest traders; (3) such protection might create a complex and undesirable overlap between trade marks and other forms of intellectual property, in particular, designs law.[30]

(i) Signs and Shapes

The first objection, that shapes are incapable of acting as signs, was raised early in the history of registered trade marks, in *Re James's Trade Mark*, decided in 1885.[31] This case concerned a registration for the figure of a black dome as a mark for graphite used for polishing, known as "black lead". The evidence was that the owners of the trade mark impressed an image of the dome on each block of black lead, many of the blocks themselves being made in the shape of a dome, although the owners also sold their blocks in cylindrical form.[32] In the course of an action for infringement, the defendants applied to rectify the register by expunging the mark. At first instance Pearson J. agreed that the mark was invalid and ordered the mark to be expunged on the grounds that the mark was merely a representation of the product and hence lacked distinctiveness.[33] The plaintiffs appealed. The defendants, who had given up the black lead business, were not represented at these proceedings. The Court of

---

[27] As to the practice of the Registry, see *Coca-Cola Trade Marks* [1986] R.P.C. 421 at 423–30, 450.
[28] *ibid.*
[29] See *Report of the Department Committee on the Law and Practice Relating to Trade Marks* (Goschen Committee) Cmd 4568 (1934); *British Trade Mark Law and Practice* (Mathys Committee) Cmnd 5601 (1974).
[30] In addition to these three principal objections some concern was expressed about the ways in which a three-dimensional trade mark might be represented for the purposes of registration. See, in particular, *Sobrefina SA's Trade Mark Application* [1974] R.P.C. 672. Also see *Swizzels Matlow's "Chewy Sweet" Application* [1998] R.P.C. 244.
[31] (1886) 33 Ch.D. 392.
[32] See (1885) 31 Ch. D. 340 at 341.
[33] *ibid.* at 343–344. As to the requirement of distinctiveness see Trade Mark Registration Act 1875 (c. 91), s. 10.

Appeal unanimously upheld the appeal, emphasising that the appellants were not seeking to claim a monopoly in the shape in which black lead was sold, but only the right to use the image of a dome as a trade mark on black lead sold in any shape. In the course of his judgment Lindley L.J. said:

> [a] mark must be something distinct from the thing marked. The thing itself cannot be a mark of itself, but here we have got the thing and we have got a mark on the thing, and the question is whether the mark on the thing is or is not a distinctive mark within the meaning of that Act. Of course the plaintiffs in this case have no monopoly in black lead of this shape. Anybody may make black lead of this shape provided he does not pass it off as the plaintiff's black lead. There is no monopoly in the shape, and I cannot help thinking that this has not been sufficiently kept in mind. What the plaintiffs have registered is a brand, a mark like a dome intended to represent a dome.

Lindley L.J.'s *dictum* was subsequently invoked by the Registry to justify its practice of refusing to register shapes and containers as trade marks.[34] It was also cited with approval by Lord Templeman in *Coca-Cola*.[35]

It is important to note, however, that Lindley L.J.'s judgment was primarily concerned with the question of distinctiveness. The issue before the Court of Appeal was whether a representation of one of the shapes in which a product is sold can be distinctive of those products. The plaintiff never claimed an exclusive right over the shape of their products and apparently no submission was made on this point. Lindley L.J.'s statement, of which so much has been made, was therefore *obiter* and was delivered without the benefit of full argument. Moreover, although the *dictum* has been cited with approval in later cases, there has been no attempt to explain or elaborate on the reasoning behind this statement. What then are we to make to this century-old piece of off-the-cuff judicial reasoning? As the 1994 Act now expressly declares that the shape of a product or its packaging can act as a trade mark,[36] the temptation must be to ignore a nineteenth century judicial statement to the contrary.[37] Nevertheless, the temptation to ignore Lindley L.J.'s *dictum* should be resisted since, as will be seen, despite the wording of the Act the question of whether a shape can act as a sign has been raised in

---

[34] See *Coca-Cola Trade Marks* [1986] R.P.C. 421 at 425.
[35] *ibid.* at 457–8.
[36] s. 1(1) of the 1994 act provides, "A trade mark may, in particular, consist of words (including personal names), designs, letters, numerals or the shape of goods or their packaging".
[37] Moreover, as we have already noted, it was sometimes possible to use the law of passing off to protect a three-dimensional mark, so that even before the 1994 Act came into force courts in the UK were not consistent in denying that a shape could act as a sign. See note 12, above.

recent cases, albeit unsuccessfully. More importantly, however, it forces us to confront the issue of how shapes are perceived by consumers, which, in turn, focuses our attention on the question of distinctiveness.

(ii) The Semiotics of Shapes: Three-Dimensional Marks under the 1994 Act

The most recent case in which the ability of a shape to act as a sign has been challenged is *Philips Electronics N.V. v. Remington Consumer Products Ltd*,[38] which touches on most of the issues we will be considering. The plaintiff, Philips, is the manufacturer of the "Philishave" shaver, which consists of three rotary shaving heads arranged in a equilateral triangle. The action was brought after the defendant, Remington, began producing a rival three headed rotary shaver. Philips had previously held a number of patents for aspects of their shavers, although these had expired by the time the action was brought. It also held a registered design over the shape and configuration of one version of its shaver, which it alleged the defendant had infringed. Finally, but most importantly for our purposes, Philips had obtained registered trade mark protection for a drawing of the face of their three headed shaver, which it also alleged had been infringed by Remington. Both parties agreed that his drawing also covered three-dimensional reproductions and the judge at first instance, Jacob J., agreed that this was the correct approach.[39] The registration was therefore treated as being for the shape of the head of the shaver. Remington's main defence to the trade mark claim was that the registration of the mark was invalid.

Remington's first argument was that the shape of the head of the shaver was not a sign. Jacob J. summarised the question he had to decide in language reminiscent of Lindley L.J.'s *dictum* in *Re James's Trade Mark*, the question was "can the thing itself also be a sign". Unsurprisingly, given the wording of the Act, it was held that the shape of the shaver could be a sign for trade mark purposes. Jacob J. emphasised the broad and open-ended definition of a sign found in both the Act and the Directive and concluded, "a sign is anything capable of conveying information".[40] Since the picture of the shaver head undoubtedly conveyed a message it was unarguably a sign. He also emphasised that the argument that something could never be a sign of itself was based on a metaphysical distinction, which is "hardly the sort of thing appropriate for a law designed for men of

---

[38] [1988] R.P.C. 283 (Patents Court); [1999] R.P.C. 809, CA.
[39] *ibid.* at 290. This issue was not dealt with by the Court of Appeal but this approach would not seem beyond question. In particular, it can be doubted whether Philips's mark had been adequately represented since it would not have been immediately apparent from looking at the register that a monopoly over use in three-dimensions was also being claimed.
[40] *ibid.* at 298.

commerce".[41] The Court of Appeal declined to elaborate on the meaning of "sign" in this context, but implicitly accepted that the head of the shaver could be a sign and was apparently content with Jacob J.'s formulation of a sign as being anything with an informational content.[42]

Given that signs consisting of the "shape of goods and their packaging" are now expressly included in the list of potential marks it would be plainly unarguable to contend that the shape of the shaver was incapable of acting as sign. Moreover, Jacob J.'s point concerning the inappropriateness of relying on metaphysical distinctions when interpreting a commercial statute has considerable force. However, the fact that the Act expressly recognises that *some* shapes are capable of acting as trade marks does not exhaust the difficulties surrounding the way shapes are perceived and understood, since the plaintiff/applicant will still have to demonstrate that the mark is distinctive of its goods. In applying a test of distinctiveness we are not concerned with what the message a sign conveys "is", but only with how the public perceives the mark. Nevertheless, the practical effect of the requirement of distinctiveness is to force us to reopen the question of if and when a shape can act as a sign, albeit from a different, consumer oriented, direction.

The argument that the head of the shaver lacked distinctiveness formed the basis of Remington's second objection to the mark.

(iii) The Distinctiveness of Shapes

Ultimately it was held, both at first instance and on appeal, that Philips's mark lacked distinctiveness. The reasoning was not, however, entirely consistent and a number of important issues remain to be clarified.

Prior to the decision of the Court of Appeal in *Philips v. Remington*[43] it had been thought that the requirement that the mark be "capable of distinguishing" did not add anything to the requirement that the mark have a distinctive character.[44] It was therefore thought that (at least in theory) an applicant would always be able to show that its mark was distinctive, provided it could establish sufficient public recognition; it was said that "there is no pre-set bar saying no matter how it is well proved that a mark has become a trade mark, it cannot be registered."[45] In contrast, in *Philips*

---

[41] *ibid.*
[42] [1999] R.P.C. 809 at 817; *cf. Qualitex v. Jacobson Products* 131 L Ed 2d 248 (1995) at 253: "human beings might use as a 'symbol' or 'device' almost anything at all that is capable of carrying meaning".
[43] [1999] R.P.C. 809.
[44] See *British Sugar v. James Robertson & Sons* [1996] R.P.C. 281 at 305 *per* Jacob J. This was said to be true "at least in relation to any sign within section 3(1)(b)-(d)."
[45] *ibid.* Jacob J. went on to add, "[t]hat is not to say that there are some signs which cannot in practice be registered. But the reason is simply that the applicant will be unable to prove that the mark has become a trade mark in practice—"Soap" for soap is an example. The bar . . . will be factual not legal."

v. Remington, Aldous L.J. (for the Court) came to the conclusion that the wording of the Act suggested that "different criteria" were to be applied when deciding whether the mark is "capable of distinguishing" to when deciding whether the mark has a distinctive character. The consequence of this is that there are now some marks that will not be registrable despite evidence that the public has come to regard the mark as a badge of origin. In other words, the apparent effect of this judgment is to re-create a requirement of distinctiveness at law, in that there are now marks which will remain unregistrable even though 100% distinctive in fact.[46]

Aldous L.J. then went on to give an example of the sorts of mark that would not even have a capacity to distinguish. A mark such as WELDED MESH would not even have the capacity to distinguish, so that "[w]hatever the extent of the use, whether or not it be monopoly use and whether or not there is evidence that the trade and public associate it with one person, it retains its primary meaning, namely mesh that is welded. It does not have any feature which renders it capable of distinguishing one trader's welded mesh from other traders' welded mesh."[47] By contrast, WELDMESH would be capable of distinguishing since, "despite its primary descriptive meaning, [it] has *sufficient capricious alteration* to enable it to acquire a secondary meaning" (emphasis added).

The (re)introduction of a separate requirement that the mark be capable of distinguishing does fit a literal reading of the Directive and the Act. There are, however, a number of problems with such a requirement. Most obviously, there is the problem of determining when there has been "sufficient capricious alteration".[48] The conclusion that there would be a sufficient alteration in the case of WELDMESH suggests that the threshold is set at a very low level, but if this is the case then it is no longer clear that a separate requirement of distinctiveness at law serves any useful purpose.[49] Moreover, even the attempt to draw a clear distinction between WELDMESH and WELDED MESH is open to question, since the latter in no way represents an "absolute" description of the product

---

[46] Described by Jacob J. as a "Pickwickian position": *British Sugar PLC v. James Robertson & Sons Ltd.* [1996] R.P.C. 281 at 305. *Cf. York Trade Mark* [1984] R.P.C. 231. The Trade Marks Act 1994 seems to have been intended to modify the previous position where a mark could be refused registration on the basis that it was incapable, in law, of distinguishing the applicant's goods even when absolutely distinctive in fact, a position described as "unattractive": see *Reform of Trade Marks Law* Cm (1203), citing Blanco White and Jacob (eds), *Kerly's Law of Trade Marks and Trade Names* (12th ed., Sweet & Maxwell, London, 1986) at p. 130.
[47] [1999] R.P.C. 809 at 818.
[48] Given high degree of labour, skill and judgment involved in the creation of a successful mark the idea that alteration must be *capricious* is itself unfortunate. As to the difficulties involved in developing a successful mark, see Blackett, *Trademarks* (Interbrand London, 1998).
[49] *cf Wrigley's "Light Green" Application* R 122/98-3, where the Third Board of Appeal at the OHIM indicated that capacity to distinguish was a separate ground of objection, but one which is easily met, since the mark will be capable of distinguishing if it could perform a trade mark function "in any given hypothetical and conceivable circumstance.".

and we can, for example, imagine still more descriptive marks.[50] This is not to say that WELDED MESH ought to be registrable, rather it suggests that there is a continuum of descriptiveness/distinctiveness and both WELDED MESH and WELDMESH fall somewhere along this line. Jacob J.'s approach in *British Sugar* would seem to reflect this underlying reality rather better, since it does not entail the construction of an artificial boundary between those signs which can only ever be descriptive and those which can acquire a secondary meaning.

Leaving aside the general difficulties created by the introduction of a requirement of distinctiveness at law, when we come to apply the test of "capricious alteration" to shapes we face yet further difficulties. In deciding that the shape of the head of the shaver was not even capable of distinguishing Philips' goods, Aldous L.J. stated that the effect of the capricious alteration test is that "a shape of an article cannot be registered in respect of goods of that shape unless it contains some addition to the shape of the article which has trade mark significance." The problem with this formulation is that it seems to require some conception of what the shape "is" before we can ask whether there has been a three-dimensional addition to that shape.

Taken literally, the above formulation would seem to rest on precisely the kind of distinction that Jacob J., at first instance, described as being out of place in a commercial statute. It might, therefore, be better to ask whether there has been a capricious *selection* of features in these cases.[51] The ideal solution, however, would be to return to the *British Sugar* position and apply a single test of distinctive character. The obvious reply from the perspective of those who wish to see policy considerations built into the test of distinctiveness is that it is far more honest to build such concerns into a separate requirement of distinctiveness at law, in that the mark will be treated as lacking distinctiveness, irrespective of the level of public recognition. Whilst this point has some force, it does not outweigh the difficulties that we have identified and, in any event, it seems that the Court of Appeal was also prepared to see policy considerations built into the distinctive character test.

We now turn to consider the question of when a mark will have a distinctive character. There are in fact two separate questions which need to be addressed here: first, the circumstances in which a consumer will treat a three-dimensional sign as a badge of origin; and second, the extent to which our approach to the question of

---

[50] *e.g.* MESH MADE BY WELDING METAL RODS TOGETHER. Also see *Weldmesh TM* [1965] R.P.C. 590.
[51] Such reformulation might also be useful in cases where a mark denoting geographical origin has come to acquire a secondary meaning, since in these cases it is the selection of the word in the first place which involves a capricious element. This would have the effect of ensuring that cases like *York Trade Mark* (fn. 46, above) would not be excluded on the basis that they lacked the capacity to distinguish.

distinctiveness should be modified in order to take policy objectives into account.

(v) Capturing the Consumer

As we have already noted, despite the fact that three-dimensional marks could not be registered in the United Kingdom prior to 1994, some protection for such marks was available through the law of passing off.[52] It was therefore in the context of passing off actions that United Kingdom courts first had to consider how consumers react to different sorts of shapes. In a number of cases, claims for passing off have failed since consumers usually do not buy an article of that type because they associate its shape with a particular manufacturer, but because they find the particular shape to be attractive. For example, in *British American Glass Co. Ltd. v. Winton Products (Blackpool) Ltd* it was held that a purchaser of an ornamental glass dog would be primarily concerned with what the product itself looked like.[53] Similarly, where the issue concerned the appearance of the plaintiff's furniture, there was no evidence that the appearance of the furniture was associated by the public with any particular manufacturer.[54] In such cases, consumers do not regard the shape as an indication of source.[55]

These cases illustrate precisely the sorts of difficulties that now confront the courts when deciding whether a three-dimensional mark is distinctive: how can consumer reaction to the shape of goods or packaging be assessed? This enquiry is complicated by the fact that the goods or the packaging will almost invariably be accompanied by a word or device mark, so that it can be difficult (and highly artificial) to attempt to determine what consumers understand by the shape in and of itself.

More generally, it needs to be recognised that there is probably an element of circularity in attempting to assess what consumers understand by a particular shape, since it seems likely that their understanding will itself be partly determined by what we allow to be protected as a trade mark. That is to say, if we allow certain types of shapes to be monopolised, consumers will come to understand shapes of that type as denoting the goods of a particular manufacturer. If, on the other hand, we refuse to recognise certain

---

[52] See generally, Wadlow, *The Law of Passing Off* (2nd ed, Sweet & Maxwell, London, 1995) at pp. 426–61; Evans, "Passing Off and the Problem of Product Simulation" (1968) 31 M.L.R. 642.
[53] [1962] R.P.C. 230 at 232. See also *Politechnika Ipari Szovetkezet v. Dallas Print Print Transfers Ltd.* [1982] F.S.R. 529 at 538–9 (shape of cube puzzle); *Universal Agencies (London) Ltd. v. Swolf* [1959] R.P.C. 247 at 248 (corkscrews in shape of lady's face/clown's head).
[54] *Hensher Ltd v. Restawhile Upholstery Ltd* [1975] R.P.C. 31 at 38–9; *Benchairs Ltd. v. Chair Centre Ltd.* [1974] R.P.C. 429 at 434–6. See also *Blundell v. Sidney Margolis* (1951) 68 R.P.C. 71 at 72 (bubble gum in shape of false teeth).
[55] See *Hodgkinson & Corby Ltd. v. Wards Mobility Services ltd.* [1994] I.W.L.R. 1564 at 1573–4; *Tot Toys Ltd v. Mitchell* [1993] 1.N.Z.L.R 325 at 352–3.

types of shapes as trade marks, consumers will be forced to look to other ways of distinguishing between manufacturers.

In practice, it seems that the courts may try to avoid many of these difficult questions by assuming that three-dimensional marks lack distinctiveness and refuse the registration in the absence of distinctiveness acquired through use. This was the approach adopted in *Philips v. Remington*, where Jacob J. assumed that a "picture of an article is equivalent to a description of it", an approach subsequently endorsed by the Court of Appeal. The Court of Appeal also recently upheld the hearing officer's rejection of applications for composite marks consisting of the shape of a bottle, a label and its colour in class 3 (polishing, scouring and abrasive preparations; detergents and soaps; bleaching preparations).[56] These applications were refused on the ground that the subject-matter of each application was devoid of any distinctive character and hence objectionable under section 3(1)(b).[57] Whilst the Court of Appeal did not go so far as to say that three-dimensional marks or, as in this case, the get-up of a product will always lack inherent distinctiveness, a number of statements seem to point in this direction. This also seems to be the approach adopted by the UK Registry, as can be seen from a number of recent decisions.

In *Jaleel's Application* there was an attempt to register a bottle for non-alcoholic beverages in class 32.[58] The bottle was said to be distinctive because it had an unusual base and a low height to circumference ratio, giving it a spherical or "chubby" appearance. In rejecting the argument that these features were in themselves sufficient to render the bottle distinctive, the hearing officer stated "[t]here is no evidence before me as to whether the public would perceive the mark applied for as a badge of trade origin, nor is there any evidence that, even if the height to width ratio is lower than other bottles, it is so different as to be memorable and therefore distinctive." He added, "I do not say that the mark is unregistrable but in the absence of any evidence of recognition as a trade mark by the public or evidence of distinctiveness acquired through use made of it I, consider that it would be inappropriate to grant a monopoly in this particular bottle shape".[59]

In other cases the hearing officer has concluded that the marks lacked distinctiveness even though the applicant adduced evidence of acquired distinctiveness. For example, in *Wickes Application*[60] the

---

[56] See *Hodgkinson & Corby Ltd. v. Wards Mobility Services Ltd.* [1994] 1 W.L.R. 1564 at 1573–4; *Tot Toys Ltd v. Mitchell* [1993] 1 N.Z.L.R. 325 at 352–3.
[57] *Ibid.*, pp. 385. On the scope of s. 3(1)(b), Robert Walker L.J. (*ibid.*, at 382) stated "despite its position in s. 3(1) of the 1994 Act, para. (b) performs a residual or sweeping-up function, backing up paras (c) and (d)."
[58] O/221/98.
[59] *ibid* at 5. Also see *Procter & Gamble's "Soap Tablet" Application* [1998] R.P.C. 710: "bone shape" of the applicant's soap was merely one of a number of variants of the traditional rectangular soap pattern and there was no evidence that the public regarded any of these variants as a badge of origin.
[60] [1998] R.P.C. 698.

applicants adduced trade evidence to the effect that their "square catalogue" shape had been extensively distributed and was unique in the DIY industry. This did not assist the applicants, however, since it did not establish that the *public* regarded the shape as a badge of origin.[61]

In *Chatham's Application* it was held that sales and advertising data did not establish the distinctiveness of a jam jar since "the evidence shows that the jar is always used with other distinguishing matter... and there is no reason to conclude that it is capable of distinguishing alone".[62] Evidence as to the impact of the jar alone was insufficient to establish distinctiveness, since the respondents to a questionnaire only represented a small proportion of the relevant public and although there was some evidence of association between the shape and the applicants it fell "far short of establishing that the relevant public regard the sign applied for as a badge of origin".[63]

The fate of applications for three-dimensional marks at the Community Trade Mark Office (OHIM) provides some evidence that the OHIM may also start with the presumption that shapes lack distinctiveness. In *British Petroleum Co. Plc's Application*,[64] the Second Board of Appeals rejected BP's appeal against the examiner's finding that the shape of two containers for oils and fuels lacked distinctiveness. Concluding that "an undertaking may not generally be granted the exclusive right to the use of material containing utilitarian or functional features which its competitors and others need for their goods",[65] the Board of Appeals went on to say that signs consisting of "shapes of essential things of everyday use such as bottles and containers for liquid, should require a very high degree of distinctiveness to be entitled to registration."[66] This conclusion could be justified by an analogy with the exclusion from registrability of shapes resulting from the nature of the goods themselves.[67] It was not sufficient to establish inherent distinctiveness to show that certain elements of the shape were arbitrary. Rather, there must be something "conspicuously different" about the shape that distinguishes it from other containers of that

---

[61] *ibid.*, at 706.
[62] O/157/98 at 4. This case concerned a jam jar with an unusual lip and pattern around the base, and an unusually high height to circumference ratio.
[63] *ibid.* at 5. Also see *Swizzels Matlow's "Love Heart" Application* O/155/98, in particular, at 4; *Swizzels Matlow's "Chewy Sweet" Application* [1998] R.P.C. 244 at 247–248; *Yakult's Application* O/269/98: evidence that the shape alone had attained a reasonable level of public recognition in the South East of England did not assist the applicant since this primarily related to distinctiveness acquired after the date of application; *Roho's Application* O/169/98: public would not see functional shape of an air-cushion designed to prevent pressure sores as a trade mark "without a considerable amount of education".
[64] [1999] E.T.M.R. 282.
[65] *ibid.* at 287. For an account of the U.S. doctrine of functionality and its role in assessing whether a shape is protectable as a trade mark, see note 38 below and the accompanying text.
[66] *ibid.* at 287–8.
[67] *ibid.*

type, so that consumers of the product regard the shape "primarily as an indication of origin".[68]

In contrast, the OHIM has recently accepted LEGO's building block for registration as a three-dimensional mark consisting of the product itself. Once again, however, the OHIM denied registration on the basis of inherent distinctiveness. The mark was only accepted on the basis of distinctiveness acquired through use.[69]

We can see from the above decisions that a presumption against registrability can be justified by reference to consumer psychology. The argument is that consumers will not normally understand a shape to be a badge of origin, in particular, because shape marks will normally be "supporting"[70] or "limping"[71] marks: consumers will still differentiate the product by reference to more traditional forms of mark. Consumers will therefore have to be "educated" into understanding a shape as a badge of origin, so that, in the absence of proof of such education, the sign will lack distinctiveness.

The difficulty with the above argument is that it rests on the sort of untested assumption about consumer psychology which seems to have dogged so much of trade mark theory.[72] In addition, as we noted above, it seems to involve a degree of circularity: there is no recognition that consumer reaction can itself be partly determined by the sorts of signs we allow to be monopolised. The presumption against distinctiveness also places a good deal of emphasis on the fact that in the case of a three-dimensional mark the public will first have to be educated into understanding that the shape is a sign, before it can educate the public as to the origin of goods. Yet it seems likely that even in the case of our paradigmatic two-dimensional trade mark, the invented word, there will be some minimal need to educate the public into understanding that the word is intended to act as a trade mark.[73] The distinction therefore seems rest on the degree of preliminary education required, rather than any truly intrinsic difference between the two types of mark.

A further level of artificiality has been imposed in cases where for

---

[68] *ibid.* at 288. BP were also prevented from adducing evidence of acquired distinctiveness, since they had not submitted any such evidence to the examiner and it would be undesirable to allow applicants to bring forward such evidence at the appeal stage since "if such a situation were to be permitted, applicants would simply be disposed to make submissions on inherent distinctiveness at the examination stage of the process and, only if unsuccessful, undertake the more burdensome task of trying to demonstrate factual distinctiveness . . . at the appeal stage": *ibid.* at 289.
[69] Application No. 000107029. See further, oami.eu.int/en/news-3Dm.htm
[70] *Philips v. Remington*, above, note 47 above at 817.
[71] *Philips v. Remington*, above, note 5 per Jacob J.
[72] See Pickering, *Trade Marks in Theory and Practice* (Hart, Oxford, 1998), in particular at pp. 153, 157.
[73] In many cases this education will flow from the context in which the sign is used and its positioning on the goods. The fact that this will often happen automatically, however, shows the importance of cultural norms in this context—when we see a mark used in a certain way we "know" that it is a trade mark. Yet this merely takes us back to the point we made earlier, that these expectations are themselves partly determined by the type of sign that we allow traders to monopolise.

a long period there has only been one manufacturer of a particular product, as may well be the case if the product is initially protected by a patent and/or a registered design. In relation to descriptive and laudatory words there seems to be an assumption in such cases that mere association in the minds of the public between the (descriptive) name of a product and a particular manufacturer will not be sufficient to establish that the public understands the name as a trade mark.[74] At first instance in *Philips v. Remington*, Jacob J., in finding that the mark lacked distinctiveness, applied the same approach in relation to shapes, stating "[t]o some if no word mark is used, it also suggests manufacture by Philips. However, that is because no-one hitherto had made such shavers—a matter hardly to the point". Unfortunately, Jacob J. failed to explain why the view of some consumers is "hardly to the point". After all, if some consumers understand a particular shape as "suggesting manufacture" by a particular producer this would seem *exactly* to the point.[75] A similar approach was adopted by the hearing officer in *Roho's Application*.[76] Although the hearing officer accepted that there was considerable evidence of the public "associating" the shape of the air-cushion with the plaintiffs, this was not sufficient to establish that the public regarded the shape as a badge of origin, because such association was inevitable given that the applicants were for a long period the only persons entitled to manufacture the goods.[77]

As we will see, there are good reasons to support a general presumption against distinctiveness in the case of three-dimensional marks, and particularly good reasons for supporting such a presumption in cases where the product has previously been protected by some other intellectual property right. (A similar principle with a long lineage applies in respect of the names of patented products). At the same time, however, it would seem entirely artificial to attempt to draw a distinction between when consumers associate a shape with a particular manufacturer and when they understand goods of a certain shape as having been produced by a particular manufacturer. Indeed, the limitations of this distinction were exposed by the hearing officer in *Roho*. In attempting to distinguish between association and distinctiveness, he cited a passage from *Unilever Limited's (striped toothpaste No.2) Trade Mark*,[78] where Hoffman J. said that association could not be equated with distinctiveness since "the fact that members of the public now associate that feature with his product tells one nothing about what

---

[74] See, in particular, *British Sugar v. Robertson* [1996] R.P.C. 281 at 302; *Shredded Wheat Co. Ltd. v. Kellogg Co. of Great Britain Ltd* (1939) 57 R.P.C. 137. A similar principle applies in the law of passing off: Young, *The Law of Passing Off* (3rd ed., Longman, London, 1994) at 31–4.
[75] The Court of Appeal seems to have broadly supported Jacob J.'s approach, note 47 above.
[76] O/169/98, see note. 64 and accompanying text, above.
[77] *ibid.* in particular, at 16, 19. The hearing officer also held that the mark was in any event unregistrable since the shape achieved a technical result. This aspect of this decision is dealt with below.
[78] [1987] R.P.C. 13.

they would think if a product with a similar feature came upon the market". Not only is this statement at odds with the principle that we view the question of distinctiveness at the date of application,[79] read literally it is also meaningless, since it could be said that all trade marks will lack distinctiveness when compared with an identical sign that a future trader might come to use on identical goods. Hoffman J.'s statement is therefore probably best understood as indicating that the question of distinctiveness has to take account of the needs of potential competitors and as such is really a statement of underlying policy.

Moreover, it is not necessarily easy to justify a presumption against distinctiveness given the structure and wording of the Directive and the Regulation, since it is a presumption which is dependent on a prioritisation of more traditional forms of trade marks: the question that will be asked seems to be "is this shape distinctive of the applicants goods, given that it is used alongside a word/device mark?" However, given the structure of both the Regulation and the Directive, it would be equally possible to ask the opposite question, that is, "is this word/device mark distinctive given that it is used alongside a shape mark?"

It is also clear that a less restrictive approach has been adopted in other European countries. For example, in *Ide Line A.G. v. Philips Electronics*[80] the Swedish Court of Appeal upheld the validity of Philips's registration for its shaver head, relying on the finding, supported by survey evidence, that the shaver had a "strongly established" reputation in the market.[81] Similarly, it seems that a more relaxed approach has been adopted in the Benelux countries, where a three-dimensional sign will apparently be treated as distinctive "provided the public *could* (reasonably) perceive the sign as being distinctive of the product of an undertaking",[82] suggesting that there is no automatic presumption that the mark is descriptive in the absence of proof of acquired secondary meaning.[83]

Given that the latter approach seems to fit more comfortably with the wording of the Directive, how can the alternative (emerging U.K.) approach be defended? We believe that the answer lies in the need to ensure that trade mark protection is kept within appropriate

---

[79] See *Re Minnesota Mining and Manufacturing Co.* (1924) 41 R.P.C. 237 at 240 but *cf. Avon Trade Mark* (1985) R.P.C. 43 at 47–8 (Registry). See generally, Blanco White and Jacob, above, at p. 98.
[80] [1997] E.T.M.R. 377.
[81] *ibid.* at 385. This point is also discussed in *Philips v. Remington* [1998] R.P.C. 283 at 303.
[82] Strowell, "Benelux: A Guide to the Validity of Three-dimensional Trade Marks in Europe" [1995] E.I.P.R. 154 at 156. Authors' emphasis. See, *e.g., Kabushiki Kaisha Yakult Honsha v. Danone Nederland BV* [1998] E.T.M.R. 465 at 475 (District Court, The Hague) (shape of milk container found distinctive on facts).
[83] A further level of uncertainty is added by the French Intellectual Property Code, which treats the specific exceptions to the validity of three-dimensional marks (considered below) as factors to be considered when assessing the distinctiveness of the mark, which are not subject to evidence of acquired secondary meaning. See Strowell, *ibid*, p. 155 arguing that the French legislature has wrongly interpreted the Directive.

limits. Whilst this is also the role of the express exclusions, as Jacob J. has pointed out, there is nothing to stop similar factors being taken into account when considering the requirement of distinctiveness.[84] It seems, therefore, that it would be better if we concentrated less on consumer psychology and instead focused on a second justification for a presumption against distinctiveness that we can isolate from the U.K. cases, namely, that we must strive to protect other honest traders.

In order to justify and illustrate the above, policy oriented, approach to the question of distinctiveness, we will now turn to consider the following questions: (1) What are the potential dangers created by the registration of three-dimensional marks which might justify a presumption against distinctiveness? (2) What is the role of the express exclusions in minimising these dangers? (3) Given the existence of the express exclusions can Jacob J.'s assertion at first instance in *Philips v. Remington* that there is nothing to stop similar factors being taken into account when considering the requirement of distinctiveness really be justified? (4) If it is permissible to build policy considerations into the test of distinctiveness, how should such a test be applied? A consideration of the first question leads us back to the objections to three-dimensional trade marks that we initially identified. Again, it is to be hoped that an understanding of these objections will help us to clarify the issues that need to be resolved today.

(vi) Manufacturing a Monopoly

The gravest potential danger created by the registration of three-dimensional marks which might justify a presumption against distinctiveness is the risk that the registration of shapes may lead to the creation of overly broad monopolies. Concerns about the monopoly implications of allowing three-dimensional marks to be registered were first raised by the Goschen Committee.[85] Having considered the suggestion that the definition of a mark should be extended so as to include containers, the Committee stated:

> We are unable... to recommend the inclusion of containers as "marks". The protection afforded by registration under the Acts may be of indefinite duration, and we think that the grant of monopolies for indefinite periods for the shape of say a bottle or jar might prove embarrassing to other traders and to the public generally.[86]

---

[84] *Philips v. Remington* [1998] R.P.C. 283 at 302.
[85] *Report of the Departmental Committee on the Law and Practice Relating to Trade Marks*, above, note 29. Similar concerns had been raised in the context of passing off actions. See, *e.g.*, *Edge & Sons Ltd. v. Nicolls & Sons Ltd* (1911) 28 R.P.C. 53.
[86] *Goschen Committee*, note 29 above, para. 13.

Three-dimensional Trade Marks: Should the Directive Be Reshaped? 157

A similar point was made forty years later by the Mathys Committee.[87] When considering whether the definition of a mark should be broadened so as to include the shape of the goods and/or their containers, the Committee said:

> Whilst there are theoretically an infinite number of shapes available, in practical terms the choice must be limited by manufacturing techniques and by the necessity of finding a readily recognisable form which consumers could identify in the course of ordinary trade... [W]e can visualise a sequence of events starting with the arbitrary choice of shapes of the goods and promotion of these shapes leading to perpetual monopolies and a consequent restriction on shapes available to all other traders in a way which we believe to be entirely unacceptable.[88]

It is clear from other parts of the report that the "sequence of events" the Committee referred to was a reference to the potentially damaging effects for competition of the cumulative effect of the appropriation of shapes by different traders.[89] Although the Committee did not say so expressly, this problem is presumably most likely to arise in relation to new products, since there are unlikely to be shapes which lack distinctiveness by virtue of their customary use in the trade.

The above danger can be illustrated by imaging a nascent chocolate industry. We can imagine that as new traders place their products on the market, more and more packaging shapes become appropriated. For example, cylinders (Smarties), spheres (Terry's Chocolate Orange), triangular prisms (Toblerone), ovoids (Kinder Egg), rectangular boxes (After Eight) and square based pyramids (Ferrero Rocher) might all be eligible for registration as trade marks. Although some of the above may be registrable given the chocolate industry as it exists today, the danger of monopoly is limited since a number of the above shapes will lack distinctiveness, so that a new manufacturer will always have a number of (presumably affordable) packaging shapes from which to choose. In our imaginary industry, however, this would not be the case, so that manufacturers would be forced to seek out ever more exotic shapes with the result that a new manufacturer might find it commercially impossible to enter the marketplace.[90]

Fears about the monopolisation of shapes were also one of the main justifications for the House of Lords decision in *Re Coca Cola Trade Marks*, where an attempt to register the shape of the Coca Cola bottle failed. The application to register the shape of the bottle as a

---

[87] *British Trade Mark Law and Practice* Cmnd 5601 (1971), above, note 29.
[88] Mathys Report, para. 58.
[89] Mathys Report, para. 55.
[90] A similar point was made by Aldous L.J. in *Philips v. Remington*, above, note 47 above at 818.

trade mark was, according to Lord Templeman, an "attempt to expand the boundaries of intellectual property and to convert a protective law into a source of monopoly",[91] raising "the spectre of a total and perpetual monopoly in containers and articles".[92]

(vii) Trade Marks by Design

A related objection to the registration of three-dimensional marks is that this would create a complex and undesirable overlap between trade marks and other forms of intellectual property, in particular, designs law. The undesirability of this overlap was mentioned by the Goschen Committee,[93] and the Mathys Committee subsequently associated itself with the Goschen Committee's view.[94] Surprisingly, the Departmental Committees seem to have taken it as self-evident that an overlap between different intellectual property systems is undesirable and therefore failed to spell out their reasoning. This is unfortunate, since overlap would seem to raise three interrelated objections.

One potential objection is that any overlap would unnecessarily complicate the law by creating alternative methods of protecting the same subject-matter. These alternate routes would provide different periods of protection, different tests of infringement and different exceptions and defences. This first objection is therefore based on a desire to preserve the separateness of legal structures.

The second potential objection takes the function of the registered design and patent systems as its starting point. The most common understanding of the function of registration is that it places the design/invention in the public domain after a certain period of time has elapsed. The process of registration and the accompanying disclosure to the world can therefore be seen as the *quid pro quo* for the granting of a monopoly. On this view of the rationale behind the patent and design systems, it is possible to say that once the period of registration has expired the public has a right to use the invention/design and it should not be possible to use trade mark law to interfere with this right.[95] This objection would apply with even more force in cases where the owner of the design is able to

---

[91] [1986] R.P.C. 421, 456. *Cf. British Leyland Motor Corp Ltd v. Armstrong Patents Ltd* [1986] 2 W.L.R. 400, esp. 413, 419–21 and 435–7.
[92] [1986] R.P.C. 421, 457.
[93] See Goschen Report, above, note 29, para. 13.
[94] See Mathys Report, above, note 29, para. 60. It is also noteworthy that the owners/applicants had previously held registered designs for their products in both the *James's Trade Mark* and *Coca-Cola* cases. This was also true in *Sobrefina's Application* [1974] R.P.C. 672.
[95] See Goschen Report, above, 29, para 13; Mathys Report, above, note 29, para. 60. Also see *Qualitex v. Jacobson Products* 131 L Ed 2d 248 (1995), in particular, at 254. It should also be noted that there are alternative views of the function(s) of the registered design system. For example, it has been argued that one function of registration is to centralise information about design in such a way that the registration system operates as a "collective memory". See Bently, "Requiem for Registration" in Firth (ed.), 1 *Perspectives on Intellectual Property: The Prehistory and Development of Intellectual Property Systems*, in particular, at 44–46.

use the period of monopoly to acquire distinctiveness as a trade mark—the owner of the design would be using a monopoly intended to benefit the public for private gain.

The third objection is closely related to the second, but focuses on the trade mark applicant's state of mind, rather than on the cost to the public. From this perspective it would be unconscionable for the owner of a registered design to seek trade mark protection, since the registered design would have been obtained on the understanding that at some point the design would fall into the public domain.[96]

It is important at this stage to note an important difference between the objections. The first objection, which focuses on the purity of legal structures, would apply with equal force irrespective of whether the trade mark applicant had ever held a patent or registered design. By contrast, the third objection would only apply where the trade mark applicant owned an earlier intellectual property right and was seeking overlapping or sequential protection. The second objection also applies with most force in cases where the applicant has previously enjoyed patent or design protection, since in these cases the public is directly deprived of a benefit it could have expected to enjoy. But more generally, overly broad trade mark protection might make other intellectual property systems redundant, so that few inventions/designs fall into the public domain.

The courts have at various times shown an awareness of all three objections we identified. At the same time, however, some degree of overlapping protection has always seemed inevitable, since the discrete statutory and common law regimes are not, generally speaking, mutually exclusive,[97] and the balance of authority favours the view that there was never an absolute prohibition on the registration of a trade mark in cases where the applicant had previously enjoyed some other form of intellectual property right over the substance of the mark applied for.[98]

The question of whether there should be an absolute prohibition on the registration of shapes protected by other forms of intellectual property under the 1994 Act arose at first instance in *Philips v. Remington*.[99] Remington argued that it would be contrary to public policy to allow a shape protected by a patent to be registered as a trade mark and, as such, the shape of the shape of the head of the

---

[96] *cf.* Jacob J.'s discussion of the "election and "dedication" theories. See *Philips v. Remington* [1998] R.P.C. 283 at 310.
[97] *e.g.*, it has always been possible to claim copyright protection for an artistic work which is used as a trade mark. But see Copyright Act 1956, s. 10; Copyright, Designs and Patents Act 1988, ss. 51, 236: forcing an owner to rely on copyright *or* designs law.
[98] See, most recently, *Interlego AG's Trade Mark Applications* [1998] R.P.C. 69 at 114. Also see *Sobrefina SA's Trade Mark Application* [1974] R.P.C. 672; *United States Playing Card Company's Application* [1908] 1 Ch. 197. But *cf. Charles Goodall & Son v. John Waddington* (1924) 41 R.P.C. 658; *Moore's Modern Methods Application* (1919) 36 R.P.C. 6.
[99] This point was apparently argued before the Court of Appeal, but was not dealt with in the judgment.

shaver had been registered contrary to section 3(3)(a).[1] Remington sought some support for this view from the White Paper which preceded the 1994 Act,[2] which suggested that the trade marks system should not confer "an automatic and indefinite extension of the monopoly conferred by a patent design or copyright".[3] Jacob J. rejected this argument and concluded that the exclusion under section 3(3)(a) was confined to matters of *ordre publique* and was "not concerned with economic grounds of objection.[4] He also concluded that the White Paper could not be used as an aid to the construction of the Act, since the Act was intended to implement an E.C. Directive.[5] Thus, in relation to shapes under the 1994 Act, the same rule has been adopted as in relation to other types of mark under previous legislation. There is no rule which prevents a mark being registered simply because it has previously enjoyed some other form of intellectual property protection. This is undoubtedly the correct approach given that the Directive and the Act set out exhaustively the criteria for registrability. However, as will be seen, the desire to force right owners to rely on the most appropriate form of protection (having regard to term, scope of protection, defences and so forth[6]) does inform the interpretation of the specific exclusions contained in sections 3(2)(a)-(c).[7]

(viii) Managing Monopolies

As should be clear from what has already been said, section 3(2) of the Act contains three express exclusions which are specifically designed to limit the scope of trade mark protection for shapes. In

---

[1] S. 3(3) provides, "A mark shall not be registered if it is—(a) contrary to public policy or accepted principles of morality".
[2] *Reform of Trade Marks Law*, Cm. 1203 (1990).
[3] *ibid.* at para. 2.20.
[4] *Philips v. Remington* [1998] R.P.C. 283 at 310.
[5] In *British Sugar plc v. James Robertson & Sons Ltd.* [1996] R.P.C. 281, Jacob J. justified his refusal to take the White Paper into account by reference to the fact that when considering the meaning of the Directive the ECJ would not refer to a document which is "merely opinion on the meaning of the Directive and not part of the *travaux preparatoire*". It is submitted, however, that this approach may not be correct. In particular, Jacob J. does not seem to have considered the argument that although the ECJ would not refer to a U.K. White Paper, national Governments do have an opportunity to intervene before the ECJ and through such interventions the ECJ does take their views into account. Since national governments do not normally have an opportunity to express their views on the meaning of a Directive before a national court, it is at least arguable that national courts should be prepared to look at other sources to discover the view of a national government. This would suggest that courts should not only be prepared to look at British White Papers and the like, but also equivalents documents from other European countries, although such documents would have to be treated with much greater caution than would be the case if you were construing a domestic Act. In any event, it might be noted that the White Paper did not provide Remington with much assistance as the statement about overlap arises in the context of a discussion of the specific exclusions now contained in s. 3(2) of the 1994 Act.
[6] *cf.* Jacob J.'s discussion of the "election and dedication" theories. See *Philips v. Remington* [1998] R.P.C. 283 at 310.
[7] This is apparently what the Government intended. See *Reform of Trade Marks Law*, above, note 2 p. 160, paras 2.20–2.21.

Philips v. Remington, Remington argued that the shape of the head of the shaver fell within all three of the section 3(2) exclusions. That section provides:

> A sign shall not be registered as a trade mark if it consists exclusively of-
> (a) the shape which results from the nature of the goods themselves,
> (b) the shape of goods which is necessary to achieve a technical result, or
> (c) the shape which gives substantial value to the goods.

Before turning to look at the reasoning at first instance and on appeal in detail, it is worth emphasising the presence of the world *exclusively* in the opening words of this subsection. This would suggest that provided that some features of the mark fall outside the exclusion then the mark is registrable. In *Philips v. Remington* the parties apparently agreed that this meant that "if any feature of the shape which is not trivial does not fall within one of the exclusions, the exceptions do not apply".[8] As a result, the exclusivity requirement received only very limited consideration. In particular, the difficult issue that is left open relates to how the courts will approach the question of infringement. For example, we can imagine a scenario where a shape as a whole is registrable due to the presence of some non-trivial feature which does not fall within one of the exclusions. Could a defendant infringe by copying only the excluded features? The most obvious way of approaching this question would be to treat the excluded matter as if it were subject to a disclaimer.[9] However, neither the Act nor the Directive expressly mandates this result.

As to the first of the exclusions, shapes which result from the nature of the goods themselves, the most difficult issue is deciding what "the goods themselves" are in this context, since the answer given to this preliminary question would seem to be determinative of whether the mark is excluded. To take two extremes, if we treat the goods themselves as being all articles which can be used to shave, then it is clear that the shape of Philips's shaver does not result from the fact that it is such an article. In contrast, if we treat the goods themselves as being all three-headed rotary shavers with the shaving heads arranged in a equilateral triangle then it is clear that the shape does result from the fact that it is such a shaver.

At first instance, Jacob J. said that the correct approach is to ask how the goods are viewed as articles of commerce.[10] In this instance the goods themselves were held to be all electric shavers since "such

---

[8] *Philips v. Remington* [1998] R.P.C. 283 at 304.
[9] See, as to the effect of a disclaimer, *The European v. Economist* [1996] F.S.R. 431. Also see Registered Designs Act 1949 s. 7(6), but *cf. Granada TM* [1979] R.P.C. 303, in particular at 306.
[10] *Philips v. Remington* [1998] R.P.C. 283 at 305.

shavers are seen as a single type of commercial article."[11] The shape of the Philips shaver obviously did not result from the fact that it was a type of electric shaver. On appeal, Aldous L.J. agreed that "the goods" in this case were electric shavers, but Jacob J.'s commercial equivalence test was implicitly rejected. Rather, the Court said that the words "the goods" refer to the goods in respect of which the trade mark is registered.[12] Aldous L.J. went on to state that the purpose of the section is "to exclude from registration basic shapes that should be available for use by the public at large".[13] He added, "it is difficult to envisage such shapes, except those that are produced in nature such as bananas".[14] If this interpretation is correct then it seems that the first of the section 3(2) exclusions is without purpose or effect, since shapes produced in nature would in any event lack distinctiveness.

A literal reading of the second exclusion, that is the shape *of goods* which are necessary to achieve a technical result, suggests that this provision does not apply to packaging shapes. This reading can be further reinforced by contrasting the wording of this provision with the wording of the other two exclusion, both of which refer to "the shape" rather than to "the shape of goods". If this interpretation is correct then it seems this provision could not be used to exclude packaging features which, for example, helped to preserve perishable goods. More generally, this provides us with an indication that the express exclusions may not provide an adequate set of safeguards in the case of packaging shapes, even though, as we have seen, the progressive monopolisation of such shapes may be just as harmful to competititors as allowing manufacturers to monopolise the shapes of products themselves.

However, the most difficult issue is determining what "necessary" means in this context. A literal interpretation might suggest that a shape will not be *necessary* to achieve a technical result if there is any other way of achieving that result, no matter how functional the applicant's shape may be.[15] This interpretation was accepted by the Swedish Court of Appeal in the *Ide Line* case,[16] but was rejected by both Jacob J. and the Court of Appeal in *Philips v. Remington*.[17] Instead they interpreted the section as meaning that a shape would be excluded if its dominant features result from the fact that it achieves a technical effect.[18] As Aldous L.J. put it, the exclusion will

---

[11] *ibid.*
[12] Above, note 47 at 820.
[13] *ibid.* at 18.
[14] *ibid.*
[15] Philips argued that a number of different configurations could be used to produce the same effect at an equivalent cost. See further, *ibid.*, at 820.
[16] *Ide Line Aktiebolag AG v. Philips Electronics NV* [1997] E.T.M.R. 377 at 387–90.
[17] Above, note 5, in particular (at first instance), at 308: "One can hardly think of any object which *must* be of a particular shape to perform a function". He might have added that any example we can think of would almost certainly be caught by the first exclusion.
[18] But *cf.* note 8, above, and accompanying text: s. 3(2) will in any event only apply if the mark consists exclusively of excluded subject-matter.

apply if "the essential features of the shape are attributable only to the technical result."[19] Significantly, he also stated that these "are the types of shapes which come from the manufacture of patentable inventions."[20]

Until the European Court of Justice (ECJ) pronounces on the correct interpretation of this provision it is impossible to know how important this exclusion will be in practice. However, even if the ECJ supports the broader U.K. interpretation, this will still only take us so far. In particular, it imposes an unreal obligation on trade rivals who are forced to try to distinguish between the essential and non-essential features of the shape and then ask whether any of the former elements were attributable to capricious selection rather than to achieving the technical function itself. How, for example, would one determine whether the triangular formation of the blades in the Philips case (as opposed to the shape of the blades themselves) was attributable only to the technical result given that a number of other equally effective shapes were available? What if Philips had previously registered a two-dimensional triangle in respect of its products and had chosen the triangular formation of the shaving heads so as to continue the theme?

The final exclusion, that of shapes which give substantial value to the goods, was also considered in *Philips v. Remington*. One important preliminary point to note about this exclusion is that it is also unlikely to exclude many containers, since consumers are presumably unlikely to spend more on a product because of the shape of its packaging.

However, the main difficulty with the interpretation of this provision lies in determining what is meant by "value" in this context and how different types of value are to be distinguished. It seems obvious that value cannot here include "trade mark" value. That is to say, it cannot include value attributable to the fact that consumers recognise a shape as denoting the products of a particular enterprise and are prepared to pay more for a product because it emanates from that enterprise. As Jacob J. put it, "what is meant is an exclusion of shapes which exclusively add some sort of value . . . to the goods disregarding any value attributable to the trade mark (i.e. source identification function)."[21]

More controversial is the question of whether value in this context includes functional as well as aesthetic value. At first instance, Jacob J. concluded that all types of non-trade mark value were included in this exception. He went on to find that Philips's shape did give

---

[19] In *Roho's Application* the hearing officer concluded that the air-cushion fell within this second exclusion even though "there were other shapes available from which the same technical result could be obtained": above, fn. 64 at 6. Also see *Swizzels Matlow's "Chewy sweet" Application* [1998] R.P.C. 244 at 247: sweet on sticks were not registrable since the stick had a functional purpose: "it assists the consumer to ear the product with a minimum of mess".
[20] Above, note 47 at 821.
[21] Above, note 5 at 309.

substantial value to the goods since it was recognised as having an engineering function. The Court of Appeal rejected this conclusion and held that value in this context only means aesthetic value. Since the value of the shape of Philips's shaver flowed from its functionality it was not caught by this subsection. According to Aldous L.J., the intention was to exclude shapes which appeal to the eye which "should be protected as registered designs or the like protection, not by trade mark registration".[22]

If Aldous L.J.'s approach is correct then it becomes necessary for us to distinguish between three types of value: trade mark value, functional value and aesthetic value. The exclusion will only apply in cases where the aesthetic qualities of the shape give "substantial value" to the product.[23] Yet, any attempt to distinguish between different types of value is potentially artificial, since a successful design may achieve a number of aims simultaneously. Moreover, whilst some attempt to separate trade mark value from other types of value is probably inevitable, the Act does not require a distinction to be drawn between functional and aesthetic value, which involves the creation of a dichotomy between form and function which is alien to many schools of design. It also seems likely that the distinctions drawn between different types of value will ultimately be dependent on untested assumptions about consumer psychology.

The latter difficulty can be illustrated by reference to a number of Benelux cases, where, in drawing a distinction between trade mark value and aesthetic value, it has been held that foodstuffs are normally purchased for their taste and not because of their shape, so that shape marks for food will generally be registrable.[24] However, this conclusion would seem to rest on a number of questionable assumptions. How can we be certain that foodstuffs are purchased for their taste and not their shape without the benefit of extensive consumer surveys? Even a casual observer can, perhaps, doubt the truth of the assumption in respect of foodstuffs aimed at children. Can the shape of a product affect its flavour? That is to say, can the shape of a product have a subconscious impact on what the product tastes like?

Returning to *Philips v. Remington*, Aldous L.J. concluded that the shape of the shaver was not excluded by this third subsection. Yet, even working on the assumption that "value" in this context only means aesthetic value, it is still not obvious that Philips's shaver should not have been excluded under this heading, Aldous L.J. stating that the evidence did not establish that "the shape has any more value than other shapes which were established to be as good

---

[22] Above, note 47 at 822.
[23] It is clear from the context that substantial here cannot simply mean more than merely insubstantial. Presumably, therefore, substantial in this context bears its ordinary dictionary meaning, namely, "of ample or considerable amount of size; sizeable, fairly large": *Shorter Oxford English Dictionary*. *cf.* Copyright, Designs and Patents Act, 1988, s. 16(3).
[24] See Strowel, above.

and as cheap to produce". Without a detailed knowledge of the evidence that was presented, it is impossible to assess this conclusion adequately. It could, however, be said that the number of alternative shapes available suggests that the particular shape in question may have been chosen with aesthetic considerations in mind. Nor did Aldous L.J. refer to the fact that Philips had successfully sought registered design protection for the shape and configuration of their shaver, even though such protection is dependent on the shape having eye-appeal, suggesting that at least some aspects of the shaver must have been designed with aesthetic considerations in mind. We might at least expect such a finding to create a presumption that the design did give aesthetic value to the goods. The question would then become whether this additional value was "substantial".

(ix) Summation

We have seen that trade mark protection for shapes may have a number of undesirable consequences. In recognition of these potential difficulties the Act provides three express exclusions which are designed to ensure that trade mark protection for shapes remains within appropriate limits. On closer inspection, however, it appears that these provisions may not provide sufficient safeguards. More specifically, we have seen that the first of the exclusions has been interpreted out of existence. Neither the second nor the third exclusion would seem adequate to prevent the monopolisation of packaging as opposed to product shapes, even though the monopolisation of such shapes could have an equally detrimental effect on competition,[25] and even though applications for packaging shapes have thus far been much more common.[26] Moreover, even in the case of product shapes the second and third exclusions present a number of difficulties of interpretation such that it will be difficult to determine in advance whether a shape falls within one of the exclusions, to the extent that the actual conclusions reached in *Philips v. Remington* still seem open to question even once we understand the tests to be applied.

Given the difficulties with the express exclusions that we have identified, we believe that it is important to apply an additional safeguard through the test of distinctiveness, by operating on the assumption that three-dimensional marks lack distinctiveness.[27]

---

[25] Indeed, it should be remembered that the Goschen Committee's remarks were only directed at containers and packaging. See note 86 and accompanying text, above.
[26] See notes 59–65 and accompanying text, above.
[27] *cf. Reform of Trade Marks Law* Cm 1203 (1990) para. 2.19: "As with colours or sounds, it is likely that evidence of factual distinctiveness will be required in most cases."

(x) Reconceptualising Distinctiveness

We have already seen that the U.K. and Community registries and the courts in the United Kingdom already operate on the assumption that three-dimensional marks lack distinctiveness. However, we have also seen that they have tended to justify this starting point by reference to consumer reaction to shapes. We have seen that this justification is problematic for a number of reasons. First, it rests on largely untested and partially circular assumptions about consumer reaction. Moreover, even if there is some truth in the assumption that consumers currently place more importance on textual signs, if the "communicative predominance of linguistic matter is really coming to an end,[28] then we will reach a point where this assumption no longer reflects any sort of "reality". Secondly, we have seen that even the difference between consumer reaction to invented words and to shapes would seem to be a matter of degree and thus an inappropriate basis on which to draw a bright line between the two types of mark.[29] Thirdly, the prioritisation of two-dimensional marks and the related assumption that it is the three-dimensional mark which is "limping" or "supporting" is impossible to justify on the wording of the Directive alone. Therefore we need to be quite clear about the policy reasons that underpin our prioritisation of two-dimensional marks. Finally, in the case of patented products, a presumption against distinctiveness based on consumer reaction involves some fairly tortuous logic.

Our argument therefore is that whilst a presumption against distinctiveness should be maintained, this should be done on a much more overtly policy oriented basis. Such as approach would not require a radical change in existing judicial practice. On the contrary, courts in the United Kingdom and the Registry have emphasised on numerous occasions that the test of distinctiveness should be partly determined by reference to what other honest traders may legitimately wish to do. For example, in the more recent cases we have considered, we find statements to this effect in *Philips v. Remington*.[30] Similarly in *Roho's Application* the hearing officer emphasised that since the applicant's cushion was made up of functional features, other traders "will have a legitimate reason to wish to make their own goods in like shape".[31] More generally, it is worth referring to what was said in *Elvis Presley Trade Marks v.*

---

[28] See Dinwoodie, above, note 9.
[29] As was decided by the US Supreme Court in *Two Pesos, Inc. v Taco Cabana Inc.* 505 U.S. 763, 120 L Ed 2d 615, 112 S Ct 2753.
[30] When considering the test of distinctiveness at first instance Jacob J. stated that Philips's application raised "the question of the extent to which trade mark law, conferring a perpetual monopoly, can interfere with the freedom within the European Union of manufacturers to make an artefact of a desirable and good engineering design." [1998] R.P.C. 283 at 299. See also *Re Procter & Gamble's Trade Mark Application* [1999] E.T.M.R. 375 at 384.
[31] 0/169/98, p. 11.

Shaw,[32] where all three members of the Court of Appeal apparently took monopoly considerations into account when deciding the question of distinctiveness.[33] The importance of a policy based approach to the question of inherent distinctiveness therefore lies in the honesty and conceptual clarity that such a reconceptualisation would bring. It would also serve to insulate the presumption against distinctiveness against the criticisms of the consumer psychology based approach that we previously identified.

It must be recognised, however, that the presumption against distinctiveness which we wish to see maintained does not come without a cost. Writing in the context of the United States, Professor Dinwoodie has argued that the United States Supreme Court was right to conclude that three-dimensional marks may be inherently distinctive, thereby abandoning the presumption against distinctiveness which had previously been applied in a number of U.S. cases.[34] In particular, and contrary to our argument, Dinwoodie states that there is no "conceptual connection" between the test for distinctiveness and competition concerns. He therefore argues that such concerns are more properly left to the functionality doctrine.[35] Drawing in part on what was said by the Supreme Court in *Two Pesos*,[36] he points out that a "general requirement of secondary meaning" (as opposed to a finding that a mark is inherently distinctive) would "make investment in trade dress vulnerable in the

---

[32] *sub nom. Elvis Presley Trade Marks* [1999] R.P.C. 567.
[33] Robert Walker L.J. referred to the judgment of Lord Parker in *Registrar of Trade Marks v. W & G Du Cros* [1913] A.C. 624, who famously stated that an applicant's chance of success in establishing distinctiveness will "largely depend on whether other traders are likely, in the ordinary course of their business and without any improper motive, to desire the use of the same mark, or some other mark nearly resembling it, upon or in connection with their own goods. It is apparent from the history of trade marks in this country that both the legislature and the courts have always shown a natural disinclination to allow any person to obtain by registration under the Trade Marks Act a monopoly in what others may legitimately desire to use." Whilst accepting that this statement now needs to be treated with caution Robert Walker L.J. still regarded the passage as providing "a convenient summary of a complex point". Above, note 32, page 167 at 579.
[34] See Dinwoodie, "Reconceptualizing the Inherent Distinctiveness of Product Design Trade Dress" (1997) 75 *North Carolina L. Rev.* 471 commenting on the decision in *Two Pesos v. Taco Cabana* 505 U.S. 763 (1992). As to the reasoning of the Supreme Court see, in particular, pp. 770–5.
[35] Dinwoodie, at p. 505. The functionality doctrine holds that 'a design is legally functional, and thus unprotectible, if it is one of a limited number of equally efficient options available to competitors and free competition would be unduly hindered by according the design trademark protection.... This serves to assure that competition will not be stifled by the exhaustion of a limited number of trade dresses': *Two Pesos v. Taco Cabana* at 775. See also *Restatement, Third, Unfair Competition* (St Paul, Minn, 1995), para. 17: 'a design is "functional"...if the design affords benefits in the manufacturing, marketing, or use of the goods or services with which the design is used, apart from any benefits attributable to the design's significance as an indication of source, that are important to effective competition by others and that are not practically available through the use of alternative designs'. See generally, *ibid. Comments b* and *c* and the references cited. Also see Horton, "Designs, Shapes and Colours: A Comparison of Trade Mark Law in the United Kingdom and the United States" [1989] 9 E.I.P.R. 311.
[36] *Two Pesos v. Taco Cabana*, above.

early stages of product marketing and development."[37] This might be particularly hard on small companies who could find that their investment had been appropriated by larger enterprises with established distribution channels.[38] Accepting that shapes may be inherently distinctive and abandoning a general requirement of secondary meaning might also reduce the costs of obtaining registration and bringing an infringement action, as in some cases there would no longer be a need to adduce survey evidence.[39] Finally, he argues that building competitiveness concerns into the test of distinctiveness might be counter-productive in that the effect on rival manufacturers is the same irrespective of whether the applicant can establish secondary meaning.[40]

In response to the above criticisms it might be pointed out that it is essential that competitiveness considerations be built into the test of distinctiveness in the United Kingdom since there is no other stage at which such concerns can be adequately taken into account, the express exclusions in section 3(2) being too restricted for this purpose.[41] By contrast, the functionality doctrine in the United States is far more flexible and thus better suited to providing a one state competitiveness test. The importance of not excluding competition concerns from our test of distinctiveness can also be illustrated by reference to other types of non-traditional mark. For example, it is generally accepted that it would be undesirable to allow someone to register an olfactory mark in respect of perfume.[42] But, in the absence of any exclusion prohibiting the registration of olfactory marks which give substantial value to the goods, the only basis on which such a mark could be excluded is on the grounds that it lacks distinctiveness.[43] Again, by contrast, in the United States the functionality doctrine might be sufficiently flexible to prevent registration of an olfactory mark in these circumstances.[44]

Moreover, Professor Dinwoodie's point about the lack of any conceptual connection between the distinctiveness test and competition concerns applies with much less force in the United Kingdom. As we have seen, there is a long history in the United

---

[37] Dinwoodie, above, at p. 494.
[38] Dinwoodie, above, at p. 497.
[39] Dinwoodie, at pp. 497–498.
[40] Dinwoodie, at p. 503.
[41] The only other possibility would be for the courts to adopt an expansive view of the scope of the descriptive use defence in s. 11(2) (Art 6(1)). The difficulty with this solution is that it would not prevent the mark from being registered and the mere presence of a mark on the register can stifle competition since a potential competitor who is concerned about the risk of litigation will be deterred from entering the marketplace. As to the possible operation of a section 11(2) defence in these circumstances see *Philips v. Remington*, above, note 5, at 313 (Jacob J.) at 824 (Court of Appeal).
[42] See Firth, *Trade Marks: The New law* (Jordans, Bristol, 1995) para. 2.15; Cornish, *Intellectual Property* (3rd ed, Sweet & Maxwell, London, 1996) para. 17–20.
[43] Alternatively it might be argued that such a mark is not even a sign: Firth, *ibid*. However, given the very wide definition of sign adopted by Jacob in *Philips v. Remington* this argument is now unlikely to succeed. See above, page 168, note 40 and accompanying text.
[44] See above, page 168, note 35.

Kingdom of applying competition concerns in the course of assessing distinctiveness. It is true to say that such concerns have traditionally been raised in the context of a separate requirement of distinctiveness at law.[45] However, there is no reason to suppose that competition considerations cannot be built into unified test of distinctive character if, as we advocate, a separate requirement of distinctiveness at law is abandoned. A unified approach would have the advantage of allowing us to take consumer association/reaction and competition concerns into account simultaneously. This would in turn allow us to develop a much more nuanced understanding of the effect of allowing any given mark to be registered.

The final point also relates to Dinwoodie's argument that competitiveness concerns should not be built in to the test of distinctiveness since the effect on rival manufacturers is the same irrespective of whether the applicant can establish secondary meaning. Whilst as a matter of strict logic this may be true, the advantage of the approach we advocate is that it recognises that there is no absolute divide between those signs which may adversely affect competition and those which should be registrable. That is to say, it recognises that all trade marks may adversely affect potential competitors to some extent. Deciding which marks should be registrable should therefore involve a consideration of the consequences for competition of allowing the mark to be registered in contrast with the likely confusion of consumers if rival manufacturers start using similar or identical signs. This weighing up of competing interests can be achieved through the distinctive character test by varying the level of acquired distinctiveness that has to be established according to the likely effect on competitors. Thus, just as we demand a very high level of acquired distinctiveness in the case of common laudatory words, when considering the distinctiveness of a three-dimensional mark which other traders have a legitimate and strong desire to use, we might set our secondary meaning threshold at a high level.

It is also worth pointing out that the claim that investment in trade dress is rendered vulnerable in the early stages of development rests on two assumptions: first, that such investment should be protected and second, that in the absence of trade mark protection no other way of protecting this investment can be found.

Nevertheless, despite some of the doubts we have raised about the desirability of removing policy concerns from the test of distinctiveness, this is not to say there might not be some advantage in such an approach. In particular, there is considerable force in Professor Dinwoodie's argument that abandoning a general requirement of secondary meaning might reduce the costs of obtaining registration and bringing an infringement action. We do

---

[45] See *Elvis Presley Trade Marks*, above, page 167, note 32 and see above, page 167, note 33 and accompanying text.

not, however, believe that this is sufficient to justify an abandonment of a presumption against distinctiveness of three-dimensional marks or the related policy oriented approach to the question of distinctiveness.

4. Conclusion

The Directive and hence the Act reflect the view that, in certain circumstances, the shape of goods or their packaging perform the orthodox trade mark function of indicating the source of a particular manufacturer's goods, thereby allowing consumers to identify the key characteristics of the goods which distinguish them from other manufacturers' goods. However, an analysis of the historical objections to the registration of product and packaging shapes reveal a number of tensions inherent in extending registered trade mark protection to three-dimensional signs. The Directive and section 3(2) of the Trade Mark Act 1994 contain three express exclusions which attempt to ensure that protection for shapes does not extend beyond its proper bounds, but it is at least open to doubt whether these aims have been successfully achieved. Whether this means that the First Council Directive on trade marks should be reshaped if, or when, a Second Directive is proposed, is a matter for debate. In the meantime, it is to be hoped that the European Court of Justice will ensure that policy considerations are taken into account when assessing distinctiveness.

In relation to place names used as trade marks, the European Court of Justice has adopted a somewhat ambiguous attitude towards the relationship between public policy and distinctiveness. On the one hand, the European Court of Justice has recognised the importance of the policy considerations that lie behind the test of distinctiveness.[46] On the other hand, by refusing to vary the test of distinctiveness by reference to the perceived importance of keeping a geographical name available for use by others, the ECJ has demonstrated a reluctance to apply the distinctiveness test in such a way as to give these policies best effect.[47] This reluctance can perhaps be explained in part by the national court's terms of reference,[48] but to the extent that this reflects a more general position it is to be hoped that the ECJ will abandon its reluctance and will move towards a more overtly policy oriented test.

---

[46] *Windsurfing Chiemsee Produktions—und Vertriebs GmbH v Boots—und Segelzubehör Walter Huber and Franz Attenberger* [1999] E.T.M.R. 585 at 595.
[47] *ibid.* at 599.
[48] The German Court framed its questions in terms of prior German practice. The ECJ is inevitably going to be reluctant to interpret the Directive by reference to old national law.

8. Collectivity, Control and Joint Adventure—Observations on Marks in Multiple Use

Alison Firth

Collectivity, control and joint adventure—observations on marks in multiple use

Collective marks

The Trade Marks Act 1994 introduced into U.K. law an apparently new species of registered mark—the collective mark.[1] This form of registration is available to a mark that is or will be employed by a number of users to indicate their membership of an association. For example, the designations "Chartered Patent Agent", "Chartered Patent Attorney" and "CPA" indicate membership of the Chartered Institute of Patent Agents and hence professional qualification.[2] Other instances would include membership of a buying co-operative or a trade association. In each case, membership of the organisation in question will say something about the standing of the users and conversely their (proper) use of the mark will raise the profile of the organisation and its other members. The collective mark is explained in the Trade Mark Registry's Manual as a mark that has multiple proprietors.[3] Or, as Rozas and Johnston put it, "the owner is not a single person but a collectivity".[4]

However, the statute envisages that the association, rather than its members jointly, will be registered as proprietor.[5] If the association has legal personality, this is relatively straightforward, conceptually and in practice. In the case of the Community collective mark, Annand and Norman[6] point out that Article 64(1) of the Community Trade Mark Regulation[7] requires legal personality.[8] If an association is unincorporated, its name may be used on the U.K. register[9] as a

---

[1] s. 49 and sched. 1.
[2] Boff J. "Regulations for marks" [1996] C.I.P.A. 905. Boff cites advertisement of the marks in the *Trade Marks Journal*, [1996] T.M.J. 6144, at 12208 and [1996] T.M.J. 6150 at 13784.
[3] *Trade Marks Registry Work Manual*, June 1996, Ch. 13, para. 6. This may not always be technically correct—see below—but it gives the flavour of collective interest in use of such a mark.
[4] Rozas & Johnston, "Impact of certification marks on innovation and the global market-place" [1997] E.I.P.R. 598.
[5] s. 49(1) and Sched. 1, para. 2. For example, the Chartered Institute of Patents Agents is a body incorporated under Royal Charter of 1891.
[6] *Blackstone's Guide to the Community Trade Mark* (1998) at p. 280.
[7] Council Regulation 40/94 on the Community trade mark.
[8] Certainly the description of unincorporated associations in *Currie v. Barton, The Times*, February 12, 1998 by O'Connor L.J. that "they cannot be sued or sue in their own names. You cannot make a contract with the body, because in law it does not exist. It consists of all its members" is inconsistent with the requirements of Art. 64(1).
[9] Gold *et al.*, (eds) *ITMA UK Trade Marks Handbook*, at para. 103.24.4 state that enquiries indicate that the Registry now accepts applications in the names of unincorporated bodies and continue to accept applications in the name of registered charities. Alternatively officers of the

kind of shorthand, but the mark will indeed be owned collectively by the members, subject to the contractual arrangements which bind them as members of the association. All members, *qua* members, may use the mark. The problems which this latter scenario presents at common law were manifest in *Artistic Upholstery Limited (on behalf of itself and all other members of the Long Eaton Guild of Furniture Manufacturers) v. Art Form Limited*.[10] In that case, Lawrence Collins Q.C. had to consider the status of the mark LONG POINT which had been used for a number of years to denote a furniture show organised by members of an unincorporated Guild. He decided that the Guild members held goodwill in the mark, in that capacity and in accordance with the Guild's constitution and rules. The defendant, a founder member who had been expelled from the Guild, even perhaps wrongfully expelled, was not entitled to register or use the mark for its own independent purposes.

Goodwill generated by the defendant's use of LONG POINT appears not to have been distinct or severable.[11] In *Dawnay Day & Co Ltd v. Cantor Fitzgerald*[12] Lloyd J. granted an injunction to restrain the successor in business to a member of the Dawnay Day group of companies from trading under the name DAWNAY DAY. He found it unnecessary to decide whether goodwill in the name was owned by the holding company, was shared by all the group members or was jointly or severally owned by the group members, although he did treat the position as analogous to a licence to group members to use the name whilst within the group.

Rozas & Johnston observe that "Ownership and trading are different, and so a collective trade mark cannot be licensed by a member of the collectivity". Indeed the Trade Marks Act 1994, by s. 23(4), provides that co-proprietors of an ordinary trade mark may not license, assign or charge their shares without the consent of the other co-owners. In this regard, a collective mark resembles other forms of intellectual property in joint ownership. However, in the context of licensing, Wilkof asserts that "Trade marks are different."[13] This is perhaps borne out indirectly by Marchese's excellent article *"Joint Ownership of Intellectual Property"*.[14] Marchese deals specifically with the joint ownership of patents and copyright but not of trade marks. Trade marks carry out their functions by means of dialogue

---

association or other nominee members may be named as proprietor on the register, holding property in the mark on behalf of all members and in accordance with the association's constitution. See, *e.g* Gold, para. 104.7.

[10] (Lawrence Collins Q.C. sitting as a deputy High Court Judge) [1999] 4 All E.R. 277.

[11] For problems in a corporate setting see Watson-Gandy "The fame game: when pop groups split" (1996) 16 *Lit.* 47. For a case involving shared goodwill where, curiously, one co-owner was refused registration whilst another's registration was allowed to stand, see *Gromax Plasticulture Ltd. v. Don & Low Nonwoven Ltd* [1999] R.P.C. 367. Such divergence between the common law position and that under the Trade Marks Act 1994 is unsatisfactory in this author's view.

[12] Noted by Benjamin [1999] E.I.P.R. N-178.

[13] [1995] *Trade Mark Licensing*, 25.

[14] [1999] E.I.P.R. 364.

with customers; in that sense they are always in multiple use. However, a mark may also be used by a multiplicity of traders to communicate with actual and prospective customers.

The collective mark is one of a varied grouping of marks in this kind of multiple usership. Others include licensed marks and "house marks". This chapter seeks to compare collective marks with other forms of multiple usership, and to ascertain whether collective marks in fact could have enjoyed registration in the U.K. prior to 1994. The Trade Marks Registry states[15]

> Examples of associations who have applied to register collective marks are professional bodies such as Chartered Institutes, trade associations, educational institutes and hotel chains. These organisations were unable to obtain a meaningful ordinary trade mark registration as the services or goods are actually provided to the public by their members.

The ambit of the phrase "collective mark"

Collective marks and certification marks

As well as having the narrow meaning of "association mark", as outlined above,[16] the phrase "collective mark" is often used to denote both "association" marks and certification or guarantee marks,[17] which indicate objectively defined characteristics of goods or services. A number of different undertakings may be interested in certification marks. As Dawson puts it

> Sometimes, however, increasing his market share at his competitors' expense will not be [a trader's] only concern and he may find that it pays him to join with his trade rivals in an effort to protect the integrity of their particular industry or line of business. If he and his competitors produce goods which have some feature in common, they are all equally vulnerable to penetration of the market by traders who dishonestly pass their goods off to the public as having the feature in question. In such cases, trade mark law permits an entire industry or trade to protect itself by the registration of a *Certification Trade Mark* to act as a warranty that goods bearing the mark meet a certain standard or possess a particular characteristic.

---

[15] *Work Manual*, June 1996, Ch. 13, para. 1.2.
[16] The phrase "association mark" was sometimes used to describe the certification mark: *Report of the Departmental Committee on the Law and Practice relating to trade marks* (Goschen Committee) Cmd. 4568 (1934) at para. 223. It is not so used here.
[17] For an analysis of distinctions between these types of mark, see Joseph, "Certification Marks, Collective Marks or Guarantee Marks" (1979) 1 E.I.P.R. 160; *British Trade Mark Law & Practice* Cmnd. 5601 (1974) para. 197 (Mathys Committee).

In this case the proprietor's job is to permit others to use the mark if their goods or services have the requisite qualities and, conversely, to refuse or prevent use of the mark if not. Examples of certification mark include the British Standards Institute's "Kitemarks" and the Woolmark administered by the International Wool Secretariat and its national organisations.[18] Rozas and Johnston[19] point out that environmental certification marks, which indicate a product's impact on the environment, are of increasing importance. Contrary to the historical scepticism of the distinguished commentator, Schechter,[20] Rozas and Johnston argue that certification marks are pro-competitive.[21] Belson observes[22] that where a product attains the status of an industry standard, the trade mark which starts out denoting origin may approach the status of a certification mark, as a result of extensive licensing.

Precursors to certification marks

Certification marks governed by statute in the U.K. constitute a trading mechanism which may be regarded as a successor to the powers to regulate trade and to maintain standards[23] formerly enjoyed under charter by the guilds and craft companies. The Mathys Committee observed[24] in 1974 that the guilds' powers had generally fallen into disuse or had been incorporated into wider arrangements. The Committee recommended the abolition of the Sheffield Register,[25] maintained by the Cutlers' Company in Hallamshire for metal marks. Mathys also recommended closure of the Manchester Branch of the Trade Marks Registry, for cotton marks.[26] Other bodies with mark-related powers include Assay

---

[18] For details of these and other certification mark registrations see Dawson, *Certification Trade Marks: law and practice* (1988) Ch. 5.
[19] Rozas & Johnston "Impact of certification marks on innovation and the global market-place" [1997] E.I.P.R. 598.
[20] Schechter, *The historical foundations of the law relating to trade-mark* (New York 1925) and "Trade morals and regulation: the American scene" (1937) 6 *Fordham Law Review* 190.
[21] Guidelines for the treatment of intellectual property under the Competition Act 1998 are awaited at the time of writing. Where parties entered into an agreement pursuant to Regulations for the use of a certification mark approved by the Secretary of State, the Restrictive Trade Practices Act 1976 was usually disapplied: s.28 and Sched.3, para. 4.
[22] Belson "Brand protection in the age of the Internet" [1999] E.I.P.R. 481 at 483. Belson points out a problem with this analysis—in the USA, as in the U.K. the owner of a certification trade mark must not trade in the products itself. He praises Australia for departing from this principle in its Trade Mark Act 1995, s.169.
[23] Even Schechter, somewhat critical of the guild system, admits this function: *The historical foundations of the law relating to trade-marks* (New York, 1925) p.164, cited in Azmi, Maniatis and Sodipo "Distinctive signs and Early Markets: Europe, Africa and Islam" in Firth, ed. *The Prehistory and Development of Intellectual Property Systems* 1997 (Perspectives on Intellectual Property, Vol. 1.) at p. 139. Certification marks were called 'standardisation' marks in the Trade Marks Act 1995.
[24] *British Trade Mark Law and Practice*, Cmnd. 5601 (1974), para. 17.
[25] Applications could be made either to the Registry or to the Cutlers' Company, which acted as intermediary between the applicant and the Registry, maintained the Sheffield Register, and protected the designation "Sheffield", *ibid.* para. 218.
[26] Charming examples of cotton marks and historical accounts of the Manchester Branch and

offices for precious metal hallmarks[27] the Garter or Lyon (Scotland) Kings of Arms, who regulate the use of heraldic devices[28] and advise the Trade Marks Registry on heraldic matters. The grant of a Royal Warrant might be regarded as grant of the right to use a mark by royal prerogative.[29] Perhaps the history of regulation by the guilds[30] and the (then) continuing existence of special arrangements for textile and metal marks explain a curious fact noted by Dawson.[31] She observes that "standardisation marks", as certification[32] marks were called in the Trade Marks Act 1905, "slipped into our legal system virtually unnoticed, except by those closely interested in the work of the Trade Marks Registry".

Dawson points out that standardisation marks were not discussed in the Report of the Select Committee of the House of Commons on the Trade Marks Bill of 1905, nor in parliamentary debates. They were, however, the subject of much evidence submitted to the Merchandise Marks committee under the chairmanship of Mr Harry Greer, M.P., between December 1919 and March 1920.[33] Provisions of the Trade Marks Act 1905 relating to standardisation marks had been amended by the Trade Marks Act 1919,[34] in particular so as to remove the requirement for the proprietor to examine goods before certifying them, and to change the criterion for approval of registration by the Board of Trade from "public advantage" to "competen[ce] to certify" on the part of the proprietor. The Greer Committee's remit was firstly to consider the need to amend the Merchandise Marks Act 1887,[35] which imposed criminal penalties for the false marking of goods and for the importation of such goods, as regards indications of origin. The Greer Committee also considered the usefulness and effect of national marks of origin and similar "collective marks" and the need for international action to prevent

---

Sheffield Register can be found in the Patent Office's 1976 publication *A Century of Trade Marks*, at pp. 32–40.

[27] For a brief account of hallmarking see Marrett *Intellectual Property Law* (1996) at p. 188. See also Gormley "Quantitative restrictions and measures having equivalent effect: all that glitters is not gold?" [1996] E.J. Rev 44, a commentary on Case C-293/93 *Houtwipper* [1994] E.C.R. I-4249; Ward, "700 year old legislation helps fight modern-day crime" (1992) 48 *Magistrate* 69.

[28] See report of Mathys Committee, British Trade Mark Law & Practice, Cmnd. 5601 (1974) para. 219.

[29] Cases on Royal Warrants are rare. In *Imperial Tobacco Co Ltd's TMS* [1915] 2 Ch. 27; [1915] 32 R.P.C. 40 a registered mark was attacked on the ground that its device included Prince of Wales feathers.

[30] For a summary see Ida, Maniatis and Sodipo "Distinctive signs and Early Markets: Europe, Africa and Islam" in Firth (ed.) *The Prehistory and Development of Intellectual Property Systems* 1997 (Vol. 1, *Perspectives on Intellectual Property*) at pp. 138–140.

[31] Dawson, *Certification Trade Marks–law and Practice* (1988), at p. 15.

[32] Oddly, "certification" was one of the forms of connection between marked goods and proprietor listed by the Trade Marks Act 1905 for "ordinary" trade marks. However, it was held in *Prorace v. le Brasseur* (1927) 44 R.P.C. 73 that if certification were the only function performed by the proprietor, the mark should be registered as a standardisation mark. Nonetheless, use of an "ordinary" registered mark to indicate quality served to avert revocation for non-use: *John H Andrew & Co Ltd v. Kuehnrich* (1913) 30 R.P.C. 677.

[33] Minutes of Evidence were published in 1920 by HMSO.

[34] s. 12 and Sched. 2.

[35] As amended by Acts of 1891, 1894 and 1911.

the false marking of goods. The minutes of evidence show that feelings ran high on these topics. Some took the view that collective marks would be inimical to ordinary trade marks, whilst others strongly desired the creation of a British Empire mark[36] of origin. French and Swiss national marks of origin (UNIS and SPES respectively) seem to have been the objects of envy as well as disquiet. A combination of suspicion of foreign collective marks and fear of disadvantage also appears to have underlain the objections to registration of the French indication of origin UNIS,[37] as Dawson explains.[38]

"Collective mark" and its meanings

In this essay, "collective mark" will be used in the narrow sense of association mark, although use in other senses is widespread. For example, the WIPO training manual "Introduction to trademark law and practice—the basic concepts"[39] stated

> A collective mark may be used in connection with either goods or services. Unlike a trademark or service mark, however, the goods or services... are provided by different enterprises. A collective mark, therefore, does not distinguish between different concerns, but serves to distinguish goods or services with common characteristics from goods or services without those characteristics.

This seems more apt to describe a certification mark than an association mark. Searching national laws in Olsen and Maniatis[40] reveals widespread use of "collective mark" to denote certification marks, including geographical indications of origin.[41] Rozas and Johnston[42] note that in France "collective marks" have a special subcategory of "collective mark of certification".[43] Likewise in

---

[36] From 1926 to 1933 the British Empire Marketing Board promoted "British national marks" and supported the Ministry of Agriculture's national marks campaign in 1927: see Report of the Imperial Economic Committee, Cmnd. 2493 (1925), p. 6 and Hansard, H.C. Vol. 195, Cols 88–967, May 12, 1926.
[37] Re an application by Union Nationale Inter-Syndicale des Marques Collectives [1922] 2 Ch. 653; (1922) 39 R.P.C. 97.
[38] Certification Trade Marks–law and practice (1988) at pp. 17–19.
[39] Geneva, 1997, World Intellectual Property Organization, para. 2.5.
[40] Olsen & Maniatis, Trade Marks, Trade Names and Unfair Competition: World Law and Practice (London 1996).
[41] On which see, for example, Beier & Knaak "The protections of direct and indirect geographical indications of origin in Germany and the Community" (1994) 25 I.I.C. 1; Bendekgey & Mead "International protection of appellations of origin and other geographic indications" (1992) 82 T.M.R. 765.
[42] Rozas & Johnston "Impact of certification marks on innovation and the global market-place" [1997] E.I.P.R. 598.
[43] Code de la Propriete Intellectuelle, (1992) Art. L715–2.

Portugal, collective marks can be either association marks or certification marks.[44]

It seems clear that the phrase "Community collective mark" in the Community Trade Mark Regulation[45] refers only to association marks and not to certification/guarantee marks; as earlier draft provisions for "community guarantee marks"[46] were deleted.[47]

Collective marks and trade

In contrast to a certification mark,[48] a collective mark registered under the Trade Marks Act 1994 may have a trading proprietor. However, it is designed to be used in trade, to distinguish the services or goods of undertakings that are members of the proprietor association from the services or goods of other, non-member, undertakings.[49] The scope of protection of a registered collective mark is governed by the general infringement sections[50] of the 1994 Act; subsections 10(1)-(3) all refer to infringement by use[51] in the course of trade.

Two questions arise here. Firstly, what if the proprietor is an "umbrella" association, whose members are themselves associations? In that case it is the members of the latter who may wish to use the mark in trade. No guidance is given in the Act or Rules, but a joint statement by the Council and Commission of the European Communities and entered in the minutes of adoption of the Community Trade Mark Regulation indicate that such arrangements would fall within the definition of the Community collective mark.[52]

Secondly, is there scope for registration of collective "membership" marks which are not used in the course of trade by the members of the proprietor? The U.S. Trademark Manual of Examining Procedure describes this species of mark in the following terms[53]:

> Membership marks are not trademarks or service marks in the

---

[44] Law 16/95, *Code of Industrial Property*, Arts 171–4, 175.
[45] Council Regulation 40/94 on the Community trade mark, Art. 64.
[46] On which, see Joseph, "Certification Marks, Collective Marks or Guarantee Marks" (1979) 1 E.I.P.R. 160.
[47] See, *e.g.* Rozas & Johnston Impact of certification marks on innovation and the global market-place [1997] E.I.P.R. 598.
[48] In respect of which the Trade Marks Act 1994, Sched. 2, para. 4 states "a certification mark shall not be registered if the proprietor carries on a business involving the supply of goods or services of the kind certified."
[49] Trade Marks Act 1994, Sched. 2, para. 2.
[50] s. 9, *et seq.*, subject to minor modifications as set out in Sched. 2, paras. 11&12.
[51] On use (and misuse) of marks, see Maniatis, below at p. 231 *et seq.*
[52] OHIM O.J. 5/96 at 619, cited by Annand & Norman *Blackstone's Guide to the Community Trade Mark* (1998) at p. 279. Laddie J. in *Wagamama v. City Centre Restaurants* [1995] F.S.R. 713, decided before 1996, doubted the usefulness of such statements. See also *Antonissen* [1991] E.C.R. I–745.
[53] *Trademark Manual of examining Practice* (1997 release) at para. 1304.01; see also *Aloe Crème Laboratories Inc v. American Society for Aesthetic Plastic Surgery* 192 U.S.P.O. 170, 173 (TTAB 1976) to similar effect, cited in the Manual at para. 1302.

ordinary sense; they are not used in business or trade, and they do not indicate commercial origin of goods or services. Registration of these marks fills the need of collective organizations which do not wish to use the symbols of their organisations on goods or services but which wish to protect their marks to prevent use by others. The rationale for registration of collective membership marks is set forth in *Ex parte Supreme Shrine of the Order of the White Shrine of Jerusalem*, 109 USPO 248 (Comm'r Pats. 1956)

That appears to have been on the basis that there was legislative intent to permit registration of fraternal names. One may ponder as to whether legislation[54] thus interpreted would fall under the constitutional powers to regulate interstate and foreign commerce which underpin Federal trademark legislation in the United States. Whatever the position may be in the United States, it is submitted that fraternal marks would only be registrable as collective marks in the United Kingdom if they were intended for use in the course of trade by or with the consent of their proprietors. An oblique reference to what appears to be a membership mark application[55] appears in a decision on the admission of additional evidence under Rule 13(8).[56]

Types of multiple usership[57]

Licensing

Collective marks are used in consequence of a horizontal relationship between their users. However, the most common form of multiple usership is probably the result of a vertical relationship—the licensing[58] by its proprietor of an "ordinary" trade mark[59]. Here the nexus between the users is a contract referable to the mark itself. Clearly permitted by statute in the United Kingdom since 1938,[60] a licence may be express or implied. Even the express licence creates some dilemmas—whether quality control provisions are adequate to maintain connection between the proprietor and the marked goods or services[61]; whether a licensee should be able to sue for

---

[54] s. 4 of the "Lanham Act" of 1946 15 U.S.C.A. para. 1054.
[55] *Application No: 2051417 in the name of Supreme Grand Lodge of the Ancient and Mystical Order Rosae Crucis Inc* (1999) 28 C.I.P.A. 152.
[56] Of the Trade Marks Rules 1994 (S.I. 1994 No. 2583). Evidence of the contents of a radio interview with a member of the association was not admitted.
[57] For an excellent analysis of shared or qualified ownership of the goodwill generated by multiple use of marks, see Wadlow *The law of passing off*, (2nd ed. 1995) paras 2.80–2.86.
[58] For an extensive treatment, see Wilkof, *Trade Mark Licensing*, (1995).
[59] The term "trade mark" will be used to embrace both trade and service marks, as in the 1994 Act.
[60] Trade Marks Act 1938, s. 28.
[61] Norman "*Trade Marks Licences in the UK–time for Bostitch to be re-evaluated?*" [1994] F.I.P.R. 154.

infringement[62]; whether use by the licensee is to be regarded as use by the licensor.[63]

Agency and implied licences enjoyed by distributors

In the case of an agent, in the true sense,[64] who is actually or using the mark on behalf of a principal, there is a simple answer to the last question. However, the implied licence to use a mark enjoyed by distributors of goods and others down the commercial chain have caused problems over the years. The Paris Convention envisages that a local agent or representative may wrongfully register marks against a "true" (foreign) proprietor's interest.[65] The editors of *Kerly's Law of Trade Marks and Trade Names*[66] observe that the courts have tended to require little evidence to show that goods' real trade connection is with their manufacturer. More recently, the extent and manner of use of marks by distributors and repairers have led to references to the European Court.[67] Implied consent formed the basis of a free-trade decision in *Davidoff*.[68]

House marks

Groups of companies may involve a network of horizontal and vertical relationships. As Wadlow explains,[69] some corporate groups

---

[62] ss. 30 and 31 of the Trade Marks Act 1994, as did its predecessor, empower the licensee to sue in specified circumstances. The 1994 Act contains a potent provision that enables the court, in infringement proceedings brought by the licensor, to take account of damage to licensees. Equivalent provisions for collective and certification marks are to be found in Sched. 1, para. 12(6) and Sched. 2, para. 14.

[63] It is submitted that this is implicit in s. 46 (revocation) of the 1994 Act, which refers to use by a proprietor or with his consent. However, section 28(2) of the Trade Marks Act 1938, which provided that use by a registered user was deemed use by the proprietor was repealed by the 1994 Act and not explicitly re-enacted. A wise licensor will make contractual provision to that effect. In *"Goodwill Hunting: Assignments and Licences In Gross after Scandecor"* [1999] I.P.Q. 264, Lane points out that

there is also no immutable principle in English law that a licensee's use accrues to the licensor either in passing off or for registered trade marks. Whether it does so depends upon how the mark is presented to the public. If the manner of use makes the mark distinctive of the licensee rather that the licensor, that is the licensor's look out. [citing *Oertli v. Bowman* [1959] R.P.C. 1 at 5 and contrasting *Aktiebolaget Manus v. RJ Fullwood and Bland* (1948) 65 R.P.C. 329].

This question becomes particularly acute in the context of parallel imports of "grey goods".

[64] The self-employed commercial agent, within the meaning of Regulation 86/653 and the Commercial agents (Council directive) Regulations 1993 (S.I. 1993 No. 3053) may be such a creature, but may better be classed along with distributors and "agents" in the looser sense.

[65] Paris Convention for the Protection of Industrial Property 1883 and revisions, Art 6 *septies*; implemented in the U.K. by Trade Marks Act 1994, s. 60. In *TRAVELPRO* [1997] R.P.C. 864 it was held that "agent or representative" includes a distributor. For an earlier example, see *Zoppas* [1965] R.P.C. 381.

[66] Blanco White & Jacob (12th ed.) at para. 2–21, citing *Inescourt* (1928) 46 R.P.C. 13 and *Warschauer* (1925) 43 R.P.C. 46. *cf. Diehl* [1970] R.P.C. 435.

[67] For example in *Parfums Christian Dior v. Evora* [1988] E.T.M.R. 26; *BMW v. Deenik* [1999] E.T.M.R. 339. See, *e.g.*, Maniatis, below, at p. 254.

[68] *Zino Davidoff SA v. A&G Imports* [1999] E.T.M.R. 700.

[69] *The law of passing off*, (2nd ed. 1995) at para. 2.83.

are held out to the public in such a way as to emphasise that the group is a single enterprise. He cites the tobacco and spirits trades as examples.[70] A "house" mark, which is often a stylised form of a company name common to the group, may be used by several or all members of the group, without apparent damage to the origin function of the mark; at least where there is adequate intragroup control.[71] This is so in the United Kingdom despite the strength of the corporate veil. In *William Grant v. Glen Catrine Bonded Warehouse*,[72] the Scots Court of Session went so far as to express the view that goodwill attaching to the whisky mark GRANT'S belonged to every part of the group business.

Of course the phrase "house mark" may also describe a mark used by a single company on an extensive line of goods or services. Thus a department store or fashion house will use its name on a wide range of products, often in conjunction with other marks for the specific goods or services. Sometimes one type of "house" mark will metamorphose into the other. For example, VOLKSWAGEN, the name of the German motor manufacturer, has been known for many years as a mark used on its many models of motor vehicle. More recently, motor manufacturers which have been taken over by the Volkswagen group are advertising the fact by reference to the Volkswagen name.[73] Either way, the "house mark" is still a trade mark,[74] used to denote origin in the classic manner.

Partnerships and other joint adventures

A "horizontal" nexus between users is present when two or more persons are in partnership, carrying on business under the mark in common with a view of profit.[75] Although a partnership in England and Wales does not enjoy legal personality as an entity distinct from the partners,[76] use of a mark in the course of partnership business will be use by or on behalf of the partners collectively. Many joint business ventures are automatically partnerships by virtue of the

---

[70] And also cites, *inter alia*, *Revlon Inc v. Lee* [1980] F.S.R. 85.
[71] *Radiation* (1930) 47 R.P.C. 37; *GE* [1970] R.P.C. 339; both discussed by Norman in Trade mark licences in the UK–time for Bostitch to be re-evaluated? [1994] E.I.P.R. 154; *Dawnay Day & Co Ltd v. Cantor Fitzgerald International* [1999] E.I.P.R. N-178.
[72] [1995] S.L.T. 936.
[73] Thus, Skoda may refer to its position as a member of the Volkswagen group. Ever-changing examples may be sought on the Volkswagen website at http://www.vwvortex.com/news/index.html.
[74] As pointed out by Vandenburgh, *Trademark Law and procedure* (1959) at para. 1.50 (US).
[75] This being the statutory test for the existence of partnership—Partnership Act 1890, s. 1.
[76] The fact that a partnership changes every time a partner joins or leaves, causes inconvenience when it comes to marks used in connection with partnership business. This does not render the marks deceptive to the public: *Leather Cloth Co v. American Leather Cloth Co* (1865) 11 E.R. 1435, HL. However, it does make it difficult to record the proprietor of a mark on the Register. Gold *et al.* editors of the U.K. Trade Marks Handbook, at para. 103.24.5, express caution at the new Registry practice of allowing applications in the partnership name, without filing a list of partners. It also appears [*ibid.*] that filing in the name of nominee partners, the practice under the Trade Marks Act 1938, continues.

1890 Act. Lloyd[77] points out that the 1905 Trade Marks Act did not specifically provide for joint registration, although it was allowed. In *Isola Ld's application*[78] the Comptroller-General considered whether the parties concerned were in partnership (no) or engaged in some other form of joint venture under the mark. Since any joint venture had terminated upon the outbreak of the First World War, the applicant was not entitled to be named as co-proprietor of the mark. Interestingly, several cases show that parties in the relationship of supplier and distributor were regarded carrying on a joint adventure. Such was the case in *TARANTELLA*[79] and in *Namlooze*.[80] In both these cases the distributors had devised the marks in question. This, however, was stated not to be the ground of the decision in *Namlooze*.[81] Not every alleged joint adventure resulted in joint registration; in *Baptistin Bodrero's Application*[82] a patent license was held not to be a joint adventure for trade mark purposes. In *Elliot Optical Coy's application*[83] a distributor was held not to be jointly entitled with an applicant for registration who also sold the goods directly. It was observed in *PALMOLIVE TM*:[84]

> In my view, before a mark can be registered in the joint names of a manufacturer and a merchant or selector on the ground that they are engaged in a joint adventure, it must be shown that all the goods upon which the mark is to be placed are to pass through the hands of both the parties.

This view echoes the early case of *Robinson v. Finlay*[85] and was echoed in turn in the Trade Marks Act 1938. The 1938 Act made specific provision for the registration of jointly owned trade marks in section 63, provided the co-proprietors were only entitled to use the mark

(a) on behalf of both or all of them, or

---

[77] Lloyd, (ed.) *Kerly's Law of Trade Marks and Trade Names* (8th Edition, 1960) at p. 259, citing *Namlooze Vennootschap Fabriek van Chocolade en Suikerwerken J C Klene & Co's application*, (1923) 40 R.P.C. 103 and *Re TARANTELLA TMs* (1910) 27 R.P.C. 573 (order discharged by consent 762), CA.
[78] (1922) 39 R.P.C. 171.
[79] *Re TARANTELLA TMs* (1910) 27 R.P.C. 573 (order discharged by consent 762) CA.
[80] *Namlooze Vennootschap Fabriek van Chocolade en Suikerwerken J C Klene & Co's application* (1923) 40 R.P.C. 103.
[81] Likewise in *Al Bassam* [1995] R.P.C. 511 devising the mark was held not to be conclusive of ownership.
[82] (1938) 55 R.P.C. 185.
[83] (1952) 69 R.P.C. 169; registration was refused in this case because the mark SYNOPTOPHONE had become the common name by which formerly patented article was known.
[84] (1932) 49 R.P.C. 269.
[85] (1877) 9 Ch. D. 487, applied in *William Grant v. Glen Catrine Bonded Warehouse* [1995] S.L.T. 936. In *Van Zeller v. Mason, Cattley & Co* (1907) 25 R.P.C. 37, use of the mark KOPKE RORIZ for wine was restrained where the wine sold by the defendants under the mark no longer came from the plaintiff's Quinta de Roriz vineyard.

(b) in relation to an article with which both or all of them were connected in the course of trade.

A classic business joint venture, which would appear to satisfy section 63, is to be found in the facts of *Shell-Mex & BP and Aladdin Industries v. R & W Holmes*.[86] Aladdin selected Shell-Mex's "White May" paraffin oil as suitable for use in their heaters. Shell-Mex supplied and distributed it. Aladdin supplied a pink dye to be added to the oil. The dyed oil was sold to the public as "ALADDIN" paraffin. Thus the product sold under the mark was connected with both parties, who were also probably using the mark on behalf of them both.[87]

Other bases for multiple use

The nexus between users of a mark may be weaker or indirect. For example, the users may all participate in an event,[88] without there being any similarity in their roles. Perhaps for this reason the Olympic symbol is protected by designated legislation in the United Kingdom,[89] rather than by relying on general trade mark law.

The nexus may be geographical. The Molony Committee on Consumer Protection[90] expressing the view that many characteristics certified by standardisation or certification marks had been trivial, singled out place of manufacture for particular mention as an example. It is submitted that a geographical denomination may speak volumes about regulation of additives or non-use of child labour[91] or environmental impact in the case of manufactured goods, just as it may indicate qualities of soil, water, pasture, standards of animal husbandry, and so forth in the case of foodstuffs. Indications of (geographical) origin may be administered by Government bodies,

---

[86] (1937) 54 R.P.C. 287.
[87] Wadlow opines that the arrangement was in the nature of a licence from Aladdin to Shell-Mex: *The law of passing off* (2nd ed., 1995) at pp. 134–5.
[88] Gold *et al.* editors of the *U.K. Trade Marks Handbook* suggest that two or more parties might combine their individual marks into a composite mark to indicate joint sponsorship of a sporting event. This is regarded as co-proprietorship and not a "classic licence/licensee situation". In this scenario there may in fact be an element of cross-licensing, a concept well-recognised in patent and competition law but rarer in the sphere of trade marks.
[89] The Olympic Symbol, etc. (Protection) Act 1995, The Olympic Symbol, etc. (Protection) Act Commencement Order 1995 (S.I. 1995 No. 2472); the Olympic Association Right (Infringement Proceedings) Regulations 1995 (S.I. 1995 No. 3325). See also Orr *Marketing Games: the regulation of Olympic indicia and images in Australia* [1997] E.I.P.R. 504; Sydney 2000 Games (Indicia and Images) Protection Act 1996.
[90] Cmnd. 1781 (1974) cited by Mathys Committee, *British Trade Mark Law & Practice*, Cmnd. 5601 (1974) at para. 191.
[91] As to propriety of labour conditions, the U.S. Patent & Trademark Office explains on its website that a U.S. certification mark may certify that the work or labor on the goods or services was performed by members of a union or other organisation. "Some frequently asked questions (FAQ) about trademarks" http://www/uspto.gov/web/offices/tac/tmfaq.htm.

by semi-public bodies or statutory bodies, or by non-public associations of traders.[92]

No nexus or spent nexus

Earlier paragraphs have considered some of the problems that occur when the nexus between formerly connected users no longer is present.[93] Others may arise, for example as a result of a division of entitlement when businesses carried on under the mark become divided or by partial assignment of the marks themselves.[94] Where formerly shared goodwill has been severed, it appears that each owner may sue in passing off without joining the other(s).[95] In *Accurist Watches v. King*,[96] manufacturers applied a trade mark to watches produced for a registered user of the mark. Upon the insolvency of the customer, the manufacturers, who enjoyed retention of title in the watches pending payment, retook possession of the watches. Millett J. held that the necessary connection between the registered user (and hence the proprietor of the goods) and the goods had survived and so the goods could be sold under the mark.

Lastly, there may be concurrent use of identical or similar marks by traders with no connection whatsoever. It is clear that at common law[97] and under the Trade Marks Acts honest concurrent users may use, register[98] and defend their marks.[99]

Multiple ownership of property rather than multiple use

Several persons may be interested in a trade mark as an object of property without being interested in its use. For example, a lender may take an assignment of a trade mark by way of security, on the basis that the borrower/assignor shall have the exclusive right to use unless the financial arrangements go awry. A trustee may hold legal

---

[92] As was pointed out by a witness to the Greer Committee, *Minutes of Evidence* (HMSO, 1920) at p. 11.
[93] See, *e.g.* above, note 10 and accompanying text above.
[94] *Imperial Tobacco Co of India v. Bonnan* [1924] A.C. 755; *IHT v. Ideal Standard* [1994] E.C.R. I-2789; [1994] 3 C.M.L.R. 857; [1995] F.S.R. 59; Lane, "Goodwill hunting: assignments and licenses in gross after *Scandecor*" [1999] I.P.Q. 264; Norman "Trade Marks Licences in the UK– time from Bostitch to be re-evaluated?" [1994] E.I.P.R. 154; *JOB TM* [1993] F.S.R. 118. For the extraordinary history of proprietorship of Rolls Royce and Bentley marks, see Maniatis, below, p. 243, note 59.
[95] *Dent v. Turpin* (1861) 70 E.R. 1003; *Southorn v. Reynolds* (1865) 12 L.T. 75, cited by Wadlow, who regards the issue as one of distinctiveness rather than goodwill: *The law of passing off* (2nd ed., 1995) at p. 135, n. 81.
[96] [1992] F.S.R. 80.
[97] *e.g. Evans v. Eradicure Ltd* [1972] R.P.C. 808; [1972] F.S.R. 137. In *Vine Products v. Mackenzie* [1969] R.P.C. 1 it was held that 100 years' use sufficed at common law.
[98] Subject to opposition by the senior proprietor, Trade Marks Act 1994, s.7. For a recent example of honest concurrent user registration, see *MERLIN* [1997] R.P.C. 871.
[99] Trade Marks Act 1994, ss. 7, 11(1); Trade Marks Act 1938, ss. 12(2), 4(4).

title and be registered as proprietor, but the beneficiary[1] may be the person entitled to use the mark. These arrangements, it is submitted, involve split ownership, but no element of collective interest in using the mark as an instrument of trade.

Might collective marks have been registered under earlier U.K. legislation?
Joint adventure basis

The notion of collective interest in a mark may be relevant here—on whose behalf is a collective mark used? Clearly each authorised user may mark its own particular goods or services, but it appears that the goodwill generated by that use will belong to the collectivity,[2] as well as property in any registration of the collective mark. This suggests that use is in fact on behalf of all members of the grouping. If this analysis is correct, the collective "association" mark would fall within the first limb of section 63 of the Trade Marks Act 1938[3]—a mark in which two or more people are interested, where their relations are such that no one of them is entitled to use the mark except on behalf of all of them. Section 63 went on to state that nothing in the Act authorised the registration as joint proprietors of two or more persons who used a trade mark independently. But a collective mark is by its very nature employed *dependently*—upon the rules of the association between its users. The "joint adventure" is the association itself. From a survey of the case law it appears that no such collective mark was registered under section 63 of the 1938 Act, but it is submitted that the possibility existed. Some slight indication may be detected in the Report of the Departmental Committee on the Law and Practice relating to trade marks.[4] There it was stated, apropos of the recommendation that proprietors of certification marks should not be permitted to trade in the goods or services concerned,[5] "We think that adequate provisions is made in the Act for the registration of trade marks to associations or persons who actually trade in goods". However, this was probably directed to marks used in the course of the association's own trade, rather than that of its members.

---

[1] Or the recipient of an equitable assignment: Fitzgerald & Firth "Equitable Assignments in relation to intellectual property" [1999] I.P.Q. 228.
[2] See comments above on *Artistic Upholstery Limited (on behalf of itself and all other members of the Long Eaton Guild of Furniture Manufacturers) v. Art Forma Limited*, (Lawrence Collins Q.C., sitting as a deputy High Court Judge) [1999] All E.R. 277.
[3] See above, pp. 183–4.
[4] Cmd. 4568 (1934), para. 229(ii) (Goschen Committee).
[5] The recommendation was implemented as the proviso to s.37 (1) of the 1938 Act.

Licensing

An association could have registered a mark either for its own use or under the provisions of section 29(1)(b) of the 1938 Act as a mark proposed to be used by registered users.[6] If member licensees were registered as users, section 28(2) ensured that their use would accrue to the association as licensor.

Certification marks

In *UNIS*[7] an oft-quoted case concerning certification marks, the facts suggest a hybrid arrangement with controls more akin to those for a collective mark in the "association" sense than the arrangements normally found for certification marks. The marks UNIS, UNIS FRANCE and devices were used to signify goods of French origin. The applicants sought registration in 50 classes. The applicant association was a union of French industry syndicates. Users were not the syndicates themselves, but rather manufacturer members of the syndicates or French manufacturers who subscribed to the regulations of their relevant industry syndicates. The case raised several points of difficulty. Firstly, the marks denoted a quality, country of production, but the method of certification was indirect. However, the criterion for registration of a standardisation mark[8] had already been amended[9] from the examination and certification of goods to "undertaking to certify" by the applicant plus competence to certify. The latter question fell solely to be considered by the Board of Trade.[10] In the Court of Appeal the case turned on whether the applicant "undertook" to certify in the sense of making that its business. Despite the remoteness of the arrangements for certification, Warrington L.J. was prepared to assume that, by making and insisting upon its rules, the Union did make it its business to certify the French origin of the goods.[11] Younger L.J. expressed a healthy scepticism as to whether the Union's intended practice complied with the statutory requirements, but eventually drew back from dissenting with the majority view in favour of registration. The Union was observed to be an unincorporated association.

In accepting delegated control over use of the mark, the decision in *UNIS* foreshadowed the much later case of *Molyslip*,[12] in which it

---

[6] At least on genuine registered user was needed in order to mount such application: *Pussy Galore* [1967] R.P.C. 265.
[7] *In the matter of an application by Union Nationale Inter-Syndicale des Marques Collectives to register trade marks* (1922) 39 R.P.C. 346.
[8] Under s. 62 of the Trade Marks Act 1905.
[9] By the Trade Marks Act 1919.
[10] The equivalent function now resides within the Registry under the 1994 Act.
[11] (1922) 39 R.P.C. 346 at 361.
[12] [1978] R.P.C. 211.

was held that a licensor could exercise effective quality control by delegating it to a technically competent licensee.

Were the *UNIS* applicants to apply for registration today, would they be entitled to a collective mark? If the CTM construction were applied, it would be no problem that members of members were the actual users. However, adherence to syndicate regulations rather than full membership of the syndicates sufficed under the arrangements described by the Court of Appeal. Nonetheless those syndicates in turn were affiliated to the applicant association. It is submitted that the UNIS marks could be registered as collective marks under the new regime.

Conclusion

Collective marks might in fact have been registered prior to commencement of the Trade Marks Act 1994, whether as certification marks, joint adventure marks or under registered user arrangements with members. However the current, explicit, regime, seems far more satisfactory. It remains to be seen how much use will be made of the new provisions in the years to come.

9. Schecter's *The Rational Basis of Trade Mark Protection* Revisited

Helen Norman

Schechter's *The Rational Basis of Trade Mark Protection* Revisited

Introduction

As long ago as 1927, Frank Schechter postulated[1] that besides acting as an indicator of origin, a trade mark could fulfil advertising and guarantee functions. Taking as his starting point the orthodox definition that "the primary and proper function of a trade mark" was "to identify the origin or ownership of goods to which it is affixed",[2] Schechter asserted that such definition may have been accurate historically,[3] but was no longer so. Even by 1927, he said, courts had adjusted to the notion that, thanks to the complexities of modern trade, the average consumer did not know (or indeed care) precisely whence the product originated.[4] Schechter reasoned that the trade mark's prime function was not to designate source but to create and retain custom. Quoting from H.G.Wells[5] about how the mark reached over the shoulder of the retailer and across the counter straight to the customer, he argued that "the mark sells the goods". From that he concluded that the action for dilution, to preserve the selling power of the mark, was the only rational basis of trade mark protection, and not the narrow infringement action to prevent damage to goodwill by diversion of custom:

> To describe a trade mark merely as a symbol of goodwill, without recognising in it an agency for the actual creation and perpetuation of goodwill, ignores the most potent aspect of the nature of a trade mark and that phase most in need of protection.[6]

---

[1] Schechter, "The Rational Basis of Trademark Protection" (1927) 40 Harv.L.R. 813.
[2] *Hanover Star Milling Co v. Metcalf* (1915) 240 US 403 at 412.
[3] Ironically, the guild system (see note 8 below) promoted the guarantee function of the trade mark long before the source function came to be predominant.
[4] Schechter, above, quoted extensively from U.K. cases to support this argument, namely Lindley L.J. in the *Yorkshire Relish* case (*Powell v. Birmingham Vinegar Brewery Co* (1896) 13 R.P.C. 235 at 250) and from the submissions of Sir Duncan Kerly and the judgment of Warrington L.J. in the NUVOL case (*McDowell's Application* (1926) 43 R.P.C. 313 at 337). Such *dicta* received statutory recognition in s. 68(1) of the 1938 Act ("whether with or without any indication of the identity of that person"). More recently, Jacob J. has opined ". . . certainly Joe Soap seeing a trade mark on the goods of a multinational is not concerned with the fine detail of the multi-company structure of the group": *Northern & Shell v. Condé Nast & National Magazine Distributors Ltd* [1995] R.P.C. 117 at 124.
[5] H.G. Wells, *The World of William Clissold: a Novel at a New Angle* (Bernhard Tauchnitz Leipzig, 1927).
[6] Schechter, above, at 818.

The implications of Schechter's proposition (apart from the necessity to recognise dilution as a form of trade mark infringement) are, first, that the trade mark is more than a mere adjunct of goodwill. It has an independent, inherent value of its own which is worthy of protection, making it (in some respects) more akin to patents and copyright. Second, the rationale of trade mark protection should focus on shielding the trade mark owner against forms of harm beyond the diminution of goodwill caused by origin confusion. Logically, the trade mark infringement action should be concerned with the misappropriation of property and with notions of unfair competition or even unjust enrichment.

This paper attempts to assess whether Schechter's theory has found any acceptance in the law relating to registered trade marks in the United Kingdom over the last century. Are judges prepared to recognise that the trade mark right can be infringed not just by "piracy" of the mark (in the sense of diverting custom) but by misappropriation? This latter term is used to indicate that the defendant "free rides" on the value of the plaintiff's mark in order to promote its own brand. It will be shown that United Kingdom trade mark law suffers not only from its historical legacy, but from an unwillingness on the part of the judiciary to indulge in any sort of policy debate about what the proper basis of protection *ought* to be. Cases discussed below reveal a judicial tendency to fasten on to the literal meaning of successive Trade Marks Acts without regard to commercial reality—namely, that the defendant's conduct might be regarded by the business community as unfair competition. Such narrow-mindedness may well, it will be argued, hinder the full reception of the underlying thinking of the Trade Marks Directive[7] and ultimately prevent harmonisation of trade mark law in Europe in the twenty-first century.

The Historical Legacy

Space does not permit an examination of the use of trade marks in medieval England as either proprietary or production marks,[8] nor of the eventual decline of the guild system (under which compulsory marking of goods was the means of providing consumer protection, hence a guarantee of quality) nor of the accuracy of treating *Southern v. How*[9] as the first trade mark decision of the common law courts.

---

[7] First Council Directive 89/104 to approximate the laws of the Member States relating to trade marks, [1989] O.J.L 40/1, as amended by Annex XVII to the Agreement establishing the EEA [1994] O.J.L 1/3.
[8] Those wishing a fuller discussion of this aspect of trade mark history are referred to Schechter, *The Historical Foundations of the Law Relating to Trade Marks* (Columbia University Press, 1925, New York, 1925).
[9] The decision is blessed with five different law reports, none of which agrees with any certainty as to when it was decided: (1618) Croke's Reports (Jac. 1) 468 (hearings in Hilary Term, 14 Jac. 1 and Trinity Term, 16 Jac. 1); Popham's Reports 143 (hearing in Trinity Term, 15 Jac. 1); Bridgman J. 125 (hearing in Hilary Term, 13 Jac. 1, with further hearings in Hilary

Prior to the introduction of the registration system by the Trade Marks Registration Act 1875, the haphazard evolution of trade mark law during the nineteenth century (precipitated by the industrial revolution with the consequent physical separation of the consumer from the manufacturer), reflected the divergence of law and equity. The courts of common law, in cases such as *Sykes v. Sykes*,[10] *Blofeld v. Payne*[11] and *Crawshay v. Thompson*,[12] adhered to the notion that infringement of a trade mark was analogous to the tort of deceit, so that fraudulent intent on the part of the defendant had to be proved. The Court of Chancery wavered between two contrasting views. Influenced by Lord Langdale, in cases such as *Perry v. Truefitt*,[13] *Croft v. Day*[14] and *Burgess v. Burgess*,[15] it stayed firmly wedded to the idea of misrepresentation, somewhat wider, as might be expected, than common law notions of deceit, but nevertheless tortious in nature. However, Lord Westbury, in three decisions of 1863,[16] denied the need for fraud and assumed that trade mark infringement was a species of trespass to property.[17] There was little analysis of what this right of property entailed, other than the assertion that there was no exclusive ownership of a trade mark apart from its use in trade to indicate the origin of goods. The trade mark action was said to correspond to the infringement of a patent or copyright.

After "fusion" in 1875, the equitable view of trade mark infringement eclipsed that of the common law. Lord Westbury's views, being later than those of Lord Langdale, should have prevailed. Subsequent cases, notably *Reddaway v. Banham*,[18] *Spalding v. Gamage*[19] and *Singer Manufacturing v. Loog*,[20] returned to the premise that the essence of the infringement action was a misrepresentation that the defendant's goods were those of the plaintiff. The resultant damage was to the right of property residing

---

Term, 15 Jac. 1 and Trinity Term, 16 Jac. 1); 2 Rolle 5 (Hilary Term, 15 Jac. 1); 2 Rolle 21 (Trinity Term, 16 Jac. 1). The facts reveal that this was an unsuccessful action on the case brought in the King's Bench by a disgruntled factor against his principal concerning the sale of allegedly counterfeit jewels. Its only link with trade mark law lies, as Schechter pointed out (above, note 8, at p. 123) in "an irrelevant reminiscent dictum" by Doderidge J. concerning a half-remembered trade mark case involving the sale of counterfeit cloth. Not only does the dictum not explain by whom the action was brought (the disappointed consumer or the trade mark owner), the reasons for the inclusion of the dictum are obscure and its utterance is barely established by three out of the five reports. Its value must be negligible, as no mention of the dictum appears in Bridgman's reports, Bridgman being counsel for the defence in *Southern v. How*. It is therefore highly surprising that *Southern v. How* should be cited without question by Aldous L.J. in *British Telecommunications plc v. One in a Million Ltd* [1998] 4 All E.R. 476.
[10] (1824) 3 B. & C. 541.
[11] (1833) 4 B. & Ad. 409.
[12] (1842) 4 Man. & G. 358.
[13] (1842) 6 Beav. 66.
[14] (1843) 7 Beav. 84.
[15] (1853) 3 De G.M. & G. 896.
[16] *Hall v. Barrows* (1863) 4 De G.J. & S. 150; *Edelsten v. Edelsten* (1863) 1 De G.J. & S. 185; *Leather Cloth Co. v. American Leather Cloth Co.* (1863) 4 De G.J. & S. 137.
[17] On the authority of Lord Cottenham in *Millington v. Fox* (1838) 3 My. & Cr. 338.
[18] [1896] A.C. 199 *per* Lord Herschell.
[19] (1915) 32 R.P.C. 273 *per* Lord Parker.
[20] (1880) 18 Ch.D. 395 at 412 *per* James L.J.

in the goodwill of the plaintiff's business, not in the mark itself. The absence of any definitive ruling as to the basis of the judicial protection of trade marks before 1875 was compounded by subsequent legislation which assumed that registered trade marks were a form of personal property whilst at the same time defining infringement in terms of the trade mark's function as an indicator of origin. In the case of unregistered marks, Lord Parker's view in *Spalding v. Gamage* that what was protected was not the name but the goodwill associated with it, is still accepted as correct.[21]

The 1905 Act: the First Statutory Definition of Infringement

The Trade Marks Act 1905 was the first to contain a statutory definition of infringement.[22] The opening limb of section 39 read as follows:

> Subject to the provisions of section 41 of this Act and to any limitations and conditions entered upon the register, the registration of a person as proprietor of a trade mark shall, if valid, give to such person the exclusive right to the use of such trade mark upon or in connection with the goods in respect of which it is registered.

Registration therefore appeared to confer upon the trade mark owner the right to exclude or prevent others from using the mark in connection with the goods of its registration, the phrase "in connection with" seeming to indicate a fairly wide range of activities. However, the decision of the House of Lords in *Irving's Yeast-Vite Ltd v. F.A. Horsenail*[23] resulted in the scope of the provision being severely curtailed by the definition of "trade mark" in section 3 of the same Act.

The plaintiffs were the registered proprietors of YEAST-VITE for pharmaceutical preparations. The defendant sold a preparation labelled "Yeast Tablets–a substitute for YEAST-VITE" which had a composition different from that of the plaintiffs' product. The plaintiffs argued that to constitute an infringement of the exclusive

---

[21] See the criteria for a claim of passing off in *Erven Warnink v. Townend* [1979] A.C. 731 and *Reckitt & Colman Products Ltd v. Borden Inc* [1990] 1 W.L.R. 491. The inability or unwillingness of English law to recognise any right of property in a name (see *Day v. Brownrigg* (1878) 10 Ch.D. 294) has caused problems in those passing off cases dealing with character merchandising. The problem may be alleviated by treating copyright rather than goodwill as the property right being infringed: *Mirage Studios v. Counter-Feat Clothing Ltd* [1991] F.S.R. 145. Arguably, Browne-Wilkinson V.C. in this case goes against the principle established by Lord Parker in *Spalding v. Gamage*, above, note 19.
[22] There was no such provision in the Trade Marks Registration Act 1875, the Trade Marks Registration Amendment Act 1876, the Trade Marks Registration Extension Act 1877, the Patents Designs and Trade Marks Act 1883 nor the Patents Designs and Trade Marks Act 1888.
[23] (1934) 51 R.P.C. 110.

right conferred by section 39, it was not necessary that the word should be used as a trade mark, that is, for the purpose of indicating that the goods had "by virtue of manufacture, selection, certification, dealing with or offering for sale"[24] their origin with the alleged infringer. The exclusive right conferred by section 39 was not confined to use for a particular purpose. The House of Lords decisively rejected the argument. Lord Tomlin said this:

> The phrase 'the exclusive right to the use of such trade mark' carries in my opinion the implication of use of the mark for the purpose of indicating in relation to the goods or in connection with which the use takes place, the origin of such goods in the user of the mark by virtue of the matters indicated in the definition of 'trade mark' contained in section 3.[25]

Thus, regardless of the defendant's misappropriation of the value residing in the plaintiffs' mark to sell their own goods, because what they had done did not satisfy the implicit criteria for trade mark use in section 3, there was no infringement. Needless to say, although the case happened some seven years after the publication of Schechter's seminal article, there was no debate on whether the harm done to the plaintiffs or the gain made by the defendants *ought* to have been considered as a form of trade mark infringement. History dictated that origin confusion was all.

That is not to suggest that notions of unfair competition were totally unknown to courts dealing with the 1905 Act. A clear-cut case was *Teofani & Co Ltd v. Teofani*[26] where the defendant had misappropriated the plaintiff's trade mark for cigarettes in such a way that the relevant defence in section 44 of the Act (use of the defendant's own name) was held not to apply. Another was *Newton Chambers & Co Ltd v. Neptune Waterproof Paper Co Ltd*,[27] where the defendant's use of the plaintiff's mark IZAL (to indicate that the plaintiff's product had been used to treat the defendant's toilet paper) was held not entitled to the benefit of the descriptive use defence found in the same section. Whereas the defendant in *Teofani* had been subjectively dishonest in using his own name on a rival product, in the *IZAL* case the defendant's conduct (evidenced by the disproportionate size of lettering used to highlight the plaintiff's mark) was judged objectively by what were considered to be commercially acceptable standards of behaviour.

---

[24] The wording of s.3 of the 1905 Act.
[25] (1934) 51 R.P.C. 110 at 115.
[26] (1913) 30 R.P.C. 446.
[27] (1935) 52 R.P.C. 399. An analogous set of facts occurred in *Kimberly-Clark v. Fort Sterling Ltd* [1997] F.S.R. 877. An unfortunate concession by counsel that s. 10(6) of the 1994 Act applied to exempt the defendants resulted in the case being decided on the grounds of passing off and not trade mark infringement.

The 1938 Act and "Importing a Reference"

The Trade Marks Act 1938[28] presented a knotty problem of statutory interpretation. Parliament had seen fit to adopt the same legislative technique as that previously used in relation to the Law of Property Act 1925, in that there was a still-born amendment Act (the Trade Marks Amendment Act 1937) which was repealed on the day it was brought into force by the 1938 Act which was declared to be a consolidating measure.[29]

In an effort to reverse the *Yeast-vite* decision,[30] section 4(1) of the 1938 Act defined the trade mark proprietor's exclusive right in a provision of "inordinate length"[31] and "fuliginous obscurity".[32] Nevertheless, it is arguable that the phrase "the exclusive right to the use of the trade mark" in section 4(1) was limited by the definition of "trade mark" in section 68(1) ("a mark used or proposed to be used in relation to goods for the purpose of indicating, or so as to indicate, a connection in the course of trade between the goods and some person having the right . . . to use the mark") in like manner as section 39 of the 1905 Act had been constrained by section 3 of the same. The inevitable conclusion must be that despite the purported reversal of *Yeast-vite*, the exclusive right to the use of the mark was, at least on the wording of the Act, still limited by its defined role as an indicator of origin. The so-called trade mark "monopoly" could go no further.

The 253 words which made up the single sentence of section 4(1) entailed two provisions, a general and a specific. The general provision (hereafter, "the first part of section 4(1)"), as already noted, corresponded to the wording of its predecessor, apart from its reference to certification marks and its limitation to Part A of the Register. This was hardly surprising for a consolidating Act. The specific provision (hereafter, "the second part of section 4(1)") commenced "and without prejudice to the generality of the foregoing words" (implying that the general provision indicated the absolute extent of the trade mark monopoly) and gave two instances of when the exclusive right was deemed to have been infringed. The only other difference between section 4(1) and section 39 was the

---

[28] As amended by the Trade Marks (Amendment) Act 1984 and the Patents, Designs and Marks Act 1986. As the amendments do not alter the *substance* of the trade mark right declared by s. 4 of the 1938 Act, references in this paper are, for the sake of convenience, to its original version.
[29] For an example of how such legislative device should be interpreted, see the consideration by the House of Lords in *Midland Bank v. Green* [1980] A.C. 513 of the repeal and replacement of the Law of Property Amendment Act 1922 by the Law of Property Act 1925.
[30] On the recommendation of the Goschen Committee, *Report of the Departmental Committee on the Law and Practice Relating to Trade Marks*, Cmd 4568 (1934).
[31] Kerly, *Law of Trade Marks and Trade Names* (12th ed, Sweet & Maxwell, London 1986) at p. 261.
[32] *Bismag v. Amblins (Chemists) Ltd* (1940) 57 R.P.C. 209 at 237 *per* Mackinnon L.J.

substitution of "in relation to those goods" for the "upon or in connection with the goods".

The examples of infringement in the second part of section 4(1) were stated to occur when (in summary) any person, other than the proprietor or registered user,[33] used either the identical mark, or a confusingly similar mark, in the course of trade in relation to goods in respect of which the mark was registered in such a way that one of two inferences could be made. The first inference (in section 4(1)(a)) was that the mark was being used as a trade mark–that is, to indicate origin. The alternative inference (in section 4(1)(b)) was that the mark was being used to "import a reference" either to the person entitled to use it or to the goods with which that person was connected.

"Importing a Reference" through Comparative Advertising

The first case in which the "new" provisions of section 4(1) could be examined was *Bismag Ltd v. Amblins (Chemists) Ltd*.[34] The plaintiffs were the registered proprietors of BISURATED for medicinal preparations. The defendants, besides selling their own medicines, sold proprietary medicines of other manufacturers, including the plaintiffs. In order to demonstrate that such proprietary medicines were generally over-priced, they published a pamphlet. This contained two columns, one listing the names of "advertised patent medicines" with an analysis of their contents and price, the other showing the names of their own products, again describing contents and price. Opposite the plaintiffs' BISURATED product the defendants listed their own BISMUTHATED brand of tablets which was cheaper than the plaintiffs'. The issue was therefore whether this pamphlet "imported a reference" either to the plaintiffs or their goods.

At first instance, Simonds J. agreed that the first part of section 4(1) did not differ from its predecessor. He found it difficult to allocate a meaning to the second part of the subsection if it was to add rights not conferred by the first part. The question before the court, he said, appeared to be the following: "Does the use by the defendants of [the trade mark] in their pamphlet constitute a use by them of the Mark in relation to goods in respect of which it is registered in such a manner as to render the use of the word likely to be taken as a reference to the Plaintiffs or their goods?".[35] The conclusion had to

---

[33] The reference to the registered user was necessitated by s. 28 of the 1938 Act which permitted licensing of trade marks for the first time, although because of the stigma attached to licensing as a result of the House of Lords' decision in *Bowden Wire Co. Ltd v. Bowden Brake Co. Ltd* (1914) 31 R.P.C. 385, the word "licence" was eschewed.

[34] (1940) 57 R.P.C. 209. Although comparative advertising is dealt with elsewhere in this volume, the case is a useful vehicle to explore judicial attitudes to the proper scope of the trade mark right.

[35] *ibid*, at 217–8.

be that there was no infringement as the defendants were protected by section 4(3). Simonds J. found it difficult to imagine cases within section 4(1)(b) that were not within section 4(1)(a). To prohibit traders from comparing prices of rival products (which was basically what the plaintiffs' claim entailed) would put the whole trading community at risk. Clearly, freedom of competition was to be preferred over the prevention of unfair competition or unjust enrichment.

In the Court of Appeal, three distinct judicial attitudes could be detected. There was a valiant attempt to apply section 4(1)(b) on the basis that, however obscurely worded, this was what Parliament intended (Lord Greene M.R.); a stubborn refusal to allot any meaning to the section at all (Mackinnon L.J.); and an assumption that it must change the law (despite its location in a consolidating Act) without any real effort at analysis (Clauson L.J.).

Lord Greene[36] began by asserting that as the defendants had done precisely what had been done in the *Yeast-vite* case, before the passing of the new Act the plaintiffs would have had no claim. The problem was to determine what change had been made to the trade mark owner's monopoly by section 4(1), bearing in mind that the 1938 Act was a consolidating measure.

His analysis proceeded thus. The second part of section 4(1) was not identical with the first, so it must be assumed that Parliament intended to change the law despite obscurity of language. Part (a) of section 4(1) was the old type of infringement ("piracy" of the mark), therefore part (b) must be new. The phrase "in relation to" must be given a wide meaning and considered different from "upon or in connection with". No explanation was offered as to what this difference might be, nor was any observation made on the fact that Lord Tomlin in the *Yeast-vite* case appeared to use both terms interchangeably.[37] Lord Greene continued by saying that part (b) was "turgid and diffuse" and "far from happy",[38] but its meaning could be discerned, namely "use of a mark identical with the registered mark or so similar as to deceive or cause confusion in the course of trade in relation to the registered goods, either on the goods, or in physical relation thereto, or in advertising, in such a way as to indicate a reference to the proprietor or his goods." It must be assumed that Lord Greene's mention of "confusion" (like its appearance in the section) referred to whether the defendant's mark was confusingly similar, not whether there was a likelihood of origin confusion, since in cases of comparative advertising there can never be origin confusion. The consumer is aware that there are two different sources of supply.[39] If the requirement of origin confusion

---

[36] *ibid* at 231.
[37] See the quotation at note 25 above.
[38] (1940) 57 R.P.C. 209 at 234.
[39] Which is why comparative advertising can never amount to passing off: see Buckley L.J. in *Bulmer v. Bollinger* [1978] R.P.C. 79 at 107.

had been an over-riding pre-requisite for infringement of a Part A mark under the 1938 Act, the Goschen Committee's intended effect of section 4(1)(b) could never have been achieved. Arguably, however, such a requirement did exist in relation to Part B marks (at least in regard to the relief to be granted) because of the particular defence in section 5(2).[40]

Lord Greene added that the use of the mark must be trade mark use, not on the defendant's goods (which was covered by part (a)), but on the plaintiff's goods. However, the section did not extend to non-trade mark or descriptive use, otherwise the plaintiff would have had a complete monopoly. Again, no explanation was given as to what "trade mark use" meant under section 4(1)(b) if it was not to indicate origin as the definition of trade mark in section 68(1) predicated. His conclusion was even more contradictory. He stated that the defendants' conduct infringed the general words of section 4(1) as well as the specific words of section 4(1)(b). This conclusion, of course, rendered section 4(1)(b) redundant, and produced a totally illogical argument which went something like this. The defendants, on the basis of the *Yeast-vite*, would not have been liable before 1938; the first part of section 4(1) was no different than its forerunner, section 39; the defendants were liable under the second part, because they had "imported a reference" under section 4(1)(b); but because they had infringed section 4(1)(b) they were also liable under the general wording in the first part of the section; therefore the general wording in section 4(1) was wider than that in section 39! And as already pointed out, the only difference of substance between the two sections was the substitution of "in relation to" for "in connection with", a difference asserted but not explained by Lord Greene. Nevertheless, if one ignores this defective reasoning, Lord Greene appeared to point the way, perhaps unwittingly, towards a view of trade mark infringement which equated to unfair competition.

The illogicalities of Lord Greene's approach were highlighted by the dissenting judgment of Mackinnon L.J.[41] His by now famous comment on the subsection is worth repeating:

> In the course of three days' hearing of this case I have, I suppose, heard section 4 of the Act of 1938 read, or have read it for myself, dozens if not hundreds of times. Despite this iteration I must confess that, reading it through once again, I have very little notion of what the section is intended to convey, and particularly the sentence of 253 words, as I make them, which constitutes subsection (1). I doubt if the entire statute book could

---

[40] See *Montana Wines v. Villa Maria Wines* [1985] R.P.C. 412 concerning the equivalent provisions in New Zealand.
[41] (1940) 57 R.P.C. 209 at 236.

be successfully searched for a sentence of equal length which is of more fuliginous obscurity.[42]

Applying basic principles of statutory interpretation, he reminded his brethren that it was implicit that Parliament did not change the law except by the use of clear wording. He relied on Coke's four points of statutory interpretation: what was the law before; what was its mischief; what was Parliament's remedy; and what was the reason for the remedy?[43] Unlike Lord Greene, Mackinnon L.J. found no real difference between "in relation to" and "in connection with" and agreed with Simonds J. that the basic idea of infringement was the use of the registered mark in relation to the infringer's goods, in other words origin confusion and no more. The defendants had used the plaintiffs' mark in relation to the plaintiffs' goods and their own mark on their own goods and what was wrong with that? He had earlier[44] commented that the defendants had engaged in "sharp business competition", although by those words, he stressed, neither underhandedness nor immorality was to be implied. For Mackinnon L.J. therefore, as for Simonds J., origin confusion was the sole test of infringement. That the defendants might have been unjustly enriched at the plaintiffs' expense by relying on their reputation to sell an alternative product was of no concern to the law of trade marks.

Clauson L.J.[45] adopted a different approach. He pointed out that "trade mark" was given a new definition and that "in relation to" was deliberately wider than "in connection with". It was no longer necessary to use the mark on a particular physical object as section 4(1) contemplated its use in advertising matter. Moreover, he emphasised the use of the phrases "any goods" and "those goods" in the fifth and seventh lines of the section. The basic trade mark monopoly had been widened so that the plaintiffs had, under section 4(1)(a), the exclusive use of the word BISURATED in relation to chemical substances prepared for use in medicine and pharmacy. This would not, however, give an absolute monopoly over the use of the word, as there would only be infringement by use in the course of trade. The defendants were not liable under section 4(1)(a) (because they had not used the plaintiffs' mark to indicate the origin of their own goods), but were liable under section 4(1)(b), which, he inferred, was in addition to section 4(1)(a). Section 4(3) could not be relied on by the defendants because that subsection applied only to straightforward not comparative advertising. For Clauson L.J. then, the criterion for trade mark infringement appeared to be "use in

---

[42] ibid. at 237.
[43] ibid. at 238, quoting the mischief rule as enunciated by Sir Edward Coke.
[44] ibid. at 236.
[45] ibid. at 239.

trade" rather than "trade mark use", so that the exclusive right extended beyond origin confusion.[46]

Other Forms of "Importing a Reference"

Cases on other ways in which an infringer could "import a reference" did little to improve the understanding of section 4(1). In *Pompadour Laboratories v. Fraser*,[47] the plaintiffs had registered POMPADOUR for shampoos. The defendants had previously manufactured hair lacquer for the plaintiffs, and advertised their product as "manufactured for Pompadour Laboratories for several years". One problem was whether hair lacquer was within the plaintiffs' specification of goods.[48] Interlocutory relief was, however, principally refused because the defendants had referred not to the plaintiffs' mark but to their company name, so that there was no trade mark use as required by the section. The court did not consider the points that the trade mark in question was *part of* the company name and that under section 4(1)(b) the reference which was to be imported could be to the product *or* the proprietor.[49] As in *Bismag*, the question of what was "trade mark use" for the purposes of section 4(1)(b) was not addressed, although in the context of an application for interlocutory relief this was hardly surprising. In another decision, *AUTODROME Trade Mark*,[50] Plowman J. held that to use a trade mark as the name of a building where second-hand cars were sold was not trade mark use because it was not use "in relation to" cars for the purposes of section 4(1)(b),[51] despite the remark by Clauson L.J. in *Bismag* that because of the phrase "in relation to", the mark does not have to be physically affixed to the goods.

The claim under section 4(1)(b) did succeed in the case of *British Northrop Ltd v. Texteam Blackburn Ltd*.[52] The defendants manufactured and sold spare parts for the looms manufactured by the plaintiffs, their price list containing the following statement: "Every part shall be inspected and approved by engineers with many years experience in the manufacture of NORTHROP parts". With regard to the plaintiffs' claim under section 4(1)(b), Megarry J., remarking that

---

[46] It is not proposed to consider the subsequent decisions on comparative advertising under the 1938 Act, namely *Compaq Computers Corp v. Dell Computer Corp* [1992] F.S.R. 93 and *Chanel Ltd v. Triton Packaging Ltd* [1993] R.P.C. 32.
[47] [1966] R.P.C. 7.
[48] An issue which would not arise today because of the way in which s. 10(2) has broadened the scope of the infringement action by permitting the registered proprietor to enjoin use on "similar goods".
[49] A similar difficulty arose in *Duracell International Inc v. Ever Ready Ltd* [1989] F.S.R. 71. It remains to be seen whether the use of the word "sign" in s. 10 of the 1994 Act overcomes this particular problem.
[50] [1969] R.P.C. 564.
[51] Such difficulty has now been overcome by s. 10(4) of the Trade Marks Act 1994, which may also help to address some of the issues in *Re Dee Corporation plc* [1990] R.P.C. 159.
[52] [1974] R.P.C. 57.

"nothing save duty would have carried me thus far through that press of words",[53] held that the mark had been used by the defendant in the course of trade in relation to goods in respect of which it was registered. The reasoning from *Bismag* was applicable here. The defendants' use was for the purpose of selling their own goods. They had used the plaintiffs' mark to obtain for themselves a benefit from the reputation enjoyed by the plaintiffs' goods sold under and identified by the plaintiffs' trade mark. There had clearly been trade mark use (though what was meant by "trade mark use" other than "use in the course of trade" was not explained). Moreover, the defendants were not entitled to rely on section 8(b) as a defence, because although the use of the mark had been a bona fide description of the character or quality of their goods, the wording of the price list "imported a reference" to the plaintiffs and so was caught by the exception to the provision.

One of the last cases to discuss section 4(1)(b) in any detail was *News Group Newspapers v. Rocket Record Co Ltd*.[54] The plaintiffs, who published, *inter alia*, The Sun newspaper, had registered PAGE THREE for records and cassettes as part of their promotional activity to support one of the main features of their paper. The defendants were proposing to issue an album and a single by a group called the Lambrettas. The song "Page Three" would be one of the twelve tracks on the album and the title of the single. Slade J. rejected the plaintiffs' first contention that the defendants were using the name as a trade mark to indicate a connection in the course of trade within the first part of section 4(1):

> The defendants are, in my judgment, manifestly not using the mark PAGE THREE in *this* trade mark sense. Their use of the mark PAGE THREE is clearly not for the purpose of indicating a connection in the course of trade between the relevant records and the defendants themselves, the users of the mark[55] (emphasis supplied).

He likewise rejected the plaintiffs' second contention that the defendants were in breach of section 4(1)(a). Relying on *Bismag*, this was the "old type" of infringement which required the alleged infringer to use the mark in relation to its own goods in such a way that it would be likely to be taken as use as a trade mark—that is, to indicate their origin—which again the defendants had not done.[56]

The final part of the plaintiffs' argument was that their rights were deemed to be infringed by the defendants' use of an identical mark in the course of trade in such a way as to import a reference to the

---

[53] *ibid.* at 77.
[54] [1981] F.S.R. 89.
[55] *ibid.* at 98.
[56] *ibid.* at 98.

plaintiffs. Slade J. began[57] by relying on Lord Greene M.R. in *Bismag* as to the meaning of the phrase "importing a reference":

> In substance what is meant, as it appears to me, is that the mark must be used in what I may call a trade mark sense, not, of course, as a trade mark for the infringer's own goods (that is provided for by paragraph (a)), but as a trade mark identifying the complainant's goods.[58]

Slade J. continued by emphasising the need to show that the mark had been used in a trade mark, and not merely descriptive, sense, so as to take the present case out of the area covered by the earlier decisions in the *AUTODROME* and *Pompadour* cases. Once again he relied on the Master of the Rolls in *Bismag*:

> In short, the respondents are using the appellants' trade mark for the purpose of advertising and compendiously describing the virtues of their own goods and thus obtaining for themselves a benefit from the reputation enjoyed by the appellants' goods sold under and identified by the appellants' registered trade mark.[59]

In other words, the gist of the complaint was that the defendants used the plaintiffs' mark in a trade mark sense, to commend and sell the defendants' goods. The conclusion was that PAGE THREE, when used as the title of a single record, would be likely to be regarded by a number of persons as indicating a connection in the course of trade between the record and the plaintiff proprietors of *The Sun* newspaper. There would be a substantial number of readers of *The Sun* who knew of the plaintiffs' promotional activities who would make the necessary inference of trade connection. The same conclusion could not be drawn in respect of the album where the name PAGE THREE was one of a dozen or so titles. No inference of trade connection would be made.

It is interesting to note the tacit assumptions made by Slade J. in the above case. He assumed that section 4(1)(b) was not only wider than section 4(1)(a) (which in itself was not remarkable) but that it was wider than the general words in the first part of section 4(1). The conclusion was also reached that there was no "trade mark use" as required by the first part of section 4(1) and by section 4(1)(a), yet there was sufficient "use in a trade mark sense" to satisfy the requirement of "importing a reference" under section 4(1)(b) (apparently, something which would lead to the inference of trade connection albeit not source confusion). Such an approach may help to resolve the difficulties raised by *Bismag* and *Northrop* as to what

---

[57] *ibid.* at 99.
[58] (1940) 57 R.P.C. 209 at 234.
[59] *ibid.* at 230.

was meant by "trade mark use" for the purposes of section 4(1)(b). Nevertheless, there remains the problematic point of statutory interpretation, namely whether section 4(1)(b) could ever cover conduct not already prohibited by the general wording of the section in view of the phrase "without prejudice to the generality of the foregoing". In conclusion, however, Slade J's reliance of the various dicta of Lord Greene M.R. demonstrated a readiness to accept that "free riding" may constitute trade mark infringement.[60]

A Valediction for Section 4

That section 4 of the 1938 Act has departed the statute book should be a matter for rejoicing. Had it continued in force, several aspects awaited clarification by a higher court. Was the general wording the same as that of its predecessor or did the substitution of "in relation to" for "upon or in connection with" make a difference? Did the general wording control the areas covered by section 4(1)(a) and section 4(1)(b) or not? Did section 4(1)(b) really entitle the proprietor to recover for the sort of misuse of his mark which was not actionable before 1938? The answers to all of these questions given by lower courts in the cases discussed above depended on whether a narrow or wide view was taken as to the scope of the trade mark right—yet nowhere is there a discussion of what the policy of the law should have been.

The 1994 Act: A Fresh Start?

Those sections in the Trade Marks Act 1994 dealing with the infringement of registered marks and the defences thereto had to implement the provisions of the Trade Marks Directive.[61] The Directive is stated to be a partial harmonisation measure,[62] so that certain matters are left to the discretion of Member States, whilst in the case of others the Directive lays down a minimum standard, Member States having an option to adopt a higher, but not lower, level of protection.[63] Nevertheless, in relation to infringement, Recital 9 to the Directive declares "it is fundamental . . . to ensure that henceforth registered trade marks enjoy the same protection under the legal systems of all the Member States". The Court of Justice of the European Communities, using the Recital, has emphasised the

---

[60] For a similar outcome to that of the *PAGE THREE* case regarding the collective title of a series of books (as opposed to a single volume) see *Games Workshop v. Transworld Publishers* [1993] F.S.R. 705.
[61] Above, note 7.
[62] Recital 3.
[63] See, for example, Art. 4(4) which permits Member States to recognise dilution and earlier used but unregistered rights as two of the relative grounds for refusal of registration. Both of these have been adopted by the United Kingdom: see, respectively, ss. 5(3) and 5(4)(a) of the 1994 Act.

absolute nature of Article 5(1) in spelling out the scope of the trade mark right.[64] Further, the need for uniformity becomes even more crucial in view of the parallel provisions in the Community Trade Mark Regulation which creates a unitary trade mark right effective in all Member States.[65]

When the relevant provisions of the 1994 Act, namely sections 9, 10, 11 and 12 are compared with the text of Articles 5, 6 and 7 of Directive, certain discrepancies become apparent. For example, section 10(5), section 10(6) and section 11(1) do not have any counterparts in the Directive, section 11(3) is a somewhat idiosyncratic enactment of Article 6(2), and the single provision in Article 5(1) is spread between section 9(1) to (3) and section 10(1) and (2). The present discussion will focus solely on the mismatch between Article 5(1) and sections 9 and 10.[66]

Article 5(1) begins by stating that "the registered trade mark shall confer on the proprietor exclusive rights *therein*. The proprietor shall be entitled to prevent . . .", suggesting that this is a non-exhaustive indication of the right to prevent specified infringing activities. By contrast, the opening words of section 9(1) bear an uncanny resemblance to the 1905 and 1938 Acts, when they state "the proprietor of a registered trade mark has exclusive rights in the trade mark *which are infringed by use of the trade mark* in the United Kingdom without his consent" (emphasis supplied). The insertion of the subordinate clause beginning with the word "which" arguably has a restrictive effect on the scope of the right, especially when linked to section 9(2) ("references . . . to the infringement of a registered trade mark *are to any such infringement of the rights of the proprietor*") (emphasis supplied). As with its predecessors, section 9(1) inevitably directs the reader's attention to the definition of a trade mark in section 1. Admittedly, this section does not mention indicating origin as such, but its "new" criterion of differentiating the products of one undertaking from those of others can be regarded as

---

[64] Case C-284/95 *Silhouette International Schmied GmbH v. Hartlauer Handelsgesellschaft mbH* [1998] 2 C.M.L.R. 953 at paras 23–7.
[65] Council Regulation 40/94 on the Community Trade Mark [1994] O.J.L 11/1. The need for national trade mark law to conform to Community standards is of particular importance when it is remembered that national courts which are deemed to be Community trade mark courts under the provisions of Arts 91–101 of the Regulation are obliged, by virtue of Arts 14 and 97, to apply Community trade mark law to trade mark disputes with which they are seized. As to the need to ensure conformity between national law based on the Directive and the Community trade mark regime, see Advocate General Jacobs in Case C-284/95 *Silhouette International*, above, note 64.
[66] The other most serious discrepancy is s. 11(1) (a registered mark is not infringed by the use of another registered mark) which was inserted during the Report Stage of the Trade Marks Bill before the House of Lords in order to protect the owners of registrations entered on the Register pursuant to s. 12(2) of the 1938 Act and s. 7 of the 1994 Act (honest concurrent use). Just as s. 7 conflicts with Art. 4 of the Directive (see Annand & Norman, *Blackstone's Guide to the Trade Marks Act 1994* (Blackstone Press, London, 1994) at pp. 109–111), so s. 11(1) must conflict with Art. 6, which together with Art. 7 establishes a finite list of derogations from the exclusive right in Art. 5. Such derogations must be narrowly construed: see Advocate General Jacobs in Case C-284/95 *Silhouette International*, above, note 64.

merely a modernised version of "indicating a connection in the course of trade".

The restrictive effect of the grammatical structure of section 9 is compounded by the use of the phrase "in relation to" which appears in each of sections 10(1), 10(2) and 10(3). The cumulative effect of splitting the substantive provision, of the use of the subordinate clause in section 9(1) with its qualification in section 9(2) and the use of the phrase "in relation to" points the way to an unwitting re-enactment of the old law in a new guise, minus (of course) the infringing act of "importing a reference".[67] So why did Parliament do it this way? The answer given by the Government was simply "drafting technique".[68]

United Kingdom decisions on the scope of the new infringement provisions have not yet been obliged to consider head-on the proper scope of the trade mark infringement action, having been primarily concerned either with the validity of the mark,[69] with the correct interpretation of section 10(2)[70] or 10(3),[71] with the application of the defences in section 11[72] or with the threats action in section 70.[73] Nevertheless, the legislative style adopted in the 1994 Act seems to have distracted the judiciary from its task of appreciating the impact of the Directive on the culture of trade mark law. Familiarity has bred contempt.

Some of the wrong turnings taken by U.K. courts have been corrected by the Court of Justice in references for preliminary rulings from the courts of other Member States. Thus the assumption in *BASF plc v. CEP (UK) plc*[74] and *Baywatch Production Co Inc v. The Home Video Channel*[75] that liability under section 10(3) (based on the optional Article 5(2)) depended on there being origin confusion has been refuted by the Court of Justice in *Sabel BV v. Puma AG*,

---

[67] Although infringement by "importing a reference" had been recognised before the passing of the 1938 Act: *J.B. Stone & Co Ltd v. Steelace Manufacturing Co Ltd* (1928) 45 R.P.C. 127.
[68] Hansard, HL/PBC, col. 24 January 18, 1994. The remark by Jacob J. in *British Sugar plc v. James Robertson & Sons Ltd* [1996] R.P.C. 281 at 291 that s. 9 is merely a "chatty introduction" to s. 10 must be questioned in view of the way that both sections are derived from Art. 5(1) and the need for the latter provision to be taken as the definitive statement of the trade mark right.
[69] *British Sugar plc v. James Robertson & Sons Ltd* [1996] R.P.C. 281; *Philips Electronics NV v. Remington Consumer Products Ltd* [1998] R.P.C. 283 (Jacob J.) and [1999] R.P.C. 809 CA.
[70] *Origins Natural Resources Inc v. Origin Clothing Ltd* [1995] F.S.R. 280; *British Sugar plc v. James Robertson & Sons Ltd* [1996] R.P.C. 281; *Wagamama Ltd v. City Centre Restaurants plc* [1995] F.S.R. 713.
[71] *BASF plc v. CEP (UK) plc*, [1997] E.T.M.R. 51; *Baywatch Production Co Inc v. The Home Video Channel* [1997] F.S.R. 22; and (to a lesser degree, as it was decided principally on the basis of passing off) *British Telecommunications plc v. One in a Million Ltd* [1998] 4 All E.R. 476.
[72] *Bravado Merchandising Services Ltd v. Mainstream Publishing (Edinburgh) Ltd* [1995] F.S.R. 205; *British Sugar plc v. James Robertson & Sons Ltd* [1996] R.P.C. 281; *Allied Domecq Spirits v. Murray McDavid Ltd* [1997] F.S.R. 864; *The European Ltd v. The Economist Newspaper Ltd* [1998] F.S.R. 283.
[73] *Trebor Bassett Ltd v. The Football Association* [1997] F.S.R. 211.
[74] [1997] E.T.M.R. 51.
[75] [1997] F.S.R. 22.

Rudolf Dassler Sport.[76] The action for dilution remedies a form of harm different from that caused by deception to customers, namely injury to the selling power of the mark. At least in this regard, Schechter's hypothesis is being fulfilled.

Another area where U.K. judges will have to acclimatise to change is in relation to the assessment of likelihood of confusion in section 10(2). Admittedly *Sabel* has confirmed Laddie J.'s view in *Wagamama Ltd v. City Centre Restaurants plc*[77] that the proper interpretation of Article 5(1)(b) is that "likelihood of association" is included within the concept of likelihood of confusion and does not extend to "merely calling to mind" the plaintiff's mark in the absence of direct or indirect origin confusion.[78] Yet the same case, together with the ruling in *Canon KK v. Metro-Goldwyn-Mayer Inc (Formerly Pathé Communications Corporation)*,[79] has utilised Recital 10 to the Directive to produce an outcome diametrically opposed to that in *British Sugar plc v. James Robertson & Sons Ltd*[80] with regard to how likelihood of confusion is to be assessed. The step-wise approach posited by *British Sugar* and *Origins Natural Resources Inc v. Origin Clothing Ltd*[81] assumes notional and fair use of the registered mark in the future and considers likelihood of confusion *after* examining the similarity of the mark and the goods. *Sabel* and *Canon*, on the other hand, require the application of a global test in which the strength of the mark (whether innate or acquired) can affect the scope of protection with regard to similarity of goods.[82]

The view of Jacob J. in *British Sugar*[83] that the criterion of similarity of goods should be restrictively interpreted must be open to question—as must the view of Laddie J. in *Wagamama*[84] that to broaden the scope of trade mark protection would mean creating a new, unjustified monopoly. To use the strength of the mark to determine the scope of protection, as *Sabel* and *Canon* do, stretches the origin function almost beyond recognition and comes close to Schechter's ideal of protecting the mark against dilution, not just by use on dissimilar but by use on similar goods. Those who argued for a wide interpretation of likelihood of association[85] may have lost that particular battle, but the new "global" test for likelihood of confusion

---

[76] Case C-251/95 [1997] E.C.R. I-6191 at paras 20–1.
[77] [1995] F.S.R. 713.
[78] [1997] E.C.R. I-6191 at para. 26.
[79] [1999] 1 C.M.L.R. 77.
[80] [1996] R.P.C. 281.
[81] [1995] F.S.R. 280.
[82] [1997] E.C.R. I-6191 at para. 23; [1999] 1 C.M.L.R. 77 at paras 16–9.
[83] [1996] R.P.C. 281 at 295.
[84] [1995] F.S.R. 713 at 731.
[85] As to the "Benelux" view on "likelihood of association" and whether it should form part of Community and hence United Kingdom trade mark law, see the various articles on the decision of Laddie J. in *Wagamama* by: Harris [1995] E.I.P.R. 601, [1995] *Trademark World*, October 12; Kamperman Sanders [1996] E.I.P.R. 3, [1996] E.I.P.R. 521; Gielen [1996] E.I.P.R. 83, [1996] *Trademark World*, February 20; Prescott [1996] E.I.P.R. 317, [1997] E.I.P.R. 99.

means that despite this, the nature of the trade mark right has changed.

It is in relation to the operation of the defence found in section 11(2)(b) that United Kingdom courts seem to have experienced the greatest difficulty. The issue for the court, fundamentally, should be how to draw the line between fair use of the plaintiff's mark to describe the defendant's goods and unfair use which misappropriates the selling power of the mark. As the IZAL case[86] demonstrated, this should hardly be a novel experience.

The difficulty with section 11(2)(b) originated with a concession by counsel in *Bravado Merchandising Services Ltd v. Mainstream Publishing (Edinburgh) Ltd*[87] that in order to infringe under section 10(1) (and by implication, section 10(2)) there has to be "trade mark use". This concession was accepted by Lord McCluskey as correct, relying on the authority of *Bismag* and *Mars GB Ltd v. Cadbury Ltd*.[88] Such acceptance may have been too hasty because, as shown above, *Bismag* is by no means conclusive as to what "trade mark use" meant in relation to section 4(1)(b) of the 1938 Act. Having decided that use of the registered mark as the title of a book was nevertheless "trade mark use", Lord McCluskey ultimately found for the defendants on the basis of section 11(2)(b).

Jacob J. in *British Sugar* thought this result to be right in principle but wrong on the construction of the Act—or rather the Directive. He opined that the concession by counsel was unnecessary, preferring instead to say that there had been no use "in relation to"[89] the unauthorised biography in dispute in *Bravado*. In view of the structure of sections 9 and 10 explained above this, with all respect, is tantamount to saying there had been no "trade mark use".[90] Yet having said that "trade mark use" is not required for section 10(1) or section 10(2),[91] *Bravado*, *British Sugar* and *The European Ltd v. The Economist Newspaper Ltd*[92] all accepted without question that section 11(2)(b) is not available to a defendant who uses the plaintiff's trade mark in a trade mark sense rather than in a "purely" descriptive manner. Jacob J. further stated in *British Sugar*[93] that Recital 10 to the Directive (the function . . . of which is to guarantee the trade mark

---

[86] Above, note 27.
[87] [1996] F.S.R. 205.
[88] [1987] R.P.C. 387, where the phrase "treat-sized" was held not to be trade mark use for the purposes of s4(1)(a).
[89] As noted above, a phrase left poorly explained by *Bismag*.
[90] Similar reasoning was used by Rattee J. in *Trebor Bassett Ltd v. Football Association* [1997] F.S.R. 211.
[91] Nor is trade mark use required for s10(3): see Aldous L.J. in *British Telecommunications plc v. One In a Million Ltd* [1998] 4 All E.R. 476 at 499.
[92] [1998] F.S.R. 283 at 291, Millett L.J. By contrast, Aldous L.J. in *Philips Electronics NV v. Remington Consumer Products Ltd*, [1999] R.P.C. 806, CA, declares that "any use not falling within that list will infringe."
[93] [1996] R.P.C. 281 at 298, having previously (at 292) rejected counsel's argument that regard should be had to Parliamentary debates and the White Paper published before the Bill which became the 1994 Act (*Reform of Trade Mark Law*, Cm. 1203 (1990)).

as an indicator of origin) reflects the *sole* purpose of a trade mark. It should, he said, permeate the whole Act.

Such assertion begs a number of questions. If it is the sole purpose, why does the Recital use the phrase *in particular*? And why is section 10(3) included? If it permeates the whole Act, why is Recital 10 not needed for section 10 but is needed for section 11(2)(b)? Such circularity of argument mirrors that found in *Bismag*. It proves that, even after 70 years, Schechter's hope that the origin function could be left behind as the criterion for trade mark protection was misplaced.

Conclusion

This paper proposed at the outset that Schechter's theory required trade mark infringement actions to be based on the concept of unfair competition. This is not so radical as may first appear. After all, states belonging to the Paris Convention for the Protection of Industrial Property 1883 (as do all E.U. Member States) are obliged to "assure to nationals [of countries of the Union] effective protection against unfair competition".[94] "Unfair competition" is defined as "any act of competition contrary to honest practices in industrial or commercial matters"[95] with a non-exhaustive list of examples being given.[96] This definition forms the proviso to Article 6(1) of the Directive, thus governing the scope of the defences to trade mark infringement. It is therefore repeated as the proviso to section 11(2) of the 1994 Act and as the proviso to section 10(6) (as already noted, an entirely domestic provision). Further, Article 5(5) (which seems so far to have received scant attention) permits Member States to grant protection "against the use of a sign other than for the purpose of distinguishing goods or services where use of that sign without due cause takes unfair advantage of, or is detrimental to, the distinctive character or the repute of the trade mark". This provision appears to be considerably wider than Article 5(2), and extends beyond the use of the mark to indicate origin (which is covered by Article 5(1)) to the legality of the defendant's use of the mark in other forms of commercial conduct. Is this the new form of "importing a reference"?[97]

The structure of the Directive therefore invites any court, when confronted by one of its exhaustive list of defences,[98] to consider

---

[94] Art. 10bis (1).
[95] Art. 10bis (2).
[96] Art. 10bis (3).
[97] For a discussion of Art. 5 (5) see Case C-63/97 *BMW v. Deenik* [1999] All E.R. (E.C.) 235 at para. 40. The Article is mentioned in passing by Aldous L.J. in *Philips Electronics NV v. Remington Consumer Products Ltd*, [1999] R.P.C. 809, CA, where he declares (without explanation) that Art. 5(5) "presupposes that infringing use is trade mark use".
[98] See note 66 above.

whether the defendant has misappropriated the value of the registered mark. Such invitation has rarely been accepted by United Kingdom courts, with the notable exception of Megarry J. in *British Northrop*.[99] How much simpler would it have been, in cases like *Bravado*, for the question of infringement to be dealt with as follows. Was there use in the course of trade (meaning merely use in commerce)[1]; did the defendant's conduct *in fact* fall within either sub-sections (1), (2) or (3) of section 10 (or Articles 5(1) and (2)); could the defendant rely prima facie on the defences in section 11(2) (Article 6); or was the defendant's use of the plaintiff's mark nevertheless an act of unfair competition? Such an approach would avoid the pitfalls of having to debate "trade mark use" and of having to decide what "in relation to" meant. An indication that this may be the correct way to tackle the Article 6 defence appears in *BMW v. Deenik*.[2] The drawback is that the court would have to debate where the boundary line should be drawn between legitimate and unfair competition—a task which United Kingdom judges seem unprepared to accept. It seems likely, for the foreseeable future, that Schechter's theory will remain as an item of academic interest only— to the ultimate loss of the trade mark owner.

---

[99] See the text accompanying note 52 and 53 above.
[1] See the original proposal for a Convention to establish a Community Trade Mark, published in 1964, (which evolved into the twin track approach of the harmonisation Directive and the Community Trade Mark Regulation) which contemplated "use in commerce".
[2] Case C-63/97 [1999] All E.R. (E.C.) 235 at para. 64. The case appears to align the proviso to Art. 7(2) (legitimate reasons to object to further commercialisation of the goods) with the proviso to Art. 6 (legitimate reasons to object to descriptive use of the mark).

10. Commercialising the Personality of the Late Diana, Princess of Wales–Censorship by the Back Door?

Charlotte Waelde

Commercialising the Personality of the late Diana, Princess of Wales—Censorship by the Back Door?[1]

After the death of Diana, Princess of Wales (Diana) in 1997 there was perhaps surprisingly little evidence of commercial activity exploiting her image. There were certainly some memorabilia, T shirts, mugs and dog bowls which bore her image, but on the whole there was not the frenetic activity one might have expected. The reason for this soon became clear. The Trustees of the Memorial Fund[2] set up in the memory of Diana had made applications to the Trade Mark Registry for registration of a large number of images of Diana in both black and white and in colour, and of her name and signature and were prepared to use their prospective rights to prevent the unauthorised exploitation of those images and signature by others.

Such are the fluid boundaries of our trade mark law that had these applications succeeded,[3] the Trustees would have had complete control over the exploitation of Diana's image in the market place, leading inexorably to the conclusion that they could censor and control the way in which society was permitted to view Diana as a person after her death.

The purpose of this article is to examine the boundaries of registered trade mark law in the sphere of character merchandising illustrating the argument by reference to the attempts to control the personality of Diana.

Personality, Publicity, Privacy

Historically in the U.K. no specific framework has developed for the legal protection of a personality.[4] A rather fragmented development has provided only limited protection under the general head of

---

[1] I am grateful to Professor Hector MacQueen, Professor of Private Law, University of Edinburgh, for his useful and thought-provoking comments on earlier drafts of this chapter. I alone remain responsible for any errors or omissions.
[2] It is thought that the applications to register these marks may have been made by a number of different groups or entities. For the purposes of this article we will assume that the applications were made by the Trustees of the Memorial Fund, a charity set up in Diana's name to raise money for good causes.
[3] The application to register the image of Diana was turned down by the Patent Office in February 1999 http://news2.thls.bbc.co.uk/hi/english/uk/newsid_272000/272380.stm. The reasons for declining the application have not been made public. It is understood that had the Fund decided to appeal the decision, then the reason for the initial refusal would have been publicly available.
[4] W. R. Cornish, *Intellectual Property* (3rd ed, 1996, Sweet & Maxwell), para. 16.33 *et seq*.

character merchandising. This industry is divided into a number of categories:[5] the merchandising of real characters, the merchandising of fictional characters, and the merchandising of fictional characters played by real persons. Each of these categories has elements in common, the most basic of which is the purpose behind exploiting a particular character, building an affinity in the mind of a consumer between the character and the products in the market and to encourage consumer purchases based on that affinity. Exploitation can occur in a variety of ways, from the quite simple application of images of well known fictional or real characters to a wide variety of goods and memorabilia such as pictures of the pop group Abba on T-shirts or badges,[6] to stuffed toys created in the likeness of a character,[7] to the more complex rendition of a pop song by an Elvis Presley look alike at a public concert.[8] What or who is being exploited will determine which branch of intellectual property is relevant to protect elements of that character. Those seeking to protect fictional characters, for instance, will use copyright, design right, trade mark law and passing off to protect different facets of the whole character.

By contrast, other jurisdictions do have developed personality protection. For instance in a number of states in the United States, there is a developed "right of publicity" for commercial figures, through which a public figure may exploit image for commercial gain, and which has been "embraced enthusiastically by courts and commentators".[9] In tandem with this is a right of privacy whereby a celebrity has a legally enforceable right to be free from public disclosure of intimate affairs. These rights are in turn subject to a "newsworthiness privilege" which allows discussion of celebrity

---

[5] The World Intellectual Property Organisation (WIPO/INF/108 December 1994) defined character merchandising as "the adaptation or secondary exploitation, by the creator of a fictional character or by a real person or by one of several authorised third parties, of the essential personality features of a character in relation to various good and/or services with a view to creating in prospective consumer a desire to acquire those goods and/or to use those services because of the consumers' affinity to that character", p. 6. (Hereafter, WIPO Report), Heijo E Ruijsenaars. "The WIPO Report on Character Merchandising" (1994) 25 I.I.C. 532. The International Association for the Protection of Industrial Property (AIPPI) has called character merchandising "the use, among other things, of names or images of characters, real or fictional persons, events, groups, entities of the most varied kinds, literary and artistic works, their titles and other distinctive elements, in order to enhance the promotion or sale of products and services. This comprises four aspects; character merchandising, personality merchandising, event merchandising and brand merchandising", Heijo E Ruijsenaars, "Legal Aspects of Merchandising: The AIPPI Resolution" [1996] 6 E.I.P.R. 330. John Adams defines character merchandising as "the use in the marketing or advertising of goods or services of a fictional personality or situation". "Personality merchandising involves the use of the true identity of an individual...in the marketing or advertising of goods or services...[and] between these two types lies a rather unclear area where fictional characters played by real actors are used" Adams, *Character Merchandising* (2nd ed, 1996, Butterworths), xiv.
[6] *Lynstad v. Annabast Products Limited* [1975] F.S.R. 488.
[7] *Children's Television Workshop Inc. v. Woolworths (N.S.W.) Limited* [1981] R.P.C. 187.
[8] *Estate of Elvis Presley v. Russen* 513 F. Supp. 1339 (D.N.J. 1981).
[9] Madow, "Private Ownership of Public Image: Popular Culture and Publicity Rights" 81 *Calif. L. Rev.* 125, who argues that the right of publicity in the U.S. facilitates censorship; *Douglass v. Hustler Magazine, Inc.*, 769 F.2d 1128, 1138 (7th Cir. 1985 Posner J.).

gossip.[10] Thus, the U.S. television personality Johnny Carson can invoke his right of publicity to prevent the marketing of "Here's Johnny" portable toilets,[11] but not stop a story by a newspaper about his marital discords.[12] Tabloid newspapers can discuss Bette Midler's weight, but may not make use of a Midler "sound alike" in a TV commercial.[13] Martin Luther King's family can stop the marketing of a plastic bust having inherited the right of publicity,[14] and impersonators of Elvis can be enjoined because of his descendible right of publicity.[15]

The advantage of having a separate right of publicity intertwined with a right of privacy is that commercial exploitation of a personality takes place within a framework developed to meet the ends for which is used. However, the attendant disadvantages are that the right can be used to suppress unwanted information. Residents of those States which have not traditionally had this right have at times lamented its absence, particularly when they have been unable to control exploitation of an image in the marketplace which might portray the celebrity in an unfavourable light. Thus, in New York State, where there was no right of publicity, John Wayne's children objected to a greeting card which had a picture of John Wayne wearing a cowboy hat and bearing the legend "Its such a bitch being butch". Objections were raised not only because of the economic gain being made through this exploitation, but also because such exploitation was seen as tasteless and demeaning of their father's hard earned macho image.[16] They wanted to suppress what they perceived to be the negative comments and image about their late father.[17] The Trustees of the Memorial Fund had fundamentally the same aim: to control the image of Diana and suppress what they considered to be unwanted and unsavoury use while at the same time themselves (or through others) exploiting her image, albeit for charitable purposes.[18]

---

[10] Madow, above, p. 131.
[11] *Carson v. Here's Johnny Portable Toilets Inc.* 698 F.2d 831 (6th Cir. 1983).
[12] Madow, above, p. 131.
[13] *Midler v. Ford Motor Co* 849 F.2d 460 (9th Cir. 1988).
[14] *Martin Luther King Jnr., Ctr. for Social Change, Inc. v. American Heritage Prods., Inc.* 296 S.E. 2d 697 (Ga. 1982).
[15] *Estate of Elvis Presley v. Russen* 513 F. Supp. 1339 (D.N.J. 1981). In some States the question has now moved on from "should there be a right of publicity" to whether it should be a descendible right, and if it is descendible, should there have been exploitation during life, and how long the right should last. Madow, above, p. 130.
[16] Madow, above, p. 143.
[17] See also the discussion of the use of the late Fred Astaire's name and face on condoms in California: http://news2.thls.bbc.co.uk/hi/english/special_report/1999/03/99tom_brook/newsid_396000/396298.stm.
[18] There has been some criticism of the Fund for spending a large amount of money in pursuit of Franklin Mint which they claim is manufacturing unauthorised replicas of the image of Diana: http://news2.thls.bbc.co.uk/hi/english/uk/newsid_352000/352146.stm.
The courts in the past have not looked favourably on charities taking expensive legal action. In *British Diabetic Association v. Diabetic Society and Others* [1996] F.S.R. 1 Walker J. (at pp. 5–6) said: "A passing off action by one charity against another is on the face of it . . . a deplorable, even scandalous thing to occur. Charities solicit donations from the public . . . in the

Name and Image Control

In seeking to protect elements of the character (in the loosest sense) of Diana, and in the absence of any law against personality appropriation, the Trust turned to the law of registered trade marks. Exclusive rights are given to the holder of a registered trade mark to use it in connection with the goods and services for which it registered; to prevent others coming into the market using a similar trade mark in connection with the same goods or vice versa; and to prevent the use of similar signs where the registered mark might be tarnished or diluted.[19] In addition, the control of a trade mark in the marketplace and within the framework of the legislation can be perpetual.[20] The elements of Diana which the Trust sought to protect were her name and her image. What might have been the consequences?

Once the right to use a name can be exercised to the exclusion of others, competition in the marketplace may not only be hampered but eliminated. Imagine an absolute right to use the name "Diana". Would this then preclude competition by anyone who might wish to use her name in association with reporting a story, in a book about her life, or in association with competing or even non-competing goods? The same questions would have to be asked in relation to an image. If there was an absolute right to exploit Diana's image, then could absolute control follow?

A related, but crucial question is how far this control could extend to manipulate the ways in which we as a society are permitted to view and thus to think about the character being exploited? Some of the memorabilia which exploits the image of Diana has been described as "tacky", the clear implication being that such memorabilia should not be permitted in the marketplace—or indeed elsewhere. But who has, or indeed should have the right to dictate to others what memorabilia is or is not tacky? Tackiness is, after all, in the eye of the beholder. If you have complete control over the use of a name, an image, and every form of reproduction of any likeness of a particular celebrity, you are then able to dictate when and under what conditions the celebrity is exhibited to the public. If therefore you wanted the celebrity only to be seen in a positive light, you could veto any use of an image that might conflict with that goal. Fortunately, as a result of the rejection of the registration as a trade

---

expectation that donations will be well spent on furtherance of the charity's purposes. Even for a lawyer it is a difficult mental feat to recognise this very expensive litigation as helping th[ose] . . . whose subscriptions and gifts will be the ultimate source for payment of the lawyers' bills." This perhaps explains why the Fund were keen to emphasis that the litigation was being funded purely from the income generated from one of their commercial arms, rather than public donations.

[19] Trade Marks Act 1994, s. 10.

[20] The first ever trade mark to be registered on the U.K. trade mark register consisted of the words "Bass & Co's Pale Ale" and the red triangle. This was registered in 1876 and is still a live trade mark today: http://webdb.patent.gov.uk/cgi-bin/cbpatent1.1/cb_cgi.

mark of the images of Diana, and the likely rejection of her signature this is not as yet the case in our society. However, a little conjecture: if it were possible under our law to exert such control, should we then be considering other rights to balance this control, such as a right of publicity, and a right to free speech, so that those who disagree with the image of the character being portrayed may say so freely?

A chasm appears: The divergence between the functions of a registered trade mark and the aims of the character merchandiser.

Registered trade marks exist within the consumer society and not in a vacuum. Hence, in many reported cases as to whether the criteria for registration are met, reference will be made to the function of trade marks. If these functions are not being performed, then there is no trade mark. Nevertheless the matter is far from settled.[21] Historically, the function of a trade mark was (and still is) to indicate the origin of goods of a particular trader.[22] But a trade mark does fulfil other functions as recognised by changes made in the Trade Marks Act 1994.[23] The omission of any reference in the 1994 Act (as compared with the Trade Marks Act 1938) that a mark should be used to indicate a "connection in the course of trade", together with the disappearance of the provisions on trafficking in trade marks and the *laissez faire* attitude taken to prescriptive requirements in licences, had led commentators to argue this reflects the acceptance of the expansion in the underlying functions of trade marks. Thus, in the modern consumer society a trade mark also fulfils an advertising role and acts as a guarantee of quality.[24]

Why did the Memorial Fund apply for registration of the name and images of Diana? There is usually one prime motivation for seeking such protection: to secure a monopoly of commercial exploitation of the goods and services registered in connection with the mark. There may be a subsidiary motive: as means of controlling privacy[25] or to

---

[21] Schechter, "The Rational Basis of Trade Mark Protection" (1927) 40 Harv. L.R. 813.
[22] *Aristoc Ltd v. Rysta Ltd* (1945) 62 R.P.C. 65. "[A trade mark] serves to distinguish trade marked products originating from a particular firm or group of firms from the products of other firms. From this basic function of the trade mark are derived all other functions which the trade mark fulfils in economic life."
[23] The Trade Marks Act 1994 was introduced as a result of the E.C. Council Directive of 21 December 1988, to approximate the laws of the Member States relating to Trade Marks, 89/104 [1989] O.J. L40/1. The 1994 Act repealed the earlier legislation relating to trade marks contained in the Trade Marks Act 1938 as amended by *inter alia* the Trade Marks (Amendment) Act 1984, the Patents, Designs and Marks Act 1986 and the Copyright, Designs and Patents Act 1988.
[24] Annand & Norman, *Blackstone's Guide to the Trade Marks Act 1994* Blackstone Press 1994, p. 64. Cornish, above, para. 15–21.
[25] Frazer, "Appropriation of Personality—A New Tort?" (1983) 99 L.Q.R. 281. *Re Elvis Presley Trade Marks* [1999] R.P.C. 567 569, Robert Walker L.J.

put it another way, to censor unauthorised use. Both of these may be applicable to this discussion.

Take first the commercial purposes. Let us assume that the Fund applied for registration so that those who wished to purchase memorabilia containing Diana's image in association with her signature would know that it had come from a recognised source—the Memorial Fund. This exemplifies the traditional "origin" function of a trade mark and would appear unobjectionable. Or at least it certainly would be the case where the Memorial fund produced goods, such as T-shirts bearing an image of Diana along with her signature. But what of the position if they allowed others to use the mark in association with their own goods, either by way of licensing or for the purposes of raising funds for the Memorial Fund through sponsorship such as the appearance of the signature on Flora margarine tubs or on lottery cards, or the use of her pictures adorning postage stamps? This use of a registered trade mark does not signify origin in the traditional sense. The margarine does not originate with the Trustees, and neither do the postage stamps. Rather the images are being exploited on these products for the purpose of boosting the funds of the Trust; a far cry from the traditional origin function of trade marks.[26]

Some concern has been expressed by the Trustees of the Memorial Fund and others, that certain items of memorabilia which are available are unacceptable, such as dog bowls with a photograph of Diana printed on the base.[27] Thus, a second commercial aim of registering a series of images as trade marks would appear to be the ability to exercise quality control over the type of product on which her image is placed, a shift from the "quality" function of a trade mark recognised by the European Court in *Ideal Standard GmbH*: "It must be stressed that the decisive factor is the possibility of control over the quality of goods...."[28] Here, the quality of the goods refers to the quality of the goods produced under the mark and with the consent of the trade mark holder, not to the type of goods considered of sufficient quality by a body of unelected Trustees to bear the image and name of Diana—Flora margarine versus dog bowls. If the second and wider interpretation is taken, then the monopoly changes from a limited monopoly in the link between the mark and the goods for which it is registered to a monopoly in the mark itself. What appeared to be the intention of the Trustees of the Memorial Fund is that the Fund would only have allowed use of the (registered) logo and images of Diana if the Trustees approved of

---

[26] Such uses would be more akin to those which fell foul of the provisions on trafficking in trade marks under the 1938 Act, s. 28(6): *Re American Greetings Corporation's Application* [1984] 1 All E.R. 426; [1984] R.P.C. 349. These provisions on trafficking have not been carried through to the 1994 Act. Nonetheless, the antipathy of the courts towards similar behaviour under the 1994 Act albeit in different circumstances clearly remains deeply rooted: *BT v. One in a Million* [1998] 4 All E.R. 476; [1999] R.P.C. 1.
[27] *Sunday Times*, February 15, 1998.
[28] *CNL-Sucal v. Hag* [1990] E.C.R. 1–3711, para. 38.

(the quality of) the products being made, whatever those products may be; in other words to exert complete monopoly control. This overlaps with the second desire of character merchandisers, a right of privacy to prevent others from exploiting or using an image either in the marketplace or at all. This in turn can cross the boundary to become a form of censorship: the right to dictate to others if and how the image of a celebrity may be used.

Finally, character merchandising illustrates the advertising function which is enmeshed with the previous functions. A trade mark in commercial life can both adorn and endorse goods. As an adornment, it does not necessarily fulfil a trade mark function, but rather simply attracts a consumer to goods or services because they find it pleasing, for example a picture on a T-shirt.[29] As an endorsement, it can fulfil a trade mark role as an indication of origin and a guarantee of quality, and can also advertise the wares of the trader. It would appear that one of the main reasons for application to register the signature of Diana, together with reference to the Memorial fund, would have been to show that the Fund endorsed and approved of the type of goods produced by a particular trader and that part of the proceeds will go to the Memorial Fund. In other words, an advertising function for the Memorial Fund[30] but out of kilter with the way the advertising function has normally been viewed. The signature would not be advertising the point of origin, but rather advertising that there is a third party link with the product and that the link is "official" in the sense that it derives from the owner of a trade mark under a form of sponsorship deal. While unobjectionable in itself, sponsorship deals form the basis of a number of sporting agreements, for example—this is not the function of a trade mark.

Protection may also be sought of the image of a character to protect privacy. Historically we do not have a right of privacy in the United Kingdom,[31] and to protect the right to privacy of a celebrity has certainly not been a goal of trade mark law. As was tentatively suggested above, it may be that a secondary reason for the desire to exert the quality control over the products that exploit an image or signature of Diana was to protect privacy in the broadest sense, having the effect of a wide ranging power of censorship.

Would the accepted commercial functions of a trade mark have been fulfilled by registration as trade marks of either the images of

---

[29] *Lyngstad v. Anabas Products Limited* [1975] F.S.R. 488.
[30] *Kodak Trade Mark* [1990] F.S.R. 49. It was decided that ancillary use of a trade mark, in this case the mark Kodak on T-shirts, where the purpose was to advertise Kodak films, was not a trade mark use for the purposes of the Trade Marks Act 1938. Judge Paul Baker said at p. 47: "A mark used on goods to advertise other goods may or may not be used as a trade mark in relation to either or both goods; it is a question of fact and degree. Here the mark advertised films and plates and its manner of use did not indicate the source of the T shirts. There cannot be a trade in goods which are merely ancillary to a wider trade—whether goods are ancillary is a matter of fact and degree."
[31] *Kaye v. Robertson* [1991] F.S.R. 62.

Diana, or her signature? These questions will be examined in association with the law on registration and enforcement.

Registration—Distinctiveness

It is said that the application for registration of the images of Diana was turned down because she was an historical figure, and not a figure of commerce; registration would not have fulfilled the traditional origin function of a trade mark. There are a number of fundamental points of trade mark law underlying this decision.

In order to be registrable, a trade mark either has to be inherently distinctive, or to have become distinctive through use: it must be distinctive by nature or by nurture.[32] Can the series of photographs of Diana be considered distinctive? The answer has to be no. Diana was often described as one of the most photographed women on earth. Pictures of her appeared on a daily basis in the press, on television and so on. The series of portraits to be registered may have been taken in formal settings so that no others are the same, and the copyright may be held by the Trustees. Nonetheless, such was the frenzy to capture her image there may be many thousands of other similar pictures and portraits but in which the copyright belongs to others.[33] Thus, the photographs cannot be said to be inherently distinctive. Neither are these photographs distinctive by nurture.[34] Postage stamps apart, they have not as yet appeared in conjunction with whatever goods they were to endorse as trade marks. There is no link in the mind of the consumer between the photographs and the Memorial Fund. If registration had been allowed, this would have subverted the function of a trade mark. It

---

[32] *A.D. 2000 Trade Mark* [1997] R.P.C. 168, where G. Hobbs Q.C. stated at p. 174: "The proviso to section 3(1) indicates that the essence of the objection to registration under section 3(1)(b) is immaturity: the sign in question is not incapable of distinguishing goods or services of one undertaking from those of other undertakings, but it is not distinctive by nature and has not become distinctive by nurture."

[33] It was variously reported that during her lifetime Diana had a love-hate relationship with the Press, on the one hand courting attention, but on the other jealously guarding her privacy. It must be that she would have liked to have more control over the numbers of photographs that were constantly taken of her. Under copyright law, copyright in photographs belongs to the person who takes the photograph, and generally, the subject of the photograph has no right to prevent copies of the photograph being made and disseminated. However, where a person for private and domestic purposes commissions the taking of photographs she has a right not to have copies of the work issued to the public or the work exhibited or shown in public or the work broadcast or included in a cable programme service without consent (Copyright, Designs and Patents Act 1988, s.85(1)(a)(b) and (c)). Supposing during her lifetime Diana had issued a call that she required all photographers to take photographs of her for private and domestic purposes. Would she then have been able to prevent exploitation of her image?

[34] *British Sugar v. James Robertson* [1996] R.P.C. 281 where the court considered the question of whether the word TREAT had become distinctive through use, and would thus satisfy the proviso to s. 47(1) of the 1994 Act. The question to be asked was whether the mark had "acquired a sufficiently distinctive character [so] that the mark has really become a trade mark." Where laudatory or common words were in question, compelling evidence was required to establish this. It had to be shown "that the mark has really become accepted by a substantial majority of persons as a trade mark—is or is almost a household word."

would no longer be to guarantee either the origin or the quality of the goods and thus provide the all-important link in the minds of the consumer. It would rather be to protect the photographs as marks in themselves, presumably with the intention to prevent others from using the same or similar images[35] on goods and services. The rationale for the trade mark disappears, and the monopoly conferred on the holder shifts from the monopoly in the link between the mark and the consumer, to a monopoly in the mark itself,[36] the image of Diana.

Let us move on to consider registration of the name Diana, whether typescript or hand-written. To protect a name is obviously important for the character merchandiser. What better way of blocking others out of the market than preventing others from using the name?[37] It certainly used to be thought that registration of personal names, whether typed or in signature style, caused no difficulty under the 1938 Act. Thus, for example the signature of Marilyn Monroe is registered as a trade mark.[38] However, the practice of registering celebrity names as trade marks has been called into question since the appeal in *Elvis Presley Enterprises Inc. v. Sid Shaw Elvisly Yours*[39] where the decision to overturn registrations of a variety of styles of the name "Elvis Presley" was upheld. The case dealt with the law as it stood under the 1938 Act. Nonetheless the judgments are relatively broad, and so it would be difficult to argue that the result would be any different had the 1994 Act been under consideration. The case decided that a celebrity name was not registrable as a trade mark as it was not distinctive. A palpable fear comes across in the case in relation to the broad monopoly power that would be conferred on traders if celebrity names could be registered as trade marks. In the words of Simon Brown L.J.: "there should be no a priori assumption that only a celebrity or his successors may ever market (or license the marketing of) his own character. Monopolies should not be so readily created".

It had been argued by counsel for the appellants, Elvis Presley Enterprises, that the general public would assume that the use of the signature of a celebrity in connection with goods and services meant that there would be a connection between the celebrity and the goods and services, and, secondly, that the only reason that another trader would want to use an image or signature of the celebrity

---

[35] For a discussion on marks with a reputation, see Carty, "Do Marks with a Reputation Merit Special Protection?" [1997] 12 E.I.P.R. 684.
[36] This is something that has been judicially recognised as a danger for a very long time. In the words of Lindley L.J. as long ago as 1886: "We must be careful to avoid confusion of ideas. A mark must be something distinct from the thing marked. The thing itself cannot be a mark of itself. . ." *Re James's Trade Mark* (1886) 33 Ch.D 392, 395.
[37] For a discussion on the protection of names generally, see Watts and Walsh, "Company Names" [1996] 6 E.I.P.R. 336.
[38] See the references in Debrett Lyons, "Elvis All Shook up by the High Court" [1997] 10 E.I.P.R. 613.
[39] [1997] F.S.R. 567 affirming [1997] R.P.C. 543.

would be to take advantage of the commercial value in the name. As was pointed out, again by Simon Brown L.J. that if this was accepted:

> ...it would apply virtually irrespective of the products being exploited...irrespective of when registration were applied for...irrespective of whether it was sought by the personality himself or his legal successors...and irrespective of what if any trading in the relevant products has previously been effected either by whoever seeks registration or by competing traders.

In other words, total monopoly control would result. And this is almost undoubtedly what the Fund were seeking in applying for registration of the name and signature of Diana, leading ultimately to censorship. Although we have not as yet heard officially whether the applications for the name and signature marks of Diana have been considered by the Patent Office, in the writer's view, the judgment in the *Elvis* case should be conclusive. The applications should be turned down.

To summarise the current position, the application for the registration of the images of Diana has been turned down, and the judgment in *Elvis Presley Enterprises Inc. v. Shaw* has thrown into doubt the registrability of both the name and signature of Diana. The next part of this essay will consider what the effects might have been had the application succeeded, which in turn raises the question as to the use to which these marks could be put, and the circumstances in which they could then be infringed by other traders. The uses made of the marks may well divorce the trade mark from its recognised functions, inhibit any use in any sphere by any other trader, leading to the inevitable conclusion that the Memorial Fund would have the right to censor the context in which we are permitted to view any image of Diana.

Infringement

The carefully balanced provisions of the 1994 Act on infringement are essential for controlling the monopoly conferred by a trade mark, and for ensuring that the trade mark retains its primary function.[40] It has been argued that section 10 of the 1994 Act, which provides grounds for infringement wider than those found under the previous legislation, will assist the character merchandiser in plying his trade.[41]

Let us, take one example where the signature of Diana is registered in connection with article of ladies' clothing and consider how this might be infringed. Would such registration prevent anyone else

---

[40] Trade Marks Act 1994, s. 10.
[41] Annand and Norman, above, chap. 10.

using that name either in association with articles of ladies' clothing or at all? The 1994 Act provides that a registered trade mark is infringed if an identical trade mark is applied to the identical goods or services for which it is registered.[42] Under this provision, an identical trade mark does not mean absolutely identical.[43] Rather the comparison is "mark for mark".[44] So the signature style could be changed by another trader, at least to an extent, but a similar style used in connection with articles of ladies' clothing would still infringe under this section without the need to show consumer confusion.

Supposing a competing trader merely wanted to use the name "Diana" to describe the nature of the product being sold, a biography, for example, but registration of the mark had been accepted in connection with books and book covers. Use of the name Diana may not have been an infringement under the 1938 Act as the mark would not have been used "in a trade mark sense". This requirement kept the link between the function of the mark and the trade mark itself. However, it does not appear in the 1994 Act. So using a signature style of the name Diana in connection with identical goods and services for which it is registered—on a book containing a biography—will infringe.[45] There is a narrow defence provision[46] where such use could be excused on the grounds that using the name Diana in these circumstances was in accordance with honest commercial practices, in the same way as applying the name of a pop group to the cover of a book in order to describe the contents.[47] So such limited use may be permitted but confined to a narrow category of mainly biographical products.

These arguments apply even more strongly if the images of Diana had been registered. The images are clearly designed to call Diana into mind. Let us suppose these are registered in connection with articles of ladies' clothing. Does this mean that no-one else could apply a different picture of Diana to a T-shirt despite the myriad of photographs in existence in which the copyright belongs to other individuals? This is undoubtedly what was intended by the registration. It was to capture her image so thoroughly that other traders would have been excluded from the market. As identity does not actually mean identity in terms of a competing trade mark, any picture of Diana would have infringed if used in connection with ladies' clothing. It is difficult to see in these circumstances how the

---

[42] Trade Marks Act 1994, s. 10(1).
[43] *Bravado Merchandising Services Ltd v. Mainstream Publishing (Edinburgh) Ltd* [1996] F.S.R. 205.
[44] *Origins Natural Resources Inc. v. Origin Clothing Limited* [1995] F.S.R. 280.
[45] *British Sugar v. James Robertson* [1996] R.P.C. 281 where it was found that a trade mark did not have to be used in a trade mark sense before there would be infringement under the 1994 Act.
[46] Trade Marks Act 1994, s. 11.
[47] *Bravado Merchandising Services Ltd v. Mainstream Publishing (Edinburgh) Ltd* [1996] F.S.R. 205. Trade Marks Act 1994, s.11(2).

limited provisions on allowing use for honest commercial practices could apply.

What of use of a similar name or signature or image used in connection with identical goods or vice versa?[48] An example might be the name "Lady Di".[49] Or a picture of Diana taken by a tourist, or one of the myriad belonging to the press; not the same as those for which registration was applied for, but a picture of Diana nonetheless. As a result of the judgment of the European Court of Justice in *Canon Kabushiki Kaisha v. Metro-Goldwyn-Mayer Inc.*[50] (*Canon*), it is likely that had registration proceeded, the Memorial Fund would have had an unassailable monopoly in all uses of the same or a similar image in connection with all goods and services. In *Canon* the dispute was over the registration of the word 'Canon' on certain types of machinery. The Court ruled that the first important factor to be determined when deciding liability in respect of similarity was the distinctive character of the mark, and in particular its reputation. The more distinctive the mark and the greater its reputation, the wider the ambit of goods and services which should be considered similar and which are therefore more likely to give rise to a likelihood of confusion. Thus a distinctive mark with a reputation will obtain protection over a wide range of goods, while a less distinctive mark with a lesser reputation will be protected over a narrower range of goods. If accepted as a mark, what could have more of a reputation than an image of Diana? Or her signature? The effect of *Canon* would be to confer a monopoly in the mark over all categories of goods and services for which marks could be registered. In addition, any sign which was or contained an image or the signature of Diana would be similar. There would be a total monopoly leading to total control of the image of Diana.

We must move inexorably to the same conclusion with respect to the third section dealing with infringement under the 1994 Act[51] which has been referred to as an "anti-dilution" provision. There is no requirement under this section that the public be confused by the use of a sign, but simply that the use of an identical or similar mark in connection with dissimilar goods or services would take unfair advantage of or be detrimental to the distinctive character or repute of the registered mark where that mark has a reputation. Case law considering this section is at present sketchy,[52] and perhaps some of

---

[48] Trade Marks Act 1994, s. 10(2).
[49] It has been reported by the BBC that "A German entrepreneur (Andre Engelhardt) is trying to win international trade mark rights to the name Lady Di". Apparently Herr Engelhardt has already secured the German trade mark and has applied to register a Community trade mark: http://news2.thls.bbc.co.uk/hi/english/uk/newsid_374000/374108.stm.
[50] [1998] All E.R. (EC) 934; [1999] R.P.C. 117; [1999] 1 C.M.L.R. 77.
[51] Trade Marks Act 1994, s. 10(3).
[52] The section has been considered in *Baywatch Production Co. Ltd. v. The Home Video Channel* [1997] F.S.R. 22. The court said that this section only applied where the requirements of the section were met, plus there had to be a likelihood of confusion on the part of the public. It has to be said that there has been some doubt expressed over this interpretation of the section as there is no reference to public confusion. However, the line of reasoning suggests

the most pertinent comments have been made in cases looking at equivalent provisions of the Act[53] concerning registration rather than infringement. *Oasis Stores Ltd's Trade Mark Application*[54] concerned application to register the mark Eveready for condoms and contraceptives. Ever Ready plc opposed this on the grounds that it would tarnish and dilute their registered marks for *inter alia* batteries torches and plugs. In giving judgment the court said that simply being reminded of a similar trade mark with a reputation for dissimilar goods did not necessarily amount to taking an unfair advantage of the repute of that mark. The section was not intended to have the sweeping effect of preventing the registration of any mark which was the same as or similar to a trade mark with a reputation[55] This is heartening, and if applied to infringement cases, would keep the monopoly conferred by the mark in infringement proceedings well within limits.

However, for the name and images of Diana, the rights flowing from registration would be more difficult to regulate. Almost instantly the marks would have had a reputation in the United Kingdom or at least the concept of the mark would have had a reputation, such was her fame during her life and indeed after her death. Any name such as "Queen of Hearts", "England's Rose" and "Lady Di" would be likely to suggest a reference to Diana and to the mark and to take advantage of that reference: why use the mark if not to suggest such a reference? Any use of the name which could be considered in any way derogatory could equally be argued as detrimental to the distinctive character or repute of the mark, particularly if it was associated in any way with derogatory comments or portrayed Diana in a way that was less than complimentary.[56] This in turn would beg the questions as to who would decide whether the use was less than complimentary? The Trustees of the Memorial Fund would wish to be sole arbiters. The effect would be that the trade mark belonging to the Trustees would be infringed any time a similar one was used in conjunction with dissimilar goods or services. The Trustees instantly would have an all-encompassing monopoly, the result of which would enable the Trustees to suppress any reference to Diana in association with any goods or services made without their consent. No longer would T-shirts adorned with a picture of Diana be available from market stalls; rather, any exploitation of her image, good or bad, positive or negative, would first have to be approved by an unelected body of

---

a reluctance on the part of the judiciary to accept that a trade mark can be infringed without this element of public confusion, a requirement for infringement of a trade mark for such a long time. Cornish, above, paras 17–97.
[53] Trade Marks Act 1994, s. 5(3).
[54] [1998] R.P.C. 631.
[55] See also *Audi-Med Trade Mark* [1998] R.P.C. 863.
[56] See for example the controversy over the advertisement for the Korean car in which a Diana look-alike is used although it has been said that the advertisement would never be shown in the U.K.: *Scotsman*, May 5, 1998.

Trustees who would have an unassailable monopoly, not just in the link between the trade mark and the consumer, but in the mark itself and in the type of product it may be used in connection with. The Trustees would have total control and ability to censor use.

And of course, the protection would not just be in this country. The Paris Convention Article 6*bis*, given effect in the United Kingdom by section 56 of the 1994 Act, gives protection to well known marks used in respect of identical or similar goods; there is no need to show a record of trading in a any particular Convention country before protection is accorded. The purpose is to give protection against pre-emptive strikes by rogue traders. The TRIPS[57] Agreement extends these provisions to services[58] and to goods or services which are not similar to those in respect of which a trade mark is registered, where the use would indicate a connection between the goods and services and the owner of the registered trade mark, provided the interests of the owner of the registered trade mark are likely to be damaged by such use.[59] Given the fame of Diana, it must be almost without doubt that that she was known in every Convention country and signatory country to TRIPS. Therefore, in trade marks terms, if registered in any Convention country her trade mark would meet the criteria for protection under both the Paris Convention and TRIPS. Therefore, depending on acceptance in individual countries as to the registrability of her name and image as trade marks, the Memorial Fund could have had almost global ability to censor the exploitation of Diana.

Conclusion

The conclusion is overwhelmingly that the decision not to register these images of Diana is correct, and that the signature and name applications should also be turned down in due course. The legislation, understandably, does not give provision for investigating the motives of those seeking to register trade marks, except to require that a registration is *bona fide*. That apart, it is up to the applicant to decide if and why. If the registrations had been, or in the case of the name are, allowed to proceed, trade mark law becomes subverted from its true intent. Instead of fulfilling the limited commercial functions outlined above, registration of a trade mark in these circumstances would give not only a complete monopoly within the marketplace but also a right to censor use by third parties with absolutely no countervailing forces acting to balance the right in favour of the public interest. We would have an overwhelming right against personality appropriation by others without a right of fair comment or a newsworthiness privilege. That

---

[57] Agreement on Trade-Related Aspects of Intellectual Property Rights 1994.
[58] TRIPS Agreement, Art. 16.2.
[59] TRIPS Agreement Art. 16.3 extending Article 6 *bis* of the Paris Convention.

right could belong not only to the celebrity in question, but to descendants, or to any third party who cared to capitalise on the image of a celebrity and who was the first to register the image; furthermore, it could be perpetual.

Are we, in the United Kingdom, now at a juncture where we should be thinking of introducing a fully-fledged character merchandising right for personalities? Certainly, the social, cultural and commercial conditions prevailing in the United States which heralded the introduction of the right are not dissimilar to those prevailing in the United Kingdom now. Madow[60] argues that the right developed in the United States because by the 1950s society as a whole had shifted from a word-based society to an image-based society; from the written word, to television and films; from emphasis on society as a whole to the importance of the individual and personal success portrayed in its most extreme form in Hollywood and its followers. Similarly, Goodenough[61] argues that this focus on the self and image have been helped by the television and other media which have created celebrity identity value leading in turn to the need to be able to exploit that value for profit. This theme of the media bring the basis for the right of publicity echoes the thoughts of Nimmer, who argued that the right of publicity developed in the United States as a response to "the needs of Broadway and Hollywood".[62]

Trends can be discerned in the United Kingdom which might suggest that the time is right for the introduction of a right of personality exploitation. Thus, the written word has certainly been eclipsed by television and films, and there have been some notable recent film successes such as *The Full Monty* and *Four Weddings and a Funeral*. But film stars are not idolised here in quite the way that they are in the United States. In the advertising world, celebrity images are used to promote products, but such is the relative rarity of this form of advertising, particularly in the more traditional areas of our economy, that when a personality endorses an advertisement for a financial product, The Economist is moved to comment on the possibility that "marketing men are trying to convert the public to the cult of personality".[63]

However, there are other forces that might suggest that the time is opportune to re-examine this area. The European Convention on Human Rights (ECHR) has now been incorporated into United Kingdom law[64] and introduces a right to privacy,[65] although how far this extends is still unclear. Also, privacy is just one part of the body

---

[60] Madow, above.
[61] Goodenough, "Retheorising Privacy and Publicity" [1997] 1 I.P.Q. 37 at 48.
[62] Nimmer, "The Right of Publicity" (1954) 19 Law & Contemp. Probs 203.
[63] *The Economist*, May 2, 1998, "Personality Investing" p. 100.
[64] Human Rights Act 1998.
[65] European Convention On Human Rights, Art. 8. For comment, see Harris O'Boyle Warbrick, *Law of the European Convention on Human Rights* (1995), chap. 9.

of law in existence in the United States governing personality exploitation. If a right of privacy is to be used, however tangentially, to control commercial exploitation in the marketplace, then we will certainly need to consider some balancing provisions to ensure that the innovation shown by our traders is not unduly stifled, and indeed that it does not become an alternative mechanism for censorship. Hence the calls for freedom of the press[66] recognised in the ECHR.[67]

One thing is certain: such a development should not be carried on under the guise of trade mark law where total monopoly power can be conferred and censorship permitted by the back door. Looking back over the history of trade mark law, the courts and legislators have never really been in favour of the monopoly rights that would be necessary for a fully-fledged right of exploitation for character merchandisers. The operation of the 1994 shows fluidity in its operation; the parameters granted by the monopoly are being tested before the Patent Office and the courts, but these bodies are standing firm at least in this area and showing a marked unwillingness to allow the Act to be extended to areas not hitherto contemplated. How long this barrier can be maintained remains to be seen. But at least in the meantime, registered trade mark law will not be used to help the character merchandiser ply her trade to attain ends for which it was never intended.

---

[66] Goodenough, above.
[67] Art. 10.

11. Aspects of Trade Mark Use and Misuse

Spyros Maniatis

Aspects of trade mark use and misuse

Introduction

The fundamental characteristic of intellectual property rights is to "constrain those who have no relationship with the right-owner. They are rights that depend for their effectiveness, to a peculiar degree, upon the speed and cheapness with which they can be enforced. This explains why, so often in the modern law, it is cases in this field that test the procedures and remedies provided by the courts. In Britain, these are matters typically within the province of the judges, who receive only a modicum of direction from Parliament. Many of the issues raised in particular cases have large implications".[1]

The expansion of European law in the same area, first with case law on cross border intra Community trade and later with direct legislative intervention through the implementation of the Trade Marks Directive (89/104: "the Directive") and the Community Trade Mark Regulation (40/94), intensified rather than lessened the importance of case law, with the jurisprudence of the European Court of Justice (ECJ) being added to the body of case law that judges must take into account. Judges are grasping, throughout Europe, with subtle variations on concepts like exhaustion and association, trying to reconcile them with their own known, tried, and trusted rationale for trade mark protection.

Often they are juggling with the interpretation of the law in order to decide what, to them, seems to be the product of common sense. In this quest cases have acquired additional relevance even when the relevant law has been superseded; they serve as the guidelines in providing "the basics", the conceptual basis, for interpreting the new legislation rather than the detailed mechanics.

According to the Court of Appeal in *Philips Electronics NV v. Remington Consumer Products Ltd*[2] the new law has been drafted with input from other Member States and should not be assumed to be the same as the old U.K. law nor to be different from it. The law must be determined from the Act construed in the light of the Directive. But, although cases decided under the old law are no longer authoritative, knowledge of their reasoning can provide awareness of the types of problems that arise during use of trade

---

[1] W.R. Cornish, *Intellectual Property* (Sweet and Maxwell, London, 1996), at p. 41.
[2] [1999] E.T.M.R. 835. See also A. Firth, *Trade Marks: The New Law* (Jordans, 1995) at pp. 73–74 predicting this approach. For a critique on the question of old law, see Annand's conclusion at p.133 of this volume.

marks and a general feel for them. Jacob J. in his first instance decision in *Philips Electronics NV v. Remington Consumer Products*,[3] has qualified his earlier strong and dismissive views on the applicability of old case law, expressed in *British Sugar v. James Robertson*,[4] by stating that

> . . . all that law has been swept away. But it does not follow that the sort of concepts and safeguards provided for in the old laws . . . have no place under the new law. On the contrary one is bound to bump up against the same sort of problems under the new law as under other laws. For some matters are basic to any rational law of trade marks.[5]

Robert Walker L.J. in the Court of Appeal decision in *Procter & Gamble's TM Applications*[6] seems to follow the same cautious approach, referring to the Opinion of the Advocate General Cosmas in joined cases C-108 and 109/97 *Windsurfing Chiemsee Produktions— und Vertriebs GmbH v. Boots-und Segelzubehor Walter Huber and Franz Attenberger*[7] and Lord Parkers's observations on distinctiveness in *W and G du Cros' Application*.[8]

Examples of this process may be found in the case law of all E.U. Member States; on the one hand, more and more trade mark cases are referred to the ECJ, whilst on the other, familiar concepts, like use, are being reinvented by judges who are trying to make sense of the E.C. legislation.

It seems, for example, that Benelux courts will keep on referring cases to the ECJ until the position on association shifts towards the Benelux understanding. In *Marca Mode v. Adidas AG & Adidas Benelux BV*[9] the Netherlands Supreme Court appeared to accept that mere likelihood of association is not sufficient to justify an injunction if likelihood of confusion can be ruled out; however it also stated that if, in view of other circumstances, it must be assumed that there exists a likelihood of confusion, then likelihood of association may be sufficient to justify an injunction, and referred a question on the interpretation of Article 5(1)(b) of the Directive to the ECJ.

In the United Kingdom, Laddie J., in *Zino Davidoff SA v. A&G Imports Ltd*[10] indirectly challenges the ECJ's decisions on parallel imports. He stated that its decision in *Silhouette International Schmied GmbH & Co. KG v. Hartlauer Handelsgesellschaft mbH*[11] has bestowed on trade mark proprietors a "parasitic" right allowing them to

---

[3] [1998] R.P.C. 283.
[4] [1996] R.P.C. 281.
[5] [1998] R.P.C. 283 at 299.
[6] [1999] R.P.C. 673.
[7] [1999] E.T.M.R. 585.
[8] [1913] R.P.C. 660.
[9] [1999] E.T.M.R. 791.
[10] [1999] R.P.C. 631.
[11] [1998] F.S.R. 729.

interfere with the distribution of goods which bears little relationship to the proper function of the trade mark right. Doubting that a properly informed legislature would intend such a result he attempted to bypass the effect of *Silhouette* on the proper construction of Article 7(1) of the Directive by relying on contract law and two old English cases on the concept of implied consent; he, too, decided to make a reference to the ECJ.

In Germany the "keep free" rationale was established in cases like *POLYESTRA*,[12] where an application to register the term for yarns, threads and textile products was rejected because of the possible monopolisation of a term of art; the word was descriptive and confusingly similar to a technical term for which a need to keep it free for other competitors to use existed. The "keep free" discussion resurfaced in cases like *Something Special in the Air*,[13] where the slogan "Something Special in the Air" for services including transportation by car, railway, ships and aircraft was rejected. It could arguably be distinctive for transport by aircraft but a distinction should be made between advertising distinctiveness and true distinctiveness revealing precisely the origin of the services. In *WHAT A DAY*,[14] WHAT A DAY was proposed for a variety of goods and services including beer, board and lodging. The application was rejected since the phrase functioned simply as means to attract the attention of the customer and was not sufficiently distinctive. On appeal it was decided that the slogan would be understood as part of the colloquial language and as such it was used as an advertising means rather than a trade mark. Unfortunately the "keep free" rationale was rejected by the ECJ in *Windsurfing Chiemsee Produktions—und Vertriebs GmbH*.[15]

It is submitted that the heritage of old case law is nowhere more helpful than in coming to grips with the concept of use.

The importance of use

Traditionally, the concept of use of a sign as a trade mark has served as a factor that is determinative, firstly, in providing one of the fundamental requirements for trade mark protection and, secondly, in delineating the scope of protection.

In the United Kingdom, systems of registration are based on use or intended use; if the mark is not put into genuine use then the

---

[12] [1968] G.R.U.R. 694, BGH. The traditional doctrine is very similar to the rationale underpinning English decisions like *York Trailer Holdings v. Registrar of Trade Marks* [1982] F.S.R. 111. Note that in a recent decision, *Polaclip TM* [1999] R.P.C. 282, the U.K. Registry decided in a case were "Polaroid" was trying to block registration of "Polaclip" that the prefix "Pola" would be seen as a reference "Polarise" and "polarising", themselves descriptive words, rather than to "Polaroid". So, signs based on descriptive words seem to enjoy a rather narrow protection.
[13] [1997] E.I.P.R. D 303.
[14] [1998] E.I.P.R. N 203.
[15] See p. 252 below.

registration becomes vulnerable to cancellation proceedings. *Imperial Group v. Philip Morris*[16] is a good example; under the 1938 Act the mark NERIT, a ghost mark aiming to protect the real, albeit not capable of registration, mark MERIT, was struck off despite token use. The Court of Appeal decided that the mark was not a trade mark within the scope of section 68: token use was not trade mark use at all because it was ephemeral and not meant to be profitable. Note that use did not have to be upon the goods themselves. Use in relation to the goods would suffice.[17] Under the 1994 Act, in *Elle Trade Marks*,[18] Lloyd J. decided that endorsing cosmetic products under other brands does not constitute use of the trade mark ELLE in relation to these specific products; offers for sale of cosmetic products branded under ELLE in the United Kingdom but available only through the foreign editions of the magazine could constitute sufficient use, provided that there was evidence of actual sales. In *Wackers TM*[19] Mr George Salthouse in the Trade Marks Registry rejected an opposition based on prior use since use in the form of two shipments of samples to the United Kingdom was regarded de minimis without creating any significant goodwill or reputation. In *Jeryl Lynn TM*[20] Laddie J. noted that a sign used in identifying a particular product that was only available from a single source would indirectly identify the source of the product as well; but in deciding whether such a sign had acquired the necessary distinctiveness for it to function as a trade mark one would have to look at the nature of the product, whether the sign had been used exclusively in relation to that product, whether it had been used exclusively as a designation of origin, and the understanding of the sign by the relevant public. A sign that overwhelmingly performed a descriptive or technical function would not be capable of distinguishing, failing section 3(1)(a) of the Act, even where there was some market recognition of the sign as a trade mark. The concept of use is also crucial in cases where there are links between the parties that may lead to the conclusion that the proprietor has once consented to the use that is later considered to be an infringement. In *Northern & Shell plc v. Condé Nast & National Magazines Distributors Ltd*,[21] where Jacob J. decided that section 9(1)

---

[16] [1982] F.S.R. 72, CA; see also *Electrolux v. Electrix* [1954] R.P.C. 23.
[17] See Mr S.J. Probert's decision at the Trade Mark Registry on *Jean' Heurs S.A. Application* No. 7117 for rectification of ODEON–Registration No. 561428, concluding that "I would have been able to walk into an ODEON shop and purchase a poster directly beneath a large ODEON sign. To my mind, that must be use of the mark ODEON in relation to paper and/or stationery, even though the poster itself carries another mark, in this case Walt Disney".
[18] [1997] F.S.R. 529.
[19] [1999] R.P.C. 453.
[20] [1999] F.S.R. 491.
[21] [1995] R.P.C. 117; see also the CA decision in *Harrods Ltd. v. Harrods (Buenos Aires) Ltd.* [1999] R.P.C. 187. *Accurist Watches Ltd v. King* [1992] F.S.R. 80 is an excellent discussion of s. 4(3)(a) of the 1938 Act by Millett L.J. whereas in *Travelpro* [1997] R.P.C. 864 Mr M. Knight provides the Registry's position on a registration obtained by a distributor in the U.K. in bad faith.

of the 1994 Act did not permit the proprietor to complain of use which had his consent. Also "use in a trade mark sense", "use as trade mark", "use in the course of trade", and other similar terms, overlapping in the way they are applied, are often employed in order to outline the extent of constraint that the registered proprietor can exercise on the ability of others to use the protected sign. Otherwise a trade mark right would give its proprietor an unlimited monopoly. But common sense, again, indicates that some terms must be left free for other traders to use and that some other terms must be left free for all, traders and non traders alike, to use.[22]

In *Profitmaker TM*[23] Laddie J. remarked that the fact that honest traders have a number of alternative ways of describing a product does not mean that the mark is capable of registration, because then all those alternative ways could, based on the same argument, also become registered trade marks. The honest trader should not be required to inspect the register to ensure that common descriptive or laudatory words, or not unusual combinations of them, have been monopolised by others. In *AD 2000 TM*[24] Geoffrey Hobbs Q.C., talking about distinctiveness by nature and distinctiveness by nurture, stressed that various promotional messages could be conveyed by "AD 2000" and as a result it could not be supported, at the time of application, to be incapable of fair and honest use by anyone else.

This short, and arbitrary in its selection, review of case law, is an attempt to show that, if we want to delineate in a cautious manner the extent of protection that a trade mark deserves, then the concept of use in its many facets can serve as a good guide.

A classic case delineating areas of use

In a classic case on the importance of use, *Aristoc v. Rysta*[25] the House of Lords had to decide on the opposition against the application for registration of the trade mark RYSTA for stockings; the applicant had been using the mark for twenty five years in connection with their repair service for stockings. The successful opposition was based on three grounds: earlier registration of the trade mark ARISTOC for the same goods; registration of RYSTA would lead to deception and confusion, as a result of its prior use for the repair service; and that use of a mark to indicate repair was not use as a trade mark within the scope of section 68(I) of the 1938 Act. Lord Macmillan stressed that a trade mark must be used in

---

[22] See E. Gredley & S.M. Maniatis, "'People you know, yet can't quite name...' Fair or Foul in the 'Wet Wet Wet' Case?" [1996] Ent. L.R. 99.
[23] [1994] R.P.C. 616.
[24] [1997] R.P.C. 168. This type of analysis appears similar to the German "keep free" doctrine.
[25] [1945] R.P.C. 65.

trade. The term, he accepted, is wide but according to his interpretation

> its meaning must vary with and be controlled by its context. A connection with goods in the course of trade . . . means in the definition section an association with the goods in the course of their production and preparation for the market. After goods have reached the consumer they are no longer in the course of trade. The trading in them has reached its objective and its conclusion in their acquisition by the consumer.[26]

Lord Wright, elaborating on the association with the goods, noted that

> the word "origin" is no doubt used in a special and almost technical sense in this connection, but it denotes at least that the goods are issued as vendible goods under the aegis of the proprietor of the trade mark, who thus assumes responsibility for them.[27]

And added that

> [t]he *Solicitor-General* on behalf of the *Comptroller*, . . . has contended that the definition of trade mark in Sec. 68 of the [1938] Act calls for a wider interpretation which would include the use of a trade mark for repairing or other services to goods even though they are already the subjects of an existing trade mark indicating origin, with the consequence that further trade marks covering the same goods might be accumulated as different services for repairs, or even more ephemeral services like the valeting or cleaning of clothes or laundry work on garments, are from time to time rendered to the goods. He has stated that the *Comptroller* has made a practice of registering such trade marks, and further that the practice is advantageous in the public interest. It is, however, clear that if such a practice does not come within the terms of the Act (and I think it does not), it is not lawful, however convenient. If the law is to be altered, that must be done by Parliament, which can consider all the different factors relative to the proposed change of the law.[28]

The provisions of the 1994 Trade Marks Act

Changes in trade mark law came, firstly, with the 1986 Act allowing registration of service marks and, subsequently, with the 1994 Act.

---

[26] *ibid.* at 80.
[27] *ibid.* at 82.
[28] *ibid.* at 83.

Especially noteworthy is the fact that infringement provisions in section 10 mirror those of section 5 on obstacles to registration based on earlier trade mark rights.

What constitutes infringement

Under the 1994 Act infringing use does not have to be in relation to the goods or services in respect of which the mark is registered; under certain conditions similar and, even, dissimilar goods or services may be covered. As a result the system of defensive registrations devised under section 27 of the 1938 Act was abolished. It should be noted that the Act requires infringing use to be in "course of trade" and does not explicitly require use "as a trade mark".

The infringement provisions seem to indicate that the scope of protection has been considerably extended. On the point of use in the course of trade Lord Strathclyde has clearly stated that "as a matter of general trade mark law it is implicit that use of a registered trade mark must be trade mark use in order that the rights given by the Bill may be enforced. The content of the 15th recital to the directive also makes that quite clear".[29] However recent cases suggest that the rationale of trade mark use is by no means settled.

Section 10(4) provides an indicative, rather than exhaustive, list of what constitutes use: affixing the sign to goods or the packaging thereof; offering or exposing goods for sale, putting them on the market or stocking them for those purposes under the sign, or offering or supplying services under the sign; importing or exporting goods under the sign; or using the sign on business papers or in advertising. Although in many of these examples it is implicit that use would be in the course of trade, section 10(4) does not provide any direction on the relevance of the message conveyed by the sign.

According to section 103(2) of the Act use does not need to be visual; aural or use by any other means is also relevant. This is a significant change from the section 68(2) of the 1938 Act under which use was limited to a printed or other visual presentation of a mark. This would often in practice ensure that infringing use was in the course of trade. Also, according to section 103(1) trade is defined as including any business or profession.

Section 10(5) provides for contributory infringement. It might be argued that references to registered trade mark and mark in subsection 5 would limit its scope to use likely to be perceived as trade mark use.[30]

---

[29] *Hansard*, HL Vol. 552, *col.* 733; see, however, the 7th recital of the Directive. Lord Peston tried, albeit without success, to narrow the scope of the provision by adding that use of the mark must be in the course of business; see in general Gredley & Maniatis above.
[30] Here the original idea belongs to A. Firth.

The importance of use; the limitations in section 10 of the 1994 Act

Sections 10(6), 11, 12 and 13 provide the restrictions to the scope of infringement and the limitations on the exercise of trade mark rights. Section 12 deals with the exhaustion of trade mark rights and section 13 with the effect of disclaimers; since they are only indirectly linked with the concept of use[31] we will concentrate here to sections 10(6) and 11.

In order to understand the scope of limitations imposed on the exercise of trade mark rights we ought to start from section 2 of the Act providing that a registered trade mark is a property right. Albeit, this property right is not unlimited or abstract, the specific rights of the proprietor are provided by the Act. Section 9 provides that the proprietor has exclusive rights in the trade mark which are infringed by use without his consent. Again, the exclusive rights are limited by the provision that acts amounting to infringement are specified in section 10. In section 10, subsections (1), (2) and (3) deal with use by the defendant of the sign in relation to goods or services irrespective of whether the goods or services are related with the plaintiff or the defendant. Subsection (1) is absolute; since there is no requirement of confusion or advantage gained by the defendant the message conveyed by the infringing sign is not relevant. In order to satisfy the requirements of subsections (2) and (3) use of the sign the message conveyed by the sign must be a reference to the defendant. Otherwise there can be no likelihood of confusion, even if we accept that association has altered the traditional concept of confusion, and no advantage that the defendant might gain or damage that the proprietor might suffer. Two possible exceptions are a case that in a common law would be a case of inverse passing off[32] or another passing off scenario where genuine goods, but of a lower quality, are sold by a retailer as genuine goods but of a higher quality.[33] Still, it remains uncertain whether such cases could fall within the scope of infringement under sections 10(2) or (3) of the 1994 Act.

The use envisaged in section 10(6) is probably different. Here it is use by the defendant of a sign as a trade mark in order to refer to the trade mark proprietor, not the defendant. The defendant wants to indicate that the goods or services are related with the trade mark proprietor. And this according to the legislator should not constitute an infringement. Of course there seems to be a potentiality of conflict with section 10(1). If a manufacturer dispatches to a retailer a batch of products some of which are inadvertently left unmarked and the retailer affixes to these unmarked products a sign that is identical

---

[31] In *Parfums Christian Dior SA and Parfums Christian Dior BV v. Evora BV* [1998] R.P.C. 166 use and exhaustion are linked; see also p. 256 below.
[32] *Bristol Conservatories Ltd v. Conservatories Custom Built Ltd* [1989] R.P.C. 455.
[33] *Spalding (A.G.) & Bros v. Gamage (A.W.)* [1915] R.P.C. 273.

with the manufacturer's trade mark without notifying the manufacturer, this would prima facie fall within the scope of section 10(1); but, can the retailer use section 10(6) as a defence?

The situation is doctrinally clearer when we look at the relation between subsections (2) and (3) on the one hand and (6) on the other, because the "home grown" section 10(6),[34] seems to aim directly at comparative advertising; it allows use of a registered trade mark in comparative advertising and at the same time seeks to strike a balance between the interests of trade mark owners, competitors, and consumers alike.[35]

The importance of use; the limitations in section 11 of the 1994 Act

Section 11(1) provides that a registered trade mark is not infringed by the use of another registered trade mark in relation to goods or services for which the latter is registered; each proprietor is exercising the rights provided by the Act. If one of the registrations is declared invalid then section 47(6) must also be taken into account. But it remains uncertain whether in a case of consent under section 5(5) use could become deceptive according to section 46(1)(d) and lead to revocation.[36] Similarly section 11(3) aims to solve conflicts between rights to use a sign; here the conflict is between registration on the one hand and a right to use a sign in a particular locality on the other, for example a case of territorially limited passing off.

Section 11(2) conceptually complements section 10(6). A registered trade mark is not infringed by (a) the use by a person of his own name or address, (b) the use of indications concerning the kind, quality, quantity, intended purpose, value, geographical origin, the time of production of goods or of rendering of services, or other characteristics of goods or services, or (c) the use of the trade mark where it is necessary to indicate the intended purpose of a product or service (in particular, as accessories or spare parts), provided the use is in accordance with honest practices in industrial or commercial matters. In this case use is probably different, the sign is used not in a trade mark sense. Note that again there is no

---

[34] The provision is the result of national legislative intent rather than the implementation of the Directive where there is no directly analogous provision.
[35] For an authoritative comment on s. 10(6)–before the surge of case law on comparative advertising–see Kitchin D. and Mellor J., *The Trade Marks Act 1994* (Sweet & Maxwell, 1995), at pp. 44–46. *The Mathys Report–British Trade Mark Law and Practice* Cmmd. 5601 (1974) provides an appraisal of comparative advertising in paragraphs 80 to 88. Implementation of Directive 97/55 on comparative advertising will be the ultimate test on the effect and scope of s. 10(6). In Germany the directive had a radical effect on the acceptability of comparative advertising; see U. Doepner & F. Hufnagel, "German courts implement the EU Directive 97/55/EC–A fundamental shift in the law on comparative advertising?" 1998 T.M.R. 537.
[36] *Scandecor Development AB v. Scandecor Marketing AB* [1998] F.S.R. 500 implies that trafficking in trade mark rights is not condoned by the 1994 Act.

indication on whether use must be in relation to goods or services of the proprietor or of the party using the mark.

So, how the sign is used is potentially crucial in determining whether use constitutes infringement. Differentiations can be subtle but it seems that the 1994 Act, in principle brings us back to the situation prior to 1938. In relation to comparative advertising, in particular, "[a]s long as the use of the competitor's mark is "honest" then there is nothing wrong with telling the public of the relative merits of competing goods and services and using registered trade marks to identify them".[37]

The pre-1938 position

A number of cases decided before the enactment of the 1938 suggest that, when use of the sign was not perceived as a reference to the user's goods or as use as a trade mark, courts were unwilling to protect trade mark proprietors.

Irving's Yeastvite v. Horsenail[38] remains one of the classic cases of use of a trade mark in trade by a competitor that did not constitute infringement. The slogan "Yeast tablets a substitute for Yeastvite" did not infringe the registered trade mark "Yeastvite"; it was understood as a reference to the plaintiff not the user and at the same time use of the term in the slogan was not use as a trade mark. A trade mark served as an indication of source; this was the purpose of the trade mark and the reason for its protection. As a result, use for some other purpose would not infringe.

Two examples of use of a sign but not as a trade mark are provided by *Young v. Grierson Oldham*,[39] where use of a sign, an ox cart device, did not infringe a trade mark registration since its use could be perceived as an indication of geographical origin rather than as an indication of trade origin in a narrow sense, identifying the trader's goods, and *Carless, Capel v. Pilmore-Bedford*[40] deciding that a lighthouse device mark, for petrol, was not infringed by lighthouse shaped petrol pumps, since the shape of the pumps did not function as an indication of origin.

In *Imperial Tobacco v. De Pasquali*[41] the court had to deal with whether a common combination of words "The Regiment", used in relation to cigarettes, constituted an infringement of "Regimental Cigarettes". Astbury J. noted that the nature of the registered term must be taken into account; "[a] distinctive invented or fancy word has a much wider scope for colourable imitation than a word primarily descriptive, especially if the latter be one in common

---

[37] Laddie J. in *Barclaycard v. RBS Advanta* [1996] R.P.C. 307 at 315.
[38] [1934] R.P.C. 110.
[39] [1924] R.P.C. 548.
[40] [1928] R.P.C. 205.
[41] [1918] R.P.C. 185.

use".[42] On the other hand, in *Stone v Steelace*[43] use of the word "Alligator" in "Alligator Pattern Belting" constituted an infringement of the registration of "Alligator" since it was found to be capable of being understood as a reference to the products of the registered trade mark proprietors. This time a commonplace word was used as a trade mark.

At the same time there is jurisprudential evidence that the courts were taking into account the parties' market positions and the actual facts of the case in deciding whether the defendants actions were in good or bad faith. For example, in *Newton Chambers v. Neptune*[44] the description of toilet paper as "medicated with Izal" constituted an infringement of "Izal" given that the "Izal" part of the statement was depicted in a much larger font; there was trade mark reference to the plaintiff in relation to the defendant's goods.

The provisions of the 1938 Act

The 1938 Act, and in particular section 4(1)(b), were the legislator's response to the rationale of *Irving's Yeastvite*. Under the 1938 Act infringement occurred only if the offending sign was used in the course of trade[45] in respect of the goods or services for which the plaintiff's mark was registered, under section 4(1). However, infringing use could be "use as a trade mark", covering under section 4(1)(a) the classic case of infringement where the sign is used on the defendant's goods, or "importing a reference", expanding under section 4(1)(b) the concept of infringement so as to cover cases where by using the sign the defendant refers to the trade mark proprietor. The infringing sign should be "identical with" or "so nearly resembling" the registered trade mark so "as to be likely to deceive or cause confusion".

Trade mark rights were "exhausted" where the trade mark proprietor or a "registered user" (licensee) has applied the trade mark or consented to its use, according to section 4(3)(a). Further defences of bona fide use of one's own name, product descriptions, etc., were provided in section 8.

---

[42] *ibid.* at 195. An analysis that is very similar to the U.S. position on strong and weak marks.
[43] [1929] R.P.C. 406.
[44] [1935] R.P.C. 399.
[45] The ambiguity of the concept of "in the course of trade" was aptly described by T.A. Blanco White and Robin Jacob in the 11th edition of *Kerly's Law of Trade Marks and Trade Names* (London, Sweet and Maxwell, 1984) at p. 243: "[t]he particular words of section 4(1) refer to use of a mark "in the course of trade"; whilst section 4(1)(a) refers to use "as a trade mark", which in turn (by virtue of section 68(1), defining a trade mark) brings in the same words. But the general words of section (4(1) contain no such words, and nor does section 68(2), defining use of a mark. The old cases were clear, that infringement required "use of the mark for the purposes of trade in the marked goods" [referring to *Levy v. Walker* (1879) 10 Ch.D. 436 and *Richards v. Butcher* (1890) 7 R.P.C. 288]; whether this is still in all cases a requirement depends on the question of interpretation discussed in the last preceding paragraph."

The position post-1938

Bismag v. Amblins[46] settled that section 4(1)(b) included use of the trade mark in advertising.[47] As a result, the defendants use of "Bisurated Magnesia Tablets" next to their own "Bismuthated Magnesia Tablets", in a table included in a pamphlet, constituted an infringement of the registered trade mark "Bisurated" by importing a reference to the proprietor of the registered trade mark.

In two more cases involving comparisons between products it was reconfirmed that referring to the trade mark proprietor by using the registered trade mark could be an infringement. In *Compaq v. Dell*[48] the claim that Dell computers functioned similarly to Compaq computers was found to infringe Dell's registered trade marks; the fact that the case was a typical example of a comparison between lemons and oranges helped the plaintiff. In *Chanel v. Triton*[49] a chart comparing smellalikes with their branded equivalents was found to infringe despite the fact that the chart was made available only to retailers and not to actual consumers, the end-customers, and there was no evidence that end-customers were misled.[50]

The policy shift was far reaching, so in a series of cases the judges attempted to limit the draconian scope of the provision. In *Pompadour v. Frazer*[51] the proprietors of the registered trade mark "Pompadour" failed in their action seeking an interlocutory injunction against the defendant using on his hair care products the statement "Frazer's Chemicals have manufactured hair lacquer for Pompadour Laboratories Limited for several years", since the reference was to the plaintiffs' name rather than their trade mark.[52] Similarly, in *Duracell International Ltd. v. Ever Ready*,[53] Ever Ready almost escaped by claiming that their batteries lasted longer than the batteries made by Duracell International Ltd rather than Duracell batteries; in addition, the batteries with which the Ever Ready batteries were compared were depicted in shades of black and white, not the registered by Duracell black and gold combination. In *Parker Knoll v. Knoll Overseas Ltd*[54] the statement "not connected with Parker Knoll plc" was clearly not an infringement of Parker Knoll, it was not

---

[46] [1940] R.P.C. 209.
[47] The juxtaposition between the two signpost cases, *Bismag v. Amblins* and *Irving's Yeastvite*, is of course an oversimplification. The views of Lord Greene M.R. on s. 4 remain essential reading for understanding the very complex and often puzzling wording and structure of the section.
[48] [1992] F.S.R. 93.
[49] [1993] R.P.C. 32.
[50] On the issue of whether there is anything wrong in copying a product it is worth comparing *Chanel v. Triton* with *Hodgkinson & Corby v. Wards* [1995] F.S.R. 169.
[51] [1986] R.P.C. 7.
[52] Contrast with *British Northrop v. Texteam* [1974] R.P.C. 57 where the statement "Every part shall be inspected and approved by engineers with many years' experience in the manufacture of NORTHROP parts" was found to infringe Northrop's registration.
[53] [1989] F.S.R. 87.
[54] [1985] F.S.R. 349.

understood as a reference in a comparative sense and it was not considered to be use in relation to goods.

In *Autodrome*[55] use of a registered trade mark for cars as a name for a building where second hand cars were sold was held not to infringe because there was no evidence that the sign was used in relation to the cars as such.

Baume & Co. v. Moore[56] tested the scope of section 8. The answer was obvious: account must be taken of the relevant market, the particular product, and the practice of other traders in the same field, as reflected to a certain extent on the trade mark register. So, a trader's use of his own name could be considered bona fide use,

> provided that the trader honestly thought no confusion would arise, and if he had no intention of diverting business to himself by using the name. The truth is that a man is either honest or dishonest in his motives; there is no such thing, so far as we are aware, as constructive dishonesty.[57]

In *Bentley v. Lagonda*[58] the owners of the trade mark "Bentley" for cars succeeded in their action for trade mark infringement against the defendants, owners of the trade mark Lagonda, based on an advertisement stating that "It is worth reflection that the products of LAGONDA and the designs of W.O. BENTLEY have not always been large cars" with the words LAGONDA and BENTLEY in a much larger font.[59]

---

[55] [1969] R.P.C. 564.
[56] [1958] R.P.C. 226, CA.
[57] *ibid.* at 235. It is worth contrasting this case with similar questions in a passing off context expressed in *Parker-Knoll v. Knoll International*, [1962] R.P.C. 265, HL and *Scandecor v. Scandecor* [1999] F.S.R. 26, CA. Lord Devlin, in *Parker-Knoll* stated, at 289, that
... the falsity of a representation does not depend (at any rate in the absence of fraud) on the meaning which the maker of the representation intended or believed it to have or upon the construction which the court itself puts upon it, but upon the way in which it would reasonably be understood by the persons to whom it is addressed . . . It is literally truthful for the appellants to say that their furniture is manufactured by Knoll International, but if that statement conveys to a member of the public that the furniture is manufactured by Parker-Knoll or some company connected with Parker–Knoll, it is a false representation.
[58] [1947] R.P.C. 33.
[59] Actually the history of Rolls Royce as a car maker is one of the best examples of the power of a brand. Charles Stewart Rolls and Frederick Henry Royce started building cars in 1904 and formed their company in 1906. Rolls died in 1910, however his name has become in this very short period part of one of the most valued and exclusive brands. Walter Owen Bentley was another car enthusiast who started selling cars and then moved to building his own cars. In 1930 his company run into financial trouble and was acquired by the British Equitable Trust Ltd. acting for an unknown company, Rolls Royce. The new company, Bentley Motors, was a wholly owned subsidiary of Rolls-Royce and Bentley became an employee of the company bearing his name. Unhappy with his position he left in 1935 and joined Lagonda designing engines for Lagondas and Aston Martins. Rolls Royce were also building engines for aeroplanes since 1914. In 1971 the company was nationalised and the motor car part–Rolls Royce Motor Cars–was floated as a separate company becoming a part of Vickers. In 1987 Rolls Royce was returned to the private sector. In 1998 Rolls Royce Motor Cars became a prize in a war between BMW and VW; they wanted the company for its expertise in building custom made cars and for its brand name, the icon of luxury and exclusivity. The company was sold to Volkswagen; however there was some uncertainty as to who owned the right to the Rolls

Finally, on the issue of whether extensive use would create the distinctiveness required for registration enabling the registration of an otherwise weak mark, one of the last cases on registrability decided under the 1938 Act, *Interlego AG's Trade Mark Applications*,[60] provided an excellent discussion. On appeal Neuberger J., confirmed the decision of Mr N. Harkness refusing registration of a number of trade marks consisting of combinations of arrangements of raised knobs and tubes applied to building bricks for building bricks. The judge underlined that what the applicants were seeking was a monopoly in toy bricks rather than a monopoly in a trade mark; this would be "contrary to principle and objectionable in practice".[61] The evidence that the public associated the bricks with the applicant was not helpful. The public did not understand the signs as trade marks; the knobs and the tubes where not "used (or recognised by the public) as the badge of origin of the bricks".[62] The brand name Lego was always stamped on the bricks, weakening further Interlego's application. In addition Neuberger J. remarked that "the decision whether to register a trade mark, at least in some cases, involve a balancing exercise, particularly in light of the very substantial benefit accorded to a proprietor if he succeeds in registering his mark and the public interest against monopolies in products (as opposed to marks) . . . the fact that an applicant has, or has had, the benefit of the protection of a registered patent in respect of the very thing which (or part of which) he seeks to register as a trade mark is a factor, which, at least in some cases, ought to be taken into account".[63]

As to whether ordinary, but still in the context of a commercial activity, use in language of a term that is also a registered trade mark in *Mars v. Cadbury*[64] it was held that the slogan TREAT SIZE did not infringe the trade mark TREETS registered for identical products. Similarly, Mothercare/Other Care, used as a title for a book, was a reference to the contents of the book rather a reference to the plaintiff's products,[65] with Dillon L.J. saying that

---

Royce name, partly engineered by Rolls Royce itself. The result is that VW bought the plant and the right to build Bentleys but BMW will become the owner of the Rolls Royce brand for cars after January 1, 2003. Ironically, the sale of Rolls Royce Motor Cars made Vickers an attractive target for Rolls Royce seeking to become a big player in marine power (*Financial Times*, September 21, 1999). Can we really trust the actual message conveyed by a name?
[60] [1998] R.P.C. 69.
[61] *ibid*. at 110.
[62] *ibid*. at 113.
[63] *ibid*. at 114. However Remington's argument based on public policy was rejected by Jacob J. in *Philips Electronics NV v. Remington Consumer Products* [1998] R.P.C. 283. The judge noted that he had to enforce a statute rather than embark on a socio-political discussion; if the legislator wished to rule out parallel protection under patents or copyright and trade marks then he would have done so. It is worth contrasting the two approaches taking into account Jacob J.'s decision in *Hodgkinson & Corby v. Wards* [1995] F.S.R. 169, decided under passing off.
[64] [1987] R.P.C. 387.
[65] *Mothercare UK v. Penguin Books* [1988] R.P.C. 113.

it stands to reason that a Trade Marks Act would only be concerned to restrict the use of a mark as a trade mark or in a trade mark sense, and should be construed accordingly. If descriptive words are legitimately registered in Part A of the register, there is still no reason why other people should not be free to use the words in a descriptive sense, and not in a trademark sense.[66]

In *Unidoor Ltd v. Marks & Spencer plc*[67] the application of the slogan Coast to Coast on T-shirts was held not to infringe registration of the same slogan, since it was not trade mark use.

Finally it is worth mentioning two passing cases in order to complete the picture on the pre-1994 situation on use of a another trader's indicia in product comparisons. In *McDonalds v. Burger King*[68] use of the slogan "Not just Big, Mac" in an advertisement of the defendants "Whopper" burger was found to constitute passing off. The consumer could be led to believe that the Whopper was a variation of a Big Mac. However, in *Ciba Geigy v. Parke Davis*,[69] where the advertisement's audience was considered to be more attentive, use of an apple (indirectly referring to the plaintiffs advertising campaign for Voltarol) together with a bitten apple (referring to the defendant's Diclomax Retard product) and the slogans "Diclomax Retard takes a chunk of your prescribing costs" "Diclomax Retard offers everything would expect from diclofenac retard with one crucial difference—The price" was not sufficient to support a passing off claim. The direct reference in the advertisement was to diclofenac retard, the generic name of the pharmaceutical product, not to the plaintiff's branded product. There was no confusion as to source and as a result there was no passing off or injurious falsehood.

The situation post-1994

Barclays Bank v. RBS Advanta[70] was one of the first comparative advertising cases exploring the limits of section 10(6). The primary objective of section 10(6), it was decided, was to allow comparative advertising provided that use of the competitor's mark is honest. The onus is on the plaintiff to show that the factors of the proviso that: use is not in accordance with honest practices in industrial or commercial matters, or without due cause takes unfair advantage of, or is detrimental to, the distinctive character or repute of the trade mark. This means that use must either give some advantage to the

---

[66] *ibid.* at 118.
[67] [1988] R.P.C. 275.
[68] [1986] F.S.R. 45.
[69] [1994] F.S.R. 8.
[70] [1996] R.P.C. 307.

defendant or inflict some harm on the character or repute of the registered mark; in any case the effect must be above a *de minimis* level. As to the required level of honesty Jacob J. decided that we do not have to look at statutory or industry agreed codes of conduct; honesty is determined by looking at what would be reasonably expected by the relevant public of advertisements for the goods or services in issue. It is submitted that the reference to the relevant public is helpful, despite the subjectivity that it introduces, because it allows a flexible approach to section 10(6); perhaps this opens the way for a similar approach in section 10(1), 10(2), and 10(3), if the public understands that the sign is used by the defendant in a way that does not induce confusion–there is no trade mark recognition on the market–then courts should take this into account.

Vodafone v. Orange[71] gave the opportunity to Laddie J. to look at a comparative advertising case from two different perspectives: injurious falsehood and trade mark infringement. On injurious falsehood he decided that in applying the "one meaning rule" (meaning that a statement is either false or true) the judge acts as a notional jury and has to decide upon a single, natural and ordinary meaning of the words used, taking into account that the public have learned to expect hyperbole in advertising. However, on the issue of applicability of section 10(6) we do not need to look at the "one meaning rule"; a comparative advertisement is not in accordance with honest practices if it is objectively misleading to a substantial proportion of the reasonable audience.[72] Laddie J. strengthened further the flexible approach adopted by Jacob J. by introducing the objectivity requirement in a way that expands rather than narrows the scope of the provision. Finally, commenting on the intricate language used in section 10(6) he stated that ordinarily the "without due cause takes unfair advantage of, or is detrimental to, the distinctive character or repute of the trade mark" half of the proviso does not add anything to the significance of the other half, "use is not in accordance with honest practices in industrial or commercial matters".[73]

British Telecommunications v. AT & T Communications[74] provided us

---

[71] [1997] F.S.R. 35.
[72] In *MacMillan Magazines v. RCN Publishing* [1998] F.S.R. 9 the plaintiff sought an application for an interlocutory injunction on the basis that comparisons were not like with like, data for the comparisons was eleven months old, some data was not objectively verified, and some allegations were untrue. The application was refused because the comparisons made by the defendant were arguably true or at least they were not obviously false; each party had an arguable case. It was mentioned that where an issue involving a question of malicious falsehood fell to be decided at the interlocutory stage the court would have regard to the fact that the defendant intended to plead justification. Where the statements complained of were not obviously untrue then the court would decline to grant the relief sought. This extended to cases where, as here, the plaintiff had also argued that the provisions of section 10(6) of the TMA 1994 did not apply. So, the balance of justice favoured neither party but it was underlined that the granting of relief would effectively interfere with the defendant's right of free speech; this tipped the balance in refusing the injunction.
[73] [1996] R.P.C. 307 at 314.
[74] [1997] E.I.P.R. D-134.

with a decodification of section 10(6). Mr Crystal Q.C. digested the existing case law as meaning that the law permits comparative advertising. As long as use of the plaintiff's mark is honest there is nothing wrong in informing the public of the relative merits of competing goods or services and using registered trade marks to identify them. The onus, in establishing the applicability of the proviso, is on the plaintiff. To determine that use is not in accordance with honest practices, and as result that the advertisement constitutes trade mark infringement, we must employ an objective test: a "reasonable" reader is given the full facts and is asked to determine whether the advertisement is not honest. Instead of taking into account statutory or industry agreed codes of conduct we should look at what is reasonably expected by the relevant public of advertisements for the goods or services in question. The general public is sophisticated enough to be used to the ways of advertisers and to expect advertising hyperbole and as a result the 1994 Act should not require the courts to enforce a more puritanical standard than the general public would expect from advertising. Finally, it was obvious that a significantly misleading advertisement would not be considered honest for the purposes of section 10(6). He then added his own findings, expanding even further the scope of section 10(6). The advertisement must be considered as a whole. At the interlocutory stage the court should not hold words used in the advertisement to be seriously misleading unless on a fair reading, in context, against the background of the advertisement as a whole they can really be said to justify that description. A minute textual examination would not be embarked upon by a reasonable reader of an advertisement. The court should not encourage a microscopic approach to the construction of a comparative advertisement at the interlocutory stage.[75]

---

[75] It is worth considering here the situation in the U.S. where in *Societe Comptoir de l' Industrie Cotonniere Etablissements Boussac v. Alexander's Department Stores* 299 F2d 33, 132 USPQ 475 (CA 2, 1962) it was found that there is no cause of action where there is no misrepresentation or confusion: the statement "Original by Christian Dior–Alexander's Exclusive–Paris–Adaptation" could be detrimental to Dior but was nevertheless true; there was nothing that Dior could do. It was stressed that the Lanham Act does not prohibit a commercial rival's truthfully denominating his goods as a copy of a design in a public domain, though he uses the name of the designer to do so. And it was difficult to see any other means that might be employed to inform the consuming public of the true origin of the design. However the adoption of an anti-dilution basis of trade mark protection may challenge this liberal position despite the fact that section 43(c) of the Lanham Act clearly provides that comparative advertising should not be affected. But comparative advertising must, firstly, be truthful, in *McNeil–P.C.C. v. Bristol–Myers Squibb* 19 USPQ 2d 1525 (1991) the defendant's claims that his Aspirin-free Excedrin "relieves pain better" than plaintiff's Extra Strength Tylenol proved to be false following clinical studies that proved that the products were equivalent. Similarly in *Tyco Industries v. Lego Systems* 5 USPQ 2d 1023 (1987) the claim that competitor's toy block "looks and feels" like Lego was found to be false. In *Castrol v. Pennzoil* 987 F2d 939, 25 USPQ2d 1666 (CA 3, 1993) it was established that there is infringement where deceptive data is used in the comparisons. And, secondly, the message must not lead to confusion on the origin of the product. In *Charles of the Ritz Group v. Quality King* 832 F2d 1317, 4 USPQ 2d 1778 (CA 2, 1987), a smell-alike case, there was evidence that there was a likelihood of confusion as a result of a slogan used on the packaging of the defendant's product mentioning "If you like Opium

The limitations to the scope of infringement imposed by section 10(6) are combined with those provided for in section 11(2). The same sign can be recognised at one point as a trade mark, at another as a non trade mark reference to the trade mark proprietor, and at another as plain use in language with or without any commercial significance attached.

In *Bravado Merchandising Services Ltd v. Mainstream Publishing (Edinburgh) Ltd*,[76] the owner of the mark "Wet Wet Wet", registered *inter alia* in class 16 in respect of books, magazines and other printed matter, sought an injunction against the use of its trade mark by Mainstream Publishing in a book entitled *A Sweet Little Mystery—Wet Wet Wet-The Inside Story.* Both parties had agreed that use "in the course of trade" meant use "in a trade mark sense" as developed under the 1938 Act. Lord McCluskey accepted this, but did not find the distinction between use in a trade mark sense and use in a non trade mark sense of great value in applying section 10 to the facts of the case. Lord McCluskey stressed that it would be a bizarre result of trade marks legislation if it could prevent publishers from using protected names in the titles of books about the company or product; use that according to our analysis, refers to the trade mark proprietor but where there is no trade mark recognition of the sign. If that had been the intention of Parliament it should have been made plain. Similarly, registration of the trade mark WET–WET–WET should not interfere with the feelings and the freedom of an unlucky travel writer who would like to produce an article entitled "Wet wet wet" after a fortnight's hill walking in the Lake District in April; use of a common sign in language without any reference to the trade mark proprietor. So he had to decide that the use of the defendant fell within the provisions of section 11(2)(b). Mainstream were using the words as an "indication" of the main characteristic of the book, *i.e.* that it concerned the pop group.

In *British Sugar v. James Robertson*[77] Jacob J. observed that section 11(2) to a certain extent overlaps with section 10(6) in that permits a fair comparison between the trade mark owner's goods and those of the defendant; and provided the comparison is honest and is part of a genuine indication of characteristics like quality or price then it falls within the provision. A trade mark functions as an indication of origin, this is what the Directive purports to protect and as a result the law should not extend the trade mark monopoly to the point of enabling the trade mark proprietor to suppress competition in cases

---

... you'll love Omni". Otherwise, it was held in *G.D. Searle & Co. v. Hudson Pharmaceutical Corporation* 715 F2d 837, 220 USPQ 496 (CA 3, 1983) that use of another party's trade mark on the packaging of one's own product is allowed unless it is likely to cause confusion. In Germany there has been a volte face following the adoption of E.U. legislation on this issue; see B. Steckler & F. Bachmann, "Comparative advertising in Germany with regard to European Community law" [1997] E.I.P.R. 578–586 (in particular 584 to 587) and S. Dittmers "An end to the "cursory average consumer"? [1998] E.I.P.R. 313; see also note 35 above.

[76] [1996] F.S.R. 205.
[77] [1996] R.P.C. 281.

where his trade mark is used in this way, as an indication of origin. But he did not follow Lord McCluskey's finding on use and decided that for the purposes of section 10(1) and (2) there was no requirement that the defendant's use of the sign be in a trade mark sense; the law only required use in the course of trade. So, use of "Treat" in "Robertson's Toffee Treat" on a label for a sweat spread was considered to be use in the course of trade. It would infringe registration of "Treat", albeit "Treat" was devoid of any distinctive character and in any case the defendant's use would fall again within the scope of section 11(2). Here use in language of a common term with some commercial meaning but probably without a trade mark reference to the plaintiff was used primarily as the basis for expunging the registration; it proved the absurdity of accepting that such a common term could be acknowledged by the public as a trade mark.

Despite *British Sugar*, in *Trebor Bassett Ltd v. The Football Association*[78] Rattee J. decided that the depiction on cards of footballers wearing the team shirt of England did not constitute an infringement of the three lion device mark appearing on the shirt. He decided that Trebor Bassett was not affixing the sign comprising the England crest to the cards and that it was not putting on the market the cards under the same crest. The case was outside the scope of section 10(4). It is submitted that Rattee J.'s approach is the one which most directly limits the scope of infringement, recognising the public's understanding of the function of the relevant sign. He took one step back and looked at the relevance of use in establishing infringement rather than condoning the defendant's behaviour.

Finally in the Court of Appeal decision in *Philips Electronics NV v. Remington Consumer Products Ltd*[79] Aldous L.J. started by noting that the fact that a trade mark has by use become such as to denote goods of a particular trader does not necessarily mean that it is capable of distinguishing as required by section 1. Capability of distinguishing depends upon the features of the trade mark itself rather on the result of its use. Accordingly,

> a shape of an article cannot be registered in respect of goods of that shape unless it contains some addition to the shape of the article which has trade mark significance. It is that addition which makes it capable of distinguishing the trade mark owner's goods from the same sort of goods sold by another trader.[80]

It is submitted that this finding has the potential of redrawing the boundaries of registrability. It seems that some signs will never be capable of registration irrespective of the public's recognition.

---

[78] [1997] F.S.R. 211.
[79] [1999] E.T.M.R. 816.
[80] *ibid.* at 826.

Aldous LJ. also considered the question of what type of use would be required for infringement to occur. "Remington drew attention to section 9 which provided that registration gave exclusive rights "in the trade mark which are infringed by use of the trade mark". They submitted that to infringe that right, the use had to be trade mark use namely use denoting origin. That was emphasised by Article 5(5) which presupposes that infringing use is trade mark use. As this case was not trade mark use there was no infringement. Their submission can be explained by taking the example of the well-known trade mark "Mothercare". They accept that the trade mark would be infringed by use of the words denoting that a book was published by the proprietor of the trade mark. However they submitted that it would not be infringed by use of the words in the title of a book, *e.g.* "Mothercare: the correct way" as that would not be trade mark use. A similar submission found favour Lord McCluskey in *Bravado Merchandising Service Ltd v. Mainstream Publishing (Edinburgh) Ltd*.[81] However it was rejected by Jacob J. in the *British Sugar* case. In the present case the judge accepted Remington's submission that the use was not use that indicated origin, but declined to decide whether trade mark use was a requirement under the Act and the Directive.

> For my part I prefer the submission of Philips that found favour in the *British Sugar* case namely that trade mark use is not essential. There is nothing in sections 9 or 10 which require an infringing use to be trade mark use and section 11(2) (Article 6) contains a comprehensive list of the exclusions that were thought appropriate. That being so, any use not falling within that list will infringe, whether or not it is trade mark use. In any case I would expect that any use which was not trade mark use to fall within the list. I therefore reject Remington's defence upon this ground.[82]

It seems that Aldous L.J. understands the difficulty of interpreting the "use in trade" requirement in a way that takes into account the function of the sign on the market place. So, first he employs use in order to narrow the scope of registrability, then he rejects the argument that infringing use must be trade mark use, but also mentions that all types of non trade mark use would fall within the scope of section 11; sensible but confusing!

A note on domain names

Use of a sign in the course of trade is also relevant in the context of the links between trade marks and domain names. Use of a sign as a

---

[81] [1996] F.S.R. 205.
[82] [1999] E.T.M.R. 816 at 832–833.

domain name may save the trade mark registration of the same sign from cancellation proceedings based on non use. On the other hand more and more conflicts between domain names and registered trade marks are brought before the courts. In the United Kingdom, *Marks & Spencer plc (& Ladbrokes plc & J. Sainsbury plc & Virgin Enterprises Ltd & British Telecommunications plc) v. One in a Million*[83] has probably become a landmark in this type of case. The plaintiffs claimed that the defendants registration of a number of Internet domain names comprising the plaintiffs' names or trade marks constituted passing off and trade mark infringement under section 10(3) of the 1994 Act. The passing off part of the action was successful. As to the trade mark infringement part, J. Sumption Q.C., sitting as a deputy judge, characterised the defendants as dealers in domain names comparing them with company registration agents.[84] For the defendants, in the absence of any actual use, there were four ways for exploiting the domain names: sell the name to the trade mark owner, sell the name to an unrelated third party (a potential user or another dealer in domain names), sell the name to a party that might have a special interest (*e.g.* a person called J. Sainsbury), or, finally, block the use of the domain name by the relevant trade mark owner. The judge decided that use by the defendants was use "in the course of trade"; the law was interpreted as requiring use by way of business rather than use in a trade mark sense. Section 10(3) was applicable, irrespective of whether likelihood of confusion was implicitly required since the plaintiffs had demonstrated a likelihood of confusion.

Before the Court of Appeal,[85] L.J. Aldous also found that there was a valid passing off claim. On trade mark infringement his lordship noted that even if section 10(3) is interpreted narrowly so as to require infringing use to be trade mark use and at the same time confusing use he can still find that

> threats to infringe have been established. The appellants seek to sell the domain names which are confusingly similar to registered trade marks. The domain names indicate origin. That is the purpose for which they were registered. Further they will be used in relation to the services provided by the registrant who trades in domain names.

Such use would take unfair advantage of, or be detrimental to the distinctive character or reputation of the respondents' trade marks

---

[83] [1998] F.S.R. 265.
[84] Indeed, straightforward "cyber squatting" cases are very similar with conflicts between trade marks and company names. The principles are similar (see for example *Glaxo v. Glaxowellcome* [1996] F.S.R. 388); however there are two distinguishing factors: the huge number of applications for registration of domain names compared with applications for company names, and the nature of the Internet as on the one hand a new market place and on the other a market for the exchange of ideas and non commercial messages.
[85] [1999] F.S.R. 1.

since the domain names were registered to take advantage of the distinctive character and reputation of the marks. "That is unfair and detrimental."[86]

In the United States, where there is a much larger number of decisions[87] dealing with this issue it is worth mentioning *Planned Parenthood v. Bucci*[88] for its interpretation of the "use in commerce" requirement. The plaintiff, a non profit organisation providing advice on reproductive health care, sued for trade mark infringement of "Planned Parenthood" the defendant, an anti-abortion broadcaster in "Catholic Radio", who registered the domain name plannedparenthood.com. Bucci argued that his use felt outside the scope of the Lanham Act being non-commercial speech within the scope of the exemption provided in section 1125(c). The court rejected this analysis, firstly, because the defendant's actions prevented the plaintiff's commercial activities, and, secondly, because the audience accessing the defendant's site would have to use interstate or international telephone lines; the second factor would of course satisfy the "use in commerce" requirement for setting any type of home page.[89]

The ECJ's approach to use

Distinctiveness acquired through use

In joint cases C-108 and 109/97 *Windsurfing Chiemsee Produktions-und Vertriebs GmbH v. Boots-und Segelzubehor Walter Huber and Franz Attenberger*[90] the ECJ firstly clarified the circumstances under which Article 3(1)(c) of the Directive could be used to block the registration of a trade mark which consists exclusively of a geographical name. The court decided that Article 3(1)(c) of the Directive protects the public interest by ensuring that some terms may be freely used by all. In particular signs or indications which may serve to designate the geographical origin of the specified products must remain available also because they may function as an indication of their

---

[86] *ibid.* at 25; he seemed to dismiss the argument that s. 10(3) requires use to be trade mark use or confusing use.
[87] For a review of case law see G.N. Verganil "Electronic Commerce and Trade Marks in the United States: Domain Names, Trade Marks and the 'Use in Commerce Requirement' on the Internet" [1999] E.I.P.R. 450 and D.M. Cendali, C.E. Forssander & R.J. Turiello Jr., "An Overview of Intellectual Property Issues Relating to the Internet" [1999] E.T.M.R. 485.
[88] 42 USPQ2d 1430 (SDNY 1997).
[89] It is worth comparing *Planned Parenthood* with the Irish case *Gallaher (Dublin) Ltd, Hergall (1981) Ltd and Another v. The Health Education Bureau* [1982] F.S.R. 464. Costello J. decided that use of a tobacco brand on packets with imitation cigarettes–rolled pieces of paper providing anti-smoking advice, constituted infringement. He remarked, at 469, that "[I]t seems to me that if it can be shown that a person used another's mark in a way which means that the registered proprietor cannot use it again on the goods for which he obtained registration, then it is highly likely the use complained of must have been in relation to the goods in respect of which it was registered, as otherwise no damage would have been to his mark".
[90] [1999] E.T.M.R. 585.

quality and other characteristics and may influence the consumer by associating in a positive way the products with the particular place. In relation to Article 6(1)(b) the ECJ found that it is not in conflict with Article 3(1)(c) but aims to resolve problems posed by registration of a mark consisting wholly or partly of a geographical name. It does not confer on third parties the right to use the name as a trade mark but merely guarantees their right to use it descriptively, as an indication of geographical origin and in accordance with honest practices in industrial and commercial matters.

In deciding whether Article 3(1)(c) is applicable the competent authority must assess whether the relevant geographical name is that of a place currently associated in the mind of the relevant class of persons with the category of the specified products, or whether it is reasonable to assume that such an association may be established in the future. However, its application does not depend on there being a real, current or serious need to leave a sign or indication free, the doctrine developed by German case law.[91]

The ECJ also decided on the requirements that must be met for a mark to have acquired distinctive character through use and in particular whether such requirements differ according to the extent of the need to keep the mark free. The court first noted that the protectable function of a trade mark does not change through Article 3(3); the mark with the acquired distinctiveness must still identify the specified product as originating from a particular undertaking, and thus to distinguish that product from goods of other undertakings. In respect of geographical names Article 3(3) simply means that they may become registrable where they have gained a new significance and their new connotation is not purely descriptive. Albeit, it is the meaning of the sign in the marketplace that determines registrability rather than its perceived importance as a geographical name that must be kept free for others to use. So, what needs to be established in such cases is that the mark has come to identify the product concerned as originating from a particular undertaking, and thus to distinguish that product from goods of other undertakings, taking into account the specific nature of the geographical name in question. A very well-known geographical name needs long-standing and intensive use of the mark by the undertaking applying for registration, and a name that is already familiar as an indication of geographical origin in relation to a certain category of goods needs evidence that the long-standing and intensive use of the mark is, also, particularly well established. Further points to be taken into account are: the market share enjoyed by the mark, how intensive, geographically widespread and long-standing the use of the mark has been, the investment in promoting the mark, the proportion of the relevant public identifying through the mark goods as originating from a particular undertaking, and

---

[91] See p. 233 above.

finally statements from chambers of commerce and industry or other trade and professional associations. The ECJ also clarified that survey evidence may be used as guidance but stressed that it is the balance between all these factors and not a reference to general, abstract data such as predetermined percentages that determines whether enough distinctiveness has been acquired through use.

Use as a trade mark

In *Bayerische Motorenwerke AG and BMW Nederland BV v. Ronald Karel Deenik*,[92] the ECJ had to define the scope of the infringement provisions. In some aspects the case is so much reminiscent of *Aristoc v. Rysta*[93] that it is as if we have reached the conclusion of a full circle. Does use of a registered trade mark by a third party, Deenik, in order to refer to services provided in relation to genuine trade marked products, repairing and maintaining BMWs and selling second hand BMWs, constitute an infringement when the registered proprietor had not registered the same trade mark in respect of the relevant services.

Looking at a number of questions referred by the Hoge Raad the ECJ interpreted the first two as essentially asking whether use of a trade mark, without the proprietor's authorisation, in order to inform the public that another undertaking carries out repairs and maintenance of goods covered by that trade mark or that it has specialised in such goods constitutes a use of that mark for the purposes of Article 5 of the Directive. Given the facts of the case, the ECJ noted that the case was about a situation where, at first sight, the relevant use was within the scope of Article 5(1)(a) of the Directive: the BMW mark was used by a third party in respect of genuine BMW goods and such use would constitute an infringement. But this prima facie reasoning could be undermined by arguing, firstly, that the relevant expressions ("BMW specialist" and "Specialised in BMWs") included the BMW mark for purposes other than for distinguishing goods or services and as a result were back within the scope of Article 5(5) of the Directive. And, secondly, that in the advertisement for "repair and maintenance of BMWs", the BMW mark was not used in respect of goods but to describe a service in respect of which the mark has not been registered. This would bring Article 5(1)(b) or (2) into play.

The court indicated that the scope of application of both Article 5(1) and (2) and Article 5(5) depends on whether the trade mark is used for the purpose of distinguishing the goods or services in question as originating from a particular undertaking, that is to say, *as a trade mark as such*, or whether it is used for other purposes. But in a situation such as that before the court, use of the same trade

---

[92] [1999] E.T.M.R. 339.
[93] See p. 235 above.

mark is intended to distinguish the goods in question as the subject of the services provided by the advertiser. Deenik used the BMW mark to identify the source of the goods in respect of which the services are supplied; he wanted to distinguish those goods from any others in respect of which the same services might have been provided; this applied both to the sale of second-hand BMW cars and to the repair and maintenance of BMW cars. As a result the answer given to the two questions was that the unauthorised use of a trade mark for the purpose of informing the public that another undertaking carries out the repair and maintenance of goods covered by that mark or that it has specialised in such goods constitutes use of the mark within the meaning of Article 5(1)(a).

However, the other two questions, according to the ECJ, were essentially asking whether Articles 5 to 7 of the Directive entitle a trade mark proprietor to prevent its use for informing the public that a third party carries out the repair and maintenance of trade marked products put on the market with his consent, or that it specialises in the sale or the repair and maintenance of such goods. In particular whether he may prevent such use only where the advertiser creates the impression that his undertaking is affiliated to the proprietor's distribution network, or whether he may also prevent such use where, because of the manner in which the trade mark is used in the advertisements, the public might be given the impression that the advertiser is using the trade mark in that regard to an appreciable extent for the purpose of advertising his own business as such, by creating a specific suggestion of quality. The ECJ had to look at the applicability of Article 6, limiting rights arising from registration, and Article 7, on the exhaustion of rights.

In relation to the advertisements for the sale of second-hand BMW cars the ECJ referred to its case law, expressed in *Parfums Christian Dior v. Evora*.[94] BMW could not prevent Deenik from informing the public that he is in the business of selling second hand BMWs, provided that the relevant cars have been put on the E.U. market with the trade mark proprietor's consent and that the way in which the mark is used does not legitimise, within the scope of Article 7(2), the proprietor's opposition. If the trade mark is used in a way that it may give the impression that there is a commercial connection between the reseller and the trade mark proprietor, this too may constitute a legitimate reason. But the mere fact that the reseller derives an advantage from using the trade mark and this attributes an aura of quality to the reseller's business does not fall within Article 7(2).

As to use relating to repair and maintenance the ECJ stated that trade mark rights are not exhausted, but may be limited under Article 6(1)(c), providing that the proprietor may not prohibit use that indicates the intended purpose of a product or service, in

---

[94] [1997] E.C.R. I-6013, [1998] R.P.C. 166.

particular as accessories or spare parts, provided that the use is necessary to indicate that purpose and is in accordance with honest practices in industrial or commercial matters. The court found that Article 6, like Article 7, seeks to reconcile trade mark protection with free movement of goods and freedom to provide services in the common market; so, under the same reasoning with that under section 7, use should also not be prohibited under Article 6(1)(c).

The ECJ's position

It is submitted that in both cases the ECJ has been cautious but direct. It rejected the applicability of the German doctrine that some terms must be kept free for others to use and copy, an unwelcome development for the sceptics amongst trade mark lawyers, but its analysis on the requirements that must be satisfied for a sign to become a trade mark through use reflects some of the German concerns. Equally, in respect of infringement, it was recognised that a trade mark may be used by third parties in order to refer to genuine marked products. This is what a trade mark does, indicate that a product has been put on the market by a specific marketer, so it would be a bizarre result of trade mark law if the same marketer could use the registration in order to stop a third party from indicating the same thing! And although the Directive lacks the equivalent of section 10(6) of the 1994 Act the limitations imposed by Article 6 appear to work effectively; the adventurous advertiser could even claim that section 11 might even cover comparative advertising. The trade mark sceptic would argue that Deenik's activities should not fall from the outset within the scope of trade mark infringement,[95] but there is some reassurance from the attitude of the court that reminded the balance between trade mark rights, free movement within the E.U., and competition. The expansionists amongst trade mark lawyers should always remember that the first wave of ECJ decisions on limiting the scope of intellectual property rights was based on competition law. Too much stretching of trade mark rights may result to a change of heart in the ECJ's current position.

Looking at the future—demarcating areas of use

Following this short review of relevant case law it has become apparent that the current trend in trade mark law is to expand the scope of trade mark protection. At the same time trade mark registration regimes are becoming increasingly easier to satisfy on issues of registrability requirements. It is submitted that the combined effect of these two approaches could be a trade mark

---

[95] See the analysis of infringement provisions in p. 238 above.

system that is overburdened and uncertain. Too many and easy-to-acquire rights arising from registration combined with an ever expanding scope of protection for trade marks that have acquired strength through use will inevitably result to more conflicts between right holders. Registrations will become meaningless unless tested in cancellation or infringement proceedings. The field of trade marks will become a field where too many non trade mark battles[96] are fought. The effectiveness of trade mark law will be eroded. One way of solving the problem is to take a step back and rethink the rationale of trade mark protection.[97] Until then a solution could be provided by constantly remembering the relevance of use in delineating the scope of trade mark protection.[98] Its potential application is exemplified by two recent cases.

Oasis Stores Ltd's Trade Mark Application[99] is a U.K. decision on a conflict between marks where "use" is ingeniously employed in order to narrow the scope of section 5(3) of the 1994 Act. Mr. Allan James in the Trade Marks Registry dismissed the opposition, of the owner of a number of "Ever Ready" word and device marks for batteries, torches, plugs, smoke alarms, etc., against the application for registration of "Eveready" for contraceptives and condoms. Following the ECJ's findings in *Sabel BV v. Puma AG, Rudolf Dassler Sport*[1] and *Canon Kabushiki Kaisha v. Metro-Goldwyn-Mayer Inc.*[2] the examiner accepted that, in principle, it was possible for an opponent to satisfy the conditions of section 5(3) without establishing that there is any likelihood of confusion.[3] However his interpretation of the unfair advantage for the applicant or the detriment to the distinctive character or the repute of the earlier trademark brought back the scope of the provision into classic trade mark law. He stressed that if a consumer is simply being reminded of a similar trade mark with a reputation this does not necessarily mean that the applicant for registration is taking an unfair advantage of the earlier trade mark's reputation. Then he narrowed further the scope of the provision by adding that normally reputation does not exist in abstract terms but rather in a specific field,[4] so, if the opponent could point to a specific

---

[96] Like battles on competition or for domain names.
[97] On this see the contribution of Helen Norman in this volume.
[98] See p. 234 above, on the relevance of use in registrability questions.
[99] [1998] R.P.C. 631.
[1] [1998] F.S.R. 199.
[2] [1999] R.P.C. 117.
[3] Contrast *Baywatch Productions v. The Home Video Channel* [1997] F.S.R. 22.
[4] Geoffrey Hobbs Q.C. however ruled differently in a similar case dealing with VISA condoms. The respondent here argued that use of the word was intended as a reference to its passport sense rather than as a reference to the name of the card network. This time however the applicant was the registered proprietor of a truly widely known mark; its notoriety was transcending diverse areas of use and perhaps this was one of the factors that influenced the decision. He was reported stating that "many people were "deeply imbued" with the Visa name, and its use on a condom would trigger associations with the card network. "My impression is that [the respondent] wanted to use a name . . . whose fame they fed upon". Reported in the *Financial Times*, October 7, 1999 by J. Eaglesham. It is worth comparing this decision with the contradicting outcome of case law in Germany

aspect of its reputation for batteries that would benefit the applicant to a significant extent,[5] this would strengthen the basis of a case established on "(non origin) association".[6] Use of the same or similar mark on dissimilar products could potentially dilute the distinctiveness of the earlier trade mark, however, section 5(3) was "clearly not intended to have the sweeping effect of preventing the registration of any mark which was the same as, or similar to, a trade mark with a reputation".[7] Instead, a number of factors should be considered in order to determine the likelihood and extent of detriment that would empower the opponent with the applicability of section 5(3), one of them being whether the, otherwise dissimilar, goods or services are in some way related or likely to be sold through the same outlets. It is submitted that using factors that are also employed in determining product similarity[8] in a different and distinct test that is applied in a section on use on dissimilar products seems to be akin to a revival of the dormant common field of activity requirement that characterised a number of passing off cases.[9] Finally, another relevant factor is whether the earlier trade mark would become less distinctive than before for the goods or services for which it enjoyed reputation; it is the distinctiveness rather than the reputation that is relevant here.[10] So, it was decided that

---

in analogous situations; see Kouker L., "Is the Purpose of Trademark Law Limited Only to Protecting Purchasers?–Analysis Under United States and German Trademark Law" [1997] T.M.R. 151.

[5] It seems that an unfair advantage that does not result to a significant benefit for the applicant would not normally fall within the provision. Note too that the value of the trade mark with the reputation should be affected in some material rather than de minimis fashion. Compare with Laddie J.'s approach in comparative advertising; see p. 246 above. On the effect of a truly well known name see N. Dawson, "Famous and Well-Known Trade Marks–'Usurping a Corner of the Giant's Robe'" [1998] I.P.Q. 350.

[6] [1998] R.P.C. 631 at 649.

[7] ibid.

[8] The test devised by Jacob J., in, *British Sugar v. James Robertson & Sons Ltd* [1996] R.P.C. 281, for determining product similarity provides that we must take into account the respective uses and users of the respective goods or services, the physical nature of the goods or acts of service, the respective trade channels through which the goods or services reach the market, and the extent to which the respective goods or services are competitive. It was approved in *Canon Kabushiki Kaisha v. Metro-Goldwyn-Mayer Inc.* [1999] R.P.C. 117, however there it was also stressed that the distinctiveness of the earlier mark, in particular the distinctiveness that has been acquired through use and the resulting reputation, is another factor that we must examine in order to determine whether there is a likelihood of confusion. As a result the two tests, the one determining similarity between trade marks and the other determining similarity between products, are not distinct from each other but instead function like communicating vessels.

[9] Interestingly the essence of the "common field of activity" requirement made another indirect comeback in *BBC Worldwide Ltd v. Pally Screen Printing Ltd* [1998] F.S.R. 665 a case where the plaintiff claimed copyright infringement and passing off against the printing on T-shirts of representations of the Teletubbies. Laddie J. refused a summary judgment on the basis of arguable defences. In the passing off part of the case he felt that there was a valid question to be asked on whether the public perceived the representations as simple illustrations rather than as an indication that the product was manufactured or marketed under the control of the plaintiff. The public's understanding, or lack of it, of the representations as an indicator of source is analogous to our discussion on how a sign can function as a trade mark at one point and in some other capacity at another point.

[10] [1998] R.P.C. 631 at 650–651.

registration of the applicant's trade mark "Eveready" for condoms and contraceptives would not affect the distinctiveness of "Ever Ready" for batteries and also that it was unlikely that "Ever Ready's" reputation would be damaged by normal and fair use of "Eveready" by the applicant. The demarcation of the areas of use of the relevant trade marks, even in the case of section 5(3), could create a type of analysis that brings us back to the basics of trade mark protection.

The second example of the potential of use is a U.S. decision on a conflict between domain names and trade marks. The U.S. District Court for the District of Massachusetts held, in *Hasbro Inc. v. Clue Computing Inc.*,[11] that a legitimate competing use of another person's trade mark as a domain name does not *per se* constitute trade mark dilution. Hasbro, the owner of the trade mark "Clue" for a mystery board game sued Clue Computing Inc. for classic trade mark infringement and dilution for adopting the name "clue.com" for its web site. In his summary judgment Judge Douglas P. Woodlock first ruled that there was no trade mark infringement since there is little similarity between Hasbro's products and Clue Computing's services. "It is 'a stretch' to assert that Hasbro's on line technical support to users of its Clue CD-ROM game is similar in any meaningful way to Clue Computing's consulting services, . . . online services are at most a small component of the Hasbro's Clue product."[12] In addition large segments of the two parties prospective customers do not overlap, and, in any case they are sophisticated enough to know the difference between the two products. As to dilution he decided that using another party's trade mark as a domain name is not a new type of dilution. There are two kinds of classic dilution, dilution by tarnishment and dilution by blurring. On dilution by tarnishment he decided that

> while use of a trademark as a domain name to extort money from the markholder or to prevent the markholder from using the domain name may be per se dilution, a legitimate competing use of the domain name is not. Holders of a famous mark are not automatically entitled to use that mark as their domain name; trademark law does not support such a monopoly. If another Internet user has an innocent and legitimate reason for using the famous mark as a domain name and is the first to register it, the user should be able to use the domain name, provided it has not otherwise infringed upon or diluted the trademark. I reject Hasbro's request for a per se dilution rule and instead turn to whether Clue Computing has diluted Hasbro's CLUE® mark under existing dilution standards.[13]

---

[11] No. 97–10065-DPW, 9/2/99, reported in BNA, *Patent, Trademark and Copyright Journal*, Vol. 58, No. 1443 at 618.
[12] *ibid.* at 618.
[13] *ibid.* at 620.

In deciding on dilution by blurring his analysis appears to complement the decision in *Eveready*

> If courts were compelled to find dilution every time a plaintiff showed that the plaintiff's and defendant's mark were similar and that the plaintiff's mark was famous, several anomalous results would follow. First, in the case of Hasbro's Clue® trademark, were it found to be famous, every third party with a trademark for the word "clue,"*** would be engaged in trademark dilution. Indeed, no other than the mark holder could ever use a trademark similar to the one found to be famous. Second, if similarity to a plaintiff's mark was sufficient, then I would have to find per se dilution for domain names that use famous marks–a proposition which I have already rejected. These sweeping consequences fly in the face of the First Circuit's assertion of a rigorous standard and McCarthy's call for caution.[14]

Indeed! Perhaps these two decisions should become essential reading for trade mark examiners, ECJ judges, and Benelux lawyers.

---

[14] *ibid.*

Contributors

Ruth Annand is a Professor of Law and Director of the Diploma in Intellectual Property Law and Practice in the Faculty of Law at the University of Bristol. She is also a practising solicitor and Associate with Humphreys & Co. where she specialises in contentious and non-contentious trade mark matters. She is a member of the Board of Directors of the International Trademark Association and chairs its sub-committee on the Community Trade Mark. Her publications include (with co-author Helen Norman) *Blackstone's Guide to the Trade Marks Act 1994* and *Blackstone's Guide to the Community Trade Mark.*

Huw Beverley Smith, LL.B., Ph.D. (Wales); Lecturer in Law, University of Wales, Aberystwyth. He is a contributor to the 14th edition of *Copinger and Skone James on Copyright*, and is currently working on a book on appropriation of personality in the major common law jurisdictions.

Robert Burrell, LL.B., L.L.M. (London); Lecturer in Law, King's College, London, formerly Lecturer in Law, University of Wales, Aberystwyth. He has written in the *Common Market Law Review*, *European Intellectual Property Review* and is a contributor to the 14th edition of *Copinger and Skone James on Copyright.* He is currently writing a book with Allison Coleman on exceptions and defences to copyright.

Hazel Carty, M.A., Barrister, Senior Lecturer in the University of Manchester since 1991. One of her main research interests is the scope and development of the economic torts. She has written extensively in the area and now edits the chapter on Malicious Falsehood, Deceit and Passing Off in *Clerk & Lindsell on Torts.* She will be publishing her text on *Economic Torts* (with OUP) in 2000.

Allison Coleman, LL.M. (Wales); Senior Lecturer in Law, University of Wales, Aberystwyth; University Advisor on Intellectual Property and Industrial Contracts; consultant on Intellectual Property Law to Margraves, Solicitors. Author of the *Legal Protection of Trade Secrets* (Sweet and Maxwell, 1992); *Intellectual Property Law* (Longman Law, Tax and Finance, 1994); co-author of *Professional Issues in Software Engineering* (2nd ed., UCL Press, 1995; 3rd ed. forthcoming); contributor to Reed: *Computer Law* (3rd ed., Blackstone Press, 1996, 4th ed forthcoming); and author of articles on Intellectual Property in, *inter alia, Law Quarterly Review*; *Legal Studies*; *E.I.P.R.*; *Law,*

Computers and Artificial Intelligence; *Yearbook of Law, Computers and Technology*. She is currently working with Robert Burrell on a book on exceptions and defences to copyright.

Liz Cratchley graduated in Physics and Maths and worked with private practice firms of patent and trade mark agents for 10 years, during which time she became a Chartered Patent Agent and a Member of the Institute of Trade Mark Agents and gained two law degrees. She then joined Unilever where she worked in the trade marks department for 20 years. She was, until recently, Chairman of the Anti-Counterfeiting Group, and is now a vice-president of the Trade Marks, Patents and Designs Federation. Liz was awarded the OBE for services to intellectual property in 1999.

Norma Dawson is Professor of Law in Queen's University, Belfast. Her research interests are in the areas of trade mark law, copyright law, commercial leases, and Irish legal history.

Alison Firth, M.A., M.Sc., Barrister, is senior lecturer in intellectual property law at Queen Mary & Westfield College, University of London. Her publications include *Trade Marks–the new law* (1995) and (as editor) the first volume of *Perspectives in Intellectual Property: The Prehistory and Development of Intellectual Property Systems* (1997).

Ellen Gredley is currently Tutor-Librarian at the Queen Mary Intellectual Property Research Institute, where she teaches Law of Trade Marks and Unfair Competition on the M.Sc. in Intellectual Property Management course and runs the Institute's specialist research library, providing information services which support the Institute's current research work. Before joining Queen Mary College in 1992 she taught information science and law at the University of North London. Her publications include articles on parody in copyright and trade mark law and the classical origins of trade marks.

Spyros Maniatis, LL.B. (Athens), LL.M. (LSE), Ph.D. (QMW) is Lecturer in Intellectual Property at Queen Mary & Westfield College, London. He is co-author of *Trade Marks, Trade Names and Unfair Competition, World Law and Practice* and *Design and Copyright Protection of Products, World Law and Practice*.

Christopher Morcom Q.C. is Head of the Intellectual Property Chambers at One Raymond Buildings. Having obtained his degree at Cambridge in 1961, he was called to the Bar by Middle Temple in 1963, and was appointed Queen's Counsel in 1991. Since the late 1960s, he has practised in all aspects of IP, and in particular in trade marks and related fields. He is involved with a number of national and international organisations in the Intellectual Property field: Member of Board of Directors of INTA since 1998; Chairman of the Competition

Law Association (the British Group of the LIDC) 1985–1999; President of the LIDC from 1996–1998; Bar representative on the Standing Advisory Committee on Industrial Property (SACIP); a member of the Board and Council of Experts of the Intellectual Property Institute and of the Council of the British Group of AIPPI.
He has written extensively in the field of intellectual property and has published widely, including the E.I.P.R. and the *Trademark Reporter*. He is author of *A Guide to the Trade Marks Act 1994* (Butterworths).

Helen Norman, a Barrister and Senior Lecturer in Law, worked for five years as an in-house lawyer for an international oil company in London, specialising in trade marks. She then taught at Bristol Polytechnic (now the University of the West of England) before moving in 1991 to the University of Bristol. She has written extensively on Intellectual Property a subject she has taught since 1982. She is co-author of *Blackstone's Guide to the Trade Marks Act 1994* and *Blackstone's Guide to the Community Trade Mark* with Ruth Annand. She is currently completing a monograph for Athlone Press on the influence of E.C. law and the European Patent Convention on the U.K. domestic law of patents; and a textbook for Oxford University Press on *Intellectual Property*.

Charlotte Waelde is a lecturer at the University of Edinburgh School of Law. She has particular interest in the areas of trade marks and copyright, and has taught, researched and written widely in these areas. Recently she has been working on the changing role of trade marks and copyright in a digital environment.

Index
(*All refernces are to page number*)

ACG, 16–17
"AD 2000", 235
Advertisement materials in newspapers, 24
Advertisements
  comparative, 197–201, 239, 240, 245–250
  generally, 4
  Schechter's theory, 191
  three-dimensional trade marks, 143
  using sign in, 237
"Advocaat" case, 23, 25, 46
"AEILYTON", 115
Agency, collective marks, 181
Agents. *See* Patent agent; Trade mark agent
"AJAX", 13
"ALADDIN", 184
Anti-Counterfeiting Group (ACG), 15, 16–17
Application for registration
  See also Filing programmes; Registrability; Trade Marks Register; Trade Marks Registry
  countries, choice of, 6
  local, 6
  multi-class, 6
  publication, 11
  unknown subsidiary, by, 6
Arabic, foreign language words as trade marks, 101
"ARISTOC", 235
Assets, brands as, 11
Assignment of trade mark, negotiations, 5
Association membership 173. *See also* Collective marks
Associations of brand owners, 15–17

Associations of brand owners— *cont.*
  Anti-Counterfeiting Group (ACG), 16–17
  British Brands Group (BBG), 17
  generally, 15
  Trade Marks Patents and Design Federation (TMPDF), 15–16
Aural use, 237
"AUTODROME", 201, 203

"BENTLEY", 243
"BISMUTHATED", 197
"BISURATED", 197
"BLOODSTREAM", 133
"BONUS GOLD", 132
Bottles, Coca-Cola, 124
"BOVRIL", 115
Brand creation agencies, growth of, 3
Brand owners, 3–18
  Anti-Counterfeiting Group (ACG), 16–17
  associations, 15–17
    Anti-Counterfeiting Group (ACG), 16–17
    British Brands Group (BBG), 17
    generally, 15
    Trade Marks Patents and Design Federation (TMPDF), 15–16
  British Brands Group (BBG), 17
  clearance of trade marks, 3–6
  counterfeiting, action on discovery of, 15
  enforcement, perspective on, 14–15

Brand owners—*cont.*
 filing programmes, 6–8
 future for brands, 17–18
 generally, 3
 management of brands. *See*
  Management of brands
 search by, 10
 selection of trade mark, 3–6
 Trade Marks Patents and
  Design Federation
  (TMPDF), 15–16
Brands
 assets, 11
 extensions, 13–14
 future for, 17–18
 global, 12–13
 house names, 11–12
 individual, 11–12
 local, 12–13
 management. *See* Management
  of brands
 owners. *See* Brand owners
 ownership, 13
 standardising, 12
 sub-brand names, 12
 valuation, 11
British Brands Group (BBG), 17
British Producers and Brand
 Owners Group, 17
"BUITONI", 12

Canada
 filing programmes
  normal commercial terms, 8
  proof of use, 8
  specification of goods or
   services, 8
Cancellation proceedings
 non-use of trade marks, 234
 token use of trade mark, 234
Capable of distinguishing
 distinctiveness, 121–122, 123,
  124, 133–134
 foreign language words as
  trade marks, 93–94
 registrability, 121–122, 123, 124,
  134
 three-dimensional trade marks,
  147–150

Certification marks
 bodies with mark-related
  powers, 177
 collective marks and, 175–176
 earlier legislation,
  registration under, 187
 environmental, 176
 examples, 176
 heraldic devices, 177
 precursors to, 176–178
 pro-competitive, 176
 royal prerogative, 177
 standardisation marks, 177
Character merchandising,
 213–228
 development of law, 213–214
 Diana, Princess of Wales,
  213–228
 distinctiveness and
  registration, 220–226
 divergence between functions
  of registered trade mark
  and aims of character
  merchandiser, 217–220
 divisions of industry, 214
 European Convention on
  Human Rights, 227–228
 exploitation, methods of, 214
 fictional characters, 214
  played by real persons, 214
 methods of protection, 214
 name and image control,
  216–217
 publicity, right of, 214–215
 real characters, 214
 reform proposals, 227
 US right of publicity, 214–215
Chartered Institute of Patent
 Agents, 173
Chinese
 foods, 101
 foreign language words as
  trade marks, 101, 102
"CIF", 12
Clearance of trade mark, 3–6
 See also Registers
 difficulties, 3–6
 historical background, 5
 immediacy, requirement of, 6

Index 267

Clearance of trade mark—*cont.*
  multi-country basis, 5, 6
  process on finding mark in other countries, 5
Co-operative, buying, collective marks, 173
Co-proprietors, collective marks, 174, 183–184
"COCA-COLA" bottle, 124
Collective marks, 173–188
  agency, 181
  ambit of phrase, 175–180
    certification marks and, 175–176
    guarantee marks, 175
    precursors to certification marks, 176–178
  assignment of share, 174
  association membership, 173
  availability, 173
  bases for multiple use, 184
  certification marks and, 175–176
    collective mark of certification, 179
    earlier legislation, registration under, 187
    precursors to certification marks, 176–178
  charging shares, 174
  co-operative, buying, 173
  co-proprietors, 174, 183–184
  Community collective mark
    legal personality, 173
    meaning, 179
  concurrent use of identical marks by unconnected traders, 185
  distributors, 181
  earlier U.K. legislation, registration under, 186–187
  fraternal names, 180
  geographical indication of origin, 178
  geographical nexus, 184
  goodwill in mark, 174, 185
  Goschen Committee, 158, 186
  guarantee marks, 175

Collective marks—*cont.*
  horizontal nexus between users, 182
  house marks, 181–182
  implied licences, 181
  introduction, 173
  joint adventures, 182–184, 186
  joint ownership, 174–175
  legal personality of association, 173
  lenders taking security, 185
  licensing, 180–181, 186
  licensing share, 174
  meaning, 173, 175–179
  membership marks, 179–180
  Molony Committee, 184
  multiple ownership, 185
  narrow sense of word, 178
  national marks, 178
  nexus between users of mark, 184
    no nexus, 185
    spent nexus, 185
  no nexus, 185
  Olympic symbol, 184
  ownership of mark, 174
    multiple, 185
  participation in event, 184
  partnerships, 182–184
  Portugal, 179
  precursors to certification marks, 176–178
  proprietor, 173, 179
  rationale for registration, 180
  scope of protection, 179
  severance of goodwill, 185
  spent nexus, 185
  trade and, 179–180
  trade association membership, 173
  trading, 174–175
  trustees, 185
  types of multiple usership, 180–185
    agency, 181
    distributors, 181
    house marks, 181–182
    implied licences, 181
    licensing, 180–181

Collective marks—*cont.*
  umbrella association as proprietor, 179
  unincorporated associations, 173–174
  use of mark, 175
    members, 174
  WIPO training manual definition, 178
Colours, Community Trade Mark (CTM), 132
Combinations of ordinary words, registrability, 117
"COMFORT", 7
Common origin, doctrine of, 9–10
  consent, 9–10
  revocation application, 9–10
Community Trade Mark (CTM)
  colloquialisms, 105
  colours, 132
  confusing similarity, 106–107
  dialectal variants, 105
  examiners, 105–106
  Examination Guidelines, 105
  filing systems, 6
  foreign language words as trade marks, 104–107
  implementation of Regulation, 231
  likelihood of association, 106
  neologisms, 105
  non-descriptive words, 105
  non-distinctive words, 105
  obscene words, 105
  operation of system, 104
  scripts, 107
Community Trade Mark Office (OHIM), three-dimensional trade marks, 152–153
Comparative advertising, 239, 240, 245–250
  rationale of trade marks protection, 197–201
Competition, influence of, 7
Compulsory search, Trade Marks Registry, by, 10
Conflicting marks
  See also Relative grounds
  use, 9

Confusing similarity
  association, likelihood of, and, 232
  Community Trade Mark (CTM), 106–107
  foreign language words as trade marks, 88–90
  use of trade mark, 238
Consent to use, 234–235
  common origin, doctrine of, 9–10
  relative grounds, 9
Conservatories, passing off, 23–24
Containers. *See* Three-dimensional trade marks
Cooling off period, proposed, 10
Counterfeiting
  Anti-Counterfeiting Group, 15, 16–17
  background, 14–15
  brand owner action on discovering, 15
  detergent, 15
  enforcement, 14–15
  exporting counterfeit goods, 14
  filing programmes and, 7
  foods, 15
  fraudulent use of a trade mark, 16
  growth in, 14–15
  holograms, 15
  knowledge, 7
  liquor, 15
  luxury goods, 15
  products, 15
  strategy, anti-counterfeiting, 15
  "SUNSILK", 15
  toiletries, 15
Crazy Horse Saloon, 69–76, 80–81
Creation agencies. *See* Brand creation agencies
CTM. *See* Community Trade Mark (CTM)
Czech, foreign language words as trade marks, 101

Danger to public health, relative grounds, 8–9

Deceptive similarity, foreign
   language words as trade
   marks, 97–98
Designs, three-dimensional trade
   marks and law of, 158–160
Detergents
   counterfeiting, 15
   filing programmes, 8
   specification of goods or
      services, 8
Diana, Princess of Wales,
   213–228
   See also Character
      merchandising
   commercialising personality of,
      213–228
   distinctiveness and
      registration, 220–226
   divergence between functions
      of registered trade mark
      and aims of character
      merchandiser, 217–220
   name and image control,
      216–217
   photographs, 220n
   refusal of registration, 213
Dilution
   passing off, 34–35, 50–52
   Schechter's theory, 191
Directive, Trade Marks, 139–170,
      192, 204, 209–210
   definition of trade mark, 139
   gesture marks, 139
   implementation, 260
   infringement, 204–205
   likelihood of association, 207,
      232
   newly registrable marks, 139
   objective, 204
   old law and, 231–233
   olfactory marks, 139
   packaging, 139
   shape of goods, 139
   sound marks, 139
   three-dimensional marks. *See*
      Three-dimensional trade
      marks
   Trade Marks Act 1994 and,
      205–209

Disclaimers
   effect of, 238
   passing off, 24–25
Distinctiveness, 111–135
   acquired through use, ECJ
      cases, 252–255
   adaptability to distinguish,
      118–120, 121, 122
   assessment, 1905 Act, 119
   capable of distinguishing,
      121–122, 123, 124, 133–134
   three-dimensional trade
      marks, 147–150
   definition, 114
   definition of trade mark and,
      111–135
   Diana, Princess of Wales,
      220–226
   essential particulars, 113, 119,
      122
   foreign language words as
      trade marks, 88–89
   meaning, 119–120
   "old" marks, 114
   place names, 170
   registrability, relationship with,
      111–135
   1883–1905, 114–118
   case law under 1994 Act,
      129–133
   current U.K. position,
      assessment of, 133–134
   Patents, Designs and Trade-
      Marks Act 1883,
      114–116
   Patents, Designs and Trade-
      Marks Act 1888,
      116–118
   signs, 125–128
   Trade-Marks Registration
      Act 1875, 112–114
   Trade Marks Act 1905,
      118–120
   Trade Marks Act 1919,
      120–122
   Trade Marks Act 1938,
      122–125
   Trade Marks Harmonisation
      Directive 1988, 125–128

Distinctiveness—*cont.*
 shapes, 147–152
  reconceptualising, 166–169
 signs, 125–128
 statutory requirement, 111
 three-dimensional trade marks, 147–152
  reconceptualising distinctiveness, 166–169
 U.K. and Community Office practices compared, 129–133
Distributors, collective marks, 181
"Doctrine of foreign equivalents", 85
Domain names
 grabbing, 25, 27–29
 use of trade marks, 250–252
Dutch, foreign language words as trade marks, 101

"ELECTRIC", 115
"ELLE", 234
Empire Trade Mark, 15–16
Enforcement
 anti-counterfeiting, 14–15
 brand owner's perspective, 14–15
 counterfeiting, 14–15
 infringement actions. *See* Infringement actions
 look-alikes, against, 14
Equity, rationale of trade marks protection, 193–194
Ethnic minorities, languages of, 101–102
European Convention on Human Rights, character merchandising, 227–228
European Court of Justice (ECJ), 231
Exclusive rights of proprietor, 238
Exhaustion of trade mark rights, 238, 241

Fabric conditioners, 7

Fancy words
 foreign language words as trade marks, 87, 90–93
 Patents, Designs and Trade-Marks Act 1883, under, 114, 115, 116
 registrability, 114, 115
Filing programmes, 6–8
 See also Application for registration
 brand owners' perspective, 6–8
 Canada
  normal commercial terms, 8
  proof of use, 8
  specification of goods or services, 8
 choices
  countries, 6
  system, 6–7
 Community Trade Mark (CTM) 6. *See also* Community Trade Mark (CTM)
 counterfeiting and, 7
 countries
  choice of, 6
  internationally, filing, 7
  priorities, 7
 detergents, 8
 expenses, 6, 7
 multi-class applications, 6
 packaging, 8
 "rolling" programme, 6, 7
 scripts, 8
 specification of goods or services, 7–8
  Canada, 8
  detergents, 8
  precision, 8
  USA, 8
 systems
  choice of, 6
  Community Trade Mark (CTM) 6. *See also* Community Trade Mark (CTM)
  Madrid Protocol 6. *See also* Madrid Protocol
 unknown products, where, 7

Filing programmes—*cont.*
  unknown subsidiary, 6
  unsuccessful products, 7
  USA
    normal commercial terms, 8
    proof of use, 8
    specification of goods or services, 8
  word mark, 8
Foods, counterfeiting, 15
Foreign language words as trade marks, 85–108
  advantages, 85
  Arabic, 101
  capability to distinguish, 93–94
  case law
    1905–1938, 94–98
    deceptive similarity, 97–98
    "ordinary Englishman", 95–97
  characters and scripts, foreign, 88–90
  Chinese, 101, 102
  Community Trade Mark, 104–107
  conclusions on, 107–108
  confusing similarity, 88–90
  consisting exclusively of signs or indications..., 100–101
  controversy, 85–86
  Czech, 101
  dead languages, descriptive word from, 86
  deceptive similarity, 97–98
  descriptive words, 90–93
  distinctive devices, 88–89
  "doctrine of foreign equivalents", 85
  Dutch, 101
  early statutory provisions, 86–87
  ethnic minorities, languages of, 101–102
  fancy words, 87, 90–93
  "foreignness" of mark, 85
  French, 101
  Gaelic, 102
  geographic names, 93–94
  German, 101

Foreign language words as trade marks—*cont.*
  Greek, 101, 102
  guidelines for twentieth century, 86–93
  Gujerati, 101
  Herschell report, 87
  invented words, 90–93
  issues involved with, 85
  Italian, 101
  Japanese, 101, 102
  Languages of Ethnic Minorities, 101–102
  Latin, 102
  Less Well Known languages, 101
  Native Languages other than English, 101–102
  "ordinary Englishman", 95–97
  Portuguese, 101
  practice of Registry, 1905–1938, 98–100
  registrability, 117
  Registry rules, 87–88
    Acts of 1905–1938, under, 98–100
  Roman characters, 89–90
  Russian, 101
  scripts, 88–90, 107
  Spanish, 101, 103
  statutory provisions
    1875–88, 86–87
    1905–1938, 93–100
    1994, 100–104
  Swedish, 101
  Urdu, 101
  USA, 85
  uses, 85–86
  Well Known languages, 101, 103
  Welsh, 102
Foreign trade mark owner, 59–81
  Crazy Horse Saloon, 69–76, 80–81
  future, 80–81
  Joburgers, 60–63
  Johannesburg
    1992, 60–63

Foreign trade mark owner—*cont.*
  Johannesburg—*cont.*
    1995, 76–80
    London, 1967, 69–71
    London and Dublin
      1901, 63–67
      1976, 71–76
    Lowestoft, circa 1907, 68–69
    McDonald's, 59–63, 78–79
    Pasadena, 1937, 59–60
    Poiret fashion house, 68–69
Fraternal names, collective marks, 180
Fraudulent use of a trade mark, introduction of offence, 16
French, foreign language words as trade marks, 101
"FRISKIES", 13, 14
"FROOT LOOPS", 132

Gaelic, foreign language words as trade marks, 102
Geographical names
  collective marks, 184
  foreign language words as trade marks, 93–94
  registrability, 115, 117
German, foreign language words as trade marks, 101
Gesture marks, 139
Global brands, 12–13
Goodwill, protection of
  collective marks, 174, 185
  definition of goodwill, 37–38
  passing off, 35, 36, 37
  Schechter's Rational Basis of Trade Mark Protection, 192
Goschen Committee, 122, 158, 186
Greek, foreign language words as trade marks, 101, 102
Greer Committee report, 177, 178
Guarantee functions, Schechter's Rational Basis of Trade Mark Protection, 191
Guarantee marks, 175
  Community, 179

Guarantee marks—*cont.*
  guild system, 191n, 192
  Schechter's theory, 191
Guild system, 191n, 192
"GUINESS", 4
Gujerati, foreign language words as trade marks, 101

Herschell report, 87, 115–116
Holograms, 15
"Horse blister", 4
House marks, 181–182
  collective marks, 181–182
House names, 11–12
"HOVIS", 14

Implied licences, collective marks, 181
"Importing a reference", 196–204, 241
Infringement actions
  See also Use of trade marks
  "as a trade mark", use, 237
  avoidance, 14
  brand owners' attitude to, 14–15
  conflicts between rights to use, 239–240
  consent to use, 234–235
  contributory infringement, 237
  cost, 14
  "course of trade", 237
  definition, 194
  Directive, Trade Marks, 204–205
  disadvantages of using, 14
  importance of use
    section 10 of the 1994 Act, 238–229
    section 11 of the 1994 Act, 239–240
  litigation costs, 14
  look-alikes, 14
  meaning, 237
  name and address, use by person of own, 239
  no use in trade mark sense, 239–240
  use, 113

Infringement actions—*cont.*
  use, list of what constitutes, 237
"INSTANTANEOUS", 5
Intellectual property rights
  effectiveness of rights, 231
  fundamental characteristics, 231
Internet, domain names, 25, 27–29, 250–252
Invented words, foreign language words as trade marks, 90–93
Inverse passing off, 43–45, 54, 238
Italian, foreign language words as trade marks, 101
"IZAL", 195

Japanese
  foods, 101
  foreign language words as trade marks, 101, 102
"JIF", 9, 12
Joburgers, 60–63
Joint ventures, collective marks, use of, 182–184

"Keep free" rationale, 233

"LADY", 13
"LAGONDA", 243
Language of trade mark
  See also Foreign language words as trade marks
  inappropriate, 4
  offensive, 4
  pronounceability, 4
"LASTING PERFORMANCE", 133
Latin, foreign language words as trade marks, 102
"LAY", 12
Lenders, collective marks, security and, 185
Licensing, collective marks, 180–181, 186
"LIFEGUARD", 8

Likelihood of association
  Community Trade Mark (CTM), 106, 232
  confusion and, likelihood of, 232
  decisions on, 232
  three-dimensional trade marks, 154–156
Liquor, counterfeiting, 15
"LIVERPOOL CABLES", 122, 124
Local authorities, enforcement of anti-counterfeiting measures, 17
Local brands, 12–13
"LONG POINT", 174
Look-alikes, 8
  British Brands Group (BBG) and, 17
  infringement actions, 14
  passing off, 14
  proposed action against, 14
  Trade Marks Patents and Design Federation (TMPDF) views on, 16

McDonald's, 12, 59–63, 78–79
"MAGNOLIA", 118, 119
Malicious falsehood
  Joburgers and, 60–63
  passing off, 36, 45n
Management of brands, 11–14
  assets, brands as, 11
  extensions, brand, 13–14
  familiarity, 13
  generally, 11
  global brands, 12–13
  house names, 11–12
  individual brands, 11–12
  local brands, 12–13
  ownership of brands, 13
  standardising use, 12
  sub-brand names, 12
  valuation of brands, 11
"MARATHON", 12
"Mark for mark" rule, 34
  meaning, 34
Marketing, descriptive trade marks, by, 4
"MASTERPIECE", 5

Mathys Committee, 123n, 158, 176–177, 184n
"MAXIMA", 133
"MAZAWATTEE", 115
"MELROSE", 115
Membership marks, collective marks, 180
"Mere puffs", passing off, 45
"Metal corset busks", 4
Misappropriation, passing off, 34, 38, 52–53
Misrepresentation, passing off. *See under* Passing off
Misspellings, registrability, 117
Molony Committee, 184
"MONKEY", 118
Multi-class applications, use, 6
Multiple use, marks in. *See* Collective marks

Name and address, use by person of own, 239
National marks, collective marks, 178
Nature of trade marks, 4–5
"NERIT", 234
Newspapers, advertisement material inserted into, 24–25
Non-use, invalidation of registration for, wide specifications, 8
Notice, relative grounds, 9
"NUTRITIVE", 129

Offences, fraudulent use of a trade mark, 16
OHIM. *See* Community Trade Mark Office (OHIM)
Olfactory marks, 139
Olympic symbol, 184
"One in a Million" case, 25–29
"OOMOO", 115
Opposition proceedings
 cooling off period, proposed, 10
 relative grounds, 10
 settlement, 10
"ORANGE", 132

"Ordinary Englishman", foreign language words as trade marks, 95–97
Origin
 See also Common origin, doctrine of
 indication, 4, 141, 142, 178
"OVAX", 14
Ownership of brands, 13

Packaging
 Directive, Trade Marks, 139
 filing programmes, 8
 "look-alikes", 8
 "PENGUIN", 14
 registration, 14
"PAGE THREE", 202, 203
"PALMOLIVE", 183
Pan-European brands, need for, 3–4
Paris Convention, Article 10, 209
 passing off, 21–22, 30
Passing off, 21–30, 33–55
 advertisement materials in newspapers, 24–25
 "Advocaat" case, 23, 25, 46
 approach, 29
 availability of action, 112
 basis, 37
 black market goods, 40
 calculated to injure, misrepresentation, 38
 characteristics of tort, 27–28
 charities, actions by, 215n
 "classic trinity", 36
 commercial misrepresentations, 35
 common field of activity, 23
 common law, 37
 connection misrepresentation, 41–43, 50
 conservatories, 23–24
 continued importance, 33–35
 control mechanisms, 37, 38
 damage, 36
  confusion dilution, 50
  devaluation of reputation, 49
  dilution harm, 34–35, 50–52
  diversion of custom, 49

Passing off—*cont.*
   damage—*cont.*
      increased heads of, 49–53
      lessening of capacity to distinguish, 50
      loss of control of reputation, 49, 50
      misappropriation, 52–53
      proof, 52
      restriction on expansion potential, 49, 50
      speculative, 49
   deceit, 35, 36, 38
   definition, 22
   development of tort, 33–55
   dilution, allegations of, 34–35, 50–52
   disclaimers, 24–25
   dishonest or unfair trading, 29
   domain name grabbing, 25, 27–29
   equity, in, 37
   fraud, 37
   goodwill, protection of, 35, 36, 37, 47–49
      definition of goodwill, 37–38
      name goodwill, 49
      product goodwill, 47
      reputation and, 47–49
      source goodwill, 47
   grey market goods, 40n
   importance, 33–35
   incorrect product equivalence claimed, 45–46
   increased head of damage, 49–53
   intention to deceive, 37
   interference with trade, 37
   inverse passing off, 43–45, 54, 238
   leading cases, 21–30
      outside the traditional form of passing off, 22–25
   limiting mechanisms, 37, 38
   list of categories not closed, 23
   look-alikes, 14
   malicious falsehood, 36, 45n
   meaning, 22

Passing off—*cont.*
   "mere puffs", 45
   misappropriation, 34, 38, 52–53
   misdescription, 53–54
      equivalence with plaintiff's products, 45–46
      plaintiff's products, 40–41
   misrepresentation, 23, 37–38
      actionable, 34, 53
      commercial, 35
      connection misrepresentation, 41–43, 50
      growth of relevant, 39–40
      misdescription of plaintiff's products, 40–41
      product misrepresentation 43–46. *See also* product misrepresentation below
      public interest, 35
      quality of plaintiff's products, 40–41, 238
      relevant, 39–40
      requirement, 36
      source, 39–40
      types, 39
   nineteenth century, in, 36–37
   "One in a Million" case, 25–29
   parallel statutory trade mark protection, 33
   Paris Convention, Article 10, 21–22, 30
   product misrepresentation, 43–46
      "drinks" cases, 46
      incorrect product equivalence claimed, 45–46
      inverse passing off, 43–45, 54, 238
      malicious falsehood, 45n
      meaning, 43
      "mere puffs", 45
      unfair competition, 43
   public interest, 35
   quality of plaintiff's products, 40–41, 238

Passing off—*cont.*
  rationale, 35–36
  registering company names
    for improper purposes,
    25–27
  reliance, 38
  representation of own goods
    as goods of somebody
    else, 23–24
  reputation of plaintiff, trading
    on, 22
  role of tort, 33–55
  "Scotch Whisky" case, 23
  source misrepresentation,
    39–40
  Spalding v. Gamage, 37–39
  "Spanish Champagne" case,
    22–23, 29
  subject of, 37
  theoretical basis, 38
  three-dimensional trade marks
    and, 141n, 150
  traditional principle, 22
  TRIPS Agreement, 22, 30
  twentieth century
    developments, 33–55
    beginning, 37–38
    goodwill, 47–49
    growth of relevant
      misrepresentations,
      39–40
    increased heads of damage,
      49–53
  unfair competition and, 34, 38,
    43
Patent agent, selection of trade
  mark by, 3
Patents, three-dimensional trade
  marks, 154
"PENGUIN", 14
"PERFECTION", 120, 121
"PERRIER", 11
Personality. *See* Character
  merchandising
Phonetic words, registrability,
  117
Photographs, 220n
Place names used as trade
  marks, 170

Poiret fashion house, 68–69
"POLYESTRA", 233
"POMPADOUR", 201
Portugal, collective marks,
  179
Portuguese, foreign language
  words as trade marks, 101
Property right, registered trade
  mark as, 238
Public health, danger to,
  "SUNDROPS" CASE, 8–9
Publication, application for
  registration, 11
Publicity, right of, 214–215

Quality
  indication of, 4
  passing off, 40–41, 238
  three-dimensional trade marks,
    141–142

Rationale of trade marks
  protection, 237
  collective marks, 180
  comparative advertising,
    197–201
  confusion, likelihood of,
    207–208
  equity, 193–194
  historical legacy, 192–194
  "importing a reference",
    196–204, 241
    comparative advertising,
      197–201
    forms of, 201–204
  infringement, 194–195
  nineteenth century, 193
  production marks, 192
  proprietary marks, 192
  Schechter's Rational Basis of
    Trade Mark Protection. *See*
    Schechter's Rational Basis
    of Trade
    Mark Protection
  three-dimensional trade marks,
    140–143
  Trade Marks Registration Act
    1875, 193
  Trade Marks Act 1905, 194–195

Index

Rationale of trade marks
  protection—*cont.*
  Trade Marks Act 1938,
    196–204
  Trade Marks Act 1994,
    204–209
  unfair competition, 195
Registered design, three-
  dimensional trade marks,
  154, 158–160
Registrability
  1883–1905, 114–118
  adaptability to distinguish,
    118–120, 121, 122
  capable of distinguishing,
    121–122, 123, 124, 134
    three-dimensional trade
      marks, 147–150
  combinations of ordinary
    words, 117
  conditions of registration
    adaptability to distinguish,
      118–120, 121, 122
    capable of distinguishing,
      121–122, 123, 124
    fancy words, 114–116
    invented word/s, 116–117
    Patents, Designs and Trade-
      Marks Act 1883,
      114–116
    Patents, Designs and Trade-
      Marks Act 1888,
      116–118
    Trade-Marks Registration
      Act 1875, 111
  decisions under Trade Mark
    Act 1994, 129–133
  definition of trade mark. *See
    under* Trade mark
  developments in, 111–135
  distinctiveness, relationship
    with, 111–135
    See also Distinctiveness
    1883–1905, 114–118
    case law under 1994 Act,
      129–133
    current U.K. position,
      assessment of,
      133–134

Registrability—*cont.*
  distinctiveness, relationship
    with—*cont.*
    Patents, Designs and Trade-
      Marks Act 1883,
      114–116
    Patents, Designs and Trade-
      Marks Act 1888,
      116–118
    signs, 125–128
    Trade-Marks Registration
      Act 1875, 112–114
    Trade Marks Act 1905,
      118–120
    Trade Marks Act 1919,
      120–122
    Trade Marks Act 1938,
      122–125
    Trade Marks Harmonis-
      ation Directive 1988,
      125–128
  essential particulars, 113, 119,
    122
  fancy words, 114, 115
  foreign language words as
    trade marks, 117
  geographical names, 115,
    117
  misspellings, 117
  parts A and B of Register,
    120–124
  Patents, Designs and Trade-
    Marks Act 1883,
    114–116
  Patents, Designs and Trade-
    Marks Act 1888, 116–118
  phonetic words, 117
  problem of, 111–112
  signs, 125–128
  Trade-Marks Act 1875, 112–114
  Trade Marks Act 1905, 118–120
  Trade Marks Act 1919, 120–122
  Trade Marks Act 1938, 122–125
  Trade Marks Harmonisation
    Directive 1988,
    125–128
  two years bona fide prior use,
    121, 122
  unused marks, 119

Registration
  See also Distinctiveness; Trade Marks Register; Trade Marks Registry; Registrability
  collective marks. see Collective marks
  Diana, Princess of Wales, image of, 220–226
  incentive, 114
  "old" marks, 114
  property right, registered trade mark as, 238
  purpose, 113
  service marks, 236
  use of new trade mark, 113
Registry. See Trade Marks Registry
Relative grounds, 8–11
  advice on, 10
  common origin, doctrine of, 9–10
  compulsory search by Trade Marks Registry, 10
  consent, 9
  danger to public health, 8–9
  dealing with, 9
  development of, 8–9
  "JIF", 9
  meaning, 8
  notice, 9
  objections, 9–11
  opposition proceedings, 10
  Registry guidance, 10
  revocation application, 9–10
  "SUNDROPS", 8–9
Revocation application
  common origin, doctrine of, 9–10
  relative grounds, 9–10
"ROWLAND'S KALYDOR", 4
Russian
  foods, 101
  foreign language words as trade marks, 101
"RYSTA", 235–236

Schechter's Rational Basis of Trade Mark Protection, 191–210
  See also Rationale of trade mark protection
  advertising function, 191
  definition of trade marks, 191
  function of trade marks, 191
  goodwill, protection of, 192
  guarantee functions, 191
"Scotch Whisky" case, 23
Scripts
  Community Trade Mark (CTM), 107
  filing programmes, 8
  foreign language words as trade marks, 88–90, 107
Search
  need for, 10–11
  purpose, 11
  Trade Marks Registry, 10
Selection of trademark, 3–6
  brand owner, by, 3–6
  difficulties, 3–4
  patent agent, by, 3
  trade mark agent, by, 3, 4
Service marks, registration, 236
Shapes 139. See also Three-dimensional trade marks
Sheffield Register, 176
Signs
  distinctiveness, 125–128
  registrability, 125–128
  use of trade marks, 234, 237
"SNICKERS", 12
"SOLIO", 117, 119
"SOMATOSE", 117
Sound marks, 139
Spanish, foreign language words as trade marks, 101, 103
"Spanish Champagne" case, 22–23, 29
Specification of goods or services
  Canada, 8
  detergents, 8
  filing programmes, 7–8
  precision, 8
  USA, 8
  wide, too, 8

Index 279

Standardisation marks, 177
Standardising brands, 12
"STONES" dry ginger wine, 4
Sub–brand names, 12
Subsidiary, unknown, filing by, 6
"SUNDROPS", 8–9
"SUNLIGHT", 3, 5, 6, 13
"SUNSILK", 15
Swedish, foreign language words as trade marks, 101

"TARANTELLA", 183
TDMPF, 15–16
Three-dimensional trade marks, 139–170
  advertising function, 143
  assessment of consumer reaction, 150–156
  assets, as, 142
  association and distinctiveness distinguished, 154–156
  capable of distinguishing, 147–150
  capturing the consumer, 150–156
  Community Trade Mark Office (OHIM), 152–153
  conclusions on, 170
  consumer associations, 141, 150–156
  dangers of registration, 139
  designs law and, 139, 158–160
  distinctiveness of shapes, 147–152
    presumption against, 147–152, 166–169
    reconceptualising, 166–169
  excluding features, infringement by, 161–162
  exclusions
    Directive, 139, 170
    Trade Marks Act 1994, 161–165, 170
  historical opposition, 143–169
    capturing the consumer, 150–156
    distinctiveness of shapes, 147–150

Three-dimensional trade marks—*cont.*
  historical opposition—*cont.*
    generally, 143–144
    managing monopolies, 160–165
    manufacturing a monopoly, 156–158
    Philishave shaver, 146–147, 160–161
    reconceptualising distinctiveness, 166–169
    semiotics of shapes, 146–147
    signs and shapes, 144–146
    summation, 165
    Trade Marks Act 1994, 146–147
  introduction of protection, 140–143
  investments in, 143
  justifications for protection, 140–143
  managing monopolies, 160–165
  manufacturing a monopoly, 156–158
  marketing power of mark, 142
  meaning, 139n
  monopolies
    managing, 160–165
    manufacturing, 156–158
  nature of goods, shape resulting from, 161–162
  opposition to protection. *See* historical opposition above
  origin, indicator of, 141, 142
  passing off and, 141n, 150
  patent protection, 154
  Philishave shaver, 146–147, 160–161
  presumption against distinctiveness of shapes, 147–152, 166–169
  quality, 141–142
  rationale for introduction of protection, 140–143
  reconceptualising distinctiveness, 166–169
  registered design, 154, 158–160

Three-dimensional trade marks—*cont.*
  scope of protection, 140
  semiotics of shapes, 146–147
  signs and shapes, 144–146
  substantial value given to goods by shape, 161, 163–165
  technical result, shape necessary to achieve, 161, 162–163
  value given to goods by shape, 161, 163–165
  value of marks, 142–143, 161, 163–165
Toiletries, counterfeiting, 15
Token use of mark, 234
Tort, passing off. *See* Passing off
Trade, definition, 237
Trade association membership, collective marks, 173
Trade mark
  definition
    Directive, Trade Mark, 139
    Patents, Designs and Trade-Marks Act 1883, 114
    Schechter's Rational Basis of Trade Mark Protection, 191
    Trade-Marks Act 1875, 113
    Trade Marks Act 1905, 118–119
    Trade Marks Act 1938, 124, 236
    Trade Marks Act 1994, 111
  essential particulars
    1875 Act, 113
    1905 Act, 119
    1938 Act, 122
  use. *See* Use of trade marks
Trade mark agent, selection of trade mark by, 3
Trade Mark Directive. *See* Directive, Trade Mark
Trade Mark Federation (TMF), 16
Trade Mark Journals, generally, 4
Trade Marks Patents and Design Federation (TMPDF), 15–16

Trade Marks Register
  See also Trade Marks Registry
  advantages, 112
  complete record, 113
  crowding in, 3
  establishment, 112
  "old" marks, 114
  Part A, 120–123
  Part B, 120–124
  purpose of registration with, 113
  Trade Marks Act 1985, under, 5
  U.K., 5, 11, 120–124
  vested rights, 113
Trade Marks Registry
  See also Trade Marks Register
  compulsory search, requirement, 10
  foreign words as trade marks, practice where, 87–88, 98–100
  search, 10
"TREAT", 129, 134, 220n
"TREAT SIZE", 244
TRIPS Agreement, 78
  passing off, 22, 30
Trustees, collective marks, 185

"UKISTON", 121
Unfair competition
  passing off, 34, 38, 43
  product misrepresentation, 43
  rationale of trade marks protection, 195
Unregistrable trade marks, use of, 4
Urdu, foreign language words as trade marks, 101
USA
  "doctrine of foreign equivalents", 85
  filing programmes
    normal commercial use, 8
    proof of use, 8
  publicity, right of, 214–215
  specification of goods or services, 8
Use of trade marks, 231–260
  See also Infringement actions

Index

Use of trade marks—*cont.*
  advertising, using sign in, 237
  affixing sign to goods or packaging, 237
  aural use, 237
  business papers, using sign on, 237
  cancellation proceedings, 234
  conflicts between rights to use, 239–240
  consent to use, 234–235
  contributory infringement, 237
  de minimis, 234
  demarcating areas of use in future, 256–260
  domain names, 250–252
  ECJ approach
    distinctiveness acquired through use, 252–255
    position of ECJ, 256
    use as a trade mark, 254–256
  endorsing cosmetic goods under other brands, 234
  examples, 237
  exclusive rights of proprietor, 238
  future position, 256–260
  genuine use, 233
  importance, 233–235
    section 10 of the 1994 Act, 238–239
    section 11 of the 1994 Act, 239–240
  importing or exporting goods under the sign, 237
  infringement action, 113
  inverse passing off, 238
  limitation on use
    section 10 of the 1994 Act, 238–239
    section 11 of the 1994 Act, 239–240
  list of what constitutes, 237
  name and address, use by person of own, 239
  offering or exposing goods for sale, 237
  post-1938 position, 242–245

Use of trade marks—*cont.*
  post-1994 position, 245–250
  pre-1938 position, 240–241
  putting goods on the market, 237
  relation to goods, in, 234
  relevance of message conveyed by sign, 237
  "RYSTA", 235–236
  scope of protection, 233–236
  signs, 234, 237
  stocking goods for purposes of putting on the market, 237
  token use, 234
  Trade Marks Act 1938, 241
  Trade Marks Act 1994, 236–240
  trade, use on, 235–236
  two years bona fide prior use, 121, 122
  visual use, 237

Valuation, brands, 11
"VASELINE", 8
"VISS", 12
"VOLKSWAGEN", 182

"WALKERS", 12
"WELDMESH", 123
Well-Known Marks
  registers, 80
  WIPO Committee of Experts on Well-Known Marks, 77–78, 79–80
Welsh, foreign language words as trade marks, 102
"WHAT A DAY", 233
WIPO Committee of Experts on Well-Known Marks, 77–78, 79–80
Word marks
  filing programmes, 8
  foreign. *See* Foreign language words as trade marks
World-wide brands, need for, 3–4

"YEAST-VITE", 194
"YORK", 124
"YORKSHIRE RELISH", 118